NICK FALDO

NICK FALDO
DRIVEN
The Definitive Biography

Dale Concannon

This book is dedicated to my good friend,
Mark McKenna.

When we walk to the edge of all the light we have,
And take that step into the darkness of the unknown,
We must believe that one of two things will happen:
There will be something solid for us to stand on,
Or we shall be taught how to fly.

'Faith' by Patrick Overtor

This edition published in Great Britain in 2005 by
Virgin Books Ltd
Thames Wharf Studios
Rainville Road
London W6 9HA

First published in paperback in 2002 by Virgin Books Ltd

First published in hardback in 2001 by Virgin Books Ltd

All photographs supplied by the Phil Sheldon Golf Picture Library, 40
Manor Road, Barnet, Hertfordshire EN5 2JQ (tel. 020 8440 1986).

Typeset by TW Typesetting, Plymouth, Devon
Printed and bound in Great Britain by
Mackays of Chatham PLC

CONTENTS

ACKNOWLEDGEMENTS

The author would like to extend his sincere and grateful thanks to the following: David Begg; David Carter; Dave Musgrove; Golden Bear Inc.; Roddy Carr; Peter Butler; Maria Acasia, Amen Corner; Tim Ward; Mizuno; Matthew Harris, Golf Picture Library; Steve Beddow; Peter Oosterhuis; Bernard Hunt; John Jacobs; Warren Humphreys; David McNeilly; Andy Prodger; Bernhard Langer; Renton Laidlaw; David Cronin; Scott Crockett; Phil Pilley; Bob Warters; Robert Aziz; John Huggan; Pete Masters, *Golf World*; Jock Howard, *Golf World*; PGA European Tour media department, especially Frances Jennings, Gordon Simpson, Vanessa Brannetti, Valerie Steele and Julie Medlock; Gaston Barras, Canon European Masters; Christina Steinmann; Ian Connelly; Lauren St John; Rosemary Anstey; Linda Milton, *Golf Weekly*; Ian Marshall; John Paramour, PGA European Tour; Walter Mechilli; Phil, Gill and Jan of the Sheldon Golf Picture Library; Jonathan Taylor of Virgin Books; and Daniel Balado.

And my grateful thanks to John Hopkins, *The Times*' golf correspondent, and Mitchell Platts, director of communications at the PGA European Tour, for permission to use selected quotes from their earlier biographies of Nick Faldo (respectively: *Nick Faldo: In Perspective*, Allen & Unwin, 1985; and *The Rough with the Smooth*, Stanley Paul and Co., 1980). Gentlemen, my respect for you has never been higher.

Finally, a huge thank-you to those who cannot be named yet were of enormous help in my research for this book. You know who you are.

Dale Concannon
February 2001

INTRODUCTION

It was November 1992. Nick Faldo walked into the grill room at the Shady Oaks Country Club in Fort Worth, Texas, the very picture of success. All eyes turned towards him as, dressed in a smart blue jacket, cashmere roll-neck and neat black trousers, he made his way over to a large table near the window. His lunch partners were already waiting, and all but one stood up to make their introductions. Glancing over at the grey-haired figure still in his chair, Faldo offered a nervous smile. This was the man he had wanted to meet most of his life.

Arranged by former PGA champion Dave Marr, it was one of the few times in thirty years that Ben Hogan had agreed to meet a fellow professional socially. Faldo had spent most of the previous night writing down things to ask the great man. By the time he fell asleep in the early hours of the morning he had filled up ten pages of hotel notepaper with queries on the swing, the mental side of the game and how to play under pressure. Whether Hogan would answer them was another question entirely.

By reputation taciturn and intimidating, the eighty-year-old Hogan turned out to be the exact opposite. Courteous and polite, he appeared interested in everything Faldo had to say. Asking about his Open win at Muirfield a few months earlier, he discussed with Faldo what elements of his game he was working on and how much modern-day equipment had changed the game over the past four decades. Relishing the chance to pick up the odd tip, Faldo pulled out his notes and laid them on the table. But true to form, Hogan was reluctant to give up any of his secrets.

They were kindred spirits, and the respect they had for each other was obvious. A generation apart, the similarities were compelling. Faldo, like Hogan, was considered to be the most complete golfer of his generation. Tough and uncompromising, he had long been known for his cold-blooded, almost scientific approach to tournament play. Nothing was ever left to chance.

Practice was regimented and physically demanding. Perfection in all things was the motto of both men, as Hogan demonstrated when asked to remember his greatest ever shot: 'I can only remember the bad ones,' he said. Faldo would undoubtedly have agreed.

A few hours later, the meeting ended with a firm handshake and an open invitation to return. Before making their farewells, Hogan was asked if he would like to watch Faldo hit some balls on the practice ground. Not surprisingly, he declined. Throughout his life, people had come to watch *him* hit balls, not the other way around. Faldo understood completely.

Like Hogan's, the Nick Faldo story is well documented. At the age of thirteen, he was inspired by the sight of Jack Nicklaus competing in the US Masters at the splendid Augusta National. A few days later he went for his first lesson. A few years later, a school employment councillor told him to forget a career in professional golf because 'only one in ten thousand ever makes it'. 'Then I'll be that one,' he said before leaving the next day.

A meteoric rise in the amateur game was followed by a successful introduction into the paid ranks. The youngest player ever to compete in the Ryder Cup, he was an accomplished tournament winner by the time he decided to remodel his swing in the mid-eighties. So-called experts thought he was crazy, but he knew he needed a more reliable method to win the majors he craved. Two backbreaking years later nothing had improved, and it began to look like his former brilliance had merely been a flash in the pan. Then, armed with his new Leadbetter-model swing, he proved them all wrong.

Stringing together eighteen straight pars in the final round, he finally achieved his ambition by winning the Open at Muirfield in 1987. Five years later he won his third over the same course. In the interim he travelled to the hallowed turf of Augusta that had inspired him as a teenager to capture two consecutive US Masters titles. Top-ranked player in the world throughout the early nineties, he returned to Augusta in 1996 to win a third. No British golfer has come even close to matching his record: six major championships, thirty-plus tournament victories and eleven consecutive Ryder Cup appearances.

Setting new standards in the game, he hit twice as many balls as anyone else, even when he was considered the best. After a round others might have considered a good one, he would repair to the practice ground to work out where things had gone wrong. The moment he finished there, you knew he would make his way to the practice putting green. After dinner, it was not unusual to find him in his hotel room, chipping on the carpet. As Arnold Palmer once said, 'Nick was the best of the best in his time and for a time he was hitting the ball sweeter than any golfer who has ever lived – including Ben Hogan!'

Away from the course, his personal life has been equally well covered. The briefest trawl through the tabloids reveals a catalogue of broken marriages, hidden affairs and unexplained rifts with former friends and associates. Stories of his apparent unpopularity with fellow players are commonplace, along with his legendary lack of patience when dealing with the press. It is a relationship soured due to many years of misunderstandings and broken loyalties on both sides, and Faldo still admits a healthy mistrust of all things journalistic: 'I think if the public knew the truth behind every story they read, they'd never buy a paper again. If they totted up what they spend at the end of the week, they'd be better off buying a pint.'

Not that his often hostile attitude has helped the situation. At Muirfield in 1992 Faldo made the mistake of using the presentation ceremony to vent his spleen on his critics. He famously thanked them, immaturely and ill-advisedly, from 'the heart of my bottom', and if he ever wants to know why his public image has suffered in the years since then, he only needs to play that video.

The problem is one of communication. His admirers, of whom there are many, have long wanted to know more about him. Faldo in turn is reluctant to give away anything other than his name, rank and numbers on his scorecard. This in turn has led to a polarisation of opinion. Respected more than loved, he remains an enigmatic and often misunderstood figure. To some he is a sporting icon who can do no wrong; to others he is an automaton more interested in his next round of golf than in maintaining his marriage vows. Saint or sinner, everyone has something to say about Nick Faldo.

A complex individual with little desire to explain himself, Faldo has long believed that people should judge him on his tournament record and nothing else. He is probably right, but that has not always proved possible. Whether talking to him, interviewing him or just listening to him in the press room after a round, you rarely get the feeling that you have the whole story. Depending on the journalists' prejudices, the impression the reader receives is often biased at worst, misleading at best. As Faldo has said in the past, he might sign 99 autographs but it is the one he refuses that gets all the attention.

Celebrity has never rested well on his shoulders. He was once labelled 'the most hated man in British sport' by a national newspaper, but it is hard to square that with the man who gives generously of his time and money with no thought for publicity: the man who gave away his winner's cheque of £100,000 to charity just moments after the 1992 World Matchplay Championship at Wentworth had ended; the man who sneaked a handful of terminally ill kids on to the same course, then played golf with them all afternoon; the man who was asked to donate a sweater to an auction to raise money for a children's hospital, then sent round several crates of unworn jumpers, shirts, gloves and trousers; the man behind the Faldo Junior series that gives under-privileged children the chance to play the game he loves.

So where does the truth about Nick Faldo lie? For that, we have to go to the people who know him best. In the end, it is only by talking to his friends, loved ones, employees and colleagues that we can get a true and accurate account of this fascinating character. Only then can we understand his motivation, his ambition, his frustration and his insatiable will to win. Striking a balance between his magnificent career and some of the more sensational aspects of his private life, this book offers a revealing portrait of both Faldo the golfer and Faldo the man. As always, you cannot have one without the other.

I know Nick Faldo always smiles when others try to psychoanalyse him. Fortunately, this book attempts nothing of the kind. What it does do is tell his story as honestly and accurately as possible, then asks the reader to make up his or her own mind about what drives him.

And what a remarkable story it is.

1. EARLY DAYS

In the late fifties, Welwyn Garden City in Hertfordshire was considered an ideal place to live and raise a family. Compared with the claustrophobic dourness of post-war London thirty miles to the south, it was a relatively prosperous town surrounded by open heath and farmers' fields. Founded in 1920 by the philanthropist Sir Ebenezer Howard, it set an example to the rest of Britain in terms of cheap, affordable housing and was still being described as a 'new' town by the time George and Joyce Faldo moved there 38 years later.

As for most couples, money was frequently short, but this was nothing new, especially for George. A Londoner by birth, he spent his early childhood in a cramped East End flat along with his four brothers and sisters. With no running water and a lavatory shared by at least two other families, it was a tough upbringing by any standards and would influence his attitude to money for years afterwards. A tall, well-built man, he cut an imposing figure and had a personality to match. Forthright and occasionally stubborn, he was not someone who suffered fools gladly. For him, time, like money, was far too precious to waste – an attitude he would later pass on to his son.

George soon left London for an accounting post in the financial planning department at ICI Plastics in Welwyn. A step up in financial terms, it also enabled him to marry local girl Joyce Smalley in 1947. Working as a cutter and pattern drafter for nearby Cresta Silks, she was an attractive, dark-haired young woman with an inquisitive mind and a strong inner desire to better herself. In that respect she and husband George made a good partnership.

Like many couples of that time, their ambition was to save up enough money to buy a house and perhaps raise a family. So when they finally moved into 285 Knella Road two years later, it was the realisation of a long-held dream. No more than a two-up, two-down, end-of-terrace council house, it also had one great advantage over many other houses in the Peartree area of the newly styled 'Garden City' – it actually had a garden!

Little could they imagine what an invaluable asset that would prove to be over the coming years.

Their first and only child was born at three o'clock in the afternoon on Thursday, 18 July 1957. He entered the world a healthy but noisy 7lb 12oz, the midwife in attendance predicting the boy would grow to be at least six feet two inches tall. It proved to be an accurate forecast. Christened Nicholas Alexander Faldo, he was the apple of his parents' eyes. After nursery school, he went to Thumbswood Primary before moving on to Blackthorn School in Welwyn a few years later. As for most kids in the area, money was tight and luxuries thin on the ground, but rarely, if ever, did Nick go without. Indulged by his parents throughout his early childhood, especially by his mother, he always had the smartest uniform and cap and the newest shoes they could realistically afford. 'I always said that if we had a roof over our heads and enough food and heat then we were okay,' said George Faldo. 'We certainly didn't believe in having anything we could not put up the money for, apart from a mortgage.'

That said, Mr and Mrs Faldo also had a taste for the high life on occasion. Passionate about the theatre, they enjoyed regular visits to the local playhouse along with occasional trips to Shaftesbury Avenue in London. A keen amateur theatrical and former Widow Twanky, George also loved Gilbert and Sullivan operettas and could often be heard singing along with some of the better-known songs when they featured on the radio. It was a passion George and Joyce were happy to share with their son, and he with them. At the age of ten Nick was taken on a trip to the Festival Hall to see the Ernest Read Saturday morning concerts for children. At Christmas, he would be taken to at least one local pantomime. He was surrounded by music and dance throughout his early childhood – singing often provided an interesting backdrop to homework nights – and it was something that would stay with him well into adulthood.

Indeed, as Nick got older, a career on the stage was becoming a real possibility, especially if Joyce had her way. 'First we wanted him to be an actor,' she told Mitchell Platts in 1980. 'We thought he'd be another Sir Laurence Olivier. We took him to dancing and elocution lessons. We tried to interest him in music. We knew he'd win the Tchaikovsky piano prize. He had smashing legs and I wanted him to be a model, so I used to take him to Harrods fashion shows. Finally, we realised he was only interested in sport.'

Like his father, Nick grew quickly into a tall, long-legged child. Yet despite his gangly appearance, he was blessed with excellent hand–eye coordination, allied already to a burning desire to win at any sport he took on.

I was four or five years old when I got my first bat and ball. We had a good-sized garden at 285 Knella Road, and I spent many happy hours there. At the age of seven I moved on to another school, Blackthorn, where my sporting life centred on throwing a cricket ball! I was pretty big in those days – certainly for my age – and I could heave the old cricket ball a good bit further than anybody else. I must admit that it was important to me to win. Then again, you have to hate losing, however well you may accept it, if you want to climb to the top in any profession.

Nick also took to swimming, at the age of six. Four years later, he became the only boy in the history of Blackthorn to get a gold medal for lifesaving. After that, he won the Hertfordshire County Boys 110 yards freestyle. Then, as he was planning a spectacular career as British sport's next Olympic gold medallist, his ambitions suffered a major blow. Having qualified to represent his county in the National Finals at Crystal Palace in 1968, he finished a distant and disappointing fourth – an absolute disaster in his young eyes.

At the age of eleven, Nick passed his exams and joined Sir Frederic Osbourn comprehensive school. Coincidentally, his first day at school was also the day on which the family moved house. The Faldos had been saving up for the necessary deposit to buy 11 Redwoods in Welwyn Garden City for £5,200; the new house had three bedrooms and was in the middle of a nice terrace at the bottom of a close. More importantly, it moved them closer to the local golf club in High Oaks Road, where Nick would end up spending much of his teenage years.

With Nick an only child, his parents were able to indulge their son's sporting interests to the full, and there were many of them. At Sir Frederic Osbourn he played both basketball and soccer. He also played cricket, though not brilliantly, despite being a champion ball thrower at his former school. A talented athlete, he excelled at 800 and 1500 metres. He also threw the discus and javelin, and on rare occasions took part in the shot putt. Away from school, he took up tennis, his parents once again finding the cash for a series of lessons and the most expensive racquet they could afford. 'My parents always wanted the best for me,' Nick would later comment.

Encouraged by his father to compete, and compete hard, Nick had the reputation of being a moody child, even a loner. He had friends, but the competitive side of his nature tended to push people away, especially when it came to team sports. For him, the frustration of playing any sport with people who took it less seriously than he did was just too much. As befitting a supporter of the dour Leeds United team of the seventies, he was often seen berating his schoolmates for their lack of effort. 'As a kid I had begun to hate playing soccer,' he later admitted, 'because I got so furious when we lost. I felt really down when I trudged off the field a loser. My parents knew how I felt because when I arrived back after a match I used to sit down and get more depressed.'

It was obvious to everyone who knew Nick that sport was his passion, his life – a fact recognised early on by his physical education teacher Mr Harvey, who wrote somewhat prophetically on his first school report: 'Nick's future will be in sport. He sets his standards high and his dedication will be the key to his success.'

As Nick got older he found an interest in more individual sporting pursuits. Introduced to coarse fishing by his father, Nick would spend all day with him on a local riverbank or reservoir searching for perch and bream. Then, at thirteen, he developed a sudden and overwhelming passion for cycling. As his interest grew, George helped him buy not only a bike for road racing but another for dirt-track racing (like a mini-speedway, this involved four cyclists going hell for leather around a shale track to win points either as individuals or for their team). He was known to dismantle both in an effort to make them race even faster. Competing against the local kids was a huge part of the fun, but for Nick winning was everything, and despite the scraped knees and bloody shins that resulted from the odd tumble, many happy evenings were spent dirt-track racing with the Welwyn Wheelers at a banked circuit near his parents' house. There were not many sports Nick hadn't tried by the time he was a teenager, but golf was one. To him, it was an old man's game, too slow and definitely too boring. But all that was to change after his father bought a new colour television set early in 1971. (At this point, his only contact with the game had come at the age of eight when his grandfather gave him a hickory-shafted iron. Unlike Seve Ballesteros, who used his to hit pebbles on the beach at Santander in northern Spain, Nick used his as a weed-whacker in the local woods.) Colour television was in its infancy, but one day he caught sight of Jack Nicklaus competing in the 1971 Masters. Leaning forward in his seat, Nick watched excitedly as the Golden Bear went head-to-head against Charles Coody and Johnny Miller in the final round. Enthused by the sport and the majestic and colourful splendour of Augusta National, he implored his parents to arrange for him to take some golf lessons with a local pro. 'The Masters of 1971 was my very first encounter with golf,' said Nick. 'I was thirteen years old and saw the last two days on television. With the Easter holidays just beginning, I told my parents that I wanted a go at the game. For me, that was the start.'

With his father busy at work, it was his mother who made the first move. 'Neither of us really knew how I should go about becoming a golfer,' recalled Nick, 'so my mother said that the only way to find out was to go up to the local club at Welwyn Garden City and simply ask. She also stressed that in return for taking me along I must have my hair cut!' Somewhat reluctantly, Nick went to the local hairdresser's in the morning, and in the afternoon paid a visit with his mother to Welwyn Garden City Golf Club. They were greeted by assistant professional Chris Arnold, who told them it would probably be best to have half a dozen lessons before buying any golf equipment. That way, a beginner could determine whether or not he wanted to continue at the price of instruction alone. It was excellent advice. Nick, like most teenagers, was raring to go. He wanted his first lesson that afternoon, but Arnold was fully booked and told him to come back the following day.

When he finally did get his first golf lesson, Nick Faldo was hooked. Sitting behind his desk at school, he would constantly practise with a wooden ruler the overlapping grip Arnold had taught him. Faldo returned every Saturday for the first six weeks for half an hour's tuition at a cost of fifty pence a time, and the two quickly became good friends. After each lesson, Faldo would go off and practise by himself, often for hours. Having imparted the basics to his young pupil, Chris Arnold then handed him over to the head professional at Welwyn, Ian Connelly. It was with Connelly that his golfing education would really begin.

By the time Faldo arrived for his first 'proper' lesson, Connelly was already coaching a number of talented young players, many of them regulars in the Hertfordshire Colts team. Born in Dundee, he was an amiable man with a strong work ethic – something he liked to instil in his pupils. Resident pro at Welwyn since 1966, he had learnt much of his instruction technique while assistant to former Ryder Cup pro Jimmy Adams at Royal Mid-Surrey. Connelly kept his teaching simple, and immediately noticed in his new charge what others had seen in him before. 'I can still remember the first time I gave him a lesson,' said the Scot. 'It wasn't so much that he had talent, Nick had something else as well – ambition. There are plenty of kids with talent but there aren't that many with both talent and burning ambition.'

But as Nick's enthusiasm for the game grew, so did the expense. Apart from the lessons there were other things to consider like proper golf shoes and gloves, all of which had to be paid for by his parents. Then, after a few weeks, it became glaringly obvious that he needed some clubs of his own to practise with. Hearing about his plight, it was next-door neighbour Graham Thomas who finally stepped in with some help. A golfer himself, he went hunting in his garage and came back with a ladies' seven- and eight-iron. These became Nick's first clubs, and he carried them everywhere in those early months.

Golf balls came to him in a similar way. Working part-time at a school in nearby Ware, Joyce happened to mention that her son had taken up golf. The following day one of the teachers sent over a selection of battered old balls. They were better than nothing, and Nick put them inside an old bag made by his mother and would carry them across the road to the nearby Monkswalk School playing field, where he would practise for hours. 'I used to strike the ball down the line of the football pitch. Just beyond the pitch, there was a long-jump pit, and I practised trying to land all the balls in the sand. I suppose it was about a hundred yards away from where I was hitting them and my record was fifteen out of eighteen. I can remember that because I used to get annoyed that I couldn't do better.'

These were joyful times for Nick Faldo. Now, it seemed to him that the game of golf offered so many advantages over other games. He did not need other kids to practise with, as was the case with team sports such as soccer and cricket, and with that knowledge came a form of freedom, a freedom he would exploit to the absolute limits over the coming years. 'I have always been content with my own company and was able to amuse myself for hours when I was a child. The solitude of the practice ground and the hours spent building a golf swing were a real pleasure to me, whether in the early days after taking up the game, or later when I turned professional.'

Having convinced his parents this was no passing fad, Nick was presented with a half-set of 'St Andrews' golf clubs on his fourteenth birthday, bought from Ian Connelly at the Welwyn pro shop for £35. Nick's excitement was obvious.

When I was given the clubs I could hardly wait to get out of the house. I raced up to the course to have my first round on my own. I was worried at the close proximity of the clubhouse and the fact that I might make a mess of things with somebody watching. But I was more worried when I reached the first green. The sprinklers were on and water was spraying everywhere. I thought, 'Hell, I shouldn't be here.' So I nipped round to the second tee and missed putting out. It was the same at the second green, and I didn't tread on a real green until I reached the third. It was a funny sensation. The grass was so soft and I felt as if I should be wearing carpet slippers and not spiked shoes. How did I fare that first time? Well, I hit the ball

*seventy-eight times but I lost three balls and I didn't count all
the putts. So I decided that as I would never do it that way
again I wouldn't count it!*

Losing golf balls was not much of a problem because, like most
of the other juniors, Nick re-used those he found by rummaging
through the bushes that separated the ninth and tenth fairways.
Not to mention the late-night golf-ball hunts he would go on
with his father during summer.

Another significant moment in Nick Faldo's young life came
in April 1972, when he took part in a Duke of Edinburgh
Outward Bound course at Ullswater in the Lake District. Held
during the Easter holidays, it was an experience he would never
forget. In addition to being woken up at 6 a.m. every morning,
freezing temperatures and ice-cold showers made it the most
uncomfortable four weeks of his life. The course also included
a three-day 'unescorted' survival test in two feet of snow. A far
cry from anything he had experienced before, it definitely had
the desired effect of 'toughening' him up. Not exactly spoilt,
Nick was certainly indulged by his parents as a young child.
Prone to moody outbursts, he changed his attitude completely
after these experiences at Ullswater. Rising to the challenge,
Nick proved, perhaps most importantly to himself, that he
could finally stand on his own two feet. Joyce Faldo often
claimed that 'Nick went away as a boy and he came back a man.'

Returning to the relative warmth of Hertfordshire, Nick was
more determined than ever to make a success of golf. Stretching
his parents' modest finances even further, he booked up for
more tuition with Ian Connelly. An average of one lesson a
week for the next two years built the foundations of a long and
ultimately successful relationship.

Like his assistant, Connelly believed in getting the fundamentals right: the grip, the set-up and the posture. 'Why start off
your golfing career with a bad grip which will require
compensations? Grip properly and other facets of your swing
will more readily fit into place. I believe in young players
developing good habits from the word go. It will stand them in
good stead later and make their development as players easier.'
From the very start Nick used the Vardon overlapping grip.

Placing his hands on the grip in the same way they would be at the moment of impact, he followed Connelly's philosophy of keeping things as simple as possible. 'It cuts down on problems in the long run,' he often insisted.

Probably the biggest 'problem' Nick suffered from early on was his posture. Typically for a tall boy – he was an inch over six feet at the age of fifteen – he had the habit of standing far too close to the ball. To compensate, he stooped over at address and, not surprisingly, crowded himself out. To help him correct this, Connelly suggested that he tilt from the waist instead of bending over quite so much, 'like a cat about to spring', as he described it. It was advice Nick would later take into his professional career. He also had a tendency to take back his club too steeply and at the top of the back swing. Also a fault linked to his size and build, he was forced as a result to drop his hands inside on the down swing to get them into the right position at impact. Inevitably, this left his swing with a slight loop, and it would be many years before he got rid of it completely.

Recognising what a special talent his young pupil had, Connelly drove Nick hard in their early years together. Praise and criticism came in equal measure, and rarely did a practice-ground meeting pass without some sort of exchange. As Faldo later remarked, 'Ian was my biggest fan and my biggest critic.' Connelly was not averse to reading the Riot Act to his pupils when the occasion called for it. Strong on discipline, he believed that golfers should behave like gentlemen; whenever he saw one of his 'lads' playing up, or throwing a club in frustration, he would admonish them in no uncertain terms. 'Not that it was ever a problem with Nick,' he said with a twinkle in his eye.

Needless to say, Nick Faldo could not avoid the odd scrape with authority. When he was fifteen, he was banned from club competition for a month after playing off the wrong tee in a monthly medal. Having joined Welwyn Garden City Golf Club as a junior member only eighteen months earlier, he was accused of 'jumping' ahead of a group of adult members coming up the ninth fairway. He chose to start his round from the tenth tee rather than hang around at the much busier first, and his winning net score of 67 was immediately disqualified. Faldo was absolutely incensed by the decision, and he would never again play another monthly medal at Welwyn.

Not that he lacked good competition there. In the summer holidays when three or four rounds a day were possible, he was just one of a group of talented youngsters who played at Welwyn in the mid-seventies. Nick, Trevor Powell, Bobby Mitchell and Bryan Lewis, all of whom would later turn professional, competed against each other and were described by Ian Connelly as his 'big four'. Add to that list low-handicap brothers Colin and John Moorhouse, who would later caddie for Faldo on tour, and you had a potentially explosive mix. As handicaps tumbled, friendly but intense rivalries grew up between them, on and off the course. They would spend hours around the practice chipping green trying to get the better of one another, testing one another's skills to the limit. Playing for side bets, usually a Mars bar or a can of Coca-Cola, they would throw balls under nearby bushes to see who could play the best recovery shot. After that, the putting green in front of the clubhouse windows would become the venue for head-to-head battles of nerve and skill. 'If I was down in a match, or I had to hole a long putt to win, it usually went in. Never mind how difficult the putt was, I always sank it. In those days I could hole anything. I really could putt then. In those days I really could see the ball going into the hole. That was the way to do it. You never hole a putt by standing there thinking, "I've got to do this, I've got to do that." You've got to see the ball go into the hole and then it just happens. I had no fear in those days.'

It seems chocolate bars, cans of fizzy pop and wrapped Dunlop 65s were not the only things Nick liked to play for. 'I used to play the odd round with Nick when he was around fifteen or sixteen,' recalled Connelly.

I remember he turned to me on the twelfth tee at Welwyn and said, 'Well, boss, that's me two-up!' I said, 'I didn't know we were playing a match,' and he turned to me stony-faced and said, 'I was!' I have never seen somebody so happy at winning a pound. That was typical Nick – competitive to his fingertips. Then, as his game improved, which it did rapidly, I made him an offer. I said that if he beat me off level I would give him £20.

And if he beat me over nine holes then I would give him £10. Of course he was rubbing his hands at the thought of taking my money until I mentioned that he had to put up some money of his own: £1 over nine and £2 for eighteen. That took the smile off his face.'

A hard-working partnership on the practice ground, Nick and Connelly gradually developed a strong bond of friendship off it. A constant visitor to the pro shop, Nick would spend hours in the winter months listening to the Scot chat away about the great players of the past, including Sam Snead, Henry Cotton and, most especially, Ben Hogan. Over the years Connelly had read every book written by the legendary American and constantly reinforced his ethos that only hard work and dedication could take someone to the top. It was another lesson Nick would never forget.

Apart from competition, what Nick enjoyed most was practising on his own. Happy with his own company, he spent hour after solitary hour on the practice ground, often hitting balls until he could hardly hold the club in his hands, so raw had they become. Even in the heart of winter, when many of the other juniors found the warmth of the clubhouse far more appealing, he would be working hard on his game, even if it meant clearing a patch of snow next to the practice nets. 'From the start he had one great asset,' recalled Connelly, 'he was willing to work and work and work. That was something you really had to admire about him. He had an incredible work ethic even as a young boy.'

Like most young boys, Nick needed a focus, something to work on. Realising this, Connelly enjoyed setting him weekly, even daily challenges. 'I would ask him to hit a low draw, then perhaps a high fade. Anything that kept him interested and focused on the job in hand. I could see he was special. He was tall, well built for a youngster and had a burning desire to do well. It was often a matter of just keeping him on the right track.' According to his teacher, these so-called challenges had a more serious purpose in that they taught Nick Faldo *feel*. 'The golf swing is based entirely on mechanics,' said Connelly. 'But if it breaks down a good player can always fall back on feel.

That's what I tried to teach Nick. By hitting all sorts of shots – high, low, draw, fade – you learn to use your hands better, and with that comes a better feel for the shots.' Not that Nick needed too much persuading to work hard on his game. 'For long periods I used to encourage Nick to practise with nothing but a six-iron. I felt it improved his hand action and rhythm, but he worked so hard he kept wearing the grooves out!'

For Connelly, who described Nick Faldo as a real 'one-off', it was this dedicated, almost professional approach to the game that really made him stand out.

Nick always listened attentively. He asked a lot of questions, and, most of all, spent hour after hour practising the fundamentals I had been preaching to him. One day, after giving Nick a lesson on the importance of tempo, I told him, only half-seriously, to go and practise it for the rest of the afternoon. Five hours later as I was about to leave for the day, Nick came marching up to me in the Welwyn car park and said, 'I've got it, boss, I've got it!' That is the stuff that champions are made of.

Another thing 'champions' have is driving ambition, and Nick Faldo certainly had that. He desperately wanted to do well, make the grade, and Ian Connelly always believed he could. Constantly stressing the importance of setting targets, something he did with all his pupils, the Scot always had lofty ambitions for his most talented pupil. For most people, it might be lowering their handicap or winning a monthly medal, but with Nick it went way beyond that. 'I set goals early on. I told him that after he made the county team, he would make the England boys' team. Then he would make the youth team and then the England senior team – all of which he did. We even talked about turning pro and playing on the United States Tour. He was so talented. For me, it was always a matter of *when*, not if.'

It was now clear that Nick loved golf to the exclusion of everything else. So it came as no surprise to his parents that on leaving school shortly before his sixteenth birthday, he expressed a desire to make the sport his career. In truth, he had little choice. His final year at Sir Frederic Osbourn had been at best half-hearted, at worst neglectful. 'I totally lost interest in school from the age of fifteen,' he said some years later. 'I just couldn't see any way in which an algebraic equation was going to help me with my golf.' That said, he possessed a natural intelligence that brought him exam passes in mathematics, English, metalwork, woodwork and technical drawing.

With these qualifications, and at the age of just sixteen, Nick of course had other options open to him (before leaving school he had considered applying for a job as a ranger for the Canadian Forestry Commission, only to be put off by the poor wages on offer). But for Nick Faldo, it was always golf or nothing.

2. CLIMBING THE LADDER

Having left school in June 1973, Nick Faldo felt relieved. Unshackled from the responsibility of boring schoolwork, he revelled in the thought of playing golf full-time, first as an amateur, then at some distant point as a tournament professional. Advised by an employment councillor at the school to forget a career in golf because 'only one in ten thousand ever makes it', Faldo famously replied, 'Then I'll be that one,' and promptly left the following day.

A few weeks later, in July, Faldo travelled with his father George to the Open at Royal Troon. It was one of the coldest and wettest championships in living memory, and father and son spent the week cooped up in a rickety caravan near the course, but his first real taste of a major championship would linger for the rest of his life. 'I remember it was so cold that I wore my pyjamas under my clothes to try and keep warm,' recalled Faldo. 'It was my second full summer of playing the game and I was absolutely hooked. So I would be out there all day watching the greatest players of that time. I remember I'd be up early and wave my dad goodbye and I'd be running all over the course, then I'd meet him somewhere in the evening.'

Indeed, within minutes of arriving an excited Faldo knew exactly how he wanted to spend his time. Running towards the practice range, he wanted to see those players he had only heard about, or seen on television. 'I watched them all. I used to love sitting on the back of the range checking everybody out – Jack Nicklaus, Lee Trevino, Gary Player, Tom Weiskopf, Johnny Miller and Tony Jacklin.' Standing behind the picket fence that separated him from the stars, he spent hours studying their technique. Making mental notes all the time, he watched how they hit the ball, how rhythmically they swung the club and how long they practised. 'Then I'd go back to Welwyn Garden City and try and copy their swings.'

As a tall, gangly youth himself, Faldo found that the player who impressed him most was the American giant Tom Weiskopf. He added his own support throughout the week, and it came as no real surprise to Faldo when Weiskopf came through to win his first major title. 'I picked Weiskopf to win because I watched him practising in his street shoes. It was late in the evening and he was hitting shots in these slippery leather shoes. He just stood there and nailed it. I was pretty impressed. So much that I said to my dad that he was going to win, and I was right.'

Marvelling over what he had seen at Troon, an inspired Nick Faldo returned home more determined than ever to succeed in his chosen profession. Within a year, he reduced his handicap from 5 to 2 and got his first game for Hertfordshire Colts. He was finally on his way up, but there was still a huge amount of work to do on his game before he could genuinely compete at national level. He was pushed all the way by his Scottish taskmaster Ian Connelly, who believed that physical strength was of huge importance for anyone considering a career in professional golf. Faldo, he said, needed some muscles.

Not for the first time taking his mentor's advice to heart, Faldo began to exercise in the hope of building up stronger wrists and forearms. Standing in front of the pro-shop window, he would idle away the time swinging a club one-handed, left and right. It was the same when he was out on the course. Selecting a thick, tangled area of rough, he would swish away until his arm ached with the effort. Naturally right-handed, he decided that more effort would be needed to strengthen his left, so a wrist exerciser was immediately purchased. Then he went through a phase of doing press-ups, but abandoned both forms of exercise when he discovered that the best way of strengthening his arm muscles was by using a specially weighted driver fashioned for him by one of Connelly's assistants. It was far too heavy to hit a golf ball with, even though he often tried, and he used it almost every day for a year.

Not forgetting his putting, Faldo developed a stiff-wristed method that he could repeat effortlessly and, most importantly, under pressure. In winter and summer he spent hours practising his stroke on the carpets at home. Still competing in club tournaments, he would select which carpet to putt on depending on where he was playing. For example, the downstairs hall carpet was textured and quite bumpy and absolutely perfect for the slower greens found at Welwyn in autumn and winter. A Persian rug upstairs was smoother and faster, but for *really* fast greens, like those found at nearby Knebworth Golf Club in Stevenage, it had to be the linoleum on the kitchen floor. 'I took a back swing of one inch to hit the ball a few feet. It was great practice. By the time I had done that for half an hour I was able to make a three-inch back swing so controlled I needed only to touch the ball to start it rolling.'

By the second summer since leaving school, Faldo had developed a steady routine. In the morning he would cycle the few miles to Welwyn Garden City Golf Club, often with his golf clubs over his shoulders. After playing eighteen holes, he would then sit down by the practice putting green and eat the sandwiches prepared by his mother the previous evening. They were neatly packed away in a plastic Tupperware container, and their fillings rarely varied from his favourite cheese and salad cream, followed by an orange, an apple or a Penguin chocolate biscuit. After playing another round in the afternoon, he would often finish off his day hitting a few balls on the practice ground or, like the other boys, practising his putting on the green next to the clubhouse before returning home in the late evening -- a routine that obviously suited the talented young golfer.

In June 1974, Faldo made his debut for the Hertfordshire senior county team. Now competing against some of the best amateurs in the country, including his future Ryder Cup colleague Ken Brown, he earned a surprise call-up for England Boys a few weeks later. This selection to play in the home internationals at Royal Liverpool proved to be a real step up in class from the county game. He lost both his matches, including one against the Auld Enemy Scotland, hardly the start he had wanted to make to his career, but instead of worrying about it he resolved to work even harder.

Not long afterwards, Faldo competed in the West of England Open strokeplay tournament at Saunton Sands. Playing in testing conditions on Devon's windy northern coast, Faldo led the tournament well into the final round before slipping down the leaderboard after a particularly poor finish. He was barely able to contain his frustration at losing out on such a prestigious title, and won himself few friends after a series of petulant outbursts. Inevitably, word got back to Connelly, and Faldo's response to defeat brought a rare rebuke from the Scot. 'He was boiling mad,' Connelly remembered, 'but as I told him, if you cannot control yourself, you cannot control your game. I think he learnt from that experience in the end.'

One of the few people Faldo did impress that week was Gerald Micklem. One of the most respected administrators in British golf, Micklem had watched Faldo in the England v. Scotland international and could scarcely believe the improvement in the young man's game. 'Something tremendous has happened,' he told six-time British amateur champion Michael Bonallack. 'I've just seen the best player I've seen for ages and ages. He's terrific.' He had already introduced himself to Faldo at Hoylake, and the two became firm friends despite the considerable differences in their backgrounds and ages.

I always listened to Gerald because he presented things so well. He spoke such good sense. It was straight to the point. He never wasted words. He would tell me what I had to do or what had gone wrong and then leave me to decide how to cope with it. I can hear him now saying to me in that distinctive way he has, 'I'll leave you to work out what the best solution is for that.' I remember I threw my clubs down in disgust [at Saunton Sands] and he came up to me later and said, 'I've just got to chat to you. I didn't like you throwing your clubs down like that. I used to do it and you can see that it never got me anywhere.' He didn't say to me, 'If I ever see you doing that again I'll . . .' and I appreciated it. At that time in my career he was the only person, apart from Ian Connelly, who if he said something to me I knew he was saying it for my own good. As a result I would try my darnedest to do whatever he suggested.

Over the winter of 1974/75 Nick Faldo practised harder than ever. As the cost of competing in amateur events grew alarmingly, Ian Connelly arranged on behalf of his protégé a part-time job with local businessman and Welwyn club member Ron Marks. A carpet fitter by trade, it was agreed that Nick would be paid two pounds a day to fetch and carry for Marks. Reasoning that it would be a good way of building up his muscles, Faldo gladly accepted and started work in September 1974. His first real job proved to be an invaluable education. A likeable, down-to-earth character, Marks helped develop some of the social skills that were sadly lacking in the seventeen-year-old Faldo. Becoming good friends with the shy, occasionally petulant youngster, Marks showed Faldo in the few months they spent together that there was a world beyond Welwyn Garden City Golf Club. (Years later, Nick would present Ian Connelly with a book on his early career with the inscription, 'Without your help I would have made a great carpetbagger! Thanks for all your help and support, Nick.')

In 1975, Faldo was determined to show that Gerald Micklem's glowing comments about him had been well founded, but the year began surprisingly badly. Starting his season in April, he had ambitions of winning the prestigious Carris Trophy, a top amateur event held at nearby Moor Park in Rickmansworth. Unfortunately, he scored a disastrous 86 in the second round and made little impact. After that, his entry for the Lytham Trophy in April was refused because his Hertfordshire County handicap of 3 was too high. Later the same month, he was overlooked for the British Walker Cup team to face the USA at St Andrews the following month. No real surprise there, but the selectors must have kicked themselves afterwards. Faldo literally exploded on to the amateur scene later that summer.

Having just scraped into the British Amateur Championship at Royal Liverpool at the end of May, Faldo took on and surprisingly beat the tournament favourite, John Davies, in the third round. It came a mere six days after Britain had suffered a humiliating 15 ½ to 8 ½ defeat in the Walker Cup, and people immediately wanted to know who this youngster was, and why he had not been playing at Hoylake – questions no one was able to answer. For the experienced Davies, losing to Faldo was a huge blow, but afterwards he was full of praise for his young opponent. 'I have just been beaten by the best amateur I have ever seen,' he said to the waiting reporters. 'What a boy! What class! He is better than all these Americans are and he is good enough to win this week. He has a great temperament. If I can find a chink in the armour of anyone I play, I'll always attack it. But there was nothing I could do about him – he had no weaknesses.'

Whether or not these comments went straight to Faldo's head is a matter for speculation. What is certain is that he was brought down to earth with a major bump fewer than twenty-four hours later. Facing the little-known and little-rated David Moffatt in the next round, he lost the match in a play-off at the first extra hole. He put it down to experience, but there was even more disappointment a few weeks later when he failed to qualify for the Open at Carnoustie by two strokes. He had wanted so much to be a part of the Open, and to lose out by such a narrow margin made the experience even more frustrating.

Yet the trip to Scotland's west coast did have its compensations. After leaving the qualifying course at Monifieth, Faldo had raced over to Carnoustie to watch part of the practice round. On arriving he met up with Willie Aitchieson, who had caddied for John Davies at Hoylake. Now working for two-time Open winner Lee Trevino, Aitchieson invited Faldo to walk the course with him and his playing partner, Johnny Miller. It was a wonderful experience. He enjoyed not only a close-up look at two golfing superstars, but was treated to the story of the talkative Mexican's life.

A few days later, Faldo arrived at the English Amateur Championship at Royal Lytham in good spirits. Compared with the dramatic splendour of Carnoustie, Royal Lytham can appear rather ordinary, yet it provides one of the sternest tests in British golf. Known for its narrow fairways and punishing rough, not to mention having the Blackpool to Fleetwood railway line acting as out-of-bounds for the opening seven holes, the course suited Faldo's game perfectly.

After a comparatively easy 3 & 2 first-round victory over one R. Pritchard, a left-hander from Coventry, Faldo sliced through his half of the draw in ruthless fashion. (Interestingly, in the same round, unknown Brian Stockdale surprisingly beat Walker Cup player and defending champion Mark James.) As if in a series of merciful executions, Faldo brushed aside Brian Winterage by two shots on his way to reaching the quarter-finals, then beat Gordon Edwards from the Wirral by 2 & 1. He now faced the unusual situation of having to play his own roommate in the semi-finals. Philip Morley, another left-hander, had shared Faldo's lodgings throughout the week, including during the earlier qualifying round. They were good pals off the golf course, but Faldo had little sympathy for him on it, cruising to victory by the comfortable margin of 4 & 3. Having made it through to his first major final, he was thankfully spared the embarrassment of taking on yet another friend, and fellow Welwyn Garden City Golf Club member, Chris Allen, who had been beaten in an earlier round by 49-year-old Reg Glading. It was now up to Faldo to bring the trophy home to Hertfordshire.

With the final of the 45th English Amateur Championship scheduled over 36 holes, Nick Faldo felt confident that he could win – and so it proved. Matched against 27-year-old David Eccleston, Faldo cruised into lunch six-up after shooting a 69. The match should have been dead and buried, but Faldo struggled to close out his opponent, finally managing it four holes from home.

Winning by 5 & 4, he was immediately hailed as the youngest winner in the championship's long history. Only nine days past his eighteenth birthday, Faldo was overjoyed. 'It felt absolutely fantastic,' he told John Hopkins in 1984. 'So fantastic I can still remember the feelings of excitement nearly ten years later. I rushed to the phone to tell my parents, but they were out. [Then] I drove home in dad's Opel Kadett with the windows down, the cup on the back seat, singing and shouting.'

The true feelings of winning can last for ages and ages. It starts at the prize-giving when you sense that people are looking at you. They're not looking at the guys who have come fourth tied, they're looking at the winner. They want to see the winner. But it can go on for longer than that. After that there's the time when people are saying, 'There's Faldo, he won last week.' And then after that the feelings of success can remain inside you for ages. There have been pressures on you to win, and so finding that you have met them is rewarding. You've pushed yourself and you've found that you're not scared of winning.

The newspaper reports made wonderful reading. Pat Ward-Thomas of the *Guardian* commented, 'It would be surprising if this success was a sudden flash of glory because there is a distinct quality of the unusual about Faldo. The exceptional strength of his wooden and iron play would stand favourably in any company, and is achieved with less effort than I have seen in any young golfer for many years. This plainly is a natural gift. For a boy, his approach to the game is uncommonly mature.'

With his win at Royal Lytham acting like a catalyst, Faldo was quite simply unstoppable for the rest of the year. Having made this breakthrough, he just kept on winning and winning. In a golden six-month period, he added a host of other tournaments to the English Amateur Championship, including the British Youths Championship, the Berkshire Trophy, the South African Amateur Strokeplay Championship, the Scrutton Jug, the Champion of Champions Trophy, the Hertfordshire County Championship, the Hertfordshire Boys Championship, the Royston Junior Championship and a tie for first place in the King George V Coronation Cup. Not to mention the Welwyn Garden City Club Championship! As Dudley Doust of the *Sunday Times* wrote, 'Few could have made a more mercurial rise than Faldo has done.'

Geoff Marks, a former Walker Cup selector, pointed out the differences that made Faldo so special. 'In those days, Sandy [Lyle] had the ability to strike the ball better than any amateur I've ever seen, but his mental approach was that of a seventeen-year-old. For example, every time he stepped on to a tee his sole idea was to get the driver out and give the ball a tremendous yahoo and hit it three hundred yards down the fairway. Nick was the reverse. He had an inferior method, but mentally was as good as anyone.'

Inferior method or not, the pressure on Faldo to turn professional was growing fast. With that in mind, he was invited to play golf with Mark McCormack over the Old Course at Sunningdale in the autumn of 1975. McCormack, the driving force behind the International Management Group (IMG), wanted to cast an eye over the promising amateur with the possibility of taking him on as a client. Impressed with his game, he said afterwards how much Faldo's swing reminded him of US Tour player Jerry Heard. More significantly, he told Faldo that he was probably worth around $100,000 a year in sponsorship deals should he ever make it as a professional. And who would argue with the man who had made Arnold Palmer, Jack Nicklaus and Gary Player into multi-millionaires?

From September until December Faldo worked hard on his game, but having enjoyed huge success that year, he knew some tough decisions would have to be made about his future. With a career in the professional ranks beckoning, he was certainly not short of offers outside IMG. He was approached by a number of other business managers eager to take him on as a client; one even offered to pay all his expenses on tour for five years in return for a percentage of his winnings. The temptation was obvious. Over £600 in the red, his father was already scraping the bottom of the financial barrel just to keep his son in the amateur events.

There was another option. One of the people who approached him was American agent Bruce Streather. He discussed representing Faldo with his father George, as all potential suitors did, and the possibility of a golf scholarship to an American university was brought up. Over the winter Faldo had received a number of similar offers, including a signed letter from Tom Weiskopf inviting him to consider Ohio State University, where Jack Nicklaus had gone to college. The University of California also made enquiries, as did Wake Forest and the University of Houston. Asked for his opinion, Streather suggested Houston. He had contacts there and would help with all the paperwork.

Still only eighteen, Faldo talked it over with his mentor, Ian Connelly. A long-time admirer of American golf, Connelly advised him to post off the forms immediately. He believed the only place to play tournaments was the United States, and what better training could any potential professional have than to play collegiate golf over there? 'I felt that Nick needed more competitive experience,' he said later, 'and there was no better way to obtain that than in America.'

Faldo was still unsure. He liked the idea of playing another season of amateur golf in Britain, perhaps even waiting until after the 1977 Walker Cup at Shinnecock Hills before he turned pro. Sadly, his finances, or lack of them, were becoming a major problem. He had recorded all his expenses in a notebook – something he was encouraged to do by his accountant father

– and it made harsh reading. As he was barred from accepting financial help as an amateur, it was obvious that he could not afford to go on for another year without seeking some sort of aid. As for his parents, George and Joyce, they would back any decision their son made. 'I wasn't worried about Nick,' his mother said confidently at the time. 'I had complete faith in his ability. Besides, George and I were reassured by what everyone said about his golf. Wherever I took him to compete in junior competitions, local golf experts used to come up to me and pour praise on Nick's head. I felt he was bound to succeed.'

In the end the choice was narrowed down to two options: turning pro or accepting the golf scholarship at the University of Houston. After consultation with Keith McKenzie, secretary of the Royal and Ancient, and Ian Erskine, secretary of the English Golf Union, the decision was made to go to Texas. Among other reasons for the decision was that the weather would be warmer there.

Faldo applied for his first passport that November. In January 1976 he packed his bags and headed off to Texas to sit his entrance exams. It was the first time he had been away from home since his trip to the Lake District in 1972. Apprehensive and excited as he flew out from London, Faldo was unsure what to expect from his American adventure, but determined to give it his best shot.

Joining him on the trip were Sandy Lyle and Martin Poxon. The three of them represented the cream of British amateur golf, and it was generally seen as a positive move for the youngsters. Written about at length in the golfing press, the experience of playing and practising in the United States would, it was thought, benefit them enormously. With American stars currently dominating the world game, it was considered a unique opportunity to study under the same system that had produced players of the quality of Jack Nicklaus, Tom Watson and Johnny Miller. Perhaps, as a result of initiatives like this, Britain might be able to produce an Open champion to follow in Tony Jacklin's footsteps.

Sadly, with the golfing hopes of a frustrated nation placed on their shoulders, they would all be disappointed. Within a few months both Lyle and Faldo had returned home. The only one to stick it out was Martin Poxon, and even he would return home not long afterwards. As far as the university was concerned, the biggest disappointment was the departure of Sandy Lyle. Considered the pick of the bunch, he was the first to leave after being told he must attend junior college while waiting for another opportunity to re-sit the entrance test, which he had failed first time round. Lyle, however, was in no mood to wait, especially as the time would be spent apart from his pal, Martin Poxon. Nick Faldo did enough to pass his entrance exam and, like Poxon, was awarded a scholarship bursary of £450 to cover lodging and tuition fees.

Despite Lyle's decision to return home to England, Poxon made the difficult decision to stay and enjoy what was on offer. 'The golf facilities were outstanding,' he said later. 'We could use almost any [golf] club in Houston and they all had so much space. There were always large practice areas, greens to pitch to and lovely putting greens.' Poxon quickly attuned to life on the campus, nicknamed 'Space City' because of its close proximity to the Manned Space Center, but Faldo did not. Expected to work for three hours each morning, studying subjects such as physical education and public speaking, he started to skip classes in favour of more time on the golf course. Used to practising six or seven hours a day at home, in Houston he could get barely half that. 'There was simply too much studying. I was missing the usual practice sessions I had at home. I was used to hitting six hundred practice shots a day. I had been doing that for three years and I was now being asked to break my routine.' Nor did Faldo like the competitive structure of American collegiate golf. With a dozen or so players vying with one another for inclusion in the six-man Houston team, most afternoons were taken up with competitive qualifying rounds, the results of which would determine who would be in the team that weekend. It was pressure Faldo could do without. 'It naturally led to a deterioration in my game,' he admitted later.

At the University of Houston, the rules were simple. To maintain his golf scholarship Faldo had to achieve a seventy per cent pass rate in a regular series of exams. Therefore he was expected to study as much as possible, and if he played in a tournament it was a case of studying more to catch up on lost time. Consequently, during the first few weeks he rarely got a chance to go and hit practice shots, and when he did, there were added complications. 'I didn't have my own transport and so had to ask for a lift to the nearest practice ground, which was twenty minutes away. This was only 220 yards long and extremely narrow. Driving ranges were good but the bags of balls were expensive. And they were all surlyn-covered Top Flites. Well, you can stand there all day hitting those and you will think that you have got it. But it doesn't turn out that you have!'

Nevertheless, he put up some creditable performances and was selected for three of the university's five matches. He also won a freshman tournament with a two-round score of 140, but that was little consolation to the hard-working youngster. 'I was losing so much time,' he recalled. 'I was so dependent on the other guys in the dorm for a lift to the course each afternoon, and at the weekends they always wanted to lie in after going to discos the night before, whereas I wanted to get going. They were so lazy! I was practising once a week, at the most, and falling behind.'

Faldo instinctively felt that endless qualifying rounds were no way to improve his game. He was used to correcting his faults through trial and error on the practice ground; the golf course was no place to try out new things. Ian Connelly had taught him that. Matters rapidly developed into a chicken-and-egg situation: when his game did deteriorate through lack of hitting practice balls, he was ordered to spend even more time out on the course.

Another problem was the emphasis the coaches at Houston placed on putting. Working on the idea that 'a great putter makes a great golfer', every lesson seemed to revolve around the practice putting green. The philosophy seemed to be that if you could hole putts you were all right. Forget good ball strikers like Faldo, Houston preferred the dogged scrambler, the player who could get up and down from the side of the green every time. Indeed, the first question he and Poxon were asked on arrival was, 'Are you a good putter?' Even the basketball coach would question him about his putting ability.

Dave Williams, the golf coach, had been at the University of Houston for 25 years. Faldo felt that Williams, a motivational specialist, lacked the technical knowledge he needed desperately to cure some of the faults that were starting to appear in his swing. It became increasingly obvious that if any of the players had a problem with their technique, it was a case of going to an outside professional and paying for it to be put right, and for the young Englishman that was a problem. He had been invited to Houston on a partial scholarship, which meant that he was given his books, tuition and accommodation free along with his meals. So when he was forced to pay for another professional to give him advice, it became almost intolerable. After all, he felt he had gone there to learn golf.

At the same time he, like the other boys, had to retain a razor-sharp edge for the regular team matches they were expected to play in. In his first match, Faldo qualified at number five to play in the Houston side against Southern Methodist University, Texas A and M and Texas University. With each university fielding a six-man team, the matches were played over 36 holes with the aggregate scores of the top four players counting. Played in typically windy conditions, the match ended with Houston winning by 760 to 771 and Faldo contributing two rounds of 81 and 74. A creditable performance, it gave him joint ninth place in the individual tournament and third place in his team. More importantly, he was now exempt for the next match and wouldn't need to take part in the regular pre-qualifying tests, sometimes played over as many as four rounds.

But 'Space City' was starting to close in on Nick Faldo. For the first time since he took up golf, he could feel his game slipping away. The limited opportunities to practise were dragging him down, and he was beginning to lose the ability to produce those shots that had brought him so much success. Worse still, he could see no hope of improvement unless he returned home and sorted things out. 'I was in America for a total of ten weeks, and in that time I had ten practice sessions. When I compared that with my routine at home I knew I was in the wrong place. I had always practised in the morning and played a round in the afternoon. It was a successful formula for me.'

Feeling unsettled and perhaps a little homesick, Faldo made the decision to leave. A phone call to Ian Connelly from

Houston airport left his teacher feeling somewhat disappointed. 'I really wanted him to stay there. I was a great fan of collegiate golf in America and they would have taught him so much. Not only golf, they had experts on public relations who would have given him lessons on how to present himself. How to react to people, a whole social education. I always thought Nick would have really benefited from that.' On hearing the news that the second of his three British golfers had returned home, coach Dave Williams also appeared disappointed. 'Nick's got a lot of potential. He's long enough off the tee but he needs lots of competition. Technically I think his swing is a little loose. He's got to get firmer.'

Back in Britain, Faldo felt nothing but relief. But if he thought all his problems were behind him, he was sadly mistaken. When the news broke that he had quit the University of Houston after just a few months, he was roundly criticised in the British newspapers for his 'selfish and immature' decision. The *Sunday Times* wrote, 'Faldo, a prodigy, is suffering a disease common to so many British golfers, both amateur and professional; things have come too easily for him. He was, perhaps still is, a glorious prospect. He has come out of it poorly and, as the reigning English champion, doubtless has left a bad taste behind him.'

Hearing about the surprise departure of Faldo from a fellow member of the Houston golf team, Martin Poxon decided to stay on in Texas and see it through. Then, towards the end of his first semester, he was given the unwelcome news that the authorities had reduced the number of scholarships and were reluctantly forced to end his. Without any money to carry him through, he had little choice but to return home. (Unlike Faldo, Poxon had struggled to make the team, playing only once in the time he was there.)

Despite the outburst of indignation from the British golfing press on his return, Faldo knew he had made the right decision. Now it was a case of proving it, and quickly. Before leaving Houston he had already asked his father to get the entry forms for the early events on the amateur circuit. Putting the whole 'American thing' behind him, he now looked forward to playing in the Lytham Trophy at the beginning of May. After that, he would defend his English amateur title a few months later.

As he had arrived home on 14 March, there were a number of other events he could enter before Lytham. A month later he travelled to the first of them, the King George IV Trophy at Craigmillar Park in Glasgow. It was his first opportunity to prove his critics wrong, and he reeled off four wonderful rounds of 68, 70, 76 and 68, winning the tournament by four strokes over George Macgregor. Faldo had made his point.

Not surprisingly, there was talk of Faldo being a certain pick for the forthcoming Walker Cup match, yet there was something about his win in Glasgow that convinced him he should turn professional. Feeling that he had wasted enough time already, Faldo desperately needed a new challenge, one that would not be satisfied by going over old ground in the amateur game no matter how successful he was. 'I felt as though everybody was expecting me to win in Scotland. And as that would have made it much harder, if not impossible, to be as successful as I'd been the previous year, I decided to turn pro.'

After consulting Ian Connelly, Faldo gave up his amateur status on 14 April and turned professional. After further discussions with his parents, he decided to begin his career without any financial help from a sponsor.

> *If you're confident and you know you're going to make it then you don't want the guy from down the road knocking on your front door saying, 'Remember me? I lent you £20,000 to play the tour and you've only repaid me £15,000. Now you've won £100,000 I want twenty-five per cent of that. It's in the contract.' That may be all right for the guy who hasn't got any ambition. He thinks, 'Great, somebody is paying my expenses and I'm able to concentrate on the tour.' But to my mind that's not breeding a champion.*

One thing Nick Faldo *did* want was an attachment to a golf club, preferably one within easy driving distance of his family home. No longer a member at Welwyn Garden City Golf Club, he needed somewhere he could play and practise without being interrupted. In May, Ian Connelly approached nearby Dyrham Park as a possible candidate. Having recently taken up the post of club professional, Connelly put Faldo's offer to the committee but it was politely refused on the grounds that 'the golf club neither desired nor needed the publicity that such an attachment would bring'.

It was only a minor setback. Faldo continued to map out his future in the professional game down to the last detail.

When I started touring my father said to me, 'If we can afford it you'd do better having a room on your own.' So I did, right from the start. I didn't worry about that from the money point of view. I didn't want to have to worry about trying to get to sleep if my roommate didn't also want to go to sleep, and I certainly didn't want to be woken up if somebody else was getting up early. I decided it would be better for my golf if I didn't share. That's how I came to be labelled as a loner.

That was not the *only* reason Faldo would be labelled a loner in his early months on the tour. Advised by Ian Connelly to keep himself to himself, Faldo took him at his word. 'I told Nick that he should not become distracted by life on tour. I said that the best times to practise were early in the morning and late afternoon. There would be less distractions that way. Of course if you do that, you are not going to see many of the other players.'

Having announced his decision to turn professional, Faldo made his debut at the French Open at Le Touquet on 6 May 1976. Two weeks earlier, he had outlined his immediate goals in *Golf Illustrated* magazine. 'If I pre-qualify I see it as the equivalent of winning a one-day amateur tournament,' he said. 'Then, if I get through to the last day of a pro tournament it will be equal to winning the English Amateur Championship.' He went into the French Open with some sound, if unexpected, advice from American Ryder Cup star Ben Crenshaw. Responding to the news that Faldo had set himself small targets on turning pro, he said pointedly:

Tell that boy to go out and win the French Open, and set his sights no lower. There was absolutely no pressure on me in my first professional tournament [the San Antonio Open in 1973] and Faldo should realise this. He should go out and play for his life before he starts to realise, as I did, the enormity of his

achievement. Maybe he will suffer the kind of relapse that hit
me when I was stupid enough to start thinking that the game
that had served me so well as an amateur was not good enough
technically for the professional game. But he must know and
believe he can win in France and think of nothing else until he
has done so.

In the end, Faldo made a solid, if not spectacular, debut by
finishing joint thirty-eighth at Le Touquet.

In July, he entered the Open at Royal Birkdale and acquitted
himself well for an inexperienced nineteen-year-old. Having
made the halfway cut, he crowned it with a final round of 69
to finish joint twenty-eighth with Gary Player, Doug Sanders
and Neil Coles. More importantly, he won a total of £335 in
official prize money.

He took to his new life like a duck to water, and it quickly
became obvious that Faldo needed professional help in hand-
ling his business affairs. Up to that point, he had continued to
jot down his expenses in a small notebook before handing it
over to his father at the end of each week to see whether he had
made a profit or not. Now there were added complications.
Sponsors approached him most weeks with tempting offers of
new clubs, gloves, balls and shoes. A far cry from his
poverty-stricken amateur days, it was obvious that he needed
some good advice to negotiate his way through this, and in
August he signed up with Mark McCormack's International
Management Group.

It was the start of a long and highly lucrative partnership. The
deal had been set up by wealthy South African businessman
George Blumberg, a personal friend of McCormack. Blumberg
had met Faldo in Durban during the British Commonwealth
Trophy tournament in November 1975 and had been suitably
impressed. Aware that Faldo was looking for a management
company, he had telephoned the Faldo family home late in July
1976 asking them to hold off making a decision until he had
spoken to IMG. A matter of days later, he had good news.
McCormack had agreed to take Faldo on a six-month trial basis,
leaving them both free to go their own way if things did not
work out. Faldo agreed, and a contract was signed.

By September the season was over in Europe, and Faldo could reflect on a solid start to his tournament career. Starting with the French Open, where he had picked up his first professional cheque for £130.83, he ended the year fifty-eighth in the money list with prize money totalling £2,339. Then, in November, at the invitation of 'Uncle' George Blumberg, he headed down to South Africa to compete in four events on the so-called 'Sunshine Circuit'. He stayed with Blumberg and his wife at their apartment in Johannesburg (along with his fellow pro Warren Humphreys), and it proved to be a good experience as well as a profitable one. He never finished higher than twenty-second place, but it gave Faldo a taste for playing overseas that would never really leave him.

The future looked bright. Having successfully made the transition from top amateur to tournament professional, Faldo could now look forward to his first full season on the European circuit – and perhaps his first win.

3. FIRST JACK, THEN SEVE

Unlike many amateurs who turn professional then struggle, Nick Faldo found that life as a tournament player suited him perfectly. Money was often in short supply, but the long hours he was able to spend on the practice ground more than compensated for the penury as far as he was concerned. He worked hard on his game over the winter of 1976/77 with Ian Connelly, and his coach was convinced that success was just around the corner. But while Faldo talked in terms of winning his first 72-hole tournament, the Scot had far loftier ambitions for his pupil. 'Let's make the Ryder Cup team,' he said. 'That should be our target for the year, nothing less.'

Faldo was astonished. A year earlier he had been thinking in terms of playing in the Walker Cup against the USA, now it was the Ryder Cup! But the more he thought about it, the more it appealed. All he had to do was finish in the top eight in the money list and he would qualify as the youngest player in the history of the event. To the outsider, it would have been interpreted as youthful bravado, but by the time he arrived at Moor Park in June for the Uniroyal tournament it was beginning to look a distinct possibility.

In a whirlwind start to the season, Faldo had finished joint third in the Madrid Open in April and joint sixth in the Colgate PGA Championship at Royal St George's in May. (He had also reached the fifth round of the Sun Alliance Matchplay at Stoke Poges before losing to the Ryder Cup captain, Brian Huggett.) As the tour moved on to Moor Park, the signs were good. Little more than half an hour's drive away from Welwyn, it was a course Faldo knew well, having played in several Hertfordshire Colts matches there during his amateur days. More importantly, he was beginning to swing it well, and Connelly felt confident this could be his week.

Opening up with rounds of 68 and 67, Faldo unexpectedly found himself four shots clear of Greg Norman. In the third round, the pressure of leading such a prestigious event started to hit home. His rhythm got faster, his ball striking more erratic, and it was left to his caddie John Moorhouse to keep reminding him to slow down. Finishing with a score of 73, he now trailed Seve Ballesteros by a single stroke with one round to play. Despite his disappointing performance the day before, Faldo felt confident he could turn things around. In the end, it was a conversation with Connelly about rhythm that made the difference. 'Nick always had a wonderful tempo,' said the Scot. 'I remember him asking me, "What should my tempo be?" So I told him that as a tall chap he should swing it slow and somehow that stuck in his mind – one-two-three up and one-two-three down. Often it was just a case of reminding him.'

With 'one-two-three up and one-two-three down' constantly playing in his head, Faldo set about closing the gap on Ballesteros, but there was a problem. Drawn with Australian Graham Marsh for that final round, Faldo found himself constantly looking over his shoulder to see how his Spanish rival was getting on behind him. It proved a frustrating task, especially as there were no leaderboards on the front nine and few on the back nine. Gradually, news filtered back via the caddie grapevine that Seve was hitting the ball all over the place but still scoring well. Nick Faldo, in contrast, was scoring well and playing well.

Convinced he was well in the lead by the time he came to the eighteenth, Faldo was shocked to find that he still trailed Ballesteros by a single stroke at eleven under. Faldo, under pressure to make birdie on the testing par-three hole, saw his tee-shot finish twenty feet past the cup. Left with a treacherously fast downhill putt, he decided to be bold. Racing down the slope, the ball hit the back of the cup dead centre and dropped in. Whether it was a stroke of fortune or not, it was good enough to put him in a play-off with Ballesteros, the first of his professional career.

With the long par-five sixteenth selected as the first extra hole, the Spaniard was given the honour. In typical style, he hit two consecutive hooks and was fortunate to find himself still in play after a lucky bounce off a spectator's heel. Faldo, in contrast, hit two wonderful shots to the back edge of the green, leaving himself an outside chance of an eagle.

As Ballesteros prowled around the left side of the green looking for somewhere to land his pitch, Faldo looked on impassively. He gave no clue as to how nervous he felt inside, barely blinking when his opponent played a miraculous chip to within three feet for an almost certain birdie. Still with the advantage, Faldo now had a putt for the title. The stroke itself seemed smooth and unhurried, but the ball seemed to gather pace as it travelled down the slope, eventually coming to a halt fourteen feet beyond the hole. Faldo looked stunned. It was still his turn, and it surprised nobody when his next putt finished short of the hole. Seconds later, Faldo could hardly bring himself to watch as Ballesteros walked up and tapped in the winning putt.

Driving home, Faldo had mixed emotions about his second-place finish. He was delighted to have played so well but disappointed to have missed out in such dramatic fashion. It was a feeling that was still affecting him at the Open at Turnberry a month later where a lacklustre performance left him languishing in joint sixty-second place behind the gap-toothed American Tom Watson. Having been on the brink of a welcome boost in his position in the Ryder Cup rankings, the twenty-year-old Faldo had spent a frustrating few weeks, but things were destined to get much better.

Despite prize-money earnings of just under £10,000 in July, finances were surprisingly tight. Consequently, the arrival of a new sponsor in Glynwed International, the brainchild of its managing director Sir Leslie Fletcher, was a welcome boost to both Faldo and his long-suffering parents. Fletcher had been tipped off about Faldo shortly before the Open. Told about this 'bright young golfer' by fellow knight Sir William Barlow, Fletcher was persuaded to watch Faldo play a few holes in the opening round. Suitably impressed, Fletcher invited Faldo and his father to his London office. The proposal was simple: in return for having a Glynwed International sticker on his bag (or their subsidiary Defy, should he be competing in South Africa), Faldo would receive just under £4,500 a year over the next three years to cover playing expenses. It was an offer he gladly accepted.

It was Glynwed's first and last venture into golf sponsorship, but Sir Leslie Fletcher remained a staunch Faldo supporter for years afterwards. Never forgetting their first meeting, he often recalled what had impressed him most about the young English golfer. 'They came into my office, and as I sat looking across at Nick I couldn't help noticing his large hands. I thought to myself, "The clubs must look like pencils in them. With hands like that he must be able to play golf."'

He was right. In August, Faldo won his first professional tournament, a 36-hole strokeplay event at Gleneagles sponsored by Skol Lager. It was scheduled as a warm-up for the Double Diamond World Golf Classic, an international team event played later the same week, and he beat Craig Defoy and Chris Witcher in a play-off after recording rounds of 67 and 71. The win was accompanied by a handsome cheque for £4,000, which lifted him into the top eight in the Order of Merit for the first time in his career. Now in position to qualify automatically for the Ryder Cup at Royal Lytham in September, all he had to do was hold on.

With two events remaining, the race to fill the automatic places came down to just three men: Nick Faldo, Sam Torrance and Doug McClelland. Based on a points-for-pounds system, Faldo led his two closest rivals by over £2,600 in the money list. Having already stated his intention to miss the Dutch Open in August – the last qualifying tournament – Faldo needed a solid finish in the German Open at Düsseldorf to confirm his place. With that in mind, PGA tournament director Tony Gray informed Faldo in Germany that there was still time to enter the Dutch Open should he need to.

In the end, it was unnecessary. Finishing with a final round of 68 and a joint-third placing, Faldo became the youngest British Ryder Cup player in the event's long history. Relieved not to have to compete in Holland, Faldo returned home to Hertfordshire to work on his game with his coach. Delighted that his pupil had made it, it was an emotional Ian Connelly who greeted Faldo on his return. (Not only had he predicted that Faldo would make the Ryder Cup side at his first attempt, he had placed a substantial wager with a member of the Welwyn club that he would.)

On the practice ground at Dyrham Park everything Faldo and Connelly did together was geared towards sharpening his game. Faldo was in good spirits and was looking forward to making his Ryder Cup debut. Then came a problem that threatened to ruin absolutely everything. Playing in a pro-am at Hill Valley in Shropshire, Faldo felt a sudden pain in his neck. Unable to carry on, he asked his mother Joyce to drive him back home to Welwyn that afternoon. The following day his doctor's initial diagnosis was a trapped nerve, but a blood test was taken as a precaution. Relieved it was nothing serious, Faldo decided to play in the Tournament Players Championship at Foxhills a few days later, and immediately regretted it. Tired and listless, he stumbled through an opening round of 80, his worst competitive round since turning professional. Partnered by Brian Huggett, it was hardly the form he wanted to show in front of the British captain. Worse still, the Welshman had been quoted as saying that he preferred experience over youth, especially when it came to the pressure of a Ryder Cup.

Having lost to Huggett in the Sun Alliance Matchplay at Stoke Poges earlier in the year, Faldo was determined to make a better impression in the second round. Feeling slightly stronger, he battled back bravely with a one-under-par 71 to make the halfway cut. Faldo saw it as a victory over the testing, tree-lined Surrey course. If it was, it was a fairly short-lived one. Twenty-four hours later he shot a horrendous 83 and immediately withdrew from the event feeling completely exhausted. Something was wrong, but what? A telephone call from the doctor to his mother gave them the bad news: Faldo had a mild case of glandular fever.

The two took the decision not to tell Faldo, who arrived at the British team hotel in Lytham two days later feeling stronger after a short rest. The only thing on his mind now was the Ryder Cup. Then, on the Wednesday, the day before the match was due to start, he woke up with a scarlet-coloured rash on his fingers. Then he noticed the same red marks on his wrists, knees and elbows. He could not believe it. Playing in the Ryder Cup was the realisation of a long-held dream, and now, with literally just hours to go, it was under severe threat. He reasoned he could cover up the rash and make out that nothing was wrong; after all, his face was clear and he certainly didn't feel ill. But what if there was something seriously wrong with him? What if he fell ill during a match? What if he collapsed in front of millions on television? Calming himself down, he sat on a chair in his hotel room trying to convince himself that he was strong enough to play. He told himself that there was no problem – until he reached over to his bag, grabbed a club and found he couldn't hold it.

The decision was made for him. Picking up the phone, he asked reception for Brian Huggett's room.

'Brian,' he said when Huggett answered. 'It's Nick. I'm covered in a rash.'

'I'll get the doctor to see you,' Huggett replied after a momentary silence. 'He's already coming over to see [Tony] Jacklin because of a cold. I'll send him up to you afterwards.'

When the doctor finally arrived, he did some tests before confirming the Welwyn doctor's diagnosis. Faldo had glandular fever. He asked about a cure and was informed very matter-of-factly, 'Attempt nothing strenuous, take lots of rest and avoid stress.'

Taking the doctor's advice, Faldo rested in his bedroom – for two hours. As the rash began to fade, he joined the rest of the British team for the final practice round. Two hours after that, Huggett informed him on the fourteenth fairway, 'You and Peter Oosterhuis are playing together tomorrow. Good luck.'

With five foursomes scheduled for day one, five fourballs for day two and twelve singles on day three, both teams needed a fast start. Drawn against Ray Floyd and Lou Graham in the foursomes, Faldo was excited about the prospect of taking on two of the United States' most experienced players. It was decided that as Faldo was striking the ball better in practice than his more experienced partner, he should hit the opening tee at the first. A testing 206-yard par three, it was a daunting prospect for any Ryder Cup rookie, especially someone who at twenty years, one month and 28 days was now officially the youngest player in Ryder Cup history.

It would be nice to say that Faldo holed this first shot, but the record books tell a different story. Having hit countless four- and five-iron shots on the practice range in preparation, he not only pulled his tee-shot left of the green, but missed the three-foot putt his partner had left him for par. One-down immediately, the British pair then compounded the error by losing the next two holes. Three-down after three was not the dream start Faldo had had in mind.

Wrapped up against a chill north-easterly breeze, Faldo and Oosterhuis seemed unable to cut into the Americans' lead. Two-up at the turn, three-up after ten, Floyd and Graham were seemingly cruising to victory when everything fell apart for them. After losing the eleventh, twelfth, fourteenth and fifteenth holes to fall one stroke behind, they looked at each other in total disbelief. Having dropped five shots to par over the previous six holes, they stumbled on to the seventeenth looking for a miracle, but none was forthcoming. Bunkered in two, on the green in three, Graham faced a short putt to save the match and, perhaps not surprisingly, missed. Victors by 2 & 1, the home team had its first point on the board and Great Britain & Ireland had a new hero in the twenty-year-old Nick Faldo. Had the American pair been complacent? Whether the British pair 'won' or the American pair 'lost' was not important. Cheered all the way to the Lytham clubhouse by a fervently patriotic crowd, Faldo had made the perfect start to his Ryder Cup career.

On day two, Faldo and Oosterhuis drew the plum American pairing of Ray Floyd and Jack Nicklaus in match three. His head still spinning after the victory over Floyd the previous day, Faldo was now lined up to play the man who had inspired him to take up golf just six years earlier. In what proved to be a memorable encounter, Faldo grabbed the lead at the second after finding the par-four green with a superb two-iron, which he then converted for a birdie. It was an advantage he was determined not to give up, and he scraped a heroic half at the third, followed by another at the sixth. Unable to prevent Floyd winning the fourth to square the match, it must have felt like an uphill battle for the young Englishman who was grimly hanging on as his partner struggled to find any rhythm. Oosterhuis finally got back into the match at the par-four eighth, hitting a superb one-iron/four-iron combination to within ten feet for a hole-winning birdie. 'I was playing so poorly that for the first seven holes Nick was on his own,' said Oosterhuis later. 'But I had no worries. He is a solid player and, as he proved, utterly dependable in such circumstances.'

Two-down at the turn, Floyd and Nicklaus won the tenth to halve the deficit. It could have been a turning point, but Faldo bounced back immediately with a long birdie putt at the next to restore their lead. In truth, that was the match right there. Six holes later, the British pair reached the penultimate hole two-up with two to play. With the wind directly behind him, Peter Oosterhuis found the green on the testing 453-yard par four with a drive and a nine-iron, going on to seal a wonderful win with a two-putt par. But celebrations were tempered by the fact that Faldo and Oosterhuis had been the only British winners in either the foursomes or fourballs.

With Great Britain & Ireland trailing by five points going into the final day, the Ryder Cup was effectively lost, but Nick Faldo had no intention of letting up. Matched in the singles against the reigning Masters and Open champion Tom Watson, he had an opportunity for even more glory. Not that anyone gave him much of a chance. In the morning newspapers, the British press speculated on how much Faldo's two wins had owed to the steadying influence of Peter Oosterhuis. Perhaps he was just lucky, they said. Floyd and Graham had been out of sorts, Nicklaus was still recovering from his loss at the hands of Tom Watson in the Open at Turnberry two months earlier. Faldo, in truth, could not have cared less. After his second win in two days he said to waiting reporters, 'I've never been beaten on this course. I won the English championship here, so I'm keen to keep my record.'

Faldo discussed his game plan with Ian Connelly the night before, and the next day made the perfect start, winning the fourth with a par and the fifth with a spectacular eagle three. He was hitting the ball better than ever; not even losing the seventh and ninth to a resurgent Watson could dent his new-found confidence. Retaking the initiative with birdies at the tenth and the twelfth, Faldo restored his two-hole advantage, but not for long. Followed by the biggest crowd of the week, the momentum in this roller-coaster match swung Watson's way again as he won the fourteenth and seventeenth to square the match. Everything would now rest on the par-four eighteenth.

Standing on the tee, Faldo felt he needed a birdie to win, but in the end a simple par was good enough. Tom Watson, normally the straightest of hitters, looked on agonisingly as his drive found a fairway bunker. He had been unable to reach the green in regulation, unlike Faldo, and his subsequent bogey was just enough to hand his opponent victory. Speaking afterwards about his incredible Ryder Cup, Faldo said, 'I never thought that I would be thrown in the deep end against all these great players, but I'm enjoying every minute. It's quite a lot of fun, and I'm not as nervous as I thought I might be.'

In a week that began with such uncertainty over his health, Nick Faldo had ended it in glory. Taking a maximum of three points from three matches played, he had taken on America's best and beaten them, including the world number one, Tom Watson. So what if the Ryder Cup had been lost? So what if the match became Europe versus the USA in two years' time at the Greenbrier, as everyone predicted? For now, Britain had a golfer who could take on the world, and that was a victory in itself.

The Ryder Cup was barely over when Faldo, flushed with confidence, won his next tournament. Competing in the Laurent Perrier Trophy, an exclusive eight-man invitation event in Belgium, he took on and beat Seve Ballesteros in the final round. Returning to England the next morning he was astonished at the praise heaped on him by the golfing press. Having played brilliantly in the Ryder Cup, then defeated the pride of European golf, Faldo could do no wrong. 'Faldo has the class to rule Europe for years,' wrote Michael McDonnell, respected golf columnist of the *Daily Mail*. 'His display was not only thrilling but also showed clear evidence that he is the stuff of champions.' Someone else who was impressed was former US Open champion Billy Casper, who finished joint second with Ballesteros in Belgium. 'Nick has more talent than anyone I have seen out of Britain. I would like him to get to the States. He gets a little hot when he misses a shot, but that's youth.'

Having made the transition from top amateur to top tournament professional so successfully, Faldo finished eighth in the end-of-season Order of Merit. It was a remarkable performance by any standards; his first full season in Europe had brought in a rich harvest. Apart from the sensational Ryder Cup debut, he had won two tournaments, finished second in another and accumulated £23,978 in prize-money earnings. He was also awarded 'Rookie of the Year' by three-time Open champion Henry Cotton at the end of the year. The future looked increasingly bright as he prepared to build on his success over the following year.

But by the time the 1978 season rolled around Nick Faldo had still not won a 72-hole tournament. A frustrating omission from his curriculum vitae, it became his main ambition as he arrived on the Algarve for the season-opening Portuguese Open in April. A month later he came close to breaking his duck after finishing a distant runner-up to Seve Ballesteros in the Martini International at the RAC Club in Epsom. The tournament was played in glorious May sunshine, but the weather turned surprisingly sour for the Colgate PGA Championship at Royal Birkdale the following week. With rain and strong winds battering the players, the practice days were a nightmare of rainproof clothing, uneven greens and tangled rough. Mercifully, the weather had cleared up in time for the opening round on Friday, and Nick Faldo took full advantage.

Opening up with rounds of 70, 68 and 70, the twenty-year-old Englishman began his final round on Bank Holiday Monday holding an unexpected four-shot lead. Paired with his nearest challenger, Howard Clark, Faldo looked nervous and apprehensive as he missed short putts on the first three holes to give the chasing pack some realistic hope. Dropping another shot to the blond-haired Yorkshireman at the par-three fourth, the hapless Faldo was having a nightmare and seemed completely unable to do anything about it. Moving into the back nine, he finally started to find his game, having been spurred into action after an incident at the eighth. Later accusing his playing partner of gamesmanship, he was annoyed that play had been held up for over twenty minutes while Howard Clark called for a rules official.

He called for a ruling, yet in my mind it was obvious that he could take a drop because his ball was simply behind a scoreboard. The European Tournament Players Division have repeatedly tried to point out to players that they should know the rules well enough not to have to call for a tournament director's ruling if it is obvious what to do. But I think Howard wanted to make me wait and lose my momentum. We sat there for twenty minutes under a blazing sun, but there was no way it was going to make me mad.

The delay made little difference to the eventual result. By the time both players arrived at the fifteenth tee, the scoreboards were showing that Faldo had a five-shot lead (in fact, the lead was only three after Ken Brown birdied the sixteenth to move into second place). Despite the steamingly hot weather Faldo was in no mood to let things slip now. After a huge drive down the 542-yard par-five fifteenth, he struck a wonderful three-iron to fifteen feet and slotted home the putt for an eagle. Now eight-under for the tournament, he followed it with another birdie on the seventeenth. Victory was assured.

Walking up the last, Faldo soaked up all the applause from the holiday crowds. This was the big win he had wanted, and it had come before his twenty-first birthday. After holing out on the final green, Howard Clark walked across to shake Faldo's hand and add his congratulations. Then, in a moment of high farce, one drunken fan came zigzagging his way towards the new champion with a glass in one hand and a bottle of champagne in the other and offered Faldo a drink. He politely refused, mainly because he had just one thing on his mind at that moment: making his way to the PGA caravan to sign his card and pick up his trophy. It was then that he began to shake. Sitting in front of the official scorer, Bill Hodge, Faldo tried to add up the figures but could not get them to make much sense. For some minutes, he barely realised that he had shot a 69 for a ten-under-par total and victory by seven clear shots.

As Faldo walked from the caravan he saw his father – neither man knew what to say. In the end, it was a bottle of champagne that roused both men to action. Before the final round, Faldo had arranged with his father that if he won he should make sure that there was a case of champagne in the press tent. Spotting the bottle in his father's hand, he asked if he could deliver it by way of thanks to the golf writers that had supported him over the past eighteen months.

The only player to break par in every round, Faldo had secured an emphatic win, and the plaudits were not long in coming. Michael Williams, writing in the *Daily Telegraph*, pointed out that Faldo was the youngest British tournament winner since Bernard Gallacher captured the Schweppes title at Ashburnham in 1969 at the age of twenty, while Pat Ward-

Thomas of the *Guardian* described his victory as 'probably the most commanding win ever by a young player in a British professional tournament'. Mark Wilson of the *Daily Express* wrote that Faldo had shown 'the five-star class of Walter Hagen and the late Tony Lema in celebrating victory by calling for champagne'. There were similar glowing tributes from writers in the other morning newspapers, including Michael McDonnell. Referring to the new breed of competitive young professionals, he said, 'What sets Faldo apart from all of them is his gift of making it all look so damnably easy.' High praise indeed.

After the initial whirlwind of telephone calls from relatives, friends and the press, things finally started to calm down in the Faldo household. Before the Ryder Cup, Faldo had been little known outside golfing circles but success had followed success and he suddenly found himself thrust into the national spotlight. Press comments were generally complimentary, but the added interest in Faldo the man rather than Faldo the golfer brought an unexpected rash of articles in the tabloids and Sunday supplements. Faldo found himself the subject of 'lifestyle' items in newspapers like the *Sun*, which featured him in a two-page centre spread with comments like, 'He lives, sleeps and dreams golf. He has that rare quality of believing you play to win.' But Faldo was flattered by all the attention. Boyishly good-looking, he was an editor's dream, and for weeks afterwards it seemed that every glossy magazine in Britain carried a story about him. Not that it was all his idea. A week after he won the Colgate PGA, he had been assigned a new manager by IMG, John Simpson. A clever operator with a sharp mind and a canny taste for promotion, Simpson would ultimately make Nick Faldo one of the richest sportsmen in the world.

They first met at the 1977 Penfold PGA Championship at Royal St George's. Brought up in nearby Broadstairs, Simpson was working in public relations for Kent County Council after obtaining a degree in business studies at Westminster College in London. Introduced by a friend of Faldo's caddie, John Moorhouse, they got on extremely well, and Faldo was happy to put in a word of recommendation when the position with IMG came up eleven months later. Given responsibility for IMG's growing band of European golfing clients, including

Faldo, Simpson took it upon himself to pay back his best-known client by arranging a series of lucrative sponsorship deals, including one with the jam-makers Robertson's. This was the first in a long line of deals the quick-witted Simpson would arrange for his client over the coming years, although the Robertson's contract was the one which would remain among the most memorable, as Faldo later explained: 'In return for the contract I displayed a golly on my golf bag and carried a golly umbrella. You can imagine all the jokes from the guys out on tour when this came out.'

Faldo's profile was high in the early summer of 1978, and with the Open at St Andrews little more than a month away, expectations were also high about a potential 'home' win. Through all the talk, Faldo appeared unconcerned. Competing in the Belgian Open in Brussels in early June, he opened up with three successive rounds of 71 leaving him well placed to record his second win on Belgian soil in eight months. In the end, however, the final round proved a huge disappointment for him and his growing army of fans. Feeling jaded, he was unable to lift his game when it most mattered. Ending the tournament with a mediocre round of 72, he finished joint sixth behind the eventual winner, Noel Ratcliffe of Australia, who shot a 66. When it came down to it, there was just not enough juice left in the tank. Returning to England, Faldo could still reflect on a remarkable few weeks. In his last thirteen competitive rounds he had scored over par only once, and that was his closing round in Belgium. Better still, twelve of those rounds had been sub-par scores, leaving him 29 under par over thirteen rounds. A wonderful record, but it was not destined to last.

The following week in the Greater Manchester Open at Wilmslow he could only manage rounds of 74, 69, 77 and 75. Finding concentration difficult, he tried to focus on the forthcoming Open, but that only added to the pressure of expectation he was now feeling. The decision was made to miss the following week's Sumrie tournament in Bournemouth in order to take a rest. At the end of June he returned to competition in the Sun Alliance European Matchplay event at Dalmahoy near Edinburgh. It would prove a frustratingly short visit. Playing in bitterly cold conditions, Faldo ran off four birdies in the first seven holes in his 6 & 5 first-round demolition of Peter Berry. In the second round he was drawn to meet Garry Cullen, and again started the match in a brilliant manner, reaching the turn in 32. But this was matchplay, not strokeplay, and despite having missed the cut in his last four events, Cullen rose to the challenge and eventually beat his better-known opponent by 2 & 1.

There was, however, one ray of sunshine in the week leading up to the Open. On the Sunday before he was due in Scotland, Faldo delighted members at Welwyn Garden City Golf Club by defeating the reigning US Masters champion Gary Player in a £6,000 winner-takes-all challenge match. Faldo shot a new course record 65 in the process, and the diminutive South African lost little time in giving his opinion on Britain's latest golf star. 'He's big and he's strong and he's got a nice swing. Now it is just up to him. In today's golf world there are many potential winners and you can liken them to a stampede of racehorses coming to the last furlong. One can shoot out of the pack – and he's got the style to be the real thoroughbred.'

In typical style, Faldo had prepared meticulously for the match, and had especially practised his tee-shot at the par-three eighteenth (a £43,000 Rolls-Royce was on offer for a hole-in-one). He hit faded four-irons into the green, but the closest he got was two feet away from the cup, yet he seemed confident that he could get it closer when the time came. He did. As the large gallery looked on, the ball pitched, bounced, ran towards the hole, hit the hole but stayed on the lip. Typically, Faldo disguised his disappointment by theatrically throwing his club to the floor. The crowd laughed as they were obviously meant too, but having prepared so diligently, he was seething inside.

Another bonus was the surprise visit of Gerald Micklem to watch the match. Full of admiration, he walked up to Faldo afterwards and unexpectedly handed over three pages of handwritten notes detailing everything any potential champion needed to know about the Old Course at St Andrews. Essentially an 'insider's guide', the document pinpointed every hump and hollow in meticulous detail. It showed what bunkers to avoid, what lines to take off the tee, and even indicated where the pin positions would be on each of the four days. By way of an introduction, Micklem wrote, 'While it is generally assumed that the Old is a hooker's course, there are holes where it is necessary to be to the right in order to get the easier shot into the green.' Not surprisingly, Micklem's generosity left Faldo bubbling with enthusiasm. 'It was better than an Ordnance Survey map,' he said many years later. 'The detail was such that I felt I knew the Old Course like an old friend. Yet I had not even set out from home and I had never set eyes on St Andrews. The only thing I could fault was his handwriting! It reminded me of the scrawl on a doctor's prescription.'

Transferring Micklem's notes to individual cards for each hole, Faldo pored over them as if they were important exam notes and began repeating them like a mantra on the car journey up to Scotland. Taking turns behind the wheel with his caddie John Moorhouse, he arrived in the old town late on the Saturday evening and lost little time in getting to know the ancient links. Having only seen the course on television, he resisted the impulse to play, preferring instead to walk a few holes with Moorhouse alongside him with a measuring wheel to chart distances. It slowly began to dawn on him that Micklem was absolutely spot-on with all his calculations. Every pot bunker was located where he had put it, each hump and hollow was accurately recorded.

That night, Faldo read through some of the more general comments Micklem had made about the Old Course.

You must never get mad at St Andrews. You must be willing to accept exactly what you get. Then you must keep on trying. Keep a clear mind all the time. For there are so many humps and hollows that it is easy to allow your mind to become tangled with frustration. Once you start seeking excuses, St Andrews has got you beat. It is no good saying that this or that is a silly hole. It is no good questioning why a hump should be here. Once you do that you can seriously forget your chances of winning. The Old Course must be treated sympathetically. Don't try to fight it, try to understand it.

Determined to obey Gerald Micklem's instructions to the letter, Faldo began working on his game in preparation for the challenge ahead. In the past, Micklem had also mentioned how St Andrews was the kind of course where you are often required to play half-shots punched low into the wind. Consequently, in those days leading up to the tournament, Faldo worked hard, often gripping down the shaft on a three-iron but using a full swing. Micklem, now resident in St Andrews, doubted whether the shot could be perfected with less than one week of practice, but Faldo was confident and soldiered on.

For the opening two rounds of the 1978 Open Faldo was paired with the former golden boy of American golf Johnny Miller and Spaniard Antonio Garrido. It was a good draw, especially as Miller had gone on record earlier in the year at the French Open saying, 'You've got a British Open champion here. The fellow can really play. He's a very talented golfer. You mark my words – he's going to the top.' Those words had generated an enormous amount of confidence in the young Englishman, and it was only a couple of weeks after Miller went on record that he won the Colgate title.

After a good opening round of 71, Faldo looked to build on this on day two. Enjoying the best of the afternoon weather, he continued his good form by reaching the turn in a four-under-par 32. He was sitting proudly on top of the Open leaderboard for the first time in his career, but there would be no time to enjoy it as he prepared to play the back nine. It was here that things started to go badly wrong. Turning into a stiffening breeze at the thirteenth, Faldo suddenly became defensive and lost his tempo completely. Constantly ballooning the ball up in the air, he racked up forty strokes for the last nine for a level-par round of 72. Resolving to fight back over the weekend, he shot a morale-boosting 70 in windswept conditions to keep himself in the hunt. These third-round heroics meant that he went into the final round just two strokes behind joint leaders Peter Oosterhuis and Tom Watson on 211. Only three strokes separated the top dozen competitors, and Faldo felt confident about making a challenge, but as the final day dawned golf was suddenly a long way from his thoughts.

Shortly before breakfast, Faldo began suffering from unexplained chest pains, possibly resulting from the enormous pressure he had been under in recent weeks. He was staying with his parents at a friend's house in Dundee, and his mother suggested a warm bath might help. Faldo was due on the first tee in just over four hours, so the tension among the family was palpable, but somehow the bath worked. The pain disappeared as mysteriously as it had arrived, and Faldo was ready for action.

Unaware of the drama that had gone on hours before, the crowd gave Faldo and his American playing partner John Schroeder a huge send-off as they walked down the first. 'The crowd seemed to applaud us all the way,' said Faldo. 'I can remember thinking to myself, "Gee, this is going to be a hell of a day."' Reaching the turn in 37 – one over par – Faldo still believed he had an outside chance of winning. He was wrong, and despite making a welcome birdie at the fourteenth, the strain of what had happened earlier that morning took its toll. Forced to settle for a 72 and a three-under-par total of 285, he finished joint seventh behind the eventual winner, Jack Nicklaus. Nicklaus was a popular winner with the enthusiastic Scottish crowd, and Faldo could only look on in admiration as the Golden Bear picked up his third Open title in thirteen years. 'What an achievement that is,' said Faldo prophetically to a waiting journalist.

Faldo paused for a few moments to chat with Gerald Micklem outside the entrance of the Royal and Ancient Clubhouse, and thanked him for his help. Assuring him that he would try to make better use of his information when the Open next returned to St Andrews in six years' time, he left him with a handshake. But Micklem needed little convincing. When asked his opinion on Faldo, his reply was short and to the point. 'I have no doubt,' he said, 'he will be the best British golfer since Henry Cotton.'

Faldo missed the Dutch Open at Noordwijk the following week, taking the decision to stay at home and work on his game with his coach, Ian Connelly. A week later, Nick Faldo arrived in Cologne for the Braun German Open rattling like a chemist's travel bag after picking up a gland infection shortly before leaving London. Currently leading the Order of Merit with £19,602, he desperately wanted to consolidate his substantial lead over second-placed Seve Ballesteros. With half a dozen tournaments still to play, he knew it was not going be easy, especially with the Spaniard coming into some promising form. Having finished top dog in Europe for the past two years, Ballesteros was equally determined not to give up his crown. Trailing Faldo by £4,832, he made his intentions clear at the pre-tournament press conference when he said, 'It's going to be tough overtaking Nick but I've got to do it because I want to be top after the Carroll's Irish Open at the end of next month.' The reason for that? The leader of the Order of Merit at the end of August automatically qualified for the World Series of Golf in Akron two weeks later, and the Spaniard had no intention of missing out on such a big-money event.

What Seve wants he usually gets, and this tournament was no exception. Setting the pace with a new course record 64, he immediately issued a challenge and it was up to Faldo to rise to it – and he did. With no better medicine than a red-hot putter and plenty of birdies, Faldo quickly warmed to his task over the 6,750-yard par-72 course at Refrath. Four under par after thirteen, he birdied the fourteenth, fifteenth, seventeenth and eighteenth to equal the Spanish maestro's spectacular round earlier in the day. His best round since turning professional, it sent a clear message that he was not going to be intimidated by Seve Ballesteros or anyone.

In the second round, Faldo struck the ball just as solidly but finished nine strokes worse with a 73. From tee to green his game was sound, but the critical factor was his putting. Seve Ballesteros, in comparison, collected three birdies in his last four holes for a round of 67, then claimed he was unhappy with his game. More mind games, thought Faldo. Gary Player, Ballesteros's playing partner that day, had a different opinion: 'After seeing that, thank goodness I've won my tournaments already. This man is changing the face of golf.'

Faldo had little hope of winning, and his challenge faded away over the weekend. He recorded rounds of 70 and 71 for a ten-under-par total, but his meagre cheque for £556 was little comfort as Ballesteros raced away to win the tournament with closing scores of 70 and 67. He picked up £6,095 in prize money, which was just enough to overtake Faldo at the top of the money list. As one reporter commented at the time, 'This race is going right down to the wire.'

For Nick Faldo, the Braun German Open was a bittersweet affair for another reason. In the pre-tournament pro-am, he had scored his first hole-in-one as a professional on the 182-yard fifteenth and was desperately disappointed to find that the prize – a £17,000 Mercedes 450 SL – was not up for grabs until the following day. Then, to make matters worse, Faldo had come within an inch of aceing the same hole in his opening round of 64. Bemoaning his luck to Tony Jacklin, he struck up an agreement with the former Open champion that should either make an ace and win the car, they would give the other £1,000. On his return to London, news filtered through that Jacklin had done just that in the final round. Faldo was delighted; it was just a pity the money did not count towards the Order of Merit.

After his hard-fought victory in Germany, a rampant Balles-teros continued his wonderful run of form by winning the Scandinavian Enterprise Open the following week, followed by the Swiss Open three weeks later. In the interim he finished fourth at the Benson and Hedges and second in the Carroll's Irish Open to secure his third consecutive number one position in Europe. Amassing over £30,000 in official prize money in just five weeks transformed the season for him and took the shine off what until that point had been a wonderful year for Nick Faldo, who finished a disappointing third in the Order of Merit.

At least the Faldo v. Ballesteros rivalry had provided some exciting headlines throughout the year. In early September, both players were brought together for a face-to-face interview for *Golf World* magazine with Renton Laidlaw of the *Evening Standard* acting as a so-called referee. In the item they spoke about issues that concerned them both, like the rapid growth of European golf, prize money and the difficulties involved in playing full-time in the United States (something only Faldo would attempt, later in his career). On a less contentious subject, Seve pointed out that he could only practise about one hour a day for fear of aggravating his notoriously fragile back, while Faldo averaged at least four hours per day on the practice ground. Afterwards they were photographed smiling and shak-ing hands, and went their separate ways. It was all very amiable, but the reality was totally different. While each player respected the other's talents, there was certainly no love lost between them on or off the golf course. Complete opposites as personalities, they maintained a distant, almost frosty relationship which made their rivalry even more fascinating to watch as the season finally came to an end.

Two days later both players were in action in Belgium for the Laurent Perrier International at Royal Waterloo. An eight-man invitational played over 54 holes, it was talked up in the press as a 'decider', Ballesteros having won the event in 1976 and Faldo the following year. On the opening day, Seve grabbed a birdie and an eagle over the closing stretch for a round of 67, while Faldo kept in touch with a 69. In the second round it was honours even, both players scoring level-par 72s. With Ballesteros now leading the tournament on eight under par, it was somehow inevitable they would be paired together in the final round.

Bunkered at the first, Ballesteros made an edgy bogey. Then, with barely an afterthought, he notched up five birdies over the next seven holes to race ahead of the select field. Faldo, now a massive seven strokes behind, struggled on manfully, then almost out of nothing came his chance. After he made birdie on the par-four ninth, there was a sudden two-stroke swing in his favour when Seve dropped a shot at the same hole after missing the green with his approach. As errors go it was a small one, but as they entered the most tree-lined part of the course, it seemed to have a disturbing effect on the temperamental Spaniard. Soon Faldo had closed the gap to just three strokes with birdies on the thirteenth and fifteenth. Under severe pressure, Ballesteros carved his tee-shot deep into the woods on the right at the par-five sixteenth and was fortunate to escape with a bogey. Now the difference was two. With both golfers trading shot for shot, the final two holes took on a matchplay feel as they approached the seventeenth.

Now it was Faldo's turn to struggle. Pulling his tee-shot into heavy rough on the left of this par-four hole, he found his ball in what looked like an old tractor rut. With his rival positioned safely in the middle of the fairway, a few tense minutes passed as Faldo asked the match referee for a free drop. It was refused, and despite further protestations, he was forced to hack it eighty yards down the fairway. Once again it seemed that Ballesteros was in control, but after a loose five-iron approach found a green-side bunker, Faldo managed to claw back yet another shot after holing a long putt for par.

Only a single stroke separated the players as they arrived on the par-five eighteenth. Faldo hit two drives to leave himself pin high on the right, while the Spaniard found himself at the bottom of a slope from where he faced a tough pitch. Managing to scramble his ball to around twelve feet from the hole, he missed the putt that would give him the title. Shortly afterwards, Faldo chipped up to four feet and holed out for birdie. All square, play-off.

At the first extra hole they both notched up regulation pars. At the tricky par-four second, Seve found his approach obstructed by a tree and was forced to play his shot low under the branches. For once he could not work his magic, and he thinned it through the green into the rough at the back. Faldo, in contrast, had no such difficulties. After a well-placed iron shot, he struck an expertly controlled wedge shot to within six feet then holed the putt to win. It was game, set and match to the Englishman, but there was little time to enjoy his victory as fate provided yet another opportunity for a Faldo–Ballesteros head-to-head.

Under normal circumstances, the Hennessy Cognac Cup offered a welcome break from the toil of strokeplay tournaments. Matching an eleven-man Great Britain & Ireland team against the Continent of Europe, it was scheduled to take place in alternate years to the Ryder Cup. Inspired by the news that from 1979 the Ryder Cup would be Europe v. America, the tournament was destined to provide some interesting and occasionally controversial competition.

At the start of the week, most of the pre-tournament debate centred on the controversial choice of venue. The Belfry, situated ten miles north-east of Birmingham, was a new championship course designed by Peter Alliss and Dave Thomas. It was also the new headquarters of the Professional Golfers Association, and from the start was universally criticised by the players for its lack of definition. The course described by Brian Barnes as little more than a 'field', wasn't helped by the weather which was freezing (the course was labelled 'Ice Valley' by the pros) and the greens which were impossible to putt on. Faldo found himself in hot water for sporting a polo-neck in his opening match when he should have been wearing an officially sanctioned short-sleeved team shirt. Promising to wear one in his singles match against Ballesteros in the afternoon, he quickly reverted the next morning after losing 4 & 2.

Despite winning Seve surprised everyone by pulling out of the event that evening, but the match itself was a fairly tight affair and not without incident. In the singles, Nick Faldo was drawn against Antonio Garrido. It was a bad-tempered match. Things threatened to get out of hand after the Spanish World Cup star asked if he could remove a leaf from a bunker on the par-three seventh. Knowing that only stones could be removed from sand traps, Faldo refused point blank, and even though it was the right decision the sour-faced Spaniard took offence at the 'arrogant' way in which he was told. Then on the back nine another problem flared up. Playing the par-three fourteenth, Garrido hit his three-iron tee-shot so close that Faldo was forced to concede the putt. Ten minutes later, Faldo holed a huge putt for a birdie and, without thinking, walked on to the next tee and hit his drive. Failing to realise that it was still Antonio's honour from the previous hole, he was accused halfway up the fairway of playing out of turn. It practically amounted to an accusation of gamesmanship. A rules official was called for as the row threatened to boil over. As the argument unfolded live on television, Nick Faldo, obviously concerned that he might lose the hole, perhaps even the match, explained the circumstances to PGA tournament director George O'Grady. A short time later, a visibly upset Antonio Garrido was told that the shot could only be replayed if the error was noticed on the tee, not halfway up the fairway. After that, the match continued on in a tense silence, Faldo eventually running out the winner (as did team Great Britain & Ireland).

As the European season ground to a close, the final event was the prestigious Colgate-sponsored World Matchplay Championship at Wentworth. It was certainly an event that Faldo had long dreamed of winning, and with international stars like Gary Player, Graham Marsh, David Graham, Tom Watson, Ray Floyd and Seve Ballesteros all competing, there was certainly no better year in which to realise his ambition. As Faldo said in the pre-tournament press conference, 'Outside of the Open, there is no event in the world that I would rather win.'

The week itself began in confusion and ended in controversy. Having driven back to his new home at Ayot St Lawrence from a tournament in Chepstow the previous Saturday evening, Faldo had requested that the chauffeur-driven Mercedes, provided by sponsors Colgate, arrive first thing Sunday morning to take him and his parents to Wentworth. But the car failed to arrive, driving instead to the mansion provided for him on Wentworth Estate for that week. Realising the error, Faldo decided to drive himself down to Surrey to begin his rather flustered preparations the following day.

That said, the tournament began brightly enough with a 6 & 5 thrashing of reigning United States Open champion Andy North. Cheered all the way back to the clubhouse, Faldo was now left to carry the flag for Britain after Mark James and Brian Waites went out in the first round. And as he had already proved in the 1977 Ryder Cup at Royal Lytham, it was a role he absolutely relished.

The following day he was listed to play against Graham Marsh of Australia, but the early-morning start was delayed by heavy fog. As competitors gathered in the clubhouse drinking coffee, it was simply a case of waiting for the mist to clear. They waited and waited. For Marsh it was no problem, but for the impatient and inexperienced Faldo it proved a difficult time. He paced around becoming increasingly edgy. 'It is simply that I had got myself ready to play,' he said afterwards, 'and all that was on my mind was beating Graham Marsh. There is a limit to how long you can stand on the putting green practising. I went to sit in the car and listened to a few music tapes.'

By mid-afternoon, the fog lifted sufficiently to play eight or nine holes. In the hope that the matches would finish the following day, the decision was taken to push back the semi-finals to Sunday. This meant the 36-hole final would now take place on the Monday, much to the consternation of many players who had already booked their flight home. Faldo had no such problems but was equally scathing about the decision, especially after falling four-down to Marsh in the holes they did play. 'In my opinion, we should not have played at all that day. The decision to play just eighteen holes upset my balance. I'm positive that I was not ready to play. My game was not as sharp as it might have been and my concentration was poor. It's terrible trying to play on a day when you have no feel or judgement.'

Not that it was any easier the following day. He was determined to turn his match around. His strategy was simple: all-out attack. Urged by Ian Connelly to use his driver more, Faldo almost made the plan work. From the eighth hole onwards, Faldo won three out of the next five holes to cut the deficit to one stroke, but the experienced Marsh always seemed to have the upper hand. Slowing down the play when it suited him, speeding it up when he won a hole, Faldo was dragged around the course like a dog on a lead. Two-up with two to play, it came as no surprise when he finally closed out his young opponent on the eighteenth green.

For Nick Faldo, losing to anyone was a major disappointment. The season had shown that he could compete with the best, but that was no guarantee of success, as he found against Graham Marsh. Reflecting on the match, he knew he had played wonderfully well to be six under par for the day, but he had still lost. How? As Ian Connelly was to remark, the only thing missing now from Nick Faldo's armoury was experience, and only time could provide that. And as the next few years would prove, that extra quality would make him a formidable player.

4. WEDDING BELLS

Since turning professional, Nick Faldo had enjoyed two spec-tacularly successful seasons. Finishing eighth in the Order of Merit in 1977 was amazing enough, but to follow that up with a third place in 1978 had been little short of sensational.

With success came opportunity. In demand from tournament sponsors eager to cash in on his youthful appeal, Faldo had embarked on a mini world tour at the end of 1977 that had taken in Morocco, South America and the Philippines. It had proved an exhausting experience and, still suffering from the after-effects of the glandular fever that had threatened his first appearance in the Ryder Cup, he had no wish to repeat it. Instead, he was looking forward to spending part of the winter of 1978 playing on the Sunshine Circuit in South Africa, but once again his plans had an unfortunate way of changing.

South Africa was a country he had liked ever since his first visit there as an amateur in 1975. As a member of the British team in the Commonwealth Trophy tournament at Royal Durban, he had tasted individual glory by winning the South African Strokeplay Championship in Cape Town. More import-antly, he felt comfortable there. He liked the people, the weather and the narrow, tree-lined courses that reminded him so much of home. So it had come as no surprise when he decided to spend his first winter there as a professional in 1976/77. Perhaps if he had stuck to his plans and played there again at the back end of 1978, the coming season might not have been quite the struggle it was. Instead, Faldo spent the pre-Christmas period on a gruelling and ultimately unsuccessful tour of Australia and New Zealand. In a lucrative deal set up by his management company, the idea was to cash in on his growing fame. Reluctantly, Faldo agreed, but he still had big reservations about making such a long trip after such a tough season – reservations that would prove well founded.

Arriving in Sydney for the first time, Faldo found the natives surprisingly hostile – especially the golfing ones. Having enjoyed good relationships with a number of Australian pros back in Europe, he was expecting much of the same. Instead, he found many of them rude, unhelpful and in some cases downright antagonistic. And it was not just the players who made life difficult Down Under. On turning up for his first event – the Australian PGA Championship – he was gleefully informed by a tournament official that his entry form had not been received, which must have come as quite a shock when he had travelled halfway around the globe just to play in the event. Eventually everything was sorted out by IMG, but the incident left a sour taste in his mouth for the rest of the trip. 'I never expected the band to be playing when I stepped off the plane,' he said later, '[but] they took the stance that Nick Faldo was on their soil and because he had done well in Europe that season it didn't mean a damn in Australia. It was my first experience of pommie-bashing.'

Three weeks later, Faldo headed for New Zealand where he found his fellow players a lot more amenable. But even there there were problems. He was still having major problems with a newly acquired set of golf clubs and failed to make the 54-hole cut in the New Zealand Open. He had been presented with them shortly before his trip to Australia, and they had felt fine in practice, but in tournament play they fell a long way short of what he expected. He found himself hitting the ball higher than normal, which made playing in the windswept conditions found on Australia's east coast almost impossible for him. The clubs were a fraction too short and a fraction too stiff, and things were made worse by the fact that there was no one around with the necessary expertise to adjust them to his needs. As one journalist eloquently put it, 'It was like asking a concert violinist to play with woollen gloves on.'

Almost in desperation, Faldo began working on them himself, but with no success. Echoing his exhausting trip to Morocco, South America and the Philippines the previous winter, this one was rapidly turning into a disaster, and after one more event in New Zealand Faldo headed for home. After that, the rest of the winter was spent quietly practising his short game in the garden of his fifteenth-century Tudor cottage in the picturesque village of Ayot St Lawrence (he had admired the house since boyhood, and had bought it in January 1978 for £60,000 after his father saw it advertised in the local paper).

Shaking off the memory of this antipodean odyssey, Faldo now looked forward to the coming season with some optimism. There was also another reason he could look forward to the future. On 14 February 1979, shortly before flying out to a tournament in Hong Kong, he proposed to his girlfriend of four months, Melanie Rockall, over a Valentine's Night dinner, and she accepted.

Not exactly a whirlwind romance, it had certainly been a stormy one up to that point. The couple had originally met via the telephone. Melanie, who worked for the Sackville Design Group – a company owned by her father – was promoting a new magazine called *Jogging* and she wanted to interview any high-profile sportsman who actually jogged. Enter Nick Faldo, who, she was told, had spent many hours running around the highways and byways near his Hertfordshire cottage. They arranged to meet after Faldo returned from his trip to Australia and New Zealand in November 1978, but their first get-together had to be cancelled after the roads around Ayot St Lawrence were blocked by early winter snow. A few days later they met up to arrange a photographic session, and the rest is history.

An attractive girl blessed with a sharp, businesslike mind, Melanie Rockall was the total opposite in character to Nick Faldo. Yet almost from the start she was attracted by the shy and slightly awkward way in which he conducted himself. Indeed, before taking the pictures, Faldo had apologised for the state of his clothing having just crashed in a heap in the snow outside. 'His single-mindedness and determination appealed to me,' said Melanie in an interview with John Hopkins. 'He seemed a very strong, relaxed character. He knew what he was doing.'

A few days later she accepted his offer to join him and some friends for dinner at the Woodside Country Club. It was deemed a great success, and they spent the following evening together watching the comedy thriller *The First Great Train Robbery* at a cinema in London. From that moment on they were inseparable. Yet the chalk-and-cheese nature of the couple brought its own problems early on in their relationship.

At Christmas, they were invited to stay at Broadstairs in Norfolk by John Simpson. After a pleasant few days together, they returned to London only to have a blazing row about what music should be played in the car on the way back. It proved to be a real crisis point for their relationship, but after splitting up for a week they decided to meet up again. It was a fairly civilised occasion and they both agreed how unsuited they really were to each other. Having worked that problem out, they then inexplicably decided to give it another go, and within two months Nick Faldo and Melanie Rockall were engaged to be married.

Considering what had happened in their short time together, they wisely decided to keep their engagement secret (indeed, the only people who had been told were John Simpson and Ian Connelly). Yet even that was to change after Faldo returned home early from his three-week trip to Asia. Having missed the 54-hole cut in Hong Kong after a third round of 80, Faldo had hopped straight on a plane and returned home. He was desperate to see Melanie and was immediately accused of acting irresponsibly, but that hardly mattered to the lovesick Faldo. When Melanie met him at the airport, Faldo told his fiancée that he wanted to tell everybody about the two of them now.

The difficult aspect to that decision was how simultaneously to keep it a secret from the press – a virtual impossibility as things turned out. Within hours of their buying a wedding ring at Brent Cross, a local reporter turned up at Melanie's house in Brookmans Park asking about the forthcoming nuptials. They both realised it would be wise to make the announcement official as soon as possible, and the next few days were spent in a whirlwind of newspaper interviews and magazine photo-graphic sessions. Despite being pressed on the matter, the couple had set no actual wedding date – there was only some vague notion of November or December. Then, after a two-week trip to Kenya accompanied by Faldo's parents, the date was moved forward to 23 June. Once again they tried to keep the date quiet, and once again it quickly became known by the press – proof, if proof were needed, that Melanie would spend the rest of her married life firmly in the public eye.

A month before the European season was to get underway, Faldo set off for the United States to play in the Greater Greensboro Open as a warm-up to his Masters debut at Augusta in April. With everything settled on the marriage front, he asked Melanie to take time off work and accompany him for the few weeks he would be away. After some initial problems gaining permission from her father, she went. She watched as her fiancé played well from tee to green, made the cut and finished tied in forty-fourth place. A decent enough performance, but he had struggled badly on the fast greens after such a lengthy winter in Britain. As for Melanie, it was an invaluable insight for someone who had only the vaguest idea about life on the professional tour. Indeed, prior to this trip she had only ever seen Faldo play golf in a friendly game with John Simpson!

Next stop was Augusta National. Hoping to soak up the atmosphere before the tournament circus arrived, they walked the fairways together. For Nick Faldo, it was probably the most romantic spot on the planet at that particular moment; perhaps less so for Melanie after she trod barefoot on a dead snake. This uneasy welcome given to her by America's supreme golf course was set to continue.

Partnered by Billy Casper, the winner in 1970, Faldo approached his 1.26 p.m. tee-off time feeling understandably apprehensive. The crowd was huge, but he made a perfect start with birdies at the first and eighth holes to move on to the leaderboard. Then, just as he began to think about posting a score of 68 or 69, he three-putted the ninth to drop back into the pack. Still one under par as he stepped on to the fourteenth tee, his world began to fall apart. Trying to decide what club to use from just over 140 yards, he debated long and hard with his caddie. A local man boasting twelve years' experience, the caddie insisted that it was nearer 160 yards and suggested two clubs more than Faldo actually wanted to use. Confusion reigned, but by way of a compromise the Englishman settled on using a seven-iron instead of the eight he had in mind. Faldo struck the ball perfectly, then watched in horror as it carried the green by at least ten yards. He was fortunate to make a bogey there, then he dropped another shot at the par-five fifteenth after his second finished in the lake fronting the green. In the end his score added up to 73, and he was fuming. Seven strokes off the pace after the opening day, Faldo followed it up with scores of 71 and 79 to fall even further behind.

Coming off the final green on the Saturday with his first Masters effectively over, Faldo felt totally deflated and headed straight to the practice ground, hardly glancing left or right as he went, with barely a word to either Melanie or Gerald Micklem, who had turned up to watch. Unsure as to how to react having never experienced this type of situation before, Melanie was advised to let her fiancé cool down by leaving him alone for an hour or so. It was advice she had no intention of taking. Grabbing a cup of Coke, she walked straight up to him and handed it over. It turned out to be the right decision. After a moment of awkward silence, Faldo smiled and told her not to worry. There was no way, he said, that he would play that badly for the rest of the season. Unfortunately, that was one promise he was unable to keep.

Back in Europe, Nick Faldo began his challenge for the 1979 Order of Merit with a lacklustre performance in the Italian Open at Monticello, near Lake Como. Despite employing a new caddie, Andy Prodger, he finished well down the field in fifty-fifth place, but repaired much of the damage the following week with a fifth place in the French Open.

After that, Faldo hoped it would be champagne all the way as he prepared to defend his Colgate PGA Championship at St Andrews in May. Having played well at St Andrews in the Open the previous year, he felt confident that he could kick-start his season in the best way possible by winning. He spent four to five hours a day on the practice range in the run-up to the tournament and his swing felt in good order, but there were still some niggling doubts about his putting – or, to be more accurate, his putter. Convinced that the soft-alloy head of his old Ray Cook mallet putter had been knocked out of alignment through constant use, he was struggling to find one he liked. At the Masters a month earlier, where he had finished fortieth, he had tried out one or two others with little success. Now, with the first round of the Colgate PGA only days away, he had a real problem.

Ever since his amateur days, Faldo liked the putter face to be slightly open with a fraction of loft. Unable to find a suitable replacement, he rummaged through his old golf bag to find the centre-shafted Bullseye putter he had used to win the Hertfordshire Boys title and the Berkshire Trophy in 1975. Instinctively, he threw it in the boot of the car with the idea that he might try it out in practice. It was the best decision he made all year. Opening up with a magnificent score of 65, equalling the course record set by Neil Coles in the 1970 Open, Faldo found himself three strokes clear of the chasing pack. Holing putt after putt, he gave a wonderful exhibition of golf, and not surprisingly drew praise from all sections of the press including Norman Mair, golf correspondent of the *Scotsman*. 'There is still a long way to go, but yesterday was unquestionably a great performance by a 21-year-old dripping with athletic and games-playing talent.'

Unfortunately for Faldo, there was a long way to go. In the second round, the young Englishman played solidly enough from tee to green but his play lacked any of the fireworks of the previous day. But working on the basis that you need a little good fortune to win any golf tournament, he certainly had his share that week. As he signed for his score of 70, the weather deteriorated, and by the close of play his lead had increased to four strokes over second-placed Andy North. Returning to his hotel that evening, Faldo had every reason to feel confident about his chances of winning, but from that point on things went downhill fast. A year before, Faldo had led the Colgate PGA Championship at Royal Birkdale by two strokes at the halfway stage, before accelerating away from the field to win. Not surprisingly, everyone expected him to do the same at St Andrews. The very last thing anyone expected was a Faldo collapse, but that is exactly what they got as he closed out with disastrous rounds of 78 and 79. He dropped back down the field to finish tenth, a result that would set the pattern for the rest of the season.

He was, needless to say, bitterly disappointed, more so when at the Martini International at Wentworth a week later he scored a highly forgettable 79 in the opening round. Faldo hit the practice ground with an almost manic zeal, desperately trying to figure out the problem. With the second day washed out by a torrential downpour he managed to regroup a little with a solid round of 72, but he still missed the cut by two strokes. It was obvious that he needed to straighten out his game, so the decision was made to miss the British Airways/Avis Open in Jersey in order to allow time to practise and prepare for the Belgian Open at the Royal Waterloo Club near Brussels, scheduled for the first week in June.

For a while it looked as if he had made the right decision. Posting a score of 69, Faldo found himself only one stroke behind the first-round tournament leader, Gavin Levenson. Now in good shape to launch a solid challenge, he followed it up with rounds of 72 and 67. Still trailing the inexperienced South African by a shot, Faldo was confident he could overtake him in the final round, but he never got within striking distance. Recording a closing score of 71, Faldo eventually finished tied second with Michael King and Bobby Cole, three shots behind first-time winner on the European circuit Levenson.

With only one event remaining before he was due to walk up the aisle with Melanie, Faldo headed off to the Welsh Golf Classic at Wenvoe Castle. But apart from a wonderful final round of 65, which lifted him up to a top-ten finish, it was yet another forgettable display on another rain-soaked parkland course.

With such a busy agenda, Faldo had little choice but to leave most of the wedding arrangements to Melanie and her mother, catching up via regular progress reports on the telephone each week. He did try to help out on his one day off per week, but more often than not it seemed far simpler to let things carry on without him – especially when you consider what happened on the wedding day itself.

With only hours to go, Faldo had one or two duties of his own to carry out, not the least of which was picking up the ring. Having safely negotiated that task, the next problem was the wedding cake. He went with Melanie to pick it up, but as he fumbled in his pocket for a car-park ticket the bottom tier of the cake plummeted to the ground. Then, in a scene reminiscent of the hit comedy show *Some Mothers Do 'Ave 'Em*, Mrs Rockall accidentally reversed her car into her daughter's. Finally, proving that bad luck does come in threes, Melanie accidentally burnt a hole in her wedding veil.

After that, everything went like a dream. They were chauffeured to St Mary's Church, North Mymms, in a 1931 open-top

Lagonda driven by Faldo's old carpet-laying pal Ron Marks, and spent their honeymoon in Stratford-upon-Avon. It was an area Melanie knew very well from her days as a student at the University of Warwick. She might have wished for longer than a couple of days, but that was something she would have to get used to over the coming years. With her husband due to tee off just 25 miles away at the Belfry in the Lada English Classic, she helped him pack. If Melanie had wanted to know just how much golf would intrude on her private life over the coming months and years, surely there was no better example than this.

For a while it looked as if Faldo was going to enjoy a belated wedding present after he began with rounds of 72 and 71 to share the lead at the Belfry. But any dreams he had of registering his first victory as a married man – indeed, his first of the year – quickly evaporated with closing rounds of 77 and 73, enough to share fourth spot with Sandy Lyle. The tournament turned out to be a runaway triumph for Seve Ballesteros, who won by six shots. As the new Mr and Mrs Faldo drove home to Ayot St Lawrence, the gap between Seve and the rest at the top of the money list was getting wider by the week. It was becoming painfully clear as they moved into July that if Faldo was to stop the charismatic Spaniard making it four Order of Merit titles in a row, he had to start winning, and soon.

For Faldo, the frustration of not winning was starting to build. Throughout the first half of 1979, he had put himself in positions to win only to watch his hard work ruined by one or two errant rounds. Then, to make matters worse, it happened again the following week in the Scandinavian Enterprise Open in Sweden. In need of a confidence boost, Faldo produced a first-round 69 to share the lead with Australian Mike Ferguson, only to slump to a demoralising 78 on day two. Faldo could not believe it. Having been in another perfect position to make a strong challenge, he was now down among the also-rans. Closing with rounds of 74 and 71, he ended the week in twentieth place, way behind the eventual winner, Sandy Lyle.

Faldo returned home deflated. He had just watched his boyhood rival record his second win of the season, and his own year was falling apart. And with the Open only a week away he was even unsure as to what part of his game to work on. He talked it over with Melanie, but just could not see a solution. In Sweden, his game had blown hot and cold, but to win an Open, something he still dreamed of doing, you had to play consistently well for all four rounds. He had not played four consistent rounds all year.

Boosted by Arnold Palmer's pre-tournament prediction that he would become the first home winner of the Open since Tony Jacklin in 1969, Faldo knew that Lytham was a golf course that suited his game. For several years now he had known that the key to a good score at Lytham was the holes around the turn. The two par-four holes under 400 yards sandwiching the short 162-yard par-three ninth were where a good round could be turned into a great one because of the birdie opportunities. As usual, nothing was left to chance. Every practice day, Faldo spent time analysing each hole, including hitting approach shots to any part of the green where he thought the pin might be located. Yet by the end of the third day of play any hope he had of winning was quickly forgotten with rounds of 74, 74 and 78. To make matters worse, he then compiled a wonderful round of 69, lifting him up to joint nineteenth behind the winner and new Open champion, none other than Severiano Ballesteros.

Nick Faldo did not know whether to laugh or cry as he reflected on how far behind Seve he was in terms of achievement. Barely three months older than his English rival, Ballesteros now had the golfing world at his feet. Not only had he won nine European tournaments compared with Faldo's single victory in the Colgate PGA, he had also enjoyed five international victories including his first win on the United States PGA Tour in the Greater Greensboro only a year before. A true golfing superstar, he had even turned down an unprecedented offer from Deane Beman to join the PGA Tour in America without going through the demanding task of qualifying. And now he had won his first major!

Feeling somewhat drained, Faldo decided to miss the Dutch Open at Noordwijk a week later. Returning to action in the Sun Alliance European Matchplay tournament at Fulford in York, he lost in the first round to journeyman pro Michael Steadman. As his season disintegrated, so the race for Ryder Cup points gathered momentum. Now under pressure to secure his place in the first ever European Ryder Cup team to face the Americans, Faldo was becoming edgy on and off the golf course. He was desperate to make one of the ten automatic qualifying spots, dreading the idea of making the team through the 'back door' in terms of a captain's wild card. It was important to him that he should qualify on his own merit, but it looked as if that might take some doing.

A week after the Sun Alliance defeat, he travelled down to the newly opened St Mellion complex in Plymouth for the Benson and Hedges International Open. Aware that he needed a top-ten finish to keep the pressure on his rivals, Faldo began with a poor opening round of 75 but recovered brilliantly with rounds of 71, 68 and 66 for joint twelfth. Then came the bad news. With Maurice Bembridge and his old Hertfordshire Boys team-mate Ken Brown finishing first and second, both players had now overtaken him in the Ryder Cup points table.

The pressure was really beginning to tell. At tournaments, especially in Britain, Faldo was increasingly being described as sullen, spoiled and surly, to such an extent that Gerald Micklem urged support for him in the media. Faldo was cast in the role of anti-hero to his long-time rival Sandy Lyle, as comparisons were made between the easy-going Scot and the seemingly dour, self-obsessed Faldo. After all, the press argued, Sandy was someone who made winning look easy without ever appearing to try too hard. Nick Faldo, they said, should take note. Throughout the rest of the summer, the press stoked up rumours of a bitter rivalry between Lyle and Faldo, comparing it with the acrimonious relationship between top British athletes Steve Ovett and Sebastian Coe.

It soon became obvious to everyone that Nick Faldo needed a break, but with such a busy schedule that was impossible. Hoping to relieve some of the pressure, Melanie divided her time between Ayot St Lawrence, where she lived with her husband and in-laws George and Joyce, and travelling with him to tournaments. She offered support whenever he needed it – helping out with hotel and flight reservations, dealing with his fan mail on a small portable typewriter set up in the dining room – but as the weeks slipped by it was not proving to be a happy time for either of them, particularly for Melanie. As she walked behind the ropes at tournaments, she began to suffer with him on and off the golf course. Bad rounds for her husband meant sleepless nights for her, and while Melanie knew little about golf, she knew exactly from his body language how well or badly he was playing. After all, since returning from Augusta in April, she had had plenty of practice.

There was not much respite for her at home either. Over the coming months the relationship between Melanie and her in-laws broke down considerably. It was obvious that the Tudor cottage was too small for them all, and like most young married couples the last thing she wanted was her husband's mother and father around while they got on with their daily lives. In the end, George and Joyce were asked to leave, which caused a rift between Faldo and his father (the two men did not speak for three years until the funeral of George's mother in 1983).

At the Braun German Open in August, Faldo's less-than-positive attitude was reflected in his seven-over-par total and thirtieth-place finish. He was thoroughly miserable, in stark contrast to the smiling Tony Jacklin, who made his way to Frankfurt-Main airport on the Sunday evening still hugging his winner's trophy. It was Jacklin's first victory in Europe for well over five years and he was applauded from the moment he entered the departure lounge. As Nick Faldo stood and clapped along with his fellow players, he could only wonder where *his* next tournament win would come from.

With just one qualifying event remaining for the Ryder Cup, the Carroll's Irish Open at Portmarnock, Faldo found himself in a precarious situation. Going into the tournament he was ninth in the table; the final two automatic places would be decided between him, Michael King, Maurice Bembridge and Howard Clark. The mathematics were simple: should Faldo not make the cut, both Bembridge and Clark would have to finish in the top three to overtake him, while King, in tenth, needed to finish in the top twenty.

In the end, Faldo need not have worried, despite opening up with a nightmare round of 78. Anxiously, he returned to the clubhouse only to receive the good news that Bembridge had virtually ruled himself out of the running after scoring an 80. Clark, however, was a different story. After three rounds, the

Leeds-born professional led the tournament with one hand on the £10,000 first prize that would catapult him above Faldo in the money list. But Faldo's luck held out and Clark's challenge evaporated, a round of 75 leaving him tied in seventh with winnings of £1,650, and that was not enough to overtake either Faldo, who finished in joint twenty-sixth place with £570, or Michael King, who took the last automatic place by ending the tournament joint ninth with £1,213.

Later that evening, European team captain John Jacobs announced that Peter Oosterhuis, as expected, had been given one of the wild-card spots along with Irishman Des Smyth. As he listened to the speeches, the relief Faldo felt at having made the Ryder Cup side was obvious. He had booked his place on the plane to America; the only problem now was finding some form before the match got underway in September.

What with missing the cut in the Swiss Open and a poor finish in the European Open at Turnberry, and hurrying back to see Ian Connelly at Dyrham Park in between, the signs over the next few weeks were not good. But as Faldo and his wife joined the rest of the European team at Heathrow, the mood was one of excitement, despite all his recent disappointments. Part of a sixty-strong party, they were met at Dulles airport in Washington by the American captain, Billy Casper. From there, a one-hour flight to Lewisburg was followed by a cavalcade of black limousines ferrying the players, their wives, team officials and press to the luxurious Greenbrier Hotel at White Sulphur Springs, a small town in the heart of picturesque West Virginia. Faldo felt at home right from the start. The hotel, one of the top ten in the United States, was impressive, but it was the practice facilities that made his heart jump for joy. Everything about them was perfect: the pristine turf, the well-placed targets at which to aim and the endless supply of brand-new golf balls. He took to staying out on the practice ground long into the evening, hitting up to five hundred balls in one session (a shocked Peter Oosterhuis came over and asked him if he *always* hit that many).

For Nick Faldo, this was golf heaven. On the telephone to Ian Connelly back in England he chatted enthusiastically about the facilities on offer, the course, even the practice putting green.

His good spirits brought a smile to the face of his boyhood coach, who had just returned from teaching juniors in near freezing temperatures. Their conversation inevitably turned to Faldo's swing. Knowing the ball would have to be hit higher to cope with the American-style course, Connelly advised Faldo to stand up to the ball more, become less stooped at address. Such a posture would in turn give him a steeper angle of attack into the ball, producing a crisper strike with more backspin. As things turned out, it proved, not for the first time, to be wonderful advice.

Having struggled to qualify for the Ryder Cup, Faldo started it in magnificent form. Resuming his successful partnership of two years earlier with Peter Oosterhuis, Faldo won three out of his four matches including a hard-fought singles tie against Lee Elder (this despite being dropped by John Jacobs from the afternoon foursomes on the opening day). After what had been a hugely disappointing season, he returned to Britain with renewed confidence, unlike his Hertfordshire colleague Ken Brown, who ran into a barrage of criticism for his petulant behaviour both on and off the course during the match, behaviour that resulted in a year-long ban from international team golf along with his partner-in-crime, Mark James.

Faldo immediately sought out Ian Connelly to try and work on some of the swing changes that he wanted to incorporate after his trip to America. There were still two more events that might offer a chance of a second tournament win, but his performance in both the SOS Talisman Tournament Players Championship and the Dunlop Masters fizzled out after a solid start. Finishing the season a disappointing twenty-first in the Order of Merit with just under £14,000 in prize money, the drop in form was blamed on his short game, especially his putting. Having worked hard on his swing in January and February, perhaps he had neglected this vital area of his game and paid the price? Or maybe the exhausting trip to Australia and New Zealand had taken more out of him than he realised? Perhaps the stress of getting married had taken its toll? The truth was that neither Nick Faldo nor Ian Connelly really knew the answer, but as they planned ahead for the new decade, both of them knew something had to change if Faldo was going to offer a serious challenge to Ballesteros and the new European number one, Sandy Lyle.

Determined not to make the same mistake as the previous year, Nick Faldo decided to spend part of the winter of 1979/80 playing the Sunshine Circuit in South Africa. He had liked the country and the people on his previous visits, and had always returned to Europe feeling refreshed and ready for action. It would be no different on this trip. Having ended his season a few weeks earlier at the Dunlop Masters in September, Faldo expected to be a little ring-rusty, but he found his rhythm almost immediately. Competing in the ICL International at Kensington on the outskirts of Johannesburg, he made his best start since the Colgate PGA back in May with opening rounds of 68 and 66. Two strokes behind home favourite, Dennis Watson, Faldo then managed to avoid his customary third round disaster with a solid round of 69. That obstacle overcome, he then blasted around the Kensington course in a new course record of 65 to win his first tournament in eighteen months. As he punched the air in delight as his final putt hit the back of the hole, the relief on his face was obvious. After eighteen barren months without a win, it could not have come at a better time.

Supported by an enthusiastic crowd including his wife and his friend George Blumberg, the South African millionaire industrialist, Faldo had been unstoppable. Striking the ball beautifully, he had trailed by six shots going into the final round and had still won – not for the last time in his career. As he received his trophy, he could not have realised what a turning point this victory in South Africa would prove to be. With his confidence fully restored, he now looked forward to the future with some relish.

of stand-up arguments were fairly commonplace on the European Tour, but despite newspaper speculation to the contrary they had remained steadfastly together. The overall feeling was that they had rushed into marriage in 1979, no doubt showing the sort of lack of caution most twenty-somethings are noted for. Faldo's father, George, once said that if they hadn't insisted on marrying before the Ryder Cup that autumn, they might not have got married at all. Joyce agreed with her husband. 'It was a very fiery courtship,' she was once quoted as saying. Yet despite their misgivings, Melanie was a popular daughter-in-law, and the feeling was reciprocated.

A real case of opposites attract, the Faldos made a formidable partnership in spite of the differences in personality, temperament and background. From the start of their marriage, Melanie proved both supportive and extremely loyal. When she first got married, for example, she wrote a stinging letter to the host of a radio phone-in programme who had described her husband as a 'bloody cry baby'. She reacted in the same way on the golf course when she overheard disparaging remarks from the crowd. On one famous occasion at Royal Birkdale, she rounded on one man who was berating Faldo for his lack of putting ability. 'If you think you can do better,' she barked at the astonished fan, 'I can arrange a challenge match with Nick Faldo any time you like!'

In truth, the role of a tournament golf professional's wife was never suited to someone like Melanie. A strong character with a fiercely independent streak, she enjoyed the initial buzz of excitement that came from travelling around the world – everything about it was fun and interesting, and she had always liked meeting new people, visiting new places and taking in new experiences – but the novelty wore off surprisingly quickly.

In those early days together on the PGA Tour in America, Melanie had a fairly typical routine. Each morning she would take out a small travelling iron and press the golf shirt her husband wanted to wear that day. More often than not, it was also a shirt she had hand-washed the night before because of his dislike of hotel laundry services. At important tournaments, she would drive with him to the golf course before parking herself in the clubhouse with a coffee while he went out to practise. After that, she would follow his progress from behind the ropes, never forgetting to smile should he need a quick boost in the shape of encouragement or congratulation. On the days when Melanie did not go to watch her husband play – an increasing number as time went by – she spent most of her time by the hotel pool. There she would scribble down her thoughts in a private journal, go for a swim or practise her tennis. A voracious reader, she would get through countless paperback books before packaging them up every couple of months and sending them back home to family and friends in England.

She was blessed with a sharp, enquiring mind, but the opportunities for sightseeing or visiting museums were also surprisingly limited. Without transport of her own, and with golf courses normally situated out in the middle of nowhere, she found travelling anywhere almost impossible. Besides, without her husband by her side, there seemed very little point. Encouraged by Faldo to socialise with the other players' wives, Melanie soon found a good friend in Alicia O'Meara. A down-to-earth lady with a lively sense of humour that matched Melanie's, they would often chat together at tournaments or go out shopping whenever the opportunity arose, but their time together was still limited. As is normal on the PGA Tour, their paths would hardly cross for weeks on end because their husbands had failed to make the cut or had taken the week off. The same applied to other players' wives with whom she had built up friendships, like Linda Watson (wife of Tom) and Polly Crenshaw (wife of Ben.) She was convinced there was more to life than this gypsy-like existence, and her growing unhappiness was obvious to everyone except her husband.

Desperate to develop a social life away from tournaments, Melanie often pleaded with her husband to go out with her in the evening when he finished playing. Nothing too taxing, perhaps a trip to the theatre or the cinema, or even to go roller-skating – anything to break the monotony. 'I was screaming out for some kind of life,' she told *The Times*' golf correspondent John Hopkins.

He would play golf for twelve hours a day, come back to the room, have a shower, go out to dinner and then go to bed.

*Somehow there was always a little voice inside me that said
something's wrong. I'd look around at the girls who were having
babies and whose husbands were on the golf tour and were
enjoying themselves and it wasn't that that bothered me. I'd
look at girl friends I'd been with at school and university and it
was seeing them beginning to make headway in their careers
that upset me. I was envious of their outlet for themselves. Being
a golf wife is a terribly secondary existence. You're always
orbiting around an enormous star. You're never shining on your
own. You exist only as a satellite.*

In 1982 they had talked half-heartedly about starting a family,
but first they needed something they could call a home in the
United States. For a while, Melanie was excited about the
prospect of having a home somewhere like Florida, somewhere
she could retreat to when her husband was away playing
tournaments, but as with so many other things in their marriage
it was not to be. Sadly for Melanie, and ultimately her marriage,
Faldo would constantly get sidetracked with his golf and the
house-hunting got postponed indefinitely.

As if to prove it was virtually impossible for him to
concentrate on anything other than his golf, while on the break
that Melanie had persuaded her husband to take, Faldo
accepted an invitation to partner Mark O'Meara in a friendly
fourball against Charles Coody and local club pro Rives McBee.
He was low on confidence and struggling with his game, but it
would be this insignificant match at nearby Los Colinas that
would transform his entire season.

Dragging one or two shots left early on, Faldo complained
bitterly that this had been his problem all year. Ian Connelly
had tried to cure it by asking Faldo to raise the club a foot or
so off the ground before swinging back, yet even after he had
devoted long hours on the practice ground to this new method,
his game was no better. Now it was down to O'Meara to offer
a solution, and to his credit he knew exactly what the answer
was. Taking Faldo off to one side, he pointed out that he was
hooding the club-face on the back swing – a problem he had
himself suffered from in the past. 'Fan the club-face open more
on the takeaway,' he kept saying before grabbing Faldo's wrists

and rotating them in the manner he had suggested. It was like shining a torch in the darkness.

Later that day, Faldo tried it out for himself. It felt awkward at first and his opening shots flew everywhere but straight, but gradually things started to work and, oblivious to everything including Melanie, he spent the next five days doing little else but hit balls on the practice range at Los Colinas. Returning to competitive action in the Byron Nelson Classic the following week, he ended the tournament tied twenty-first after rounds of 71, 69, 72 and 69. Delighted with the improvement in his ball striking, Faldo looked forward to another week of practice in Texas. Fortunately for him, that plan was changed by a frantic telephone call from Paris on the Monday asking him to replace an injured Greg Norman in the French Open. Having planned to make his European debut at the Martini International a week later, Faldo reluctantly agreed, and with the tournament starting on the Wednesday he headed straight for the airport. As things turned out, it was the best decision he made all year.

Arriving in Paris in the first week in May for the Paco Rabanne-sponsored event, the young Englishman was confident about his chances despite being described on the tournament starting sheet as 'Mick Faldo'. On the course at the exclusive Racing Club de France, he began strongly with scores of 69, 67 and 72 for an eight-under-par total, sharing the lead with David J. Russell. Happy that his revised swing was standing up to the pressure, Faldo played equally well throughout the final round but was still trailing surprise leader José-María Cañizares as he surveyed the par-five eighteenth fairway from the tee.

Now came the first indication of how much Faldo's time in the United States had toughened him up. Knowing that an eagle would give him a chance of a play-off, he produced a superb drive and two-iron to reach the green, then calmly stepped up and holed from sixteen feet for a three. The cheers back on the tee had a devastating effect on the Spanish World Cup star. Cañizares proceeded to hit a wayward drive, followed that up with an equally poor second, and ultimately missed the birdie putt that would have given him the French Open title. Shell-shocked, he walked off the final green and straight into a three-man play-off with Nick Faldo and David J. Russell.

Faldo had always worked hard on his golf; now he seemed to be working harder than ever. Often the last player to leave the practice ground, the Englishman instinctively knew how important winning the play-off would be to him and his ambitions of becoming the European number one. Deep in concentration, he barely acknowledged his two opponents as he set off down the opening hole. Even after Russell was knocked out at the first, he seemed far more interested in getting to the next tee than in shaking his hand. Halving the next, Faldo finally got his way on the third extra hole after the Spaniard found trouble off the tee. The breakthrough had been made. Faldo picked up a cheque for £8,624 for his first win on the Continent and only the fourth 72-hole victory of his career.

It was over six months since his last victory in the 1982 Haig Whisky Tournament Players Championship, and again his relief was obvious. Flying back to London, Faldo headed straight to the house of his close friend Danny Desmond. Screeching his Porsche to a halt outside, he grabbed the large silver trophy from the passenger seat before jumping out. Then, as his friend clapped, Faldo held it aloft in triumph like an FA Cup-winning footballer. It was certainly a night for celebration.

He headed north to Cheshire for the Martini International a day later. The weather was as cold and wet there as it had been in France, and also windy. Gusts of up to 45 miles an hour made life extremely difficult for all the competitors. Faldo's first practice shot flew so far off line that it smashed the windscreen of South African pro Hugh Baiocchi's car. Nevertheless, picking up in Wilmslow where he left off in Paris, Faldo opened up with a 67 and a 69 to lead the tournament. With the final two rounds scheduled for the Sunday, Faldo fortified himself against the damp weather by drinking hot soup out of a flask supplied by the landlady of a local bed and breakfast. He had suffered from a bad head cold that week, so it proved the perfect tonic for him. Racing through the field with a pair of superb 66s, he ended the day tied for the tournament lead on twelve under par. In a remarkable coincidence, Faldo found himself in yet another play-off with José-María Cañizares, whom he finally beat again at the third extra hole. Faldo was in the form of his life, a far cry from just a few weeks earlier when the 25-year-old Englishman had struggled even to make a cut.

Someone else who was delighted with his victory was his caddie, Dave McNeilly – or perhaps relieved would be a better word. Later becoming one half of the most successful partnership in European golf, the Ulster-born caddie was still relatively inexperienced at that point, and it showed. Indeed, at the Martini International he had committed the cardinal sin of all professional bagmen by accidentally turning up late on the Sunday morning. It was the latest in a series of cock-ups, and Faldo was forced to wait on the first tee while his red-faced bagman raced over from the car park. Not surprisingly, Faldo was fuming, and unbeknown to McNeilly had already decided to sack him at the end of the day. The only thing that stopped him was that he won! An extremely narrow escape for the cheery Ulsterman, and certainly not the first time it had happened – or the last.

Prior to meeting Nick Faldo, David McNeilly had attended a north London polytechnic where he did a degree course in French, psychology and economics. A single-figure handicap golfer, his relaxed, almost carefree attitude contrasted starkly with the dour, often self-absorbed Faldo. Two more opposite personalities it would be hard to find, yet almost from the start they complemented each other both on and off the golf course.

Based in Florida, McNeilly had heard through the caddie grapevine that Faldo needed a bagman for the European Tour and had telephoned him about a possible job. The phone call made for an interesting conversation, especially when Faldo asked McNeilly whether or not he owned a 'wheel', which caddies use for measuring yardages. McNeilly mistakenly thought Faldo had asked if he had any 'wheels' back in Britain. His reply went down in caddie folklore: 'No,' he answered, 'I always use public transport.' Faldo laughed it off as a joke, then offered him a temporary job on the condition that they met up in London 'on Monday'. Normally that would not have been a problem, except that it was already Friday and McNeilly was strapped for cash and in Miami. In the end, he financed the trip to Britain, ironically, by selling his car. It was a huge risk, but it proved to be the best decision of his life.

Their first tournament together was the 1982 season-opener, the Martini International at Lindrick, where Faldo finished runner-up to Bernard Gallacher. By his own admission, McNeilly was 'next to useless' during those first few months in Europe. His yardage measurement was often wrong, he rarely judged the wind direction correctly and he was hopeless at working out the putting lines, but somehow he muddled through. (It seemed a few days' caddying at the PGA Tour qualifying school was not the ideal preparation for working with one of Europe's best.) What he did bring to the relationship was a sense of humour, which with someone as intense as Faldo proved absolutely invaluable. For example, when his boss became too uptight for his own good, McNeilly had a way of snapping him out of it by offering a joke here, a gentle word of encouragement there. At least that way they managed to get through those first twelve months together without Faldo strangling his caddie at least three times a round. 'Nick would get really upset,' recalled McNeilly. 'If I gave him the wrong yardage or something he would really fly off the handle. Then he said to me at the Sun Alliance PGA Championship at Hillside in May [1982], "If I take a club out and you've got a slight doubt about it then keep your mouth shut. But if you're ninety or one hundred per cent confident that I've got the wrong club, then shout." After that, things went a bit easier.'

By July, and the Open at Royal Troon, Faldo and McNeilly had ironed out most of their problems.

Those first few months together were pretty tough, I remember. Nick was really intolerant of mistakes. If I made a mistake on the course he wouldn't hide how he felt. There was nothing subtle about it, no quiet word on the next tee. He would often say things on the spur of the moment, really quite angry things, but to give Nick his due, afterwards it's all over and done with. Each outburst, and there were quite a few in our time together, would be made in public, there and then. It would be very embarrassing for me, but more often than not he was right. It was my mistake, and because he was such a hard taskmaster I probably learnt a lot quicker than I would have done with somebody who was more tolerant.

It was no secret that Faldo looked around for another caddie throughout that year, but luckily for Dave McNeilly, nobody of suitable quality and experience was ever available. 'The only one I wanted was Dave Musgrove,' said Faldo once, 'but he was working for Sandy Lyle, so I decided to carry on with Dave.' And as results improved, so did their relationship, especially after Faldo won the Haig Whisky Tournament Player Championship at Notts Golf Club in Hollinwell in September 1982. He registered his tenth top-ten finish of the season in just twelve starts, which was the turning point in the Faldo–McNeilly partnership. And with that came the decision to pursue the relationship the following season.

Following his play-off victories in the French Open and the Martini International, Faldo turned up at Sand Moor Golf Club in Leeds for the Car Care Plan International. Looking to make it three wins in as many weeks, he kept silent as many of his fellow players complained about the poor state of the rain-soaked greens. Instead, Faldo spent hours on the practice putting green in front of the clubhouse trying to get as much of a feel for the difficult surface as he could. It obviously worked. He holed putt after putt on his way to a winning eight-under-par total with rounds of 67, 68, 68 and 69, beating off a late challenge from local favourite Howard Clark. The first prize of £10,000 left him top of the Order of Merit by a country mile.

Christened the 'Rain King' by the media for his success in Wilmslow, Paris and Leeds, Faldo was fast heading towards being crowned king of Europe. In just 21 days he had won £31,954, almost half as much as in the whole of the previous season. Having agreed to a parting of the ways with his long-time coach Ian Connelly earlier in the year, Faldo was extremely heartened by the way in which his new swing change had held up under tournament pressure. 'My swing change gave me something to concentrate on for each shot,' he said after the victory in Leeds. 'I knew if I did it, then I would hit a good shot, and if I didn't, then every shot would be a bad one. So it was simple. As I walked up to my ball I asked myself a question: "Do you want to hit a good shot? You do? Then I suggest you make sure you fan the club open on the takeaway."'

Returning to Royal St George's for the Sun Alliance PGA Championship at the end of May, Faldo felt confident that he could make it four in a row. He knew the course at Sandwich better than anyone, and after two opening rounds of 69 and 71 he was in with a realistic chance. But from third place going into the weekend, one stroke behind joint leaders Severiano Balles-teros and Des Smyth, he tumbled down the leaderboard, stumbling to a two-over-par round of 74, his worst score in weeks, and following that up with a 75. His twenty-third place was put down to competitive fatigue as Seve romped to his first win of the season. It seemed Faldo's battery had finally run flat.

Just over a month later, in July, Faldo was tipped as joint favourite to win the Open along with Tom Watson. Certainly his form in the weeks leading up to Royal Birkdale was particularly impressive: he finished third in the Silk Cut Masters at St Pierre in Chepstow; second at the Times Open at Biarritz; and third again in the Glasgow Classic at Haggs Castle. Breaking the magic 70 barrier in ten of the twelve competitive rounds these tournaments comprised, he was carrying on the form of his life (he also finished twenty-fifth in the Scandinavian Enterprise Open with rounds of 77, 67, 73 and 74, but with the Open only a week away he admitted to experimenting with different shots).

Like his hero Jack Nicklaus, Nick Faldo once again prepared meticulously for the Open. Asking Dave McNeilly to double-check every yardage, he played two practice rounds with Tom Watson and three others on his own. He hit up to three hundred balls a day, and it wasn't unusual for him to start practising at nine in the morning and finish at half-past seven in the evening. All this hard work and dedication attracted admiring glances from his fellow players, and the end result was a four-under-par total and a share of eighth place with Christy O'Connor Jr, Bill Rogers and Dennis Durnian. Four months earlier, Faldo would have been delighted with a top-ten Open finish. Now, after rounds of 68, 68, 71 and 73, he felt disappointed that he had not finished higher; the pair of double-bogeys in the first round was especially painful to recall. Ending the week five strokes behind the eventual winner, co-favourite Tom Watson, Faldo was left to reflect on a series of missed opportunities and amateurish blunders.

In particular, he remembered an incident on the eighteenth green in the third round involving Dave McNeilly. Needing to hole a ten-foot putt for par that would put him into joint second place, one shot behind Watson, he accused his caddie of giving him the wrong line.

'It's a little bit left to right,' Faldo insisted, looking for confirmation.

'If you think that, you're absolutely wrong,' said McNeilly firmly. 'I saw Arnold Palmer hole an identical putt this morning and it definitely broke from right to left.'

A worried look appeared on Faldo's face. Nevertheless, he took McNeilly's advice and was about to putt when his concentration was broken by a noisy fan shouting out, 'Come on, Nicky baby!' Faldo backed off to regain his composure. Moments later he struck the putt and looked on astonished as the ball broke left to right. He gave McNeilly an icy stare, and they barely spoke to each other for the rest of the day. When they finally met again the next morning, Faldo was carrying a newspaper that mentioned the incident beneath the headline BIG MOUTH PUTS OFF FALDO. Handing over the paper to McNeilly, Faldo remarked sharply, 'Right headline, wrong person!'

After the Open, the Faldos had planned a short break together, but that was postponed after Faldo was prevailed upon to play in the Lawrence Batley International by Lawrence Batley himself. In the end it proved to be the right decision: he compiled a magnificent 62 in the final round at Bingley St Ives to win by four strokes. His lowest ever round as a professional, it was an unbelievable nine under par for fifteen holes. Faldo opened with rounds of 71 and 69, but his last two rounds of 64 and 62 had equalled the best 36 holes ever played in a European tournament. Confirming his iron grip on the Order of Merit, the quality of his play was perhaps best summed up by his playing partner Ronan Rafferty, who said afterwards, 'He gave me the impression that he shot sixty-twos every day of the week.'

Now £31,000 ahead of his nearest challenger in the money list, Faldo's lead was almost unassailable. Yet there was still the unpredictable Severiano Ballesteros lurking in the shadows, and from past experience Faldo knew what a huge threat he could pose over the closing weeks of the season, a fear that was reinforced after the Spaniard's victory in the Carroll's Irish Open in early August. Resolving that nothing would be left to chance, Faldo decided to play as many tournaments as possible, but that would ultimately bring problems of its own – especially with his wife, Melanie.

In September, after finishing runner-up to Isao Aoki in the Panasonic European Open at Sunningdale, Faldo made the somewhat controversial decision to miss his brother-in-law's wedding in favour of playing the European Masters in Switzerland. Normally it might not have been a big problem, but Faldo had already agreed to be best man, so it most certainly was. He was absolutely determined to hold on to his number-one spot at all costs, but the ill feeling the trip to Switzerland caused in his wife's family was both considerable and long-lasting, so much so that at one point he half-decided to forget the tournament and attend the wedding, as Melanie had asked him to do. As things threatened to get out of hand, it was his father-in-law who finally persuaded him that he should play, an opinion endorsed by renowned BBC commentator David Coleman, who met Faldo by chance in Cornwall. 'You're a professional sportsman,' he told him. 'It's your job to play. Go and do it!'

The tournament was labelled by the media as a showdown between the two giants of European golf, and it was party-pooper Sandy Lyle who took all the early honours with spectacular rounds of 64 and 63 (compared with 70 and 64 by Faldo and 72 and 66 by Ballesteros). Then came one of those swings of fortune that make tournament golf so fascinating. Trailing the in-form Scot by a massive eleven shots at one point, Faldo finished his third round with three birdies and an eagle for a 68 – the same score as Ballesteros. Having reduced the deficit to just five shots with one round left to play, Faldo reduced it even further by the time he reached the turn on the final day.

With Ballesteros struggling in the group ahead, Faldo had drawn level with Lyle by the time they reached the fifteenth. He had picked up eleven strokes in nineteen holes, a fantastic comeback in anyone's language, but Lyle was not finished yet.

Typically, he fought back in tenacious style, and even had a long-range putt on the seventy-second green that would have given him outright victory. Sadly for him, it horseshoed out, leaving Faldo with a ten-foot putt for birdie to force a play-off, which he holed.

The first extra hole was halved in par, and it looked like the second would go the same way until Lyle inexplicably missed from fourteen inches. He had putted brilliantly all week at Crans-sur-Sierre, so it was a strangely anti-climactic way in which to end the tournament, but Faldo was not complaining. It was his fifth victory of the season, and with Ballesteros relegated to fourth place he was virtually assured of his first Order of Merit title. Afterwards, the Spaniard all but conceded the number-one spot to his English rival, but at the same time he could not resist a subtle dig: 'The only money list I want to win is winning more money worldwide than any other golfer,' he said, suggesting that he was morally the European number one after his victory at the US Masters and at the Manufacturers Hanover Westchester Classic, where he had amassed over £250,000.

Three weeks later, the season was over and Faldo was crowned number one. Setting a new prize-money record of £140,761 – over £27,000 ahead of second-place Ballesteros – he became the first player since Bernard Hunt two decades earlier to win five 72-hole tournaments in a season. More significantly, it was a prize that would guarantee him invitations to the US Masters, the World Series, the Suntory World Matchplay and various other big-money events. Yet what pleased him most was the discovery that he was the first British player in history to lead the world stroke averages at the end of the year, despite having missed the cut in the PGA Championship at Riviera in Los Angeles with rounds of 74 and 77. (For the record, Nick Faldo played 8,347 strokes in 119 competitive rounds taking an average of 70.15 for each one. In comparison, Ballesteros was fourth with 70.53 and Tom Watson ninth with 70.81. Faldo cut the final table out of *Golf World* magazine and had it framed. For a long while it hung in pride of place in his bedroom.)

In the autumn it was back to America for the Ryder Cup, in 1983 held at the impressive PGA National Golf Club in Palm Beach Gardens, Florida. With the Europeans now under the dynamic captaincy of Tony Jacklin, it was first class all the way as the team prepared to board Concorde at Heathrow for the journey to Orlando. No longer would the team arrive drained and shame-faced after flying tourist class from Britain. From now on, the European Ryder Cup team would travel in style, in keeping with their position as sporting ambassadors. 'Too many times in the past,' said Jacklin before leaving, 'the [Ryder] Cup had been run, it seemed, more for the officials than for the players.'

Nick Faldo, however, was not among them, as he had already flown to the United States to compete in the Walt Disney World Golf Classic. He still needed several thousand dollars to retain his player's card, but far from nervously grinding out four safe rounds he set the tournament alight with scores of 72, 65, 68 and 65 to finish tied second, two strokes behind winner Payne Stewart. Faldo had avoided the stress of pre-qualifying, and there is no doubt the $35,200 he won took a weight off his mind and left him in confident mood for the forthcoming battle against the Americans.

After the defeat at Walton Heath in 1981, some important changes had been made by the Europeans for the match at PGA National. Still without an 'away' win in the entire 56-year history of the Ryder Cup, Jacklin had demanded a number of concessions as the price of his taking on the captaincy. Apart from the first-class travel, he wanted three 'captain's picks' so that he could have a decent complement of in-form players in his team, not just those who had qualified months before only to see their game slip away. Aided by a considerable sponsorship package from Bell's Scotch whisky, he asked for another concession concerning the players' caddies, who were now an integral part of the golfing scene. European professionals felt more comfortable with 'their' man standing by giving advice, so a place on the plane was secured not only for the bag carriers but for wives and girlfriends as well. The changes demanded by Jacklin made him extremely popular with the players, but his team still lost, despite the match proving a personal triumph for

Faldo. Winning four out of his five matches, he not only forged a strong partnership with Bernhard Langer in the foursomes and fourballs, he also defeated the in-form Jay Haas in the singles, proving what a strong player he was head-to-head.

He looked forward to proving that again in the World Matchplay Championship at Wentworth in October, but having arrived in good spirits, Faldo had little idea of the controversy that was to follow. With Melanie watching from behind the ropes, he was playing against his old adversary Graham Marsh. In a tense match cheered on by a highly partisan crowd, they were all square at the par-four sixteenth in the afternoon round. Lining up his second shot from the fairway, Faldo looked to have over-hit his approach way over the back of the green when, inexplicably, his ball reappeared on the fringe within birdie range. It had been picked up and thrown by a spectator so quickly that no one had any idea what had happened – least of all Faldo, who was totally unsighted at the time. Not surprisingly, he seemed totally bemused by all the fuss, and some boos, that greeted him on the green. Unfortunately, the referee accompanying the match had seen nothing and was forced to take the word of another official who, after failing to find evidence to the contrary, ruled that the ball had not stopped moving. Therefore, Faldo was entitled to play it as it lay. Graham Marsh, while confused, accepted the ruling, but some spectators began voicing their disgust at the obvious unfairness of what had happened. Then, to make matters worse, audible cheers rang out from some home supporters after the hapless Australian missed a short putt to halve the hole. Under no stretch of the imagination was it the fault of Nick Faldo, but that is exactly how it was portrayed in the media —especially after he won the next and took the match by 2 & 1.

Having watched the replay later that night on television, Faldo was upset and embarrassed by what had happened. Subsequently, he was furious at the attacks made on him by tabloid journalists, who felt he could either have conceded Marsh's second putt or been more gracious in victory. 'What I did was right,' he said afterwards. 'I came up to the green innocent. Why should I have given him a three-foot putt when I hadn't seen what had happened? You wouldn't walk up to somebody and say, "Here is ten pounds!" I worried about it for a long time afterwards and then I realised what I did was right. So I told myself to stop worrying.'

After such a wonderful season in golfing terms, the Marsh incident heralded the start of a difficult period for Faldo both on and off the golf course. Shortly before Christmas, he was awarded the prestigious Player of the Year award by the Association of Golf Writers for his efforts over the last twelve months. He was delighted to receive the award. No one could have imagined then that just three weeks later he would be making headlines of another kind as his marriage to Melanie finally ended in a blaze of publicity.

The split, when it finally came, was painfully difficult for both of them. Faldo had spent most of the evening of 30 December 1983 lying on the sofa at Tudor Cottage watching television, while Melanie was on the telephone in the kitchen making arrangements for a New Year's Eve dinner with friends. Towards the end of the evening Faldo broke the news that he wanted out, but he was persuaded to stay by Melanie at least until he left for the United States early in the new year. After that, things calmed down a little, and by the time he was ready to leave on 7 January they were making plans about the future – or at least Melanie was.

The day before he headed down to Heathrow, Melanie, intending to remain in England, packed his suitcases, turned up six pairs of trousers and drove to Northampton to collect some golf shoes for him. They had half-discussed meeting up in America in the run-up to the Masters in April, but it was not to be. Not long after Faldo landed, he rang Melanie to say that as far as he was concerned the marriage was over. He reflected later, 'We didn't have much of a home life. We never sat down and relaxed. It was all so hectic. Come and see this, do that, see this. I'd come home, throw the clubs down and fiddle around. I just wasn't happy at home.' He also admitted that he had found someone else, and almost immediately Melanie began divorce proceedings. The news broke publicly on 9 February, the headline in the *Sun* newspaper reading STAR GOLFER NICK IN LOVE TRIANGLE. While the headline might have come as a shock to his British fans, news of their split was no great surprise to the golfing fraternity. Throughout 1983 rumours about their failing relationship had grown more definite as Faldo was seen on his own more and more, both in America and Europe.

These were difficult times for both of them. Even with George and Joyce no longer living with them, confrontations had often proved difficult to avoid. When an argument started or the atmosphere became too tense, Faldo would quickly retreat to his workshop just to escape. If that did not work, he would practise his chipping in the garden or visit clubmaker Barry Willett at St George's Golf Club in Weybridge. But even that could cause an argument.

Melanie wanted me to come home and stay at home. I would go to one end of the house and put on my music full blast. I had my snooker table there and I played on that a lot. She would be up the other end of the house, in the kitchen probably. We were in the house, but we were apart. We didn't get in each other's way. It was a means of keeping the peace. I thought that America was going to be a new horizon for me, and with my career at the stage it was I had to go and play there. Melanie hated America and hated touring.

That is why everything came to a head. Faldo felt he needed support in his efforts to establish himself on the PGA Tour in the United States, and in his opinion Melanie was clearly unable to provide it. 'I wanted someone to talk to, to help me, to share my experiences,' he said once. What he failed to mention was that he had already found someone other than his wife to offer that support.

As for Melanie, all she could do was reflect on the reasons why her marriage to one of Britain's best-known sportsmen had failed. Hoping to gain some degree of the independence she craved, she had tried returning to work earlier that year, but feelings of guilt at not being with her husband had assailed her. As a result, the work she was doing had suffered, she was back to square one, and all her frustrations came to a head. 'It was a gradual realisation that if Nick couldn't give me more of himself or employ his time with me in different ways, then I questioned what role there was for me as his wife. I never said, "I don't

was expected to do well, not, as one journalist said, to 'throw in his hand when the pot got a bit expensive'.

Worse was to come. Gill Bennett's presence at Augusta had leaked out, prompting a furious reaction from Melanie who immediately contacted her lawyers about a divorce. In truth, Melanie had been aware of a relationship between her husband and Gill for some time, but having it thrown in her face like that was the final straw. It dashed any hope she had of a possible reconciliation; it was all-out war from now on.

Perhaps what upset Melanie most was the fact that Gill was someone she had known for some time. As an assistant to John Simpson, Faldo's agent and friend, it was Gill's job throughout the 1983 season to liaise with Melanie regarding her husband's travel arrangements and tournament schedules. Almost all contact was made by phone, whether it was speaking to Faldo himself or passing messages via Melanie. It was not until the Open at Royal Birkdale in July that any of them actually met face to face, and then it was just a brief encounter in the tented village.

Gill Bennett was a bright, vivacious young woman with a winning personality and dark good looks. She had first gone to work for IMG in Australia in 1981 after being recommended by talk-show king and family friend Michael Parkinson. An invaluable member of the small team that ran IMG's operations from Sydney, she was offered a post in the legal department of the company's London office in February 1983. Relishing the chance to return home after nearly two years away, she took it, but it proved to be a fairly short-lived appointment. She was quickly spotted by IMG vice-president John Simpson who felt her talents could be better used in the role of his assistant. In one of her early phone calls to Faldo, she confessed that she knew little about golf; Faldo joked about his willingness to help her out any time. After that, they continued to swap harmless banter and occasional innuendo over the phone (to such an extent that when Gill rang, Melanie would often call out to her husband, 'Your girlfriend's on the phone!').

Having introduced herself to Faldo at Royal Birkdale, she met him a few days later at a pro-celebrity charity event at Moor Park near Rickmansworth. Faldo had driven down from Southport the previous evening; Gill arrived on the Monday looking to hand over all the congratulatory messages, birthday cards and business correspondence that had built up that week. When Faldo spotted her he seemed happy that she was there. Leaving a somewhat annoyed Melanie behind, he then asked Gill to accompany him to the players' car park so that he could put the stuff straight into the boot of his Porsche. Taking the birthday cards, Faldo noticed one signed by the office staff at IMG, including Gill, who had embellished her name with two small kisses. In typical style, he then made a joke about collecting them, causing her to blush momentarily.

Innocent or otherwise, the attraction between them at that stage was patently obvious, and it grew with time. Over the coming weeks and months, Gill spent more time with Faldo at golf tournaments. Keen on most sports, she had never actually played golf and wanted to learn all she could. At first she would carry a scorecard for each course Faldo was playing and jot down notes in between shots. 'I don't walk around with my head in the clouds,' she was quoted as saying. 'I pay attention. I'm learning all the time. Sometimes I make notes, mark down where Nick's shots have gone. I always carry a card of the course. It helps me to learn. When they start using golf terminology at the dinner table I can understand what they're going on about.'

After a while, Faldo began to see her as a good-luck talisman. During the latter half of the season, it seemed that whenever Gill turned up to watch him compete he would usually play well, which in 1983 was almost every week. Inevitably, they began to fall for each other in a big way. At first Gill resisted the relationship, but as the year went on it became more and more difficult to say no. She was aware that Faldo's marriage to Melanie had been on the rocks for some time, and they planned to tell her about the two of them early in the new year, but, as always, events overtook them. In the end, the tabloid revelations and Melanie's announcement about a divorce came as a big relief to both of them. At least now they could conduct their relationship out in the open, which is exactly what Gill wanted.

They travelled together for the remainder of the season in America, and Gill quickly fell into a tournament routine. Always wonderfully organised, she would spend the early part of the week writing letters, shopping or attending to paperwork. This meant that come the first round she was ready to watch Faldo from behind the ropes, something he really came to appreciate. 'It's nice when you come in at the end of the day and she knows that you've had a cow of a round,' he said. 'She understands, and doesn't expect you to go through it blow by blow. At least somebody is watching you who has the same feelings as you and can appreciate what you are trying to do.' After most rounds, she would wait patiently while he did his media interviews, or perhaps headed off to the practice ground for another 'quick ten minutes'. Aware of the huge pressure he was under, she tried to be both supportive and understanding, even when his mood blackened after a poor round or a disappointing result.

In an interview with respected golf writer John Hopkins in 1985, she outlined exactly what she felt her role was in the relationship. 'At this stage of my life I want to help support somebody else who in turn supports me. I'm old-fashioned enough to believe I should stay with him. I would only get a job if I could go off and be with him whenever I wanted to. I don't need to go out and prove myself. I've travelled and had lots of jobs. I'm quite happy to sit back now. I don't think my role is secondary. I don't feel inferior. I can't go out and play golf for Nick. That's something he has to do for himself.' Faldo was equally forthright about the significant role she played in his life compared with his former partner. 'Gill and Melanie are total opposites,' he said. 'She enjoys travel, perhaps because she is the daughter of a pilot. When I say we're going away, she says, "Oh good, we haven't been on a plane for a week." She gets on better with the other wives. We both like the same sort of music. We make instant decisions, whereas before we used to have to have a stewards' inquiry before we did anything. Life is much less complicated now.'

But in April 1984, life was still very complicated for the couple as they travelled from Georgia to South Carolina on the Monday after the Masters. Faldo was scheduled to play in the Sea Pines Heritage Classic at Hilton Head Island, though it was not a tournament he was looking forward to playing in, especially as it preceded a trip home to England. Starting with the Bob Hope Classic in mid-January, he had now been on the road for fourteen weeks, competing in eleven straight tournaments, and he wanted a break. Plum tired after the gruelling Masters campaign, he believed a degree of caution had crept into his game over the past few weeks. Gill, upbeat as ever, told him if that was his attitude then he had absolutely nothing to lose at Hilton Head by going for everything. Faldo agreed, calculating that the worst that could happen was missing the cut and flying home early. He immediately felt liberated from the stresses and strains of expectation. 'It's either going to go very right or very wrong,' he remembered thinking at the time.

In keeping with this carefree approach, he decided to practise less and relax more. Before the tournament, he would only amble over to the range before casually swiping away seventy or eighty balls, a fraction of his normal routine. There was also a change in the putter department. Shortly before the first round, he decided to ditch the Diawa model he had used at Augusta in favour of the trusty Ping Pal he had wielded so successfully in Europe the previous season. For the totally dedicated Faldo, it was a complete turnaround in attitude.

Amazingly, it worked. He shot a five-under-par 66 in the opening round, which remained the best score of the day until Gil Morgan returned a 64 late in the afternoon. After his round, Faldo was out on the practice putting green when his former caddie, Andy Prodger, wandered over for a chat.

'Have you heard the nickname the British press gave you after the Masters?' he asked half-jokingly. 'They reckoned you folded on Sunday, so they nicknamed you "El Foldo"!'

Faldo was steaming. Already upset over the coverage his marital problems had been given since February, he went straight on the offensive. Storming over to the media centre at Harbour Town he immediately confronted Dai Davies of the *Guardian*, the only British golf correspondent attending the tournament. This gentle giant of a man was astonished by what Faldo had to say and denied knowing anything about his new nickname, after which the matter was dropped. (It subsequently turned out that no British newspaper had referred to him in print as 'El Foldo', but journalists, having seen the reaction it provoked from Faldo, would use it over and over again in the future.)

He discussed the matter with Gill that evening over dinner, and made the decision to forget about the 'El Foldo' jibe and get on with winning the tournament – and he was in a good position to do so. Nine under par at the halfway stage after a superb 67, he followed it up with a 68 in the third round. His scores were getting progressively worse, but they were still enough to lead the tournament by four strokes going into the last day. But with Tom Kite in second place, it was not an unassailable lead. As Faldo lay in bed that night, he felt the first twinges of anxiety. Apart from the minor skirmish with the press, he had been relaxed all week, but now the pressure was really on. Concerned that anyone would doubt his competitive nerve, he wondered what the reaction would be if he lost after holding such an advantage. 'Forget El Foldo,' he thought. 'It would be more a case of El Collapso.'

After nine holes of the final day the headlines were already being written. After an outward half of 35, Faldo's highest of the week, Tom Kite had halved the deficit to two shots after playing the front nine in 33. Worse was to come for Faldo as the bespectacled American made consecutive birdies at the twelfth and thirteenth to draw level. Then, unable to convert legitimate birdie opportunities on four of the last five holes, he handed the advantage back to Faldo, who regained the lead with a birdie on the fifteenth. Having kept his nerve and his game under control, the 26-year-old Englishman arrived on the testing par-four eighteenth with a slender one-shot lead.

Under the severest pressure imaginable, Faldo split the fairway with his drive before sizing up an approach from 186 yards. With Gill anxiously looking on from behind the ropes, he chose a six-iron, but it proved at least one club too many. Knowing that a par would be good enough to win, he sent his ball bounding through the green, finally coming to rest on a bare patch of ground, a collar of rough between him and the flag. Deciding to take his putter and bump it towards the hole, he judged the shot quite perfectly. As the large crowd around the green held its collective breath, commentator Ken Venturi said, 'He's made a good roll . . . what a good roll . . . what a good roll . . . what a great roll that was!' The ball had gathered pace down the slope, finally coming to a halt within tap-in

range. The tournament was over. Signing for a score of 69 to go
with his earlier rounds of 66, 67 and 68, Faldo became only the
second Englishman to win on the American PGA Tour since
Tony Jacklin in 1972.

His first victory in the United States, and only his third
outside Britain, helped dispel some of the criticism he had faced
after the Masters. By holding off Tom Kite by a single stroke
after the American's magnificent final round of 66, he had
shown that he had the nerve for the big occasion. Describing it
later as 'a great win and a great boost', Faldo lost no time in
telephoning his agent John Simpson with the good news.

Returning to England at the beginning of May, Faldo
maintained this run of form with a successful defence of the Car
Care Plan International at Moortown, near Leeds. Feeling on top
of the world, he now looked forward to defending his
number-one position in Europe with equal success. The
following week he finished third behind Bernhard Langer in the
Peugeot French Open at St Cloud – a remarkable result,
considering what had happened between the first and second
rounds. After holing his final putt on the eighteenth green on
the Thursday, he was whisked by limousine to a nearby airport.
From there he took a private jet from Paris to London to attend
a reception given by the Queen at Buckingham Palace. Flattered
at being honoured with an invitation, he was even more
flattered when the Duke of Edinburgh thanked him personally
for coming back at such short notice. He stood alongside
Olympic swimmer June Croft during the presentation, and it
proved to be a memorable occasion. 'I felt so tall talking to the
Queen I had to stop myself leaning forward. She knew I'd won
in America and we talked about that. Then the conversation
turned to swimming and I said I used to swim as well. She
looked at me and said, "You have lovely broad shoulders."'

A week later at the Whyte and Mackay PGA Championship
at Wentworth, Faldo was in far less good humour as news-
hungry reporters questioned him about his impending divorce
from Melanie. There were other problems as well. It had taken
much longer than he had imagined for his and Gill's new
'dream' house on the Wentworth Estate to be ready. With most
of Faldo's belongings in storage at his parents' house, he and

Gill had spent an uncomfortable few weeks living like gypsies in hotel rooms, rented houses or even staying with friends. Having gone through so much over the last six months, they wanted a place of refuge, somewhere they could call home, somewhere they could escape to when the press attention became too intrusive. Faldo also wanted somewhere to unwind, play his records and fiddle around with his clubs, but that was still some way off. For the time being, it was a simple matter of putting up with it.

From the end of May until October, nothing went completely to plan. After a sixth-place finish at the rain-reduced PGA Championship, the rest of the season was spent in damage limitation. In tournament after tournament, Faldo strung together four rounds that were individually acceptable yet collectively not good enough. As at Wentworth, where he followed a magnificent opening round of 67 with two mediocre 73s, any good score was often diminished by a bad one.

It was no different in America. The week before making his debut in the US Open at Winged Foot, he crashed out of the Manufacturers Hanover Westchester Classic with rounds of 74 and 76 to miss the cut. Then, moving upstate for the US Open itself, he followed a solid opening round of 71 with scores of 76, 77 and 72 to finish a hugely disappointing fifty-fifth. It was a similar story in the Open at St Andrews in July. Still in possession of Gerald Micklem's invaluable notes on how to play the Old Course, Faldo found himself in joint second place going into the weekend after rounds of 69 and 68. Once again in a perfect position to make a strong challenge, it all went horribly wrong with a morale-crushing 76.

Faldo had arrived at St Andrews with high expectations, so this was a particularly bitter pill to swallow. As he closed out his championship with a 69 for an aggregate score of 282, his frustration was obvious. For three rounds he had outplayed almost everyone in the field, yet he still ended up tied sixth behind the eventual winner, Seve Ballesteros on twelve under par (276). The simplest calculation told him that anything under 70 on the Saturday would have given him his first major victory. Instead, the record books show that it was the Spaniard's fourth major title of his career, while Faldo was still chasing his first.

Working on his game harder than ever, Faldo seemed unable to make a breakthrough. If he did spot some light at the end of the tunnel, it usually turned out to be nothing more than an oncoming train. A good example of this happened at the United States PGA Championship at Shoal Creek, a newly built club ten miles from the steel town of Birmingham, Alabama, in August. Faldo liked the course and seemed confident this would be the turning point in his year. Arriving three days before the championship was due to start, he agreed to be interviewed by a local reporter about his career and ambitions. He spoke for an hour, and apparently spent most of it criticising the British press, especially those who seemed more interested in his tortured private life than in his golf. Speaking in fairly forceful terms, he was quoted as saying, 'You can't be open, free, natural, because there will be a stupid headline the next day which will make you look big-headed, stupid.' Faldo went on to say how he felt the stories were often sensationalised, twisted in order to sell newspapers. 'They quote you out of character and then add a couple of words to your quote to make it more exciting.'

The story soon broke back in Britain under the sensational headline FALDO TAKES A SWING AT BRITISH PRESS. Afterwards, Faldo appeared genuinely surprised at the uproar his words had caused. Pleading innocence, he explained how he could never understand that if he talked to a golf journalist about a dozen different subjects he might only be quoted on one or two. To him, that was a misrepresentation of the truth. 'As soon as they ask me a question I have to sift through my mind to think what he [the journalist] is trying to get out of this, what slant is he trying to put on it?'

Did the rumpus affect his concentration? He made a good start at Shoal Creek with a 69, but his disastrous finish to the second round was probably down to poor concentration as much as anything else. Partnered by his boyhood hero Jack Nicklaus, Faldo came to the par-four eighteenth at three under par for the round, six under for the championship. With only three others ahead of him on the leaderboard – Lee Trevino, Gary Player and Lanny Wadkins – he was in a perfect position to launch a challenge over the weekend. Needing only a par or better to finish among the leaders, he recorded a quadruple-bogey eight for a round of 73. After that, he was never in contention again.

Returning to England after another disappointing perform-ance in the NEC World Series event at Akron a week later, Faldo was left to reflect on what was rapidly becoming a dreadful season. Apart from the turmoil surrounding his increasingly acrimonious divorce, he was sliding down the European money list fast. Without a victory since the Car Care Plan International in May, he had now slipped out of the top ten with prize-money earnings barely a third of what they had been the previous year. It was the same story on the PGA Tour in America. Having accumulated just over $150,000 in prize money by the start of May, including that spectacular victory in the Sea Pines Heritage Classic, Faldo saw his season go rapidly downhill. Starting with the Westchester Classic in June, he had entered six tourna-ments, missed the cut in three and won $16,074. People were now beginning to wonder if Nick Faldo, heralded as a world-beater five months earlier, was merely a flash in the pan.

Having just blown his chance of winning a major champion-ship for the third time in four months, Faldo could have been forgiven for thinking that things could not get much worse – but they could. He and Gill had been virtually homeless for months, he had had a storming on-course row with his caddie, Dave McNeilly, and for a time it seemed like everything was going wrong. Then, in September, he entered the Panasonic European Open at Sunningdale, which marked a further downturn in his fortunes.

With an end-of-season revival in mind, Faldo ran headlong into a barrage of criticism about the controversial comments he had apparently made about the British press prior to the PGA Championship in Alabama. In typical style, Faldo went on the defensive, denying that he had actually said them; if he had said anything of the sort, his comments had been used out of context. He later admitted that the story had in fact been accurately reported, but pointed out in mitigation that his comments about the press had been just a small part of an interview during which to his recollection he had also aired his views on playing in the United States, the rising standard of European golf, the Ryder Cup and a whole lot more.

Having been roasted in the press prior to the European Open, Faldo managed a superb 65 on the opening day. A brilliant performance, considering the circumstances, it proved to be a fairly short-lived triumph. On the par-five eleventh in the second round, Faldo mistakenly picked up his ball from what he thought was a lateral water hazard and moved it two club lengths sideways. In fact it was a red-staked water hazard; he should, according to the rules, have replaced his ball keeping the point where the ball had entered the hazard between him and the flag. After the round, Faldo headed off to the practice ground blissfully unaware that the incident had just been reported to PGA officials. A few minutes later he was on his way home, disqualified from the tournament.

Only four months after the greatest triumph of his career at Harbour Town, things were still bad. In Paris for the Lancôme Trophy, Faldo was asked about a report in the *Daily Mail* that he had secretly returned to the marital home in Ayot St Lawrence and removed two vanloads of household goods. Under the headline NICK NICKS KNICK-KNACKS, gossip columnist Nigel Dempster had also described how he had taken a large colour television and a food mixer rather than buy his own. 'Rubbish,' said an indignant Faldo. 'It was all arranged with Melanie beforehand. I wish he'd check his facts.'

And his problems did not end there. Increasingly being portrayed in the press as a villainous adulterer, Faldo made an easy target for any publication that wanted a cheap, attention-grabbing headline. Taking their lead from a letter published in *Golf World* magazine, several newspapers ran a story shortly before the Lancôme accusing Faldo of insulting his playing partners in the pro-am preceding the Carroll's Irish Open at Royal Dublin by practising his putting while they were still holing out. A frustrated Faldo refused to make any comment. Then came the final straw. Finding that his golf shoes had been stolen from the locker room at St Nom-la-Breteche, he finally blew his top. 'I'm fed up with it all!' he shouted. 'My game, the press, the divorce, everything!'

Desperate to escape the media spotlight, he considered refusing all interviews, something he had first thought about back in February when his divorce from Melanie was first reported. Convinced by John Simpson that this would only add fuel to the fire, he then thought about not reading the papers and magazines, but decided against that since he never believed what was reported anyway. What was needed, according to his girlfriend Gill, was a complete change in attitude. Instead of antagonising journalists with a series of barbed comments and irritating snubs, he should be less defensive, perhaps even give them what they wanted. He should be more relaxed in interviews, let his true personality come across and worry far less about what they actually wrote. It was a radical suggestion, but slowly Faldo came round to the idea.

Reasoning that things just could not get much worse, he adopted a much more relaxed attitude for the remaining weeks of the season. It was a decision that brought immediate results. A few weeks later in the Hennessy Cognac Cup at Ferdown in Bournemouth, Faldo captained an England team that included Howard Clark, Mark James and Brian Waites to a spectacular victory over the Spanish. Winning a tense final 3 ½ to 2 ½, he was in majestic form all week. In an echo of his Ryder Cup form, he made an invaluable contribution by winning both his singles, halving one fourball and losing another.

In November, Faldo was at the World Matchplay Championship at Wentworth where he faced another England v. Spain showdown. Matched against Ballesteros in the second round, the Englishman this time looked completely out of sorts with his game. Swinging badly and unable to put any lasting pressure on the reigning Open champion, he finally lost by 4 & 3. Summing up what had been a fairly dour display, his opponent said to him afterwards, 'I know you can play better than that.'

With Christmas a matter of weeks away, Faldo desperately needed a break. His form was patchy at best, and now, as winter began to close in, he needed somewhere warm and inviting to work on his game. Hence his decision to play in the Million Dollar Challenge at Sun City in South Africa. An invitational event with a growing reputation for excellence, not to mention the largest prize in golf, it would prove the right decision for many reasons. For a start, he mingled with lots of people, each of whom would have an influence on his career to a greater or lesser degree, but one would become synonymous with the name of Nick Faldo over the coming years.

David Leadbetter was in Sun City that winter.

7. LEADBETTER TO THE RESCUE

Nick Faldo arrived in South Africa for the Million Dollar Challenge with mixed feelings. He had made the perfect start to the year with tournament victories in both Europe and America, but then things had gone badly wrong and he was at a loss when it came to explaining why. The press speculated on how much his divorce from Melanie had impacted on his season, but Faldo was unconvinced. Things had been difficult all year, but his relationship with Gill Bennett was a happy one and it more than compensated for any bad publicity he had received over the past ten months. So what was the problem? Having finished number one in Europe in 1983, why had he now slipped down to twelfth place? More importantly, why was he incapable of putting together four consistent rounds in a major championship? As he prepared to end 1984 at the luxurious Sun City complex near Bophuthatswana, he desperately wanted answers to these questions and others.

Shortly before the exclusive twelve-man tournament, signs of a Nick Faldo revival were not good. Rusty from weeks of inactivity, he had travelled to Sun City more in hope than in any expectation of winning. One thing the tournament did offer, however, was superb practice facilities and guaranteed sunshine, both of which Faldo planned to take full advantage of over the coming few days. And for once, it would be time extremely well spent.

Blessed with a rhythmic, aesthetically pleasing swing, Faldo had been aware for some time that it contained flaws that urgently needed ironing out. For example, compared with other top players like Tom Watson and Greg Norman, he knew that he did not 'flight' the ball particularly well, which in windy conditions was a real problem. Increasingly envious of the crisp ball strike and piercing trajectory enjoyed by Watson, Norman and other top players, he knew important changes had to be made if he was to fulfil his potential. 'His swing was not as good as it looked,' said his former Ryder Cup captain John Jacobs.

'He was tall, handsome, and he had a good rhythm. But he used to swing back too straight and therefore his shoulders rocked in sympathy with that swing path. When he swung back so straight his right side didn't get out of the way on the back swing and his left side was in the way on the down swing. Thus he pushed some shots and hooked others.'

Faldo's free-flowing, loose-limbed technique had also shown itself to be notoriously inconsistent under the type of intense pressure exerted during a major championship. At the Open in July, Faldo had blown any chance he had of winning after a disastrous third round of 76. It was the same story in the PGA Championship in August when that quadruple-bogey eight took him out of the running. At Royal Birkdale in 1983 Faldo had had a good chance to win the Open but was unable to maintain a decent enough challenge over the closing stages. At the time his failure was put down to inexperience in the majors, as it had been on several occasions since, but Faldo was beginning to think otherwise.

Ever since he had parted company with Ian Connelly in 1982, it had been slowly dawning on Nick Faldo that his swing was not as technically sound as it might be. Even before his spectacularly successful season in 1983, he had considered giving his game a complete overhaul. Then came the lesson from his fellow pro Mark O'Meara in Texas, but from having missed three cuts in his first four events on the PGA Tour earlier in the year, he won tournament after tournament, five in all, three in consecutive weeks, and set new records for prize money and scoring averages. All thoughts of change were dismissed from his mind. Now, with the success of that year nothing but a distant memory, perhaps it was time to reconsider making those changes once again? Most importantly of all, who could he trust to help him complete those changes?

Over the past eighteen months, Faldo had spent time with a number of top coaches including John Jacobs and Bob Torrance, as well as several other teachers in the United States. While each had his own theories on how he could progress on to the next level, Faldo remained stubbornly unconvinced. 'They either wanted me to work on their ideas, which in some way or other were different to what I thought was right, or suggested I should go back to my old swing,' said Faldo later.

'On the surface, the solution was simple. "Work on that," they said, "and you will learn to handle the big occasions in due course."' Convinced that it was only a matter of time until Faldo achieved his goal of winning a major championship, they urged patience on him, patience and hard work. But as Faldo already worked harder on the practice ground than many of his contemporaries, he instinctively felt this was not the way he needed to go. It was against this background of frustrated ambition and growing self-doubt that Faldo came to South Africa. Then came a chance meeting with the man who would not only change his swing, but his entire golfing life.

Today, David Leadbetter is considered to be among the top golf instructors in the world. Coach to an elite group of tournament professionals – men and women – he is the inspiration behind many best-selling instructional books, videos and practice aids. In huge demand all over the world, he currently lends his name to some seventeen teaching academies in eleven different countries. Often more famous than those he teaches, he enjoys the type of celebrity status usually reserved for major championship winners. Boasting lucrative endorsement contracts with companies like Rolex, Mercedes and Callaway, Leadbetter is credited with singlehandedly revolutionising the golf teaching industry over the past two decades. Yet until Nick Faldo came along, very few people knew who he was.

They had first met in the late seventies, but neither of them can remember the meeting in any great detail. 'I think the first time I set eyes on him was in 1977, not long after he turned pro,' said Leadbetter. 'I was playing a tournament in Zimbabwe, near Victoria Falls, and I think he was out there with Warren Humphreys. Warren was like his minder. George Blumberg [the South African industrialist] brought him out and I remember watching this big tall fellow with a fairly languid-looking swing, but I didn't take much notice of him.' The fact that they did not recognise each other that day is not surprising. Although Faldo had achieved some minor fame as a British Ryder Cup player by 1977, David Leadbetter was just one of a faceless band of local professionals trying to scratch out a living on the Sunshine Circuit. Indeed, it was his complete lack of success as a tournament player that first gave him the idea that he might be better off teaching the game for a living rather than playing it.

Born in England, David Leadbetter moved with his family from Worthing in Sussex to Rhodesia, as Zimbabwe was called then, when he was seven. He was a sickly child who suffered from chronic asthma; it was hoped the condition would be eased by the change in climate, which it was. As he grew into a tall, wafer-thin youth, his schoolboy passion for sport belied his earlier ill health. A keen cricket and soccer player, he showed an exceptional talent for tennis before turning to golf in his early teenage years.

With hopes of being the next Gary Player, or possibly the next Tom Weiskopf considering his height (six feet four inches), Leadbetter turned professional at the tender age of eighteen. He played some events on the Sunshine Circuit in the mid- to late seventies, but also spent some time in Florida working under the legendary American coach Phil Ritson. After that, he took up his first teaching post at Staverton Park in Northamptonshire in 1977. An enthusiastic and well-liked professional, he spent the next two years there fine-tuning the teaching skills he had been taught in the United States.' It was a case of do your own thing as long as you could demonstrate that it was a good idea. So I put in a driving range, and I think at that time it was the first in a private club in Britain where you could hit your own golf balls.'

It was during this time that Leadbetter attempted to make a comeback as a tournament professional. A decent enough ball striker, he played in a number of events on the European circuit but with very little success. The problem, he later admitted, was the same one that had plagued the notoriously inconsistent Tom Weiskopf throughout his career. 'I was such a perfectionist as far as my golf game was concerned. I was a great practice-round player and it used to drive me crazy to think that I could spend all those hours on the practice tee and hit the ball well and yet get out under tournament conditions and not produce the same sort of result.'

An aficionado of the golf swing, Leadbetter began to recognise his own limitations as a player. Returning to the United States in 1979, he decided to strike out as a teaching pro, heading first to Chicago, then to Florida two years later.

Having attended as many teaching seminars as he could, he finally established a base of his own at the Grenelefe Resort, near Orlando. In 1981, he persuaded his old pal Dennis Watson to desert Europe in favour of playing the PGA Tour in America. 'He was a good player but didn't like the European weather, and I just felt his game would succeed in America,' said Leadbetter. 'We started working together and he began to play real well, and then Nick Price came over. So it was really through an association of old friends that I got started.'

Working with two such highly talented players proved to be a huge turning point for David Leadbetter – especially after Nick Price finished runner-up to Tom Watson in the 1982 Open at Troon. Leadbetter was one of the first coaches actually to join his players out on the practice ground at tournaments, so as their reputation grew so, inevitably, did his. It was this close relationship with Nick Price that drew Leadbetter to Sun City for the Million Dollar Challenge in 1984, and within a matter of days he had had a practice-ground conversation with the man who would change his life for ever, Nick Faldo.

He asked me to have a look at him. I think Nick Price had been speaking to him. Nothing was planned. It was more a case of I was there, he was there. I think he might already have spoken to Mark O'Meara about his swing at that stage and maybe wanted a second opinion. Then he said, 'Hey, would you have a look?' So I made a couple of suggestions. I told him that his swing was too steep. That he needed to get his swing a little more rounded – a little flatter. Something that would give him a little more control. I remember walking with him in a practice round at Augusta in 1982 or 1983, and noticing that when he hit his tee-shots, especially into a slight breeze, how they seemed to balloon up. There was no run on his shots and his goal at that stage was to win a major. He dearly wanted to win the Open but I thought the way he hits it high like that he is going to struggle. So my suggestion was to get the club going a little more round him and we sort of left it at that.

Having watched Nick Faldo hit some balls on the practice ground in Sun City, Leadbetter offered one or two pointers but deliberately kept things as simple as possible. As someone who saw the golf swing as a solid moving block rather than a loosely connected series of movements, he noticed that Faldo had far too many moving parts. And, like any machine, the more moving parts there were, the more things could go wrong. Instead, he explained to Faldo that many of the week-to-week problems he was experiencing could be resolved by working on his overall method. For example, he said, there were at least six faults that could easily be rectified by working on a better takeaway.

Nick Faldo was suitably impressed. Rarely had he spoken with someone with such a clear insight into the mechanics of the golf swing. 'I took to David right away. Others had told me what they thought I was doing wrong, but nobody had said this in particular is how I could cure my faults.' But he remained uncommitted about working with Leadbetter on a full-time basis. Instead, he agreed to think about what the tall Zimbabwean had said and would decide over the winter break whether he wanted to take the matter further.

In truth, Leadbetter probably never gave it another thought. Having spent a lot of time on the road with Nick Price and Dennis Watson, he was used to offering little titbits of information to anyone who asked for help, as he'd done during that walk with Faldo in Augusta, but rarely did it progress into anything more. He knew most players had their own teachers back at home, and if a player wanted his help it usually meant they had a specific problem that particular week that needed solving. Why should Faldo be any different?

Nick Faldo was in no mood to credit anyone after his success at Sun City. He finished in second place, five strokes behind the runaway leader Seve Ballesteros, and it gave him just the boost he needed with the start of the PGA Tour only weeks away.

He spent Christmas at home in England with Gill, and was still in confident mood by the time he teed up at the Phoenix Open in the middle of January 1985. He felt even more positive after opening up the new season with rounds of 67, 73, 69 and 66 for a share of fourth place and over $16,000 in prize money. Then, almost inexplicably, things started to go wrong. He missed the cut in the Los Angeles Open the following week, and the miserable run continued at the Bing Crosby Pro-Am (tied sixty-fourth), the Hawaii Open (tied forty-fifth), the Honda Classic (tied thirty-fifth), the Hertz Bay Hill Classic (tied eighteenth). There was another missed cut in the Tournament Players Championship at the end of March.

After this uninspiring start to the season, Faldo arrived at Augusta National for the Masters totally lacking in self-belief. Then, to make matters worse, he played solidly enough for a share of twenty-fifth place only to find that by finishing outside the top twenty-four he had missed out on an automatic exemption for the following year. Moving on to Hilton Head Island to defend the Sea Pines Heritage Classic title he had won in such spectacular style the year before, he must have realised it was not going to be his week right from the start.

At the start of the week, the reigning champion is asked to open proceedings by hitting a ball into the lake bordering the eighteenth green. In keeping with the 'heritage' theme of the tournament, two suitably dressed 'yeomen' light a fuse attached to a small cannon in the hope that the cannon fire and the drive happen simultaneously. Looking somewhat bemused, Nick Faldo was handed a century-old hickory-shafted wood with which to hit the ball. To his credit, he rose to the occasion admirably and struck the shot perfectly, despite the fact he was still wearing his leather street shoes. But the cannon misfired and he had to do it all over again. On the second occasion the cannon was fired a fraction prematurely, and it went off with such a colossal bang that Faldo jumped half out of his skin in mid-swing. The ancient club came down inches behind the ball, and Faldo was forced to watch as it scuttled lifelessly into the water (in truth, he was lucky to have hit it at all). In typical style, he then tried to save his and the organisers' embarrass-ment by hamming it up in front of the large crowd, acting as if he had been shot. The crowd lapped it up, although one humourless American reporter wrote in his column the next day about how the Englishman had made a mockery of the ceremony.

No doubt suffering from temporary deafness, Faldo went on to score an 80 and a 72 to miss the cut by a mile. Having failed to defend his title, he moved on to the Houston Open a week later, only to miss the cut again with rounds of 74 and 75. That meant that in 35 competitive rounds since the middle of January, he had only broken the 70 mark five times, and three of those had come in the Phoenix Open. Things improved slightly in May after a fleeting trip to Europe paid off with decent finishes at the Italian Open (eleventh), the Car Care Plan International (thirteenth) and the Dunhill British Masters (third), but by the time he arrived at the Memorial Tournament two weeks later his game had unravelled once more. 'Things had got so bad that I couldn't hit a green with a nine-iron.'

He was desperate to turn things around, and there was someone at the tournament who could help him do just that. Ping-ponging across the Atlantic in the hope of keeping his player's card on both tours, Faldo was scheduled to play just two more events in the United States before returning to Europe for the summer. Shortly after arriving at the Jack Nicklaus-inspired Muirfield Village, Faldo spotted David Leadbetter on the practice ground working with one of his growing band of pupils. Like a starving man who has just caught sight of the sweet trolley at a plush restaurant, he made an immediate beeline for the Zimbabwean and asked him to have another, more detailed look at his swing. 'I had reached the point where I knew I couldn't do it by myself, and of all the people I had talked to, Lead made the most sense.'

The diagnosis was not good. Almost from the start of his career, Faldo had dragged the club sharply inside on the back swing, then pushed it up over his head with a straight lift of the hands (as an amateur he had had a pronounced 'loop' as he adjusted from the back swing to the down swing). According to Leadbetter, this was at the root of all his problems. 'I felt he swung the club on too upright a plane. The club-face was closed initially, then very open at the top, and he would sort of slide his legs and get underneath with a very armsy-handsy-looking swing. The whole thing had a pretty big reverse-C look to it. Nick really had a swing from the seventies, which was understandable because he grew up in that era.'

After watching Faldo hit balls on the practice range for an hour, Leadbetter explained that while he had a wonderful tempo, his method would never stand up to the type of pressure found at an Open championship. Pulling few punches, he hinted that Faldo would have to rebuild his back swing completely and effectively change almost everything that had brought him such success only twelve months earlier. Then, as if keeping the really bad news to last, Leadbetter stressed that the remodelling process would take two years, and that they would both have to be incredibly determined to see it through. 'It was a risk, but at that stage I was probably a little more naive than I am now,' he said about the challenge of taking on Faldo. 'I had had a little success coaching some top players and I really did feel I could help him. I said to him, "Listen, if you want to do it, it's going to take time." It wasn't a matter of making just a few changes.'

Frustrated to the point of desperation, Faldo was still unsure whether he wanted to put himself through this golfing pain barrier. Like most professionals who go through a bad patch, he wanted a quick fix. After all, he was in much the same situation now as he had been in the spring of 1983. Back then, when he was out of form and out of confidence, a quick lesson from Mark O'Meara in Texas had turned around his entire season. For a moment he even considered the possibility of just taking on David Leadbetter's suggestions and dovetailing them into his own game, but this was never really an option and he knew it. Something drastic had to be done if he was to achieve his goals, and here, at the very least, was someone he felt he could trust.

Faldo took time to gather his thoughts on the matter, then plumped for the major surgery Leadbetter had advised. Tired of playing mediocre golf and not reaching his potential, he turned to the lanky golf instructor and said, 'Okay, you can throw the book at me!' In the tortuous months, even years, to come, David Leadbetter would do just that. 'We spoke again about how it would be a two-year job before things started to work their way into his swing and start to feel natural,' said Faldo's new coach. 'As it turned out it was a pretty good prophecy.'

After some intensive work with Leadbetter at the Memorial, Faldo began to see what a huge task lay ahead of him. He was fortunate to make the cut after opening rounds of 74 and 75, and ended the week tied for fiftieth place after weekend scores of 77 and 72. A week later his mood was hardly improved after finishing joint seventieth at the Kemper Open. He put both results down to the necessary changes he was making in his game. Then came a real setback. Competing in the Open in July at Royal St George's on the Kent coast, Faldo struggled with his long-game all week. Finishing with rounds of 73, 73, 75 and 74, he ended up joint fifty-third. Moreover, his oldest rival, Sandy Lyle, had beaten him to the winning post, becoming the first British golfer to win since Tony Jacklin in 1969.

Publicly, Faldo congratulated the new champion, but in private he felt bitterly disappointed that it was Lyle, not him, receiving all the plaudits. It was one of the lowest points of his competitive career. He had picked up news of Lyle's historic victory on the car radio as he drove back home on the Sunday afternoon. Unable to relax, he spent most of that evening practising his putting on the green in front of the old pro shop at Wentworth. Later, as he returned home, he could hear the celebrations from the Lyle household. It was a tough pill to swallow.

The following day, Faldo, like Lyle, was scheduled to play in the PGA Benevolent Society tournament at nearby Sunningdale. Looking on as Lyle paraded the Open trophy he had won fewer than 24 hours earlier, Faldo became even more determined to complete the necessary swing changes. 'Sandy's made it much harder for me now,' Faldo admitted shortly afterwards. 'Before, they used to say it was Seve who paved the way and I just had to follow him. Then came Bernhard, and now Sandy. I've got to win the Open just to keep up with them.'

By September 1985, Faldo had started to strike the ball well and he felt he was home and dry, but David Leadbetter disagreed. Certainly Faldo had improved the initial movement of his back swing, but after playing with the 'wrong' swing for so many years he had compensated by making even worse mistakes in other areas. In retrospect, under the enormous pressure of playing a minimum of fifteen tournaments just to keep a PGA Tour card, mid-season was probably not the ideal time to embark on a major course of reconstruction, but Faldo felt he had no choice. He began to suffer again from the shock of the extent of what Leadbetter had planned for him. 'We sort of laid it out with a lot of video and I made some suggestions,' Leadbetter said, recalling their first week-long session at Grenelefe.

> We started with the set-up because I felt he had a very poor set-up for a tall player – quite sort of slouchy really. So we really worked on getting his posture right, but his build dictated that things were going to be difficult. Being very long from the waist down, he had a very leggy-looking method. So the main objective was to get the club on a better plane. That meant opening it early and being more closed at the top, rather than having it shut to start with, then being more open. Then we worked extremely hard on the back swing. We really tried to get that down to a point where things started to work automatically.

One place his swing definitely did not feel 'automatic' was the Belfry a few weeks later. A controversial choice of venue, the Brabazon course was a formidable test for the 1985 Ryder Cup players. It was perfectly playable after years of reseeding, fertilisation and extensive tree planting, and great things were expected of the European team. Record crowds of 25,000 turned up each day hopeful of victory; it was their noisy support over the three days that gave the visitors cause for complaint. Peter Jacobson spoke for many of his American team-mates when he said, 'All that cheering when we missed shots. I've never known anything like it before, especially from British crowds. You expect so much more from them.'

A lot was expected of Nick Faldo too. Partnered once again by Bernhard Langer, the new Masters champion, they were considered one of captain Tony Jacklin's key pairings. But the partnership that had yielded three wins out of four at PGA National two years earlier was in obvious and terminal decline. Matched against Tom Kite and Calvin Peete in the opening foursomes, Faldo struggled from the start, his fragile game unable to handle the enormous pressure. Unexpectedly beaten by 3 & 1, Faldo went straight to Jacklin and asked to be dropped from the remaining matches. 'I was under too much pressure,' he admitted. 'Tony had picked me for the team and, as I was going through my swing changes, I decided that it was for the good of the team to give him the option to make changes.'

Faldo spent the remainder of the week battling against his own particular demons on the Belfry practice ground, and little had improved by the time the crucial singles came around on Sunday. Even with a two-point lead going into the final day, the experienced Jacklin knew that over twelve matches the Americans would still be favourites. So, unlike two years earlier at PGA National, he chose to play his best players in the middle and hope his early picks could spring a surprise or two – and they did.

The final day was a hard-fought affair, the Spaniard Manuel Pinero springing the biggest surprise with a 2 & 1 victory over the experienced Lanny Wadkins in the opening match. Two games later, a topped bunker shot into the lake at the eighteenth by Ray Floyd gave twenty-year-old Paul Way an unexpected two-up victory, raising hopes for a European triumph. In contrast to Lyle, Langer, Clark, Torrance and Cañizares, all of whom won, Faldo again struggled in his match against former US Open champion Hubert Green. Losing 3 & 1, he was fortunate that his game did not affect the eventual outcome. Faldo cut a forlorn figure as he trudged back to the clubhouse; even the cheers that echoed around the course signalling an historic 16½ to 11½ European victory brought him little comfort.

When the champagne corks finally stopped popping, it was inevitable that his critics would begin crawling out of the woodwork. The general feeling among the British press was that Nick Faldo's decision to make such drastic swing changes earlier in the season had proved a disastrous one. For him to have slipped down the Order of Merit from top spot in 1983 and twelfth in 1984 to forty-second at the end of 1985, something must have gone badly wrong, and they lost no time outlining their concerns in print. Surely the answer was simple, they bleated in unison: dump Leadbetter, forget the swing changes and take a leaf out of Sandy Lyle's book – try and relax a little more. After all, the amiable Scot had shown what was possible by capturing the Open that year.

Although these were difficult times, Faldo had few doubts that when the reconstruction was complete he would get back to winning ways. David Leadbetter agreed. 'It was just a matter of time,' he said some years later. 'I felt with his talent and aptitude for the game, being able to apply it out on the golf course once it worked itself in I didn't think was going to be a problem. I really didn't. I thought if he could play as well as he did with his old technique, how can a guy with his mental strength not play better with a better technique? That was the philosophy we worked on.'

For the first few months progress had been slow, but having gone this far, it would have proved doubly frustrating to give it up now. Besides, there was no guarantee that Faldo could get his game back if he and Leadbetter parted ways. The question now was how long it would actually take. Because if Nick Faldo thought that 1985 was a tough year, 1986 was just round the corner.

8. IN THE WILDERNESS

The first week of January 1986 began with good news on the private front: Nick Faldo and Gill Bennett finally got married. With his divorce from Melanie made final just a short time before, they made the decision to wed in secret at Stroud Registry Office in Gloucestershire. The following day they had a service of blessing at nearby St Mary Magdalen's Church in Rodborough. Considering the publicity a wedding would inevitably attract, the dates were deliberately set apart so that they could enjoy a private ceremony with just family and close friends – definitely no journalists.

After a short honeymoon in Florida, Faldo returned to competitive action at the end of the month convinced he was on the right track. But once immersed in the Phoenix Open, he quickly realised that he had a lot further to go than he had believed. He missed the halfway cut in Arizona after ring-rusty rounds of 71 and 74, then did the same the following week in the AT&T Pebble Beach Pro-Am in California where his scores of 79, 74 and 78, his worst three-round total in years, made ugly reading for someone hoping to resurrect their game that year.

Perhaps the greatest distraction Faldo had to cope with during the two-year reconstruction period from May 1985 onwards was, paradoxically, his continuing desire to play golf tournaments. Right up until the point where his swing changes began to bear rich fruit in 1987, his often fragile golf game was on constant public display. Having deserted the method that had made him the golden boy of British golf in the early eighties, he slipped further and further away from the glory and success he had once known. Attracting criticism and derision from the press and public alike, he would later describe this time as his 'wilderness years'.

On average, Nick Faldo and David Leadbetter saw each other every six to eight weeks at the start. Maintaining an exhausting schedule, Faldo would often fly down to Florida in between tournaments in the US, while his new coach would link up with him in Britain around the time of the Open in July. Then, as the end of the season approached, they would get together for a number of week-long sessions at Grenelefe. It was during these so-called 'autumn camps' that they did some of their best work. Faldo hit hundreds of practice balls each morning and afternoon, followed by a swim to cool down, and it became a regular part of their intensive programme over the next few years. Leadbetter had this to say about their early work together:

> You develop certain neurological patterns which are very hard to break. My goal was to get him to strike it solidly, have control over it, be able to do what he wanted with the ball. But he worked his rear off. I'd say conservatively, when we were together he hit five to eight hundred balls a day, every day, and that was in the heat and summer of Florida. Which was not pleasant, that's for sure. I don't know how many balls we hit in total, but it was thousands and thousands.

Needless to say, it was also a period of excruciating tedium and soul-crushing frustration. No sooner had Faldo mastered one part of the swing than the next piece had to be taken apart, analysed under a microscope then put back together again. Sometimes the prognosis was good, at others not quite so good (Faldo later admitted that he might have been better off taking six months away from competition to work on his game rather than struggle on so badly). First it was the back swing, retaining the new position at the top, then a different down swing, right through to the follow-through. Often, like some badly assembled children's toy, Leadbetter would set about taking the whole thing apart in order to reconstruct it all over again – at least that is how it must have felt at times.

Almost from the word go, the decision had been made that the restructuring of Faldo's golf swing would take precedence over everything, including results, prize money and world rankings. In the second half of 1985, tournaments on both sides of the Atlantic had become no more than a testing ground for his new method, and it would be the same throughout 1986. Competitive victories, already a thing of the past by the time he began working with Leadbetter, now became secondary to how well, or how badly, he was striking the ball. Faldo never did anything in half measures.

Not that he gave up the thought of winning completely. From the end of January, Faldo spent the next four months looking for some kind of breakthrough. Playing a full schedule on the PGA Tour proved to be incredibly frustrating, despite some noticeable improvement in his ball striking over the winter. He missed the cut in six out of the first dozen events he competed in, and the news was not much better in those events for which he did complete all four rounds. Apart from the F&G Classic in late March where he finished tied third on eleven under par, it was a real case of one step forward, three steps back.

A good example of this was the prestigious Tournament Players Championship in Florida a week later. Anxious to continue the good form he had shown in New Orleans at the F&G Classic, Faldo made the perfect start at Sawgrass with an opening round of 69, his sixth score in the sixties in his last seven competitive rounds. The dark clouds were finally starting to lift and Faldo was in confident mood, then he shot a 78 in the second round. In the space of 24 hours he had gone from challenging for the lead to missing the cut. He repeated the performance at the Sea Pines Heritage Classic in April with rounds of 71 and 80, and in the Houston Open he started with 68, 69 and 70 only to end the tournament with a heartbreaking round of 77.

Despite these failures, David Leadbetter was full of admiration for his pupil's ability to play tournaments while undergoing such major swing changes.

The amazing thing about Nick is he has always had the ability to compete. He has always had a great awareness of his body. He also has a great understanding of feel. He is a very visual person, able to picture things well. So he had a lot of things going for him [in terms of] being able to use his senses to change things if they were not going well. Most people would not have been prepared to do it. It was just him. He was just so intent on making it perfect. That was part of his make-up.

But in Europe there were tangible signs that things were slowly coming right for Faldo. In May, he finished third in the PGA

Championship at Wentworth, following that up with a fourth place in the Peugeot French Open in June. When the Open came round in July, Faldo had ambitions of mounting a serious challenge. Having failed to gain automatic qualification for the Masters in April, and having turned down the opportunity to pre-qualify for the US Open at Oakland Hills in June, Faldo arrived at Turnberry in a surprisingly positive mood. David Leadbetter had arrived earlier in the week to complete some last-minute fine-tuning, and the confidence they both felt proved more than justified. Playing in squalls and high winds, Faldo struggled manfully throughout, and despite a confidence-sapping 76 in the third round, he finished fifth behind the eventual champion, Greg Norman. In terms of what had gone before, it was a huge step forward. Another bonus that week was having his former caddie, Andy Prodger, on the bag again. Brothers in arms between 1979 and 1981, Faldo had won his first two PGA Championships with 'Prodge' by his side, and now he wanted to rekindle that past glory. The diminutive north Londoner would indeed end up being a vital piece of the Faldo jigsaw.

Andy Prodger was a former assistant professional to Bernard and Geoff Hunt at Hartsbourne Golf Club. Born in Enfield, he had long cherished his own dreams of being a tournament player like Faldo. Unfortunately, those plans suffered a major setback when he was involved in a serious car smash while attempting to qualify for the 1973 Open at Royal Troon. Six years later, having endured employment both in a factory and as a window cleaner, Prodger ended up caddying for Nick Faldo.

We first worked together at the 1979 Italian Open. I was over there on holiday thinking I might do a bit of caddying when I saw Nick Faldo out on the course during the final practice day. I couldn't believe it. Here was a British Ryder Cup player and he was pulling his bag around on a trolley that he'd hired from the pro shop. I knew he had sacked his regular caddie, John Moorhouse, and then a German boy who only lasted a practice round. To tell the truth, I think everyone else was a bit scared of asking Nick for his bag. He had this reputation for being difficult, aloof, a bit stand-offish, but I wasn't bothered. I just

*went up and asked him 'Do you need a caddie?', which he did.
Perhaps if I wasn't so new to the game I might have been too
nervous to ask. After that, Nick offered me a job for the rest of
the season.*

It was a similar story when they met up again in 1986. With
Prodger temporarily between jobs shortly before the Hawaii
Open in February, he had agreed to take over from Paul
Stephens and caddie for Faldo in Kapalua. Faldo made his first
cut of the year on the PGA Tour there so Prodger's employment
was extended to the Los Angeles Open the following week. After
that, Faldo had offered him a full-time job on his return to
Europe in May, which, to his great surprise, Prodger had turned
down. Having been sacked once already Prodger, it seemed, was
reluctant to try again. 'We got on really well the first time,'
Prodger recalled with some sadness. 'I was on the bag when he
won his first two PGAs. That was a big moment for both of us,
then I got the brush-off in September 1981. That was terrible
and hurt me a lot. He told me at the Lancôme Trophy that he
wanted a change. He said that I shouldn't get upset but he felt
that I did not communicate enough with him. Communicate? I
think that upset me more than anything else.'

With that type of past history, linking up with Nick Faldo in
1986 must have been a tough decision to make, but in the end,
it was almost made for him. Expecting to work for the extrovert
American Mac O'Grady at Turnberry, Prodger was let down at
the last minute. Faldo was 'between' caddies. They met on the
Monday before the Open and Faldo again offered him a
full-time job. Now, Prodger accepted – only this time he went
in with both eyes wide open. 'I made up my mind that I wasn't
going to listen to him any more,' Prodger said in an interview
with the golf writer and author Lauren St John. 'These golfers
will tell you if you've done wrong in no uncertain terms, so I
was determined not to get upset – because the first period of
time I got very upset! I was determined not to listen to the
nastiness, and that was the way for me to keep concentrating
on doing a good job.'

The way things went for Faldo during the second half of
1986, it was inevitable that there would be an air of frustration

about him. After a string of poor results in August and September, including a missed cut in the US PGA at the Inverness Club in Ohio, Faldo ended the season 135th on the US money list. He also languished in fifteenth place in Europe, the third consecutive year he had failed to break into the top ten. All this was balanced out, however, by the wonderful news that Gill had given birth to a daughter, Natalie, on 18 September. Fatherhood made Faldo work even harder than before. After all, he now had a family to support.

While finances were not a major problem for Faldo in 1986, the loss of a number of sponsors certainly was. While he could live without the tournament spotlight trained on him, many of his financial backers could not. In many ways their frustration was understandable. When he won the Order of Merit in 1983, Faldo was hot property. Many of his contracts were structured so that they ran through to 1985, and in some cases beyond. Inevitably, as his game fell away along with his prize-money winnings, fewer businesses considered Nick Faldo a good investment; with the notable exceptions of Pringle and Glynwed, they gradually dropped out one by one, including Pioneer Music Systems, with whom Faldo had a lucrative contract. He remained undaunted. 'What gave me the encouragement that I was on the right track was that suddenly I could hit a shot or series of shots that were better than anything before. I'd hit a drive with real penetration or some iron shots that really went the way they should go. They were the stepping stones, the little boosts that kept me going.'

Faldo made an inauspicious start to 1987. He had spent six weeks at home with Gill and new baby Natalie without hitting a shot, and his game had become surprisingly ring-rusty. He headed off to Australia at the end of January to play in his first competitive event in three months, and struggled to make any impact. After Australia he travelled to Hong Kong, where he played equally poorly. Feeling the effects of the long lay-off and increasingly concerned by his dour form, he flew down to Florida to see David Leadbetter the week before the Bay Hill Classic. If anyone could turn his game around, it was him.

As usual, they spent the whole time on the practice ground, as well as working on and around the practice greens. During his rebuilding period of the past eighteen months Faldo had thought nothing of hitting 1,500 shots a day, working from early morning to 3 p.m. He would then go away, have a swim, rest up for an hour or two and go back and work even harder. But this time it was somehow different. Faldo knew his swing was in good order, but he complained at the total lack of feel that was upsetting his game. He needed answers, and Leadbetter was not long in providing them.

It transpired that during the winter Faldo had spent hour after hour swinging a heavy-weighted club in order to build up extra muscle in his forearms (something he had done during his amateur days with Ian Connelly). This exercising had made his muscles so tight that they were unable to work properly, so a new programme was quickly designed to loosen them up. Faldo returned to the PGA Tour in early April, six weeks later, to compete in the weather-affected Greater Greensboro Open. He recorded three closing rounds of 75.

Turning up at the Grenelefe Resort for yet another session with his coach, Faldo was convinced that his swing needed little more than a fine tune-up, but Leadbetter had other ideas. Over the winter he had been studying the swings of many great players and had found that many of them brought the club back to the ball on a lower plane than the one they used for the back swing. Leadbetter described it as 'shallowing out the angle' and its purpose was to produce a consistently workable fade – something Faldo up to that point had desperately struggled to master. They went to work. 'He understands the golf swing so well,' remarked Faldo. 'It is not so much knowing why you hit a bad shot but why you hit a good one that matters.'

Leaving Leadbetter at the end of that week for the Deposit Guaranty Golf Classic at Hattiesburg, Faldo arrived at Atlanta airport to pick up Gill and ran into some players heading for Augusta National and the US Masters. An ineligible Faldo described it as a pivotal moment in his career as he watched them head off to a different terminal. 'I remember how bad it felt as they turned left to Augusta and I went right to Hattiesburg.' But after the tournament he felt an awful lot better. He had posted four consecutive rounds of 67, finishing the final round in spectacular style with four birdies over the last four holes. He was runner-up as a result of this display, and it did wonders for his confidence. The following week Faldo competed in the Sea Pines Heritage Classic where a good performance was only spoilt by a last-day stumble. However, it was the performance at Hattiesburg that ultimately proved the vital stepping stone to better things. For the first time in two years, Faldo returned to Europe with renewed zest, and after top-five finishes in the Madrid Open and Italian Open he felt ready to win.

In May, Faldo entered the Peugeot Spanish Open in southern Spain. Fresh from signing a lucrative contract with Wilson Clubs – his first sponsorship deal in over eighteen months – he was in buoyant mood. He was striking the ball beautifully; even a 'tricked-up' Las Brisas was no match for his supremely assured long-game. On the orders of tournament organiser Severiano Ballesteros, the course was to be made as difficult as possible. He was taken at his word: fairways were narrowed and the speed of the greens quickened up to near lightning pace. Even the great Jack Nicklaus, who jetted in to watch his son Jack Jr compete in the event, took one look and said that only the best players would cope with the difficult, almost impossible conditions. As Nick Faldo showed, Nicklaus would be proved right.

In a week where Faldo found eleven bunkers and only failed to get up and down once, there was only going to be one winner. Putting together consistent rounds of 72, 71, 71 and 72, he had arrived at the final hole needing a par four to win – and despite some nervous moments along the way, he did just that. It was the fourteenth victory of his professional career and his first since 1984; a feeling of utter relief passed through him as he holed out his winning putt. Turning to his caddie, Andy Prodger, all he could say was, 'I've made it! I've made it!'

He certainly had. After Spain, Faldo continued his hot streak by finishing tied second in the Belgian Open. Confidence restored, he seemed relaxed and positive about the future. It was as if a huge weight had been lifted from his shoulders. 'Earlier in the year I had tried to take photographs of him with his daughter, Natalie,' recalled his mother, Joyce, 'but I couldn't get a decent photograph at all. He looked drawn and very tired.

I suppose he was after all the work he was doing. After the win in Spain he looked much better. I got some lovely photos of them then.'

A couple of months later, Joyce Faldo would have even better snaps to put in the family album, all of them with the 116th Open Championship at Muirfield as a backdrop.

9. A DREAM REALISED

The philosopher Malcolm Cowley once said, 'Talent is what you possess, genius is what possesses you.' He might have been talking about Nick Faldo during the 116th Open Championship at Muirfield in 1987.

But just a week away from his thirtieth birthday, Faldo had a problem that needed solving. During practice for the Scottish Open at Gleneagles, he was hitting the ball far too low and was losing distance on his drives. It had been the same story in his lacklustre opening round of 71. Now, with the Open scheduled to start the following week, he was worried, really worried. Faldo came into the tournament on the back of top-five finishes in Spain, France and Belgium, but any confidence he had built up was rapidly slipping away. He got straight on to the telephone to David Leadbetter, who told him not to worry; he would fly over from Florida a few days earlier than planned and take a look.

Arriving at Gleneagles, the lanky Zimbabwean with the long, thin face and hawk-like features saw what the problem was immediately. In the cold, Scottish conditions, Faldo's swing had become too narrow, too restricted, lacking the width necessary to generate club-head speed and distance. Leadbetter advised him to widen his arc more, then swing through and under to a slightly higher finish. In truth, it was nothing new, but it did have the desired effect. Crisis over, confidence restored, Faldo began striking the ball well, and even though he finished down in twenty-first place, that was unimportant. His target was the Open, not the Scottish Open.

A few days later, Nick Faldo arrived in the sleepy East Lothian village of Gullane, home to the Honourable Company of Edinburgh Golfers and Muirfield. After Gleneagles, he was now in a positive frame of mind. 'I feel it's coming right just at the perfect time,' he said to his caddie Andy Prodger. 'I know something good is going to happen this week.' Leadbetter agreed. Having watched Faldo in action at Gleneagles, he had turned to him after the final round and said, 'You're ready – now go and do it.'

Faldo understood exactly what he meant. After two years of blood, sweat and toil, his game was finally ready to take on the best golfers in the world and win. Like some latter-day Frankenstein, Leadbetter had rebuilt his swing almost from scratch. Together, they had removed the unnecessary and the unworkable and replaced them with the efficient and the effective. Faldo's game was now the completed product of all that hard work, but as he proved at Gleneagles, he still had some inner demons to battle with. It had been the same a few months earlier as David Leadbetter explained:

Round about the time of Bay Hill [Classic], coming up for the two years – March 1987 – technically you could see it really started to look good, but he really wasn't letting it happen at all. He would go fine for a couple of holes then he would hit a poor shot, then he would be delving right into his technique. I said, 'Nick, as far as I'm concerned the way it's looking now is the way you want it to look. You're really close to swinging your best.' And he understood that because he could see his divots were getting shallower, the ball flight was more piercing and he was getting more roll on his driver. So I told him, 'Nick, to me it's just tension at address that's causing these problems.' So we worked on getting his arms as soft as possible, really trying to get him to swing it in the slot that you want to swing it in. Then we went to Hattiesburg the week of the Masters and finished second. Then subsequently, from there to Spain and won. Everything suddenly clicked into place. It was a case of 'Boom!'

Certainly, Faldo's record leading up to the Open at Muirfield in July was particularly impressive. In America, his entire season, possibly his career, had been transformed by the second-place finish in the Deposit Guaranty Golf Classic at Hattiesburg in mid-April. Although he lost out to PGA Tour regular David Ogrin, his spectacularly consistent rounds of 67, 67, 67 and 67 confirmed that he had finally turned the corner with his game after a nightmare eighteen months rebuilding his swing with David Leadbetter. In Europe, his good form had continued throughout the spring and early summer with strong perform-ances in the Madrid Open (fourth), Italian Open (third),

Dunhill British Masters (eleventh), French Open (fifth) and Belgian Open (joint second). Add to that his victory in the Peugeot Spanish Open and you had someone pretty much in the form of his life. But winning the Open was easier said than done, as Nick Faldo knew through bitter experience. So many other factors came into play, like the weather, the draw, even the luck of the bounce, but Faldo was experienced enough not to let those bother him. As Jack Nicklaus once said, 'The winner of most major championships is usually the person with the best game plan.' Fortunately for Faldo, he had one he liked.

Nick Faldo's strategy was a simple one. With the weather forecast predicting poor weather for the week, he would eliminate the risk factor as much as possible by playing for position rather than distance. Figuring the championship would be won on or around the greens, he would keep his driver in reserve, preferring instead to use long irons and fairway woods off the tee for accuracy. It was a strategy that would require enormous patience, but Faldo felt confident he could pull it off.

Unlike St Andrews, Muirfield can hardly be described as a true links, but it is no less difficult for that. Described by Gary Player as 'the finest Open championship test', the narrow fairways are traditionally bordered with acres of knee-high meadow grass just waiting to swallow up an errant tee-shot or wayward second. Compared with Turnberry, it is also a deceptively flat course. Rewarding accuracy off the tee, it also places a high premium on the angle at which a player chooses to approach the flag. At Muirfield, a perfect 300-yarder down the wrong half of the fairway can often leave a near impossible approach shot over a yawning bunker. In short, to play the 6,963-yard course successfully, a player has literally to think his way round, and Faldo was prepared to do just that.

Drawn with Nick Price and Ray Floyd, Faldo opened up with a creditable three-under-par score of 68, which provided a solid foundation on which he could build. The reputedly uptight Englishman had spent the early part of the round swapping jokes with Price. 'Not many people think of Nick as funny,' said Andy Prodger. 'But get him together with a fellow joker like Price and he cannot stop. We were standing on the first tee and the first thing he said was, "Have you heard this one, Nick?" It showed just how relaxed he was going into the Open that week.'

Having joked his way round on day one, Faldo was in far more serious mood on day two. Trailing tournament leader Rodger Davis by four shots, he pulled his drive on the par-four opening hole into a bunker and was unable to reach the green in two. Leaving himself eighty yards from the hole, Faldo appeared uncertain as to what type of shot to hit. Knowing how important it was to get off to a good start, the Englishman took plenty of time to weigh up his options. Pacing back and forth, he threw up a handful of grass to test the wind, then another, then another. Meanwhile, his playing partners, Floyd and Price, were waiting up on the green.

Then came an incident that set the tone for the entire round. Having pitched up to fifteen feet, Faldo was surprised to find Ray Floyd waiting for him as he stepped on to the green. 'I thought you were never going to play that shot,' he said pointedly. Faldo was astonished at his reaction but was unsure whether or not the American was joking. It soon became obvious that he was not. Faldo was determined to make Floyd eat his words. 'I can't remember exactly what Nick said,' commented Prodger later, 'but I know he was determined not to let Floyd get to him. He couldn't be sure it was gamesmanship, but I cannot remember seeing him so pumped about an incident in a long time.' With wind and rain sweeping in from the west, the atmosphere between the two players matched the cool conditions. Out late in the afternoon, many great shots were exchanged but hardly a word passed between them all day. Five hours later, the two old rivals barely glanced at each other as they shook hands on the eighteenth green. Moments later, they signed their scorecards and went their separate ways – Faldo with his 69 and Floyd with a 68.

While Faldo and Floyd were having their own private tussle, another battle was going on at the top of the Open leaderboard. Davis, hampered by the harsh conditions, had fallen away with a two-over-par 73; he now found himself in a four-way tie for second with Gerry Taylor (68) Payne Stewart (66) and Nick Faldo. The new championship leader, by one shot, was the little-known American Paul Azinger. Seeking to emulate Ben

Hogan (1953) and Tony Lema (1964) by winning the Open at his first attempt, Azinger had surprised everyone by confessing the previous evening that he had never played a competitive round on a links course before. Yet despite this obvious disadvantage, he looked confident as he joined Faldo on the first tee on Saturday, 18 July. The two were playing together for the first time. The tall Englishman could hardly have imagined a better way of spending his thirtieth birthday.

Greeted by the welcome news that the R&A had shortened four holes 'to give the players a chance to reach the fairways', they discovered the third round was all about survival. Wrapped in layers of waterproof clothing and Slazenger pullovers, Azinger dropped his first shot of the day at the opening hole, suggesting that he was more nervous than anyone thought. It brought him level with Faldo on five under par. After that, he made very few mistakes. Hitting back with three birdies over the next seven holes, he reached the turn in a creditable two-under-par 34. But given the opportunity to build a sizeable lead both on Faldo and the rest of the chasing pack, he failed to take full advantage. Repeating the pattern of the previous two rounds, he struggled to get to grips with the back nine. Coming home in two over par, he had to accept a level-par score of 71. It was a frustrating round. Azinger knew he should have finished more than just one shot ahead of the pack going into the final day. He had dropped shots on the tenth and twelfth holes and had been warned for slow play on the par-three thirteenth. It seemed to upset his rhythm; he seemed rushed after that. Finishing with two fives (a par and a bogey) when most of the field looked to score two fours, Azinger would now spend most of the final day looking over his shoulder.

Typically, the slow-play warning was like water off a duck's back to Nick Faldo. Like Paul Azinger, he also finished with two fives for a round of 71, and for him, that was the big disappointment. A bogey at the last meant he was now tied in second place with the South African David Frost, with the American trio of Craig Stadler, Payne Stewart and Tom Watson one shot further adrift. Worse still, his bogey at the last meant he would not be playing with Azinger in the final pairing on Sunday. Now, the honour of being able to keep one eye on the tournament leader would go to Frost after his third-round score of 70.

With Faldo out with Stadler in the pairing just ahead, a relaxed-looking Azinger began the final round brilliantly. Ignoring the damp, misty conditions that made visibility poor and everything from rubber grips to leather gloves ringing wet, he holed putt after putt on the front nine to extend his lead. Starting with a birdie at the par-three fourth from twenty-five feet, then another at the par-five fifth from half that distance, the American matched his 34 of the previous day.

Faldo, in contrast, could do little but make pars – nine in succession, in fact. Striking the ball solidly, he had been within inches of birdies at each of the opening five holes, but nothing had dropped. He needed a great start to the round in order to catch the now rampant Paul Azinger, but level par was not what he had had in mind. In desperation, Faldo turned to his caddie for help. He began to ask for a second opinion on the greens, but still nothing went his way. 'I'm hitting good putts but they're not going in,' he said to Prodger. 'Do you really think I am meant to win this thing?'

A typical piece of Faldo resilience came at the eighth. Having bunkered his tee-shot at the par-three seventh and made par, Faldo found the sand again at the next. Leaving himself about 35 to 40 yards to the pin and playing straight into the wind, reputedly the hardest shot in golf, he picked the ball clean off the sand and landed it within four feet of the hole. It was a wonderfully executed shot, and Prodger could hardly contain his delight. 'I said, "Great shot, Nick!" but he hardly noticed me. He just pulled the putter out of the bag and walked on to the green. He was so incredibly focused that day. He was desperate to win. As the caddies say, he really had the blinkers on.'

As the Open entered the final nine holes, Azinger still had the lead with a three-shot advantage over Faldo. The biggest threat now came from first-round tournament leader Rodger Davis, at that time playing the fourteenth. Returning like the ghost of Christmas past, the Australian had put together a last-minute charge with birdies at the second, eighth, ninth and eleventh. Three under par for his round, five under for the tournament, he stood joint second on the leaderboard with Faldo.

Once Davis had reached the clubhouse on four under, none of the leading players could afford to slip – Faldo least of all. Doggedly holding on to joint second place, the Englishman, clad in a lurid yellow jumper by Pringle of Scotland, came to the final holes relieved to find himself still in the hunt. He had missed two straightforward birdie putts, from fifteen feet on the 417-yard par-four fifteenth and from five feet on the 188-yard par-three sixteenth, and observers wondered whether his chance had gone. 'The worst one was the putt on the sixteenth,' recalled Prodger. 'You could really feel the crowd willing it in, but when it missed everything went flat for a second. And with Azinger [still] ahead, I thought that was it.'

In a cautious frame of mind, Nick Faldo plodded his way up the par-five seventeenth. Having hit a solid drive directly into the wind, he deliberated over his second shot for a full two minutes before choosing the safer option of playing short of the cross-bunkers instead of trying to clear them. When he came to play the shot he had left himself to the green, a lengthy five-iron approach, it barely cleared the bank on the right before toppling down on to the putting surface about 45 feet away from the cup. Forced to settle for yet another par – his seventeenth of the day – he could feel his chance slipping away. Perhaps if he had made a birdie at the previous hole it might have been different, but he seemed incapable of putting any real pressure on the tournament leader.

Having watched Faldo's progress closely all day, Azinger had seemed disturbed by the new and unexpected challenge to his supremacy by Davis. Adding to the enormous pressure he already felt, the American had begun the back nine nervously, dropping shots at the tenth and eleventh. Having also failed to birdie the 504-yard par-five ninth, he desperately needed to steady the ship with a run of par figures, which he did from the twelfth to the sixteenth. He was holding an increasingly slender-looking one-stroke lead as he stepped on to the tee of the 550-yard par-five seventeenth.

At the last, Faldo reckoned he needed a birdie to tie, but even then it might not be enough. He also knew the 448-yard par-four eighteenth would be no pushover. One of the toughest finishing holes in championship golf, the fairway was bordered by knee-length rough and needed nothing less than a long, accurate tee-shot to thread its way through bunkers left and right. On a calm day the drive is intimidating enough, but when there is a crosswind to contend with it can prove almost impossible. As Nick Faldo prepared to tee off, there was a crosswind.

He knew the ideal drive was to aim at the left-hand bunkers and hit a fade into the narrow gap. Keeping risks down to a minimum, Faldo played conservatively off the tee with a fairway wood. Having negotiated the drive, he knew his second shot, from just under 200 yards away, would require a degree of boldness as well as precision. With high-face bunkers pinching in on both sides, the entrance to the green was small and well protected. After a short debate with Andy Prodger, it was decided that a five-iron would be the right club, allowing for the distance and the amount of adrenalin rushing through Faldo's body. Pulling the club from his red and white Wilson tour bag, all he had to do now was hit it.

Not since 1983 at Royal Birkdale had Faldo been so ideally placed to have a real chance of securing the greatest prize in golf. In 1983 he had been just two strokes off the lead with one round to play, had buckled under the pressure and, in the process, highlighted flaws in his swing that had led to the well-documented changes over the past two years. And after all that hard work on his swing, it seemed as if a whole career was encapsulated in this one crucial five-iron shot.

Standing over the ball, he began his normal set-up routine: club behind the ball, move the right foot in first, then the left, square up, look at the hole, a positive waggle of the hands, then go. These simple mechanics enabled him to play the shot he did. 'I think that's what helps me,' he said later. 'When the pressure is really on, you think, I've been doing this the last seventy-one holes: rotate, set . . . You can't think about it. You have to hit it from memory.' Driving his five-iron into the back of the ball, Faldo delighted at the clean, crisp strike. Peering into the mist, he knew it was as perfect as he could have hoped as it arrowed towards the green. 'It was straight on the flag and I just wanted to shout out, "Cor, look at that!" In a way it was like driving a car and you nearly have an accident. I went hot and cold at the same time, and then it was all over.'

Well, not quite 'over'. Dead on line, the ball landed some forty feet short of the hole. He now faced a long, difficult putt for birdie across a green sloping from back to front. The scoreboard behind the grandstand told him that he needed this putt to have a chance of forcing the American into a play-off; three putts, and he would fall into a tie for second with Rodger Davis. Trying hard to banish all such negative thoughts from his mind, Faldo settled on leaving his first putt close, then tapping in for par. Then, no matter what Azinger did after him, at least Faldo would not have *lost* the Open. At least that was the plan.

Setting up to the ball in the evening gloom, Faldo struck it well, but as it reached the cup it suddenly veered away, coming to rest at least five feet beyond the hole. The nightmare vision of three-putting the last green of an Open was now a real possibility. He was forced to wait as playing partner Craig Stadler finished off his round of 75. The pressure must have been excruciating on the thirty-year-old Englishman as he surveyed his putt. 'I was so nervous because over the last five or six holes I had known that I simply could not make a mistake, or it was all over.'

His parents, George and Joyce, following the action on television at home in Welwyn, could barely watch as their son lined up what was hopefully his final putt. Placing the Ping putter he had used all week behind the ball, he was aware that this was potentially the biggest moment of his life. It was not really a case of 'this putt for the Open', but it was a vital one nonetheless. Drawing the blade back, Faldo accelerated it smoothly through the ball before daring to look up. Seconds later, a huge roar from the crowd told him what he already knew: it was in.

Somewhat shell-shocked, Faldo walked off the final green fingering the scorecard handed to him by Andy Prodger. It must have been an amazing sight − no bogeys, no birdies, nothing but pars. But if his card was without a blemish, it had been hard gained. Four times − at the seventh, eighth, tenth and eleventh holes − he had got down in two from off the green, including three times from sand. A lesson in bloody-minded resilience rather than golfing brilliance, his closing round of 71 might not have been spectacular to watch, but it was effective. 'It might look like a conservative round,' said Faldo, 'but I was going for it one hundred per cent. I played aggressively, but this is a tough course.'

The only question now was, would it be enough to put Paul Azinger under pressure?

Having chosen a driver off the seventeenth tee, Azinger had pulled his ball into a deep bunker guarding the left-hand side of the fairway. From there, he had been forced to play short of the green in three and had taken three more to get down. The result was an unexpected bogey six. Describing his decision to take a driver off the tee as the worst mistake of his career, the American said later, 'What I did at the seventeenth was ridiculous. I should never have used the driver. Also, my putter let me down in the home straight. I had birdie chances at twelve and fourteen, and if I had taken either, *nobody* would have caught me.'

Completely unaware that his closest rival was having problems of his own on the par-five seventeenth, Faldo walked off the last feeling numb. Having probably missed out on another chance to win the greatest prize in golf, how sure could he be that he would ever get another? Seconds later, the giant scoreboard behind the main grandstand clicked into life, confirming the news that Azinger had bogeyed the seventeenth. Alerted by the cheers of the partisan crowd, Faldo turned around to look and saw his name above Azinger's on the leaderboard, both golfers on five under par but Faldo on top by virtue of having finished his round. With just one hole remaining for the American, the possibility of a dramatic play-off was looming ever larger. Settling into the R&A scorekeeper's hut behind the eighteenth, Nick Faldo declined to speak to anyone until the final result was confirmed.

Moments later he was joined by Gill and Natalie in the cramped room. They exchanged a brief hug, but very few words were spoken. Ashen-faced and increasingly close to tears, Faldo then caught sight of the BBC coverage in the background but tried to ignore it. With the volume turned down, he was unable to hear Peter Alliss observing, 'How the next fifteen minutes are going to change one of these young men's lives.'

Unable to contain himself, Andy Prodger headed back to the eighteenth green. Looking down the mist-covered fairway, he could just make out Paul Azinger in his red Slazenger pullover, debating long and hard about what club to hit for his second – exactly the same dilemma faced by Faldo and Prodger a few minutes earlier. The American glanced back and forth at his caddie's yardage book. Given the circumstances, the green must have looked minute. 'A four- or five-iron?' he anxiously asked his bagman, Kevin Woodward. Neither man seemed sure.

Azinger eventually plumped for the five-iron, which ultimately proved to be his downfall. Forced to hit the ball a little harder, he dragged his approach into the left-hand bunker. As he cursed his misfortune, loud cheers rose from the huge crowd that surrounded the green. Their unsporting conduct was noted by a group of R&A officials standing in front of the clubhouse (Alistair Low, who later presented the Open trophy to the winner, would mention it in his speech). Andy Prodger was also upset by the Scottish gallery's reaction. 'I thought it was completely out of order to cheer a bad shot. After it was all over, I went over to Paul and apologised. He just said, "No problem, that's life." I'm not sure he even noticed.'

Azinger had more important things on his mind. He was the leading money winner on the PGA Tour that season; getting up and down from sand would normally not have been a problem, but these were anything but normal circumstances. As he arrived at his ball, the American's shoulders visibly slumped as he surveyed the lie (the ball was perched on a downhill slope in the back of the bunker). Having led the championship for much of the weekend, he now faced having it snatched from him at the last possible moment. The best he could do was splash it out to around twenty-five feet. He made a brave stab at the resulting putt, but as the ball rolled to a halt just inches short of the hole, his head dropped and the putter fell from his grasp. He then gathered himself, tapped in the putt and walked off the green to sympathetic applause.

Then reality dawned, and the crowd began cheering once again. Britain had itself a new Open champion.

As he emerged from the scorekeeper's hut, the first person Faldo met was the tall, gangling figure of David Leadbetter, the man who had helped rebuild his swing and provided the platform for his success that day. It was a moving moment for both men. Recalling it many years later, Leadbetter said, 'I think the words he used were, "We've done it! We've done it!" It was very much a team effort so I was really excited. It was pretty emotional.' Not surprisingly, Faldo's unexpected victory at Muirfield would impact on Leadbetter's own life over the coming months and years. 'It was interesting because I was very much an unknown up to that point although I had worked with a lot of top players [. . .] it was almost as if a lot of people who didn't know the story thought, "Gee, David Leadbetter helped this guy from nowhere and look, he's won the Open!" If only they had known how much had gone into it – all the hours and hours of hard work.'

As he waited for the presentation party from the R&A, the colour gradually returned to Nick Faldo's cheeks. Taking congratulations from his fellow players, he slowly made his way to the table situated behind the eighteenth green. Ever since his boyhood years in Welwyn Garden City, it had been an earnestly held dream to win the Open. Now, after two very long years in the wilderness, his career moving backwards, his rivals overtaking him, his sponsors deserting him, that dream had finally become reality. He lifted up the silver claret jug to the cheers of everyone present. No one could have deserved it more.

After the presentation he returned with his family to the Marine Hotel in nearby North Berwick, where the celebrations continued long into the night. After that came all the interviews and photo shoots expected of a new Open champion, followed by a fast drive to Edinburgh airport so that Faldo could take part in a charity day for the PGA European Tour Benevolent Trust at Sunningdale. The venue was close to their home at Wentworth, and here they could celebrate his triumph in the best way possible – with a delicious takeaway from the local fish and chip shop. A week later, Nick Faldo made a nostalgic trip to his former school Thumbswood in Welwyn Garden City. As befitted his new celebrity status, he went from there to nearby Hatfield to play in a special charity match with Jerry Stevens and Frankie Vaughan arranged by his old pal Ron Marks. The experience must have brought it home to Faldo just how far he had come since his carpet-fitting days back in the mid-seventies – mingled, perhaps, with thoughts of just how far he could still go.

* * *

In reflective mood after his Open triumph at Muirfield, Nick Faldo spoke of the frustration he had felt during the two years he had been working on his swing with David Leadbetter. 'Sandy [Lyle] and Bernhard [Langer] had gone ahead of me, there is no doubt about that. But I always felt that I was as good as they were and it was immensely frustrating not being able to show it.'

Well, now was the time to banish those frustrations, and in September, Faldo had another opportunity to show he was at least as good as his rivals at the 1987 Ryder Cup at the appropriately named Muirfield Village in Ohio. Arriving in America in top form, he was in buoyant mood and it showed right from the start. He partnered Ian Woosnam on day one and they won both their matches as Europe raced to a surprise 6–2 lead over the United States (in the morning foursomes against Lanny Wadkins and Larry Mize, the British pair had been four-down with nine to play but won six holes in a row to win two-up).

It was the same story the following day. After halving their foursome match against Hal Sutton and Larry Mize in the morning, they crushed Curtis Strange and Tom Kite by 5 & 4 in the afternoon. Faldo and Woosnam's dynamic play (ten under par for the match, Faldo four under on his own ball), typified Europe's desire to retain the title so hard earned at the Belfry two years earlier. 'Sometimes when you are playing with Woosie, you feel like putting a pair of reins on him and holding him back,' said Faldo afterwards. 'Not on this day. We played some unbelievable golf.'

With fans of Nick Faldo hoping to see the first win on American soil in the event's sixty-year history, Europe headed into the singles with a massive five-point lead. Unfortunately, their hero's match against the barrel-chested Mark Calcavecchia proved to be a real anti-climax. Playing his worst golf of the week, Faldo bogeyed the first and never looked comfortable. Holding a slender one-up advantage at the turn, Faldo found himself one-down by the time they reached the eighteenth. It was a scrappy affair, and both players were bunkered after two on the par-four hole, Calcavecchia to the left of the green, Faldo to the right. Playing first, the American opened the door for a possible half in the match after splashing out well beyond the hole and running his first putt three feet beyond the cup. Faldo was left with an eight-foot putt for par to halve the hole. It was exactly the type of pressure putt Faldo had been holing all year, but not this time. He watched in agony as it horseshoed around the lip of the cup and stayed out, and he lost the match. Thankfully, it made no difference to the final result as victories for Clark, Darcy and Ballesteros meant that Europe scraped home winners 15 to 13.

It had been a vintage season, but the cherry on top of this particular cake came the following month when Nick Faldo captained England to their first Dunhill Cup win at St Andrews. They beat Mexico, Spain and Australia on the way, the victory made even sweeter by the fact that they had overcome Scotland, the Auld Enemy, 2–1 in the medal matchplay final (Faldo defeated his old rival, Sandy Lyle, by 66 to 69; Gordon J. Brand won his match against Sam Torrance 64 to 69; Clark lost to Gordon Brand Junior).

Faldo ended this momentous season with five top-ten finishes in his last six events. The only prize he missed out on was the European Order of Merit, eventually finishing third with official prize-money earnings of £181,833. He had to concede that particular title to his Ryder Cup partner, Ian Woosnam, but there was always next year.

10. BROOKLINE AND LYTHAM

Having broken through at Muirfield to win his first major title, Nick Faldo was now eager to secure his place at the top of the golfing tree. Yet how could he challenge for the number one spot in the world when he could not even claim to be number one in Britain?

He enjoyed such incredible success in 1987, both individually and as part of a team, but the following season proved a strangely frustrating one for the thirty-year-old Englishman. Sandy Lyle was in rampant form, and for the first half of 1988 it must have seemed that everywhere Faldo turned, there was his boyhood rival winning tournaments and grabbing the headlines. Even before the European season had got underway in April, the big-hitting Scot had not only recorded back-to-back victories in the Greater Greensboro Open, but had topped it off by becoming the first Briton to win the US Masters at Augusta. Nick Faldo was now in the odd position of having to win another major just to stay where he was in the pecking order.

Unlike Lyle, Faldo had struggled to get his season underway despite playing some of the best golf of his career. Third in the Tournament of Champions in January, runner-up in the Barcelona Open in April, then runner-up in the Spanish Open in May, it frustrated him that he was not getting any reward for his fine play. Looking at his apparent lack of success on the greens, he began to practise using just his right hand to instil some feel into his highly mechanical putting action. He was once again searching for an answer, and felt he had something to prove by the time he arrived at Brookline for the 1988 United States Open in the third week of June.

Not surprisingly, Sandy Lyle was hot favourite to win his second major of the year at the grandly titled Country Club of Brookline near Boston. Top of the PGA Tour money list with a massive $608,478 to his name, Lyle had been unstoppable all season, and if he could just keep his errant driving under control, the title was surely his. Faldo, in comparison, had won just $43,320 – a disappointing sum considering the impressive start he had made at the season-opening Tournament of Champions at Las Costa in California. In the six PGA Tour events since then he had missed two cuts and finished outside the top 25 in the rest, including a joint thirtieth placing in the Masters at Augusta. It was hardly the form of a potential champion. Worse still, there had been a tendency among the American media to dismiss his Open victory as Paul Azinger's loss. 'How could someone shoot eighteen straight pars and call himself a champion?' whined the US press corps, but they and the watching millions on television were just about to find out how good a competitor Nick Faldo really was.

Brookline, one of the United States' premier golf courses, holds a special place in the heart of many golfers. It was here that Francis Ouimet, a twenty-year-old amateur, beat the 'British invaders' Harry Vardon and Ted Ray in a play-off in 1913 to become the first home winner of the national championship. It was a hugely significant event in American golf history, and there would be more than an echo of those bygone days as the 1988 championship moved towards a climax over the weekend. (During practice, eccentric American pro Mac O'Grady made a pilgrimage to the house where Ouimet had lived, snipped off a branch of a spruce tree growing in the garden then tucked it into his golf bag for good luck. Then, when things were going badly halfway through his opening round, he zipped open his bag and tossed the twig aside. So much for sentiment!)

Although the 1988 US Open was played over much of the same ground played by Ouimet, Vardon and Ray, the course had been changed quite considerably over the years. It wound through wooded hills and shallow valleys, and its rolling ground rarely presented the golfer with a level lie, and its greens were so small they were often difficult to hit, but as a test for the modern golfer it came up way short. In the long run-up to the championship, the club invited noted golf course architect Rees Jones to 'toughen' it up, but to his credit Jones approached the job cautiously saying that by changing the holes he would be tinkering with history. Shunning any attempt to make drastic alterations other than lengthening a few of the holes, he had support from traditionalist Ben Crenshaw, who said, 'This course is a throwback. It's very honest in so many ways, because it challenges your whole game. You pretty well go through the bag here; you hit every club and play different shots. It's a very special place.'

One problem no one had allowed for was the weather. In the weeks leading up to the US Open, New England, like the rest of the country, had been sweltering in an intense heat wave. By the Wednesday of tournament week, the temperature had risen above ninety degrees for the fourth consecutive day with the local news reporting that fourteen people had died in Boston from causes directly linked to the hot weather. In spite of the heat, the course looked in prime condition, lush and green with only a few dry spots ringed with white paint indicating ground under repair. As usual, the greens were firm and fast and conditions looked perfect for a low-scoring championship. Indeed, after some fireworks in the opening two rounds, the halfway cut fell at 146 to match the lowest ever in US Open history. With Scott Simpson showing the way with 69 and 66, both Faldo (72 and 67) and Lyle (68 and 71) were in a good position to make a strong challenge over the weekend.

Another player who had moved into contention after rounds of 70 and 67 was the enigmatic Curtis Strange. Son of the club pro at Bow Creek Country Club in Virginia, the easy-going professional had won his first tournament – the 1979 Pensacola Open – less than two years after joining the PGA Tour. Following on from a brilliant amateur career, he had finished top of the money list in 1985 and had narrowly failed to become the first player in US history to win a million dollars in prize money two years later. Strange had had his best finish in a US Open in 1984, the year Fuzzy Zoeller defeated Greg Norman in a play-off, where he finished fourth. He was placed fourth again in 1987, finishing six strokes behind the winner, Scott Simpson, but he was probably best known for having been close to winning the 1985 Masters before throwing it away on the final day. Fighting back from a disastrous opening day round of 80, Strange had climbed to the top of the leaderboard after two excellent rounds of 65 and 68. Then, with the tournament in his grasp, he had found water on the thirteenth and fifteenth on the Sunday afternoon and literally splashed out of contention. Now some experts were beginning to wonder if he ever would win a major, but despite growing doubts about his competitive nerve Strange remained upbeat about his chances at Brookline, as he made clear at the pre-tournament press conference:

> Since that 1985 Masters, I've been more interested in the majors. I picked up a lot of confidence after playing so well down the stretch against a very strong field. I've been thinking about the Open every day for the last couple of weeks; I've worked very hard preparing for it, particularly with my mental approach. You know going in you must be more patient. You know you're going to work for par and work like hell for birdies. The guys who've won in the past have been patient, steady players. It's going to be an interesting week.

He was right. The weather, which had been stiflingly hot for the first two days, was suddenly replaced by much cooler conditions and the threat of thunderstorms. More significantly, overnight rain softened the greens taking away some of their sting, but the slower, more receptive greens were not much help to Sandy Lyle. Four strokes off the lead at the halfway point, his game slipped away from him in the third round after missing far too many fairways, greens and putts. Recording a four-over-par 75, he would not be a factor again.

Also four strokes behind championship leader Scott Simpson, Faldo, in contrast, was powering his way up the leaderboard. Focused throughout, he opened up his round by dropping a five-iron within ten feet of the cup on the testing par-three second before converting the putt for a birdie. Now four under par for the championship, three strokes behind Simpson, a bogey at the fourth pulled him back to where he had started before two more birdies on the front nine brought him to the turn in 33. Meanwhile, Simpson had double-bogeyed the fifth and fallen into a tie with Faldo on five under par, three behind the new tournament leader, Curtis Strange.

For a time it was impossible to keep up with the changing situation. As the championship moved into the back nine,

Strange, Bob Gilder and Larry Mize all battled for the lead with varying degrees of success, each gaining a shot on one hole before losing it at the next. Then, almost without warning, thunder rumbled in the distance and the sky became increasingly darker. Rain seemed imminent. Strange had just saved his par on the eleventh when lightning flashed in the distance. He refused to carry on, and any possible penalty for this decision was rendered immaterial moments later when the official siren wailed out from the clubhouse suspending play. It was raining hard by this stage, and players and spectators alike scurried for what shelter they could find – under trees, next to hot-dog stands, back to the clubhouse or back to their cars and an early drive home. One hour later, the siren sounded again, telling the field to resume play. The rain had stopped, but sporadic showers affected the rest of the afternoon play making life difficult for everyone, including Bob Gilder, who complained bitterly that he and his fellow players were asked to start too quickly after the break by USGA officials. 'They kind of said, "Okay, now hit," and we weren't ready, I think.'

Perhaps he was right, because with four holes to play Curtis Strange was in total command. Moving to nine under par with his fourth birdie of the day on the fourteenth, he led by three shots over Gilder in second and looked as if he was going to have an impressive cushion going into Sunday. Then it all went wrong. Reviving speculation that he might never win a major championship, he bogeyed the sixteenth and seventeenth before limping home with a sand-save par at the eighteenth. He led by a single stroke over Gilder and Simpson, but the unexpected delay and the quick start had cost him dear. As for Faldo, he had gone into one of those strange periods when he could make nothing but pars. From the ninth onward he ran off eight of them before holing an eighteen-footer for birdie at the last for a six-under-par aggregate, also one behind Strange. The important thing was that he was still in the hunt.

The rain of the previous afternoon gave way to surprisingly pleasant weather on the Sunday with huge crowds drifting in hours before the first group was due to tee off at 9.37 a.m. Several hours later, at 2.25, tournament leader Curtis Strange teed off accompanied by Nick Faldo in a mini-Ryder Cup battle that nobody wanted to miss (Faldo was out last because he had posted his 207 before either Simpson or Gilder).

Curtis Strange opened up nervously with bogeys at the second and third holes, allowing Faldo, who made three pars, to move ahead for the first time. Then, once again enforcing his reputation among the American press as a golfing automaton, Faldo seemed incapable of taking full advantage of his faltering opponent and made no better than par for the next six holes too. Strange, in turn, continued to struggle throughout the front nine, reaching the turn in a 36 which included a much-needed birdie on the 201-yard par-three seventh. Faldo, with his nine consecutive pars, scored 35, and with neither Gilder or Mize able to mount a sustained challenge, the US Open seemed destined to be decided between Faldo and Strange.

Dead level with nine holes left to play, Strange moved ahead by holing a fifteen-footer at the tenth, but then missed chance after chance for birdie over the next few holes. The American was still holding his one-shot advantage by the time they reached the par-four seventeenth, and with the sun blazing down on both of them, it looked more than enough to hold off an uninspired Nick Faldo. Certainly that is how the unruly Boston crowd saw it as they began chanting 'USA! USA!' as both men headed down the penultimate hole. In truth, the New England crowd had become increasingly unruly throughout the day on the back of poor, almost non-existent marshalling (a problem that would famously be repeated years later in the 1999 Ryder Cup match over the same course). Fuelled by the availability of alcohol and the Britain v. America nature of the contest, fans began to chant at each other from the two big grandstands on either side of the eighteenth green. As Strange and Faldo walked down the fairway towards their balls, they could hear the off-putting sound of one grandstand full of people calling out 'Tastes great!' while the others answered, 'Less filling!' Not surprisingly, Faldo asked an official what was going on, only to hear that the crowd's words echoed a popular television advert for a beer company.

Safety first on the seventeenth, Faldo hit a one-iron/eight-iron combination to about forty feet short of the flag; pressing home his advantage, Strange went three-wood/nine-iron to finish fourteen feet beyond the hole but on the correct level. Two putts later Faldo had his par, and with a putt effectively to win the US Open, Strange stepped up to his ball. This would not be an easy shot. He faced a downhill putt on a slippery green; miss, and it could roll down the slope and on to the lower level, as had happened to Paul Azinger earlier in the day. With the crowd holding its breath, Strange tapped the ball as softly as he dared, then watched heart-in-mouth as it moved ever closer towards the hole. He could not believe what happened next. Despite the gentle contact, the ball picked up speed, missed the hole and raced seven or eight feet past. He was in shock. With glazed eyes, he studied his return putt for a long time, desperately trying to collect himself – and then missed it again. He and Faldo were tied once more.

Faldo, driving with a three-wood at the last, placed his ball in the ideal position on the fairway. Strange, still badly shaken, pulled his into the left-hand rough. By this stage the galleries had gone out of control. Ignoring instructions from the Brookline marshals, the crowds surged through the ropes lining the boundary of the hole, ran across the fairway and clustered around the anxious players. It was a frightening moment. The fans were still restive when Faldo played his approach shot into the green. Holding his concentration admirably, he ripped into a four-iron and the ball pulled up about eighteen feet to the right of the hole, cut towards the front right portion of the green. Now it was up to Strange. Expecting his ball to fly out of the rough, he chose a seven-iron, but it came up short and for the third straight day he was forced to play from the bunker guarding the front of the green. It was advantage Faldo, but not for long. Exploding from the sand, Strange's ball finally came to rest about a foot from the cup. It was a wonderful shot, and Faldo had half-expected it. Still, the Open was in his hands, and with one good putt the championship trophy would be heading back to England.

Once again the fans took a long time to settle down before Faldo could take his putt. He took a final look from beyond the hole; the line was straight and only slightly downhill. He gave it a rap and the crowd noise intensified as the ball ran towards the cup, transforming into an enormous groan as it slipped past the right edge, missing by a fraction of an inch. Strange let out a sigh of relief before tapping in his own one-footer for par. Six under par after 72 holes of tense competition, Strange had a one-over-par 72, Faldo a 71. Once again, the national championship of the United States would end in a play-off at Brookline. In 1913 it had involved an American and two Englishmen, this time only one would play.

Standing on the practice ground at 7.15 that night, Strange was troubled at having missed his chance at outright victory. 'I played horrible and putted just as bad,' he admitted to a small group of reporters. 'On the back nine I had an opportunity to put everybody away, and I just didn't do it. The only consolation is that I didn't lose the tournament.' Then, thinking about the seventeenth green where he had three-putted, he added, 'Even now I wish I could drop another ball and see if I could stop it close to the hole. I really didn't hit it hard at all. I hit the damn putt as easy as I thought I should have. The green was simply much faster than I expected. I honestly can't get upset with myself.' Then, talking about the eighteen-hole play-off the following day, he said, 'I just don't feel like I ought to be here, but I'm sure Nick's saying the same thing.'

Monday play-offs do not draw very big crowds, but Brookline was different. By the time the gates opened at eleven o'clock, three hours before play was due to begin, fans were already taking their seats in the grandstands around the eighteenth. By 1.30 the first and second holes had been encircled from tee to green, with over 25,000 spectators counted through the gates by the end of the day. It was a pity, as they looked forward to cheering Curtis Strange on to victory, that they could not have seen a more dramatic match. Under huge pressure, Strange had slept badly on Sunday night, but he showed none of the effects once play began – at least his putting didn't. Playing in swirling, blustery conditions that made approach shots hard to judge and accurate driving a lottery, the American reached the turn in a one-under-par 34. In many ways it was a remarkable display. Hitting just three greens in regulation he kept holing those nerve-racking six-footers he had to hole, and in the end that was the difference.

While Faldo had driven the ball much better, hitting six of the seven fairways compared with three for Strange, the back

nine saw the Englishman slip out of the reckoning. After a
bogey at the third, where his four-iron approach had drifted
into a bunker no more than twenty feet left of the hole, and a
birdie at the seventh, where he had matched one by Strange,
things started to go wrong at the eleventh. There, his five-iron
second bounced through the back of the green before finally
coming to rest hard against some high-standing grass that
bordered the tightly mown apron. In snooker terms he was up
against the cushion and unable to make a full ball contact, and
he bogeyed the hole. Strange, in turn, made par, and almost
without warning opened a two-stroke gap with seven holes left
to play.

Curtis Strange now looked in command, but his lead was
halved at the next after he pushed his four-iron short and right
of the par-four twelfth green. He made bogey, while his playing
partner made par. Then it was Nick Faldo's turn to make a
mistake. Driving into the right rough on the thirteenth, he
overshot the hole with his six-iron, leaving himself a viciously
quick thirty-foot downhill putt. It was impossible to stop short
of the hole, and his first putt skimmed past the cup and rolled
well down the hill. Strange, also on the green in two, reviewed
his putt from around eighteen feet before giving it a firm rap.
With Faldo looking on from the edge of the green, it first broke
right, then left, then tumbled into the hole for a birdie three.
Moments later, Faldo missed his return putt from seven feet and
his chance was gone. His opponent was three strokes ahead and
nothing could stop him now.

A birdie on the par-five fourteenth gave Faldo a glimmer of
hope, but a thinned chip across the green at the next for another
bogey dissipated any momentum he may have had. It was
followed by another dropped shot at the seventeenth after
running through the back of the green in two, and Faldo now
needed a miracle or a spectacular collapse by his opponent.
Neither looked likely. Indeed, with Strange saving yet another
par from a green-side bunker at the same hole, his sixth
one-putt par of the round, it was turning into a rout. The
American came to the last three shots ahead, the relief on his
face plain to see. Like Faldo, he had struggled all day to master
the difficult conditions and the intense pressure, and now the

trophy was finally in sight. All he wanted was to finish in style, which he did with a beautifully executed two-iron second into the heart of the green. An exhausted Faldo tried to do the same but found the front bunker, which just about summed up his miserable day. Minutes later, Strange two-putted for par and the huge crowd thundered its approval by cheering him off the green. He did have a major championship in him after all.

Relegated to a minor support role, Faldo had struggled home in 40 for a round of 75. Four shots worse than Strange, who had a 71, the next few hours were spent dealing with the press and his own bitter disappointment. The formalities of the prize ceremony over, Strange dedicated his victory to his father. Then, sitting quietly for a second in the hushed press room, he said, 'This is the greatest thing I have ever done; this is the greatest feeling I have ever had. It means a lot to me. It means that all the work and time and effort I've put into it has paid off. It got me to the next level.'

As he prepared to journey back to Britain, Nick Faldo wondered what he would have to do to reach his 'next level'. A possible stepping stone was the French Open at Chantilly, where Faldo found himself trying to come to terms with what had happened at Brookline. 'I only missed four fairways the whole week from tee to green,' he said. 'I played great but didn't have a clue what I was doing with the putter.' Then, in typical Faldo fashion, he added, 'I keep thinking about that last putt on the last green at Brookline. I have decided I am going to call it half a major.' It was an apt postscript, no doubt inspired by Curtis Strange who had advised Faldo not to dwell on his disappointment. 'You also won,' said the Virginian shortly after receiving the US Open trophy. Quite what comfort that offered Faldo is open to debate, but it would have been difficult not to dwell on the previous week's goings-on with Strange also competing in France.

In many ways the trip to Chantilly was the perfect cure for any post-major headache. A delightful little town 25 miles north of Paris, Chantilly is renowned worldwide for its lace and porcelain and as the home of thoroughbred racehorses. Certainly both players could have been forgiven if they just went through the motions. Strange had a competent but otherwise unremarkable opening 70, while Faldo was equally subdued with a 71. The lead instead fell to one of the lesser lights of the European Tour, Denis Durnian, after his superb round of 65. A lively character, Durnian used to hit golf balls off the deck of a freighter into the ocean to keep his game shipshape while working as a merchant seaman. Three days later, to everyone's surprise, Durnian's first tournament victory was looking like a mere formality as he stepped on to the seventeenth tee in the final round still two shots clear of Faldo and Australian Wayne Riley.

Faldo, playing in the group ahead, had secured his par four at the seventeenth and was preparing to drive at the 575-yard closing hole when Durnian snap-hooked his two-iron approach into a thicket short of the green. Minutes later, the 37-year-old club pro from Manchester walked off with a double-bogey six and his dream had quickly become a nightmare. Typically, Faldo was through the gap in a flash. His second to the last with a three-wood zoomed 260 yards to the heart of the green and the eagle landed on his card when he holed a snaking thirty-foot putt for a 68 and a six-under-par 274. It gave him his first victory of the season, leaving the downcast Durnian and Riley, who had par fives at the last, tied second on 276. It hardly made up for the disappointment of Brookline, but it was a timely boost to his confidence with the Open less than three weeks away.

After captaining two successive winning European Ryder Cup teams, Tony Jacklin was now considered something of a national hero. As such, he came out of semi-retirement to play in the 1988 Open at Royal Lytham and St Annes, and inevitably he was asked to tip a winner. As he looked down the list of players he certainly had a lot of choice. Everybody was there with one major exception: Greg Norman, the 1986 Open champion, was still sidelined by the sprained left wrist he had suffered in the US Open a month earlier. Otherwise, the cast was complete. 'Looking at the favourites this week,' Jacklin ruminated, 'I can't see beyond a European win and I can't see an American winning. But I'm biased. I don't think they're as good as we are now.' The Europeans understandably took this as a tribute, but the American players saw it quite differently. 'It wasn't a smart statement to make at all,' said an angry Paul Azinger. 'Jacklin's comments will certainly change the way I feel if I am in contention on Sunday. I'll be less nervous and out to prove something to him. And the other Americans will feel the same way after this.' Then, when grilled about his own chances after losing out at Muirfield, the American said diplomatically, 'You learn from experience. It took a lot out of me last year, but I overcame it pretty well.'

Inevitably, attention turned to Nick Faldo as defending champion. No doubt aware of the growing spat between the European and American players, he did his best to downplay his own chances. 'I'm not thinking of it as a defence, just another Open,' he said. 'I need more practice to sort things out. I'm just trying to get my transition between the back swing and the down swing right. Probably secretly, I was more confident last year. I just felt I was going to do it. I'm not saying whether I've got that feeling yet.'

In truth, it was that kind of week. No sooner had the name of Nick Price appeared on the leaderboard after a one-under-par 70 than talk began of his collapse down the stretch at Royal Troon in 1982. 'I'm more mature now,' he insisted. 'I've learnt a lot more.' Shooting below par on the opening day, fighting a wind he described as 'relentless', was considered a triumph. 'It was so difficult to get the ball close to the hole, whether with the wind or against it. Still, I played better than I have in the last six weeks.' Then he turned prophet. 'I [have] had two chances to win major championships since Troon, the US PGA in 1985 and the Masters in 1986. If I am in the hunt this time, I will be no stranger to it.'

Faldo, like Price, opened the defence of his title with a steady but unspectacular round of 71. It could have been so much better but a minor disaster at the notorious par-four seventeenth had proved a major setback. Standing on the tee at three under par, he had recorded his first double bogey in weeks. 'I hit a slightly bad tee-shot in that howling left-to-right gale,' he said. 'It finished in a left bunker. I came out, and then I hit what I thought was a perfect nine-iron.' Ending up in another bunker, he blasted out 25 feet short of the cup and two-putted for a double-bogey six. Worse still, he had played the last five holes in four over par after playing the first thirteen in four under par, with five birdies and a bogey. 'This is going to be a long championship,' he said later. 'The weather forecast isn't good for this week. There are going to be some screw-ups out there and I've made mine already.'

The second round, played before a record crowd of 43,111, belonged to the easy-going Nick Price. Having come within six holes of winning the 1982 Open at Troon, he was now within 36 holes of winning at Lytham after a four-under-par 67 which gave him a two-round total of five under par (137) and a one-stroke lead on first-round leader Severiano Ballesteros, who played in the heavier winds of the afternoon and was forced to settle for a 71. 'The real secret to this course,' Price said afterwards, 'is to make a good score going out, then hold on coming in.'

Stung by the comments of Jacklin, the Americans were also starting to crowd the leaderboard. Nine of them were within seven strokes of Price's lead. The closest was Craig Stadler, tied for third with Nick Faldo on 140, three behind Price after a creditable 69. Later, someone asked Ballesteros what score it would take to win. The Spaniard just shrugged and grinned. 'If I can have two seventy-ones,' he said, 'I will sign right now.' Faldo agreed with him. 'You have to birdie the so-called easy holes and par the tough holes. I have been birdie-ing the right ones and bogeying the others.' His frustration was obvious. He had missed five fairways on the back nine and taken two bogeys. That had ruined a very promising round that had begun with an outward 31, including birdies at the second, fourth, fifth and sixth holes.

So the pressure was on Nick Price now to hold his lead, which stirred up the painful memory of the 1982 Open at Royal Troon. Back then, Price was dogging the footsteps of Bobby Clampett, who had been hot through the first two rounds. When Clampett finally faded in the final round, Price found himself leading by three strokes with just six holes to play and lost. The general opinion was that he had choked, and choked badly. Price just gave a big smile and seemed determined not to make the same mistake twice. 'Remember, I was twenty-five then,' he joked, 'and how many guys at twenty-five have the opportunity to win a major championship?'

After an opening round of 79, the new US Open champion Curtis Strange was in serious danger of missing the cut, but he bore down, improved by ten strokes on the Friday to a 69, and made it with no room to spare on 148. But as he teed off early on Saturday morning he must have wished that he was back home in Virginia. The heavens around Lytham literally opened up. It rained and rained. Play was suspended at 12.20 p.m., and at 1.45 R&A officials declared play abandoned for the day. It was the first Open wash-out since 1961 at Royal Birkdale.

Plans were quickly set in motion for a double round on Sunday with players going out in three-ball matches instead of the traditional pairs, but it was never going to happen. By midnight on Saturday the fairways at the fourth, seventh, eleventh and fourteenth holes were completely waterlogged, the course in general so swamped that there were serious doubts that even one round could be played on Sunday, never mind two. For the first time in the event's long history, the final round would be played on a Monday. Early on Sunday morning course workers were out at 4.30 a.m., manning pumps and trying to repair the damage. By seven the forecast was for clouds and occasional drizzle with temperatures in the mid-sixties and a freshening wind in the afternoon. The relief among the R&A officials was obvious as the first starters went out a few hours later.

The jockeying began in earnest. With Price and Ballesteros playing solidly for rounds of 69 and 70 respectively, Faldo shot a 68, despite dropping a shot on the par-three opening hole. 'To practise all morning,' said a half-joking Faldo, 'then walk out and miss from two feet on the first hole was just stupid.' He was right, but having recovered with six birdies more than made up for any mock embarrassment he expressed in the press centre afterwards. So how confident was he of retaining his championship? 'Top secret!' he said, not a little conspiratorially. 'There are four good players there, and nobody is likely to go backwards, so it's going to be a long struggle. But if I were to be the first Briton to win two in succession, it would be everything.' What about Nick Price? the press asked. Opinion was mixed. 'Price has played in this situation before,' said Faldo, 'and he's been around a long time. The third day is the test day. If you have survived the pressure on the third day, it eases the pressure for the last day.' Ballesteros was not quite as diplomatic. 'There was pressure today,' he said ominously, 'but the pressure's not really in the third round. It comes tomorrow, on the back nine.' Seve was right. At seven under par, the Zimbabwean with a British passport only had a two-shot lead over Faldo and Ballesteros going into the final round. And with the Spanish maestro keen to make it a hat-trick of Open titles it was never going to be easy.

Monday in Lancashire was a normal working day, yet just over 15,080 people magically found their way to Royal Lytham and St Annes. And despite the gloomy weather they certainly got their money's worth as they witnessed some of the finest golf ever seen in the final round of an Open championship. With the home favourite Nick Faldo due to tee off at 12.45, it was the big-hitting Fred Couples who set the pulses racing as he stormed to the turn in 30, aided by back-to-back eagles at the sixth and seventh holes. But he was too far behind to make a real challenge, and any chance he had of winning finally evaporated with bogeys on the last two holes. He finished tied fourth with fellow American Gary Koch, and his spirited 68 was never going to be enough the way Ballesteros was playing.

It all came down to the final threesome: Price, Ballesteros and Faldo. By the time they reached the turn, it was a two-man chase: Price and Ballesteros. Nothing had changed at the first hole, all three made par, but at the second Price (missing a five-foot par putt) and Faldo (with three putts) bogeyed, while Ballesteros two-putted from fifteen feet for his par. Price's lead was now down to one, over Ballesteros. Faldo caught up with Ballesteros at the third with a birdie from eight feet. Price and Ballesteros both parred, so Price led them both by one. All three parred the fourth and fifth. It was a three-man battle for only one more hole, the sixth. All three birdied. Then began one of the great duels in Open history.

The action reached fever pitch, the pace was brutal and Faldo was first to fold. 'The seventh hole killed me,' he said later, recalling his lacklustre round of 71. 'I hit a good four-iron to the green, then found that where I was I could not even putt. I had to putt it uphill and three-putted, while the other guys were close.' Looking back, it was the 549-yard seventh hole that almost certainly ruined his chances of winning. Despite playing downwind for much of the tournament, he could do no better than make a par five each day while practically everyone else was making birdies or, as Price and Ballesteros did that day, eagles.

With Faldo falling behind by merely standing still, Price and Ballesteros now went toe-to-toe over the closing nine holes in spectacular fashion. With the Englishman now little more than a spectator, birdie after birdie was traded between the two. Coming to the last, the Spaniard found himself a stroke ahead. Still the drama was not quite over. Seve hit his approach into the left-hand rough, the 'safe' side but still thick rough about twenty yards from the pin. Nick Price in turn was on the green in two, but not near enough to threaten the birdie he so desperately needed. It was then that Seve produced his final piece of magic. Chipping up to within inches of the hole, he pumped his fist as the ball gently slid to a halt. Moments later it was all over as Price, despite three-putting, settled for second place ahead of Faldo.

Price just stood there and shook his head. Ordinarily, a leader who scores 69 in the final round will almost certainly win. But there was nothing ordinary about that day's golf. Ballesteros had just shot a six-under-par 65. It was an utter masterpiece. Before the round, Price had told his caddie, Dave McNeilly, 'Let's just go out and shoot a sixty-nine and not worry about anyone else.' It was probably good advice, and that is exactly what he did. But Faldo had long known what the Spaniard was capable of, and he just smiled when he was asked to comment on the Spaniard's brilliance. As for Seve, all he could say was, 'You can only hope for a round like that once every twenty-five, maybe fifty years. So far, it is the best round of my life. I played as good as you can hope to play this game.' Was there any reason why he shouldn't win five or six more majors? Seve grinned. 'What you think?' he said, teasing the journalist. 'This game is a piece of cake or what?' After several years in the wilderness of missed cuts, it seemed the old Ballesteros was back and European golf

was suddenly galvanised with thoughts of even more Faldo/
Ballesteros/Lyle shoot-outs. It was a delicious prospect.

Returning to the cut and thrust of the European Tour, Faldo
continued his frustrating form with yet another second-place
finish in the Benson and Hedges tournament at Fulford in York
– one of eight he would have that year. In many ways what
happened there summed up his bittersweet season perfectly.
Playing with Faldo in the final round was Peter Baker, a
twenty-year-old rookie pro from the West Midlands. Trailing
tournament leader Faldo by three strokes as they came to the
fifteenth tee, Baker calmly informed his caddie, Andy Prodger,
that he needed 'three birdies to make a play-off'. He then
proceeded to hole from three feet for a birdie on the fifteenth
moments after Faldo missed from four feet for par on the same
green. It proved a real turning point. The deficit had been
reduced to just one, which is exactly how it remained as they
came to the par-five closing hole.

Ahead, two more young players, the 22-year-old Spaniard
José-María Olázabal and the Australian Craig Parry, had finished
well, setting a sixteen-under-par total of 272. This meant that
Faldo needed a birdie at the last to win, with Baker requiring
an eagle. With the hole a gentle dog-leg stretching just over 488
yards in length, the targets set for both players looked perfectly
achievable – and that is precisely what happened. Now, for the
only time since the first tee, the pair were level. Returning with
Faldo to the eighteenth tee, Baker followed up a massive
290-yard drive with a five-iron to fewer than twenty feet from
the pin. Moments later he holed out for a second consecutive
eagle to defeat his somewhat shell-shocked playing partner.
Certainly not overawed about playing with a past Open
champion, Baker had gone into the play-off feeling he had
nothing to lose. 'Everyone was looking for Nick's experience to
tell,' he said. 'Maybe I was just lucky.'

As usual, the PGA Championship proved a wasted trip as
far as the European contingent was concerned. Indeed, Sandy
Lyle, the Masters champion and leading money winner, invited
a hail of criticism after he chose to take a week off as a holiday.
Amazed that he would pass up the opportunity to become the
first player since Tom Watson in 1982 to win two majors in

the same year, Curtis Strange voiced the opinion of many when he said, 'If he thinks he's doing what's right for him, so be it, but this is a major championship, and yes, he should be here.'

That said, you could understand Lyle's reasons for not being there. The 1988 US PGA was being played at the 7,015-yard Oak Tree Golf Club in Edmond, Oklahoma, a Pete Dye-designed course which held the highest rating of any in the country – 76.9 for its par of 71. Even before the tournament began horror stories concerning the difficulty of the course were emanating from local players like Bob Tway and Gil Morgan. It was always going to be a tough week, and not for the first time the PGA of America was brought to task by the media for continuing its policy of playing the final major of the year at some of the hottest spots in America. Why not February or March? they asked. Or perhaps May, after the Masters? Any time but August in the south of the USA. In the end none of it mattered as American Jeff Sluman turned in a superb six-under-par final round of 65 after coming from three shots off the pace to win. After matching the lowest winning final round in PGA Championship history, the journey-man pro could obviously sense the disappointment of those who wanted a big-name winner. 'I'm not going to be a Greg Norman or Jack Nicklaus,' he said modestly. 'All I can do is play my own game.'

As for Nick Faldo, he had made a momentary dash at the championship after opening up with a wonderful 67 to lead the tournament alongside Paul Azinger. Then, after further rounds of 71 and 70, it all got a little pedestrian. The birdies dried up, and despite moving to within four strokes of Sluman after eleven holes on the final day, he missed four short putts coming home and was forced to settle for fifth place. 'This putter won't be flying first-class on the way home,' Faldo said afterwards.

Returning to Europe for the Irish Open, Faldo could now reflect on what had been a remarkably good but frustrating year. After a run of second places early in the season, he had finished joint thirtieth at Augusta, recorded a win at the French Open and gone second, third and fourth in the US Open, Open and PGA. Finally, as the season drew to a close, he could also take some pleasure from a win in the Volvo Masters and from finishing second to Ballesteros in the European Order of Merit with his highest ever earnings of £347,971. Faldo was back, and while the gloss was taken off a little by losing out to his old rival Sandy Lyle in the final of the World Matchplay Championship at Wentworth, it had been a good year by any standards.

Now all he had to do was improve on it.

11. A MASTER IN THE MAKING

The Masters Tournament is all about tradition. Held each April at the exclusive Augusta National Golf Club in Georgia, it remains a privately run event for a small, highly select field of professionals. The only one of golf's four major championships to be played at the same venue each year, it has risen in stature over the past four decades to challenge the older, more historic British and American Opens as the most prestigious tournament in golf.

Tradition also means having well-established guidelines, and the Masters has more guidelines (or rules) than anywhere else in golf. A throwback to the mid-thirties when it was known as the Annual Invitational Tournament, the event is run entirely by the members for the members. An autocratic organisation, it strives to maintain the high ideals of its founder, Bobby Jones, which means that the committee not only decide who can play, but how they will conduct themselves while they are there. For example, professionals are only allowed to play one ball in practice when three or four is the norm any other week of the year. Big-money wagers are also frowned upon, as are unshaven faces, overly colourful golf attire and wrap-around sunshades – restrictions which if applied to any other tournament would have the pampered players walking out en masse.

As for the public, they are subject to even more guidelines than the golfers. For them, stepping on to the hallowed turf of Augusta means no cameras, no picnics, no excessive cheering and no asking for players' autographs anywhere on the course or practice ground. Running or walking 'in haste' is also not permitted, but as the temperature in Georgia is usually in line with the average age of a Masters season-ticket holder – about 75 – this is rarely a problem. Indeed, the only people who have been known to bend this rule are members of the press chasing an important interview. Even then, a polite but firm word from one of the small army of Pinkerton security agents who roam the estate throughout the tournament normally puts the brakes on the bravest of reporters.

Like the Championship Committee of the Royal and Ancient which organises the Open, Augusta National sees Masters week as a 'them and us' situation. An intensely private club, they are reluctant to give any interviews that do not relate directly to the tournament itself. Membership is strictly by invitation only, and while they are more than happy to open up their magnificent club to the outside world each April, the gates on Magnolia Drive remain firmly locked at all other times of the year. That said, no golf tournament in the world treats its champions quite like Augusta National. All Masters winners are automatically made honorary members. They are given their own locker room, are free to attend an annual dinner and have bestowed upon them a lifetime invitation to play in the tournament no matter what. Returning each year, they are made to feel part of a very exclusive family – unlike the rest of us, who are there under sufferance.

The first real contact the media has with the club during Augusta week is at Wednesday practice. It is there that the club chairman lays down the law. The eleven o'clock meetings are always brief and the guidelines are never open to debate. As representatives of the golf press, if you fail to abide by them it is likely you will be asked not to return – quite a deterrent if a major part of your living relies on being there as CBS anchorman, as Jack Whitaker found out to his cost some years ago. Having referred to the gallery around the final green as a 'mob' on live television, he was told that his credentials would no longer be renewed and he was not expected to return until asked. The same applied to flamboyant commentator Gary McCord, who described the greens as so slick they must have been bikini-waxed. After he followed that up with a foolish comment about needing a body bag when describing the difficulties involved in overshooting the seventeenth green, it was a case of 'don't call us, we'll call you'.

As part of the television deal with host broadcaster CBS, Augusta National charges a fraction of the estimated $25 million a year NBC pays the United States Golf Association for the US Open. In return for bestowing upon them this most prized of all sporting events, they demand some control over what is actually broadcast. For example, Augusta National demands the right to approve any commentator before he or she steps up to a microphone (see Whitaker and McCord). They permit no on-course interviews and even dictate the amount of advertising breaks permitted per hour – only four minutes' worth, even on Saturday and Sunday. Not only that, the club has influence over who can and cannot advertise during Masters coverage. Dismissing out of hand anything to do with sex, hard liquor or hamburgers, the club only wants blue-chip companies, which is why Cadillac and American Express are usually favoured this way.

On the plus side, Augusta National is a dream come true for broadcasters and photographers alike. Seen as the traditional start to the golf season, springtime in Georgia usually means astoundingly bright colours and idyllic conditions in which to play golf. Built on land that served for many years as a plant nursery, the course is a wonderful mixture of cathedral pine and oak, blooming azaleas, magnolias and white dogwood. There is rarely a blade of grass out of place; even the water hazards are dyed azure blue during Masters week to add to the overall effect. The individual holes evoke an image of glorious nature with exotic-sounding names like the Yellow Jasmine, Carolina Cherry and Firethorn.

While every hole on the back nine at Augusta is justifiably famous, it is the run of three holes at the far end of the course that grabs most attention. It is known as Amen Corner because you need the Almighty's help to get through with your score intact, and the Masters is invariably won or lost over this short stretch of holes from the eleventh to the thirteenth. Among the most photographed golf holes in the world, Amen Corner begins with the 455-yard par-four eleventh. It is named White Dogwood, and the problems really start with the second shot. Playing downhill, the player must avoid pulling the ball into the lake guarding the left half of the green while trying not to leak it right. In fact, anywhere but on the green leaves an impossible chip back towards the water.

The 155-yard par-3 twelfth is also a real test of nerve, especially on the Sunday afternoon. This is perhaps the most famous short hole in golf, the professionals playing to a shallow, kidney-shaped green sitting behind Rae's Creek. John Rae was a local man who established a sanctuary up the Savannah river to protect settlers from Indian raids in 1789, but the creek named in his honour offers no sanctuary at all for an under-hit tee-shot. With towering pines sheltering the green from any wind, the hole often requires the golfer to hit a high, floating shot into a swirling breeze. Club misjudgements are common enough and can lead to a nightmare score, as Tom Weiskopf found in 1980 when he took a horrific thirteen shots to hole his ball after tangling with both Rae's Creek and the green-side bunker.

The final hole in the loop is the 485-yard par-five thirteenth. Stunningly beautiful and lethal if you go off line, this hole is a real crowd-pleaser with anything from an eagle three to a quadruple-bogey nine the possible outcome. After a good drive down this right-to-left dog-leg, a wondrous sight appears for anyone who finds the fairway. As you play over Rae's Creek once again, you see the green set invitingly into a high bank with a mass of blooming azaleas behind it. Huge pines all the way down the left create the slight optical illusion that the green is nearer than it actually is. Inevitably, at some point over the weekend someone will birdie or eagle this hole and go on to win.

Considering its reputation, the clubhouse at Augusta National is surprisingly small at first sight. Sitting atop a steep rise, this colonial-style building vaguely reminiscent of the house in the epic film *Gone with the Wind* looks over the course below. During Masters week it remains strictly out-of-bounds to the public and media with only members and their guests allowed past the huge Pinkerton agent on the door. Harking back to the days when golf professionals were forced to change their shoes etc. in the caddie shed, a temporary arrangement is made so that the players are given access to the locker room, the dining area and main bar, but little else. The clubhouse has other quaint features, not least of which is the Crow's Nest room situated in the attic. With room enough for five beds and a bathroom it is traditionally offered to any amateur competing in the field for only ten dollars a night. Apart from an electric bulb or two, the only light is supplied via a square turret that peaks out from the tiled roof, but it offers one of the best views in golf, looking out over the course on one side and down Magnolia Drive on the other. Despite its unbeatable location, it has the reputation of not being the most comfortable place in which to spend Masters week. Without air conditioning, the temperature inside the roof space has been known to go up alarmingly making life very uncomfortable for the already nervous amateurs. (Is it any wonder, then, that the members' name for the Crow's Nest is 'the upstairs sauna'?)

One of the best traditions of the Masters comes early on the Thursday morning. While many of the players are on the practice ground working off pre-tournament butterflies, three of the game's legends are limbering up on the first tee. Winners of over a dozen major championships between them, Byron Nelson, Gene Sarazen and Sam Snead are living legends in the world of golf. All three are previous Masters winners and for many years have been given the honour of getting the tournament underway. The tee-off is scheduled for eight o'clock in the morning, but long-time starter and past club chairman Clayton Forbes always arrives ten minutes early to greet Nelson, Sarazen and Snead like the old friends they are. Despite playing a few holes at most, possibly nine, each of these gentlemen is announced on the tee as if he were going to compete in the tournament proper.

Gene Sarazen is perhaps the most famous of the three when it comes to Augusta folklore. Dressed in his trademark floppy hat and white plus-fours, the little Italian still cuts a dashing figure as he swings his old-style persimmon driver back and forth on the first tee. Behind him is the board on which the players' names are posted prior to starting their round. For the rest of the field, the figure next to it denotes the number allotted to the player's caddy, but on this occasion it shows their respective ages: 88 (Sarazen), 77 (Nelson) and 76 (Snead, the baby of the group). Treated with none of the mawkish sentimentality usually associated with similar displays of American nostalgia, this opening ceremony remains a lasting compliment to Augusta National and a most enjoyable and dignified event.

Coming into the last Masters of the eighties, Nick Faldo was not in confident mood. He had just played seven straight weeks in

America without getting the sort of results he thought his play deserved. He was hitting the ball well but not scoring, and his record for the first months of 1989 bore that out. He started his year at the Phoenix Open at the end of January, and his best finish had been tied twenty-second at the Nissan (Los Angeles) Open two weeks later in February. Yet dotted between the high finishes and mid-seventies scores, like diamonds in the dust, were some excellent rounds. He had scored a third-round 65 in Phoenix, followed by middle rounds of 68s at Riviera and a first-round 67 at the Honda Classic in March. That said, his last round before the Masters, at the Independent Insurance Agent Open in Texas, was a confidence-crushing 76. As Faldo arrived at Augusta a day later, nothing looked to have changed, and after a mediocre practice round on the Tuesday he had resolved 'just to give it a go'.

In the opening round on Thursday, veteran Lee Trevino rolled back the years with a five-under-par 67 to take the tournament lead. Nick Faldo, keeping up the pressure, also found some form to finish the day in second place after a well-constructed round of 68. On Friday, things got even better. At the turn, Faldo had played 27 holes in six under par to find himself leading the tournament by three. Then, almost inexplicably, he started moving backwards. He came home in 39 – three over par – which left him tied for the lead with Trevino on three under, behind them a group of five players at one under par including Seve Ballesteros, Ben Crenshaw and Scott Hoch.

The third round, like the second, was played in difficult conditions with most of the field struggling to match par. With rain and high winds making Augusta in April feel more like Anchorage in November, the effect on Faldo was immediate as he double-bogeyed the par-four first. Looking to repair the damage straight away, he managed to hit the green in regulation at the par-five second, but with his ball on one corner of the green and the pin on the other he was in serious three-putt territory. Then came the shot that would ultimately turn his entire week around. Putting from over a hundred feet away, Faldo holed out for a magnificent birdie. As the commentator rightly said about this miracle shot, 'That putt went through two time zones!'

Sadly for Nick Faldo, 'miracle' shots would be in short supply for the rest of the third round. He was partnered by the talkative Mexican, and by the time he walked off the twelfth green he had dropped back to level par for the tournament and was four shots behind the new leader, Ben Crenshaw. He needed a few birdies to regain his momentum, and where better to start than the easily reachable par-five thirteenth? After a solid drive followed by a second shot which scampered over the back of the green, Faldo was contemplating how to play a treacherously fast downhill chip for his third when play was suspended for ninety minutes because of lightning in the area. Then, with no sign of it clearing, play was cancelled for the day. The leading groups were asked to return first thing Sunday morning to finish off their rounds. A weather break can often prove to be a double-edged sword in such circumstances, acting either for or against a player. For Faldo the break came at just the wrong moment, but at least it gave him the opportunity to gather his thoughts and work out what had gone so wrong with his round.

Faldo resumed play at 7.35 a.m. the next day, and the first thing he faced was the chip from the back of the thirteenth green. Typically, he had found a similar spot on the putting green near the clubhouse the previous evening and had set about hitting sixty or seventy practice shots to get some feel for the shot. At 7.42 all that effort seemed to have been worthwhile as Faldo rolled his ball down the slope to within six feet. Delighted with the shot, he then undid all the good work by missing the putt for birdie. It was as if someone had pricked his balloon of concentration. After that, he three-putted the next before dropping another shot at the par-four seventeenth. Five over par for his third round, he now found himself five shots behind Crenshaw at three under with only the final round to play – which was due to start only an hour or so later.

Nick Faldo was understandably distraught. Dropping two shots to par over the closing five holes was a huge blow. Riven by self-doubt, something had to change, and for Faldo it was the putter he was using. Discarding the copper-coloured Bullseye he had used for the first three rounds, he headed out to the practice green during the lunchtime break with a selection of putters tucked under his arm. In the end he favoured a mallet-headed putter, reasoning that on slower, rain-affected greens he would need something more substantial than just a thin-bladed model. 'After my seventy-seven I was really despondent with my putter,' he recalled. 'When I came back I had a go with the Taylor Made putter, the ones with three white stripes on the top. I covered over two of them so I had just one line to set up with, and off I went.'

It was while Faldo was trying to pick out a putter that a reporter for a British newspaper made the mistake of tracking him down for a quick word. Not surprisingly, the quote he received was a short, sharp 'Fuck off!' To his credit, Faldo contacted the media centre shortly afterwards to offer an apology, but his reaction was a good indication of the pressure he was under going into that final round.

Knowing he needed something special to catch Ben Crenshaw, the 1984 Masters champion, Faldo got exactly the start he wanted. Wielding his new putter like a magic wand, he holed birdie putts from seventeen feet at the first, twelve feet at the second, fifteen feet at the fourth and twenty feet at the seventh. Four under par after just seven holes, two under for the tournament, he was back in with a fighting chance. 'I was on the front corner of the green at the first and had this tough putt right across the slope,' he said later. 'I would have been delighted just to get it close, but in it went. That sort of start is worth so much.'

The pressure was intense throughout, however, and moving into the back nine the lead kept changing hands as the quietly spoken Texan began having problems of his own. With only a handful of holes remaining, Crenshaw was overtaken by Seve Ballesteros, Mike Reid and Scott Hoch as his own putting touch temporarily deserted him. With Reid and Ballesteros leading on five under par, and Hoch just one stroke behind them, Faldo, having recovered brilliantly from a bogey on the eleventh, maintained his own challenge with further birdies at the thirteenth, fourteenth and sixteenth. Playing just ahead of the leading group, he knew the importance of continuing to post good scores and putting pressure on those behind him. He came to the penultimate hole at four under knowing that a birdie would put him in a great position.

As usual, the pin on the par-four seventeenth was in its final-day position over on the extreme right of the green. It was protected all around by severe slopes that threatened to funnel away a misdirected approach, and an overly cautious Faldo played his shot into the heart of the green, fifteen yards left of the flagstick. By that stage needing a birdie to tie with Reid and Hoch on five under, he faced a putt that had to be played over a hog's back, down the other side with a massive borrow from the left – a nightmare putt at any stage, but in the final round of the Masters, Faldo would be lucky not to bogey. Instead, he gave it a firm rap then watched as it meandered its way towards the hole. The ball literally collided with the back of the cup before dropping in (Faldo later admitted that he hit it much too hard). As one American journalist said afterwards, 'If that putt had missed, Faldo would have been lucky to have finished in the top ten!'

Needing nothing worse than a par up the last, Faldo hit a solid drive into the left centre of the fairway. Then it started raining, so hard that it seeped through his umbrella and soaked the thumb of his glove. Changing gloves would only have upset him further, so he made the unusual decision to grip the club tighter and risk it slipping in his hands. Somehow it worked, his approach stopping on the rain-sodden green fewer than twenty feet from the pin. A solid two putts later, Faldo walked off the final green with a magnificent 65. Seven under par for the round, five under for the tournament, he was leader in the clubhouse. With Ballesteros, Crenshaw, Reid and Hoch still battling it out on the course, all he could do now was wait.

When Scott Hoch birdied the fifteenth to go six under, it looked as if Faldo's score might not be good enough. Then he dropped a stroke on the seventeenth and they were back level. It was a day for mistakes. Minutes earlier Ballesteros had come to the par-three sixteenth at four under par only to pull his tee-shot into the lake, which effectively ended his challenge. It was the same story for Mike Reid, who also found water at the par-five fifteenth. Like the predator he is, Greg Norman made his move with a birdie at seventeen for a share of the lead. Needing a birdie up the last to pressure those behind, he provided more ammunition for his critics by taking a bogey, dropping back to four under. The stage was now left clear for Crenshaw and Hoch.

Coming to the final hole, the situation could not have been more clear-cut. With Ben Crenshaw having made a birdie at the seventeenth to draw level with Hoch, the destiny of the Masters now lay in their hands. If either made a birdie down the eighteenth, he would win; a par meant a play-off with Nick Faldo, and a dropped shot meant an early trip home. In a good old-fashioned shoot-out, it was Crenshaw who blinked first, making bogey to slip into a tie for third place with Norman. Scott Hoch, however, made his par, and for the second time in four major championships Nick Faldo found himself in a play-off.

In many ways the 33-year-old Scott Hoch was an unlikely figure to be facing in a play-off – especially at the Masters. He had won only three PGA tournaments in his career and the last of those had been five years ago. A controversial character, even abrasive at times, this was a man who, when he entered his first PGA tournament in 1980, wrenched his back going up some stairs before he could play an official round and had to sit out for five months. This was a man who in 1982 was tied up for an hour in his hotel room in Tucson wondering if he was going to die at the hands of a gun-wielding robber. In 1986, when Hoch won the Vardon Trophy for the lowest-scoring average of 70.08, his critics complained that not only had he not won a PGA event that year, he had also lowered his tournament average by entering marshmallow events. 'The ancient and honourable Vardon Trophy is in danger of becoming a joke,' Thomas Boswell had written in *Golf* magazine. 'And that rhymes with Hoch.' Once voted Least Popular Golfer in a poll of tour players conducted by the *Dallas Times Herald*, Hoch had revealed a more vulnerable side when he responded, 'It really hurt. It was cruel. It hurt my family and my friends. I don't know why they did it.' Not long afterwards he admitted that he could be 'kind of a smart-ass' and 'kind of hard to get to know'. In his defence, fellow PGA Tour pro Chip Beck said, 'I've known Scott since I was ten years old. Even then he'd always be in conflicts, and people would talk about him. They considered him cocky and arrogant. But that was just Scott trying to be the best he could be.'

Coming into the Masters, Hoch's form had been patchy at best. Bothered by a thumb injury, he had finished thirty-ninth at the Nestlé Invitational in March and missed the cut the following week at the Players Championship. Frustrated with his game, he had stopped playing for two weeks before the Masters, just to have time to think. One thing he decided was that he wasn't having any fun. His caddie on the tour, Rick Cesario, had already given him some unsolicited advice: 'Every day you come off the course tied up in knots. You're going to play this game for a living for, what, the next twenty-five years? Is every day going to be like that?' Maybe Cesario was right. Having left his clubs alone for ten straight days, Scott Hoch arrived at Augusta on the Tuesday, a day later than usual, with little on his mind but enjoying himself. 'I loosened up,' he said. 'I was completely at ease the whole week. I was so relaxed, it was eerie.' It was an attitude he took into the sudden-death play-off with Nick Faldo.

On the first extra hole, the par-four tenth, Faldo hit his tee-shot short and right while Hoch found the centre of the fairway over sixty yards ahead. Having failed to catch the downhill slope that can add an extra eighty or so yards to a well-hit drive, the Englishman was forced to hit his approach from just over 200 yards with a four-iron. He struck it well, but the ball caught the edge of the right-hand bunker before falling back into the sand. Having watched his opponent bunker his second, Hoch found the green in regulation, leaving himself a 26-foot putt for birdie. Fortunate to have found a decent lie, Faldo hit a good recovery but still had a sizeable twelve-footer for par. Now with a putt to win, Hoch took the safe option by coaxing his first putt up to within two feet of the hole, gambling on the fact that Faldo was going to miss his par. It was a risk that paid off. Tapping in for a bogey, Faldo could only watch as Hoch lined himself up over the ball. With just a short downhill putt between the American and victory, Faldo tried to remain positive despite his obvious disappointment. 'I wasn't willing him to miss it,' he said afterwards, 'but it's important you continue to think positively.'

It was fortunate that Faldo did maintain his concentration because Scott Hoch inexplicably, inexcusably, unbelievably missed the putt. For a moment it looked perfect, then it veered away at the last possible second, brushing the left edge of the hole as it raced down the slope. Had he misjudged the putt? Had he choked? No one watching knew, but the crowd gave out an embarrassed, painful groan as if it had just seen an actor forget his lines in the crucial scene of a play. 'When he missed, I said, "he's opened the door for me." I believed then it was my destiny.'

Adding insult to injury, the 33-year-old Floridian had ended up even further away from the hole. It was an uncomfortable moment for him; even Faldo felt a tinge of embarrassment for his opponent as he lined up his return putt from at least twice the distance. 'I remember wanting him to hole it,' he said, echoing the feelings of everyone watching Hoch that day. 'Because that wasn't the way I wanted to win.' To his credit, a 'frazzled' Scott Hoch made the five-foot return – a putt he later admitted to having no memory of. 'It was a terrible putt,' Hoch said about the first one. 'I hadn't three-putted all week. That's a nice place to do it. I had to give it a chance to go in. I'd been dropping those putts all week.'

As they moved off to the second extra hole it started to rain hard again, and there were question marks about how far the players could go in the deteriorating light. It was already gloomy by the time the play-off had begun at 7.10 p.m.; by the time they reached the eleventh tee, it was positively dark. Determined to carry on, Faldo hit a good drive on the par-four hole but still had 200 yards to the pin with the wind blowing from the right. With water on the left he took aim at the right edge of the green and saw the wind start to move the ball as it passed the trees by the twelfth tee. Landing his ball on the green 25 feet below the flag, Faldo later described it as 'just about the best three-iron I've ever hit'. Hoch, in turn, missed the green to the right. Unlike his countryman Larry Mize, who had chipped in from the same position against Greg Norman two years earlier, he then failed to pitch any closer than eight feet. Now it was so dark that it was almost impossible for Faldo to see the hole from where he was. In any other tournament they would have stopped play immediately, but no one wanted to come back the following day and finish this off. Certainly not Faldo, who had a putt to win.

'On number eleven, when he chipped up eight feet short,' Faldo recalled, 'I thought, I'm going to two-putt and I can win this. I've just got to stay loose on the putt and stroke it up there.' At least that was the plan. While lining up his putt, Faldo ushered over his caddie, Andy Prodger, to take a quick look. Not surprisingly, Prodger, who had worn dark glasses throughout the final round, felt under-qualified to offer an opinion. 'It all looks a bit too misty to me. You'd better do this one on your own,' the nervous bagman muttered as he walked away rapidly. Faldo got the hint. Having spent most of his career working up to this moment, he was now on his own.

After striking the ball towards the hole, Faldo heard the sound of it rattling into the cup and that told him it had gone in. Peering into the gloom to confirm the fact, he instantly raised his arms aloft in triumph. (Ironically, he had not managed a par on the eleventh all week, bogeying it in all four rounds before making this birdie in the play-off.) Unable to comprehend what he had just achieved, he opened his mouth but nothing came out. He had won the 53rd US Masters, and no one could have been more proud to do so, as he told reporters afterwards.

Winning the Masters means the world to me. Words do not describe it. I've seen other guys do this. You see Jack Nicklaus shoot sixty-five, then go out and win the play-off. I sit and watch TV and think it is unbelievable when that happens. Then for you to do it for yourself, it's a tough feeling to have. To think you are standing over a putt and you've got the world looking at you and you knock it in. It was ecstasy to make that putt. It was a dream. You dream it was going to happen. When it does before your eyes, you can't believe it.

In many ways it was a double celebration. Not only had Faldo won his first Masters title, but less than a month earlier, on 17 March, Gill had given birth to a baby son, Matthew. Moreover, he had now matched the record of Sandy Lyle and Seve Ballesteros by winning the Masters and the Open. Faldo felt vindicated. No longer would he feel second best to either of them again. No longer would he play his golf in the shadow of their achievements.

Sadly, the same could not be said for Scott Hoch, who appeared at the post-Masters press conference sporting an unconvincing grin. 'Well,' he said. 'I'm glad I don't carry a gun with me.' In truth, nobody seemed that worried – certainly not with his aim.

To the victor the spoils: Faldo had an appointment in Butlers Cabin to pick up his green jacket. Waiting for him there was his old rival and 1988 champion Sandy Lyle, and it was somehow fitting that it should be the big Scot who held it out for Faldo to try on. The scene was a graphic depiction of the stranglehold European golfers now had on this most American of events. Unfortunately, the jacket came up a little short in the sleeve department. 'Never mind,' quipped Faldo, 'it's the colour that counts.'

Afterwards, Faldo embarked on the usual endless round of press conferences and TV interviews. Also, as the newest member of Augusta National, he was required to attend the post-Masters dinner later that night as guest of the club's chairman, Hord Hardin, along with John Simpson. At one stage Hardin was asked by Simpson whether he thought Faldo should honour a commitment to play the following week in the Heritage or go home to his new family. After due consideration, Hardin replied, 'That's a good question, John, but I really think Sandy should stay and play.' Remembering players' names was never Hardin's strong point.

After the tournament, Hoch and his family piled into their Plymouth Voyager and drove to the next stop on the PGA Tour at Hilton Head. Stopping off for petrol on the journey, the magnitude of what had happened finally began to sink in. 'I feel like I've let you down,' he told his wife Sally, almost in tears. 'I feel like I've let you down and my parents, your parents and our friends.' Replaying his two-foot putt on the tenth green over and over again in his mind, he said 'I couldn't sleep for two nights. My dad couldn't sleep, Chip [Beck] couldn't sleep either. I guess when your friend has just blown the thing that you yourself have always dreamed of winning, it's a little hard to take.'

Faldo flew back to England after the MCI Heritage Classic (where he finished tied eleventh) and the rest of the year proved

to be equally successful. He finished the season fourth in the European Order of Merit with consecutive victories in the Volvo PGA, Dunhill British Masters and Peugeot French Open. His record was equally impressive in the three remaining majors: tied eighteenth in the US Open at Oak Hill, tied eleventh in the Open at Royal Troon and tied ninth in the PGA Championship at Kemper Lakes.

Yet the 1989 season was not without its low points. Having won just under a million dollars in prize money worldwide, Faldo had established himself as a truly world-class player by the time the Ryder Cup returned to the Belfry in September. After Europe's victory at Muirfield Village two years earlier there was a general feeling in the press that a Faldo-led side should win at a canter. After all, this was probably the strongest side ever fielded against the Americans, boasting two other Masters winners in Seve Ballesteros and Bernhard Langer. So when the USA ended up snatching a 14–14 draw on the final day, Faldo especially drew some highly unfavourable comments from the press.

Faldo had lost to Lanny Wadkins in the penultimate game in the singles, and it was hinted that once the trophy had been retained the home team had taken its foot off the accelerator. The argument was that once Cañizares had beaten Ken Green on the eighteenth the celebrations had started up prematurely, the European golfers certain in the knowledge that at least one of the four players still out on the course – Gordon Brand Jr, Sam Torrance, Faldo and Ian Woosnam – would get the point Europe needed for victory. Surely, everyone thought, with Faldo and Woosie still out there, one of them was bound to get the job done. Sadly, it was not the case. One by one they fell, and by the time both Faldo and Woosnam had found water on the eighteenth, the match was halved.

Indignant at the criticism he received in the aftermath of the match at the Belfry, Faldo hit back by saying, 'As professionals, you train yourself to keep the "what ifs" at bay, concentrating fully on one shot at a time. The fact that both Woosie and I hit the ball into the water at eighteen had nothing to do with relaxing because we had retained the cup or that there was an emotional letdown because no one was coming back to cheer us home. If anything, we ran out of steam after a long, hard week.'

Faldo knew from talking to other British sporting stars like Ian Botham and Kevin Keegan that it was typical of the British press to build someone up only to knock him or her down again. But reflecting on his remarkable year, he hardly cared. After all, he had won the prize he most wanted and was now looking forward to more success over the coming decade.

And there were many more wins to come.

12. MAJOR DOUBLE

Having established himself as one of European golf's top players in the eighties, Nick Faldo set about dominating the world game in the nineties. He was coming into his prime, and everything would now be geared towards winning more major championships. Feeling relaxed and confident, Faldo reasoned that this would be his decade, the time when all the hard work of the past few years would finally bear golden fruit on a consistent basis. Yet important changes still had to be made, the most obvious being the employment of a new caddie.

It had been on the cards for some time. Faldo needed someone with whom he could discuss things out on the course, someone to encourage him, buoy him up when things were going badly (a rare occurrence these days). Andy Prodger, although extremely able, could never be described as talkative. A shy, gentle character, he saw the bagman's job in strictly black and white terms: turn up on time, give the right yardage and keep your mouth shut. Prodger had been employed by Faldo for four and a half years and no one was more supportive of him than the diminutive Londoner. He was a fan as much as he was a caddie, so losing his job came as a horrible shock.

After going with Nick to Japan and Australia at the end of 1989, I said see you next year and went home. A short while later he phoned and said, 'We're finished.' Simple as that. It was a case of goodbye and thanks very much. We'd won five tournaments that year, including the Masters. Plus we won the 1987 Open and other events in the time I was with him, so I did something right. He said I didn't talk to him enough. What could I say? He was the one hitting the shots! In the end I didn't think I deserved to be treated that way.

Having dismissed Andy Prodger in December 1989, Faldo picked up the telephone and asked a 22-year-old Swedish girl, Fanny Sunesson, if she would be interested in caddying for him the following season. Interested in working for one of the best golfers in the world? She was ecstatic.

Born in Karlshamn, near Gothenburg, Sunesson had been introduced to golf through her parents, both of whom were keen players. She picked up her first club at the age of seven and was playing off a five handicap by the time she strolled along to the Scandinavian Open ten years later. Desperate to be part of what she saw as a glamorous lifestyle, she took up her first caddying post for the Brazilian Jaime Gonzalez a year later at the same event. After Gonzalez came jobs with Chris Moody, Mark Wiltshire, Andrew Murray, Roger Chapman, Anders Forsbrand and José Rivero. Despite being the only full-time female caddie on the European Tour, Fanny enjoyed the life and encountered few difficulties working alongside her male colleagues. Hard-working and diligent, she was already established by the time she took up the bag of Howard Clark in February 1989. A major step-up in caddying terms, she then established her own piece of history in September by becoming the first female to caddie in a Ryder Cup.

It was Clark who recommended her to David Leadbetter as a potential caddie for Nick Faldo (at the time, Leadbetter was revamping Clark's swing and it was thought that such an arrangement would suit all concerned). The message was passed on. Having seen Fanny in action at the Belfry, Faldo took little persuading. 'Fanny seemed very confident and clear and you could always hear her trying to be encouraging,' he said. 'At the time, I wasn't getting the support I needed from my caddie. I needed him to help me. I couldn't understand how he could watch me miss six putts inside ten feet and not say something.'

The likeable Swede with the trademark ponytail was just what he needed. An easygoing character with a ready smile and infectious laugh, Sunesson and her new employer hit it off straight away. Faldo needed someone who could read his moods and react accordingly. At times focused to the point of rudeness, introspective to the point of obsession, he wanted someone to lift his spirits when things were going badly, and 'Miss Funny Fanny' fitted the bill perfectly.

In January 1990 she headed off to Florida to sit in on Faldo's pre-season tune-up with David Leadbetter. She attended most of their sessions and slowly began to pick up on what they were trying to achieve – or, more correctly, what swing faults they were trying to avoid. In April, Sunesson and Faldo linked up for their first major championship together at the Masters. By that stage she had already carried for him in a number of early-season events in Dubai, Florida and Texas, and they seemed remarkably comfortable in each other's company, but in the run-up to Augusta many wondered whether their partnership would prove as successful as his previous one with Andy Prodger. As the next few days would show, they need not have worried. Fanny took to her work like a duck to water.

Masters week, as Fanny Sunesson found out, has a number of time-honoured events that set it apart from the normal run-of-the-mill PGA Tour tournaments. One of the most pleasant is the pre-Masters par-three competition. Scheduled for the Wednesday, it takes place among some of the most picturesque scenery imaginable. Treated as a relaxed knockabout by the players, the competition is played over nine holes ranging in distance from 55 yards to 140 yards. Held since 1960, the par-three competition has also proved a real two-edged sword in recent years. Records showed that no winner of this event had ever gone on to win the Masters. It was a well-known fact among the players; some of them had been known deliberately to mess up the last few holes in case they won. This year, veteran professional Ray Floyd won the tournament with a score of 23. Afterwards, he dismissed talk about being affected by the Masters hoodoo and stated that he was 'delighted to have won'.

Like Floyd back in 1976, Nick Faldo was determined to defend his title – something only Jack Nicklaus had done before, in 1965 and 1966. Arriving in Augusta on the Sunday, he immediately began fine-tuning his game under the watchful eye of David Leadbetter. (Faldo had approached committee member Jackson Stevens for permission to let Leadbetter walk alongside him during practice rounds. Not surprisingly, his request was politely refused, club member or not.) It was work they could undertake without too many distractions. 'The majors can be difficult weeks sometimes with lots of tension and hype surrounding them,' said Faldo. 'So by turning up early at least you can have some time to yourself.'

As for much of the coming season, the 1990 Masters was predicted to be little more than a Faldo/Norman shootout with the rest of the field making up the numbers. It was an easy assumption to make at the time. Already a two-time major winner, Faldo was also the defending champion while the current world number one Greg Norman had come close in the last four Masters. In horse-racing terms they were the in-form runners, with Norman the slightly stronger favourite having arrived at Augusta fresh from one of his famous Sunday charges the previous week at the J.C. Penney tournament. But West Palm Beach and Augusta National are like chalk and cheese, and almost as quickly as the shark arrived, he left. Having announced that his game had 'never felt better', he opened up with a 78 and followed that with a 72 – and then followed that with an early flight home. It was the same story for the other great British hope, Sandy Lyle. Two years after winning the Masters himself, the Scot hit three spectators in two days – one in the head, one in the eye and one in the leg. Much to the relief of the survivors in the gallery, he also missed the cut and headed home.

The early glory went to journeyman pro Mike Donald. The record holder for the amount of tournaments played the previous season – 35 in total – he holed everything and anything on his way to a superb round of 64, matching Lloyd Mangrum's 1940 record score for best opening round. Donald was so overcome at the press briefing that he was moved to tears. 'I played a lot of rounds when I was a kid, pretending it was Augusta,' he recalled. 'But I never played this good then.' Sadly, the record he set the following day was not so memorable. Dropping shots at four of the first five holes en route to a horror score of 82, he established the worst Thursday/Friday difference in Masters history (some eighteen strokes) and missed the cut.

Someone else who was trying to set a new record was 47-year-old veteran Raymond Floyd. Having made the 'mistake' of winning the par-three tournament on Wednesday, he found himself leading the Masters going into the final round after back-to-back 68s. Well set to become the oldest winner in Masters history (not to mention the first to win the par-three tournament and the main event itself in the same year), he declared, 'I'm putting no pressure on myself now. I decided I've got nothing more to prove to me. I used to be so tough on myself. Now, I'm just having fun.'

Someone else who was having fun (of a sort) was 32-year-old Nick Faldo. After a slowish start (71 and 72) as a result of which he barely made the cut, he added a superb third-round 66 to his card. His long-game was immaculate, but his putting was not; he was having trouble picking the correct lines on some of the slick Augusta greens. But if he was disappointed with the ways things had gone thus far, he certainly did not show it. Trailing tournament leader Ray Floyd by just three shots coming into the final round, with John Huston in second place a shot ahead, he knew that he needed something special to win.

He was paired on the Sunday with his boyhood hero Jack Nicklaus, so the omens looked good for Faldo, but the fifty-year-old Golden Bear had ambitions of his own. Before the Masters, his stated goal was to be the first player to win a tournament on the senior and regular tours in the same year. Now looking to add the Masters to the Tradition event he had won a month earlier in Scottsdale, he could barely disguise the gleam in his eye as he lurked only five shots behind with one round to play. But five shots is a big gap for anyone to make up, even a six-time Masters winner. Struggling from the start, Nicklaus dropped strokes at the fifth and sixth, which effectively ended his dream – for that year at least.

It was the same story for Masters rookie John Huston, who haemorrhaged shots over the first seven holes to fall out of contention. The same fate looked to have befallen Nick Faldo as he double-bogeyed the first after finding a fairway bunker off the tee and three-putting. It was far from an ideal start, but he had arrested the slide by the time he reached the eighth helped by birdies at the second and seventh. In retrospect, the disastrous first hole was just the wake-up call the Englishman needed. Another birdie on the par-four ninth further closed the gap between him and the leading group, but it was becoming a struggle. At the treacherous par-three twelfth, Faldo buried his ball in the back bunker which left him the terrifying possibilities of swiping at it to no effect or smashing it back over the green and into the creek beyond. To his credit, Faldo executed the shot well, doing just enough to save par. 'I played a great shot out, just cleared the lip of the bunker, but it still ran off the green on the other side.' Walking off the green, Faldo turned to Nicklaus and said, 'Thank God we don't have to play that hole every week.' To which Jack replied, 'Hell, I've been playing it for the last thirty-five years!' They were the first words the two men had spoken all day.

Shortly afterwards, Floyd, playing in the group behind with Huston, birdied the same hole leaving Faldo four shots adrift with six holes left to play. There was still a mountain to climb if Faldo wanted to add another green jacket to his wardrobe. It looked an impossible task, but pressure has a way of getting to the most experienced of players. Ask Ray Floyd.

The turning point, if there was one, came at the par-five thirteenth. With little to lose, Faldo went for the green in two and made birdie. Three behind. Floyd, in turn, hit a poor drive on the same hole and was forced to lay up short of the water and made par. He later admitted that even if he had hit a good one, 'I probably wouldn't have gone for it.'

At the par-five fifteenth, Faldo nailed a 234-yard two-iron over the trees and, unfortunately for him, over the green. Moments later he chipped and putted for another birdie, laying down the challenge for an increasingly timid Floyd who was considering his options back on the tee. Inexplicably, for someone who had gone into the final round nine under on the par fives, Floyd chose to lay up once again and made par. For anybody with a long memory it was an amazing turnaround. In 1976, Floyd had set a new tournament record of fourteen under on the par fives. Indeed, they were the key to his victory that year. Now he was treating them like a husband treats his new in-laws – with too much respect.

Watching his lead slowly ebb away, Ray Floyd must have sensed it might not be his day. On the fourteenth, his birdie chip was heading dead centre for the hole but hit a coin Huston had used to mark his ball. The ball missed the cup by half an inch. Floyd said later, 'Huston asked me, "How's my coin?" and I told him it was okay. I didn't think it was in my way, but it was. The ball would've gone in the hole if it hadn't been for that penny.'

After yet another birdie on the sixteenth, Faldo was only one back. He had decided before the tournament to read his own putting lines, and it was proving to be the right decision. 'The night before I dreamt I made two at sixteen and Fanny had had the same dream,' he said. 'It wasn't a difficult putt, perhaps the easiest you can get on that green, so neither of us was surprised when it went in.'

Floyd then pulled a nine-iron approach into the left half of the seventeenth green, putted up from 38 feet, then barely threatened the hole with the return from no more than six feet. The tournament was now tied. 'That putt just never lost any speed,' said Floyd about the approach putt. The momentum he had had early in the round was gone. Coming up the last, the pressure was really on, but this was an experienced campaigner. Knowing he had to make a par up the eighteenth to force extra holes, Floyd did exactly that despite finding both the fairway trap and the green-side bunker on the way.

For Faldo, it must have felt like Groundhog Day as he faced yet another Masters play-off in fading light. The only difference this time was that instead of the relatively inexperienced American Scott Hoch, he would be facing the battle-hardened veteran Raymond Floyd. It was Britain v. the USA all over again, a European Ryder Cup star against a former American captain, a 32-year-old pitting his skills against a 47-year-old. On the first extra hole, the tenth, Faldo repeated the mistake of a year before: after a weak drive down the right he dumped his three-iron approach into the bunker. Floyd got his drive down and around the corner, then hit his seven-iron approach right on to the green, no more than fifteen feet away. It was dead straight uphill too, exactly the sort of putt you would dream of if you had two to win. Memories of the previous year's encounter were fresh in Faldo's mind. 'I wasn't comfortable at all on that tenth tee,' he recalled. 'I couldn't help thinking, does this mean I'm to be done in this time?'

As Faldo surveyed his bunker shot, the defending champion instinctively knew that Floyd would certainly take no more than two putts. He might even take just one. Knowing that he had to get up and down for par obviously helped, and the subsequent trap shot to within three feet of the hole was a real masterpiece. By choosing to hole out, Faldo left the stage free for Floyd. After taking an age to line up, the American left his putt cardinal-sinfully short. 'Maybe it was the dew,' he said, somewhat lamely.

The American was still making excuses by the time he got to the eleventh green. After taking a comfort stop on the eleventh tee, Floyd found himself way behind Faldo, who was walking at his normal brisk pace down the fairway. Aware that Faldo's drive was at least twenty yards past his own, Floyd noticeably speeded up. It would cost him the play-off. No sooner had he got to his ball than he hit it – a seven-iron that will rank among the worst shots of his career. He pulled it straight left and watched in stunned silence as it splashed into the pond guarding the hole with barely a passing glance at the pin. 'Maybe I was lined up wrong,' he said. 'It didn't feel like I pulled it ten yards left.'

All bets were off. Faldo had been thinking that he might have to take on the water with his second, but now he could play safe, which in his vocabulary meant aiming at the heart of the green, rolling it up close with his first putt and tapping in for his third major. Normally a series like this was food and drink to the machine-like Englishman, but he was nervous, more nervous than he had been in a long time. Turning to Fanny Sunesson, he asked for confirmation about what club to use. They agreed on an eight-iron. Pulling the club from the bag, Faldo prepared to hit his ball.

As he walked off the green later having got his four, Faldo was greeted with a chant of 'Well done, Nick!' from a small but enthusiastic group of British supporters. He smiled back at them. Fanny Sunesson was also smiling as she replaced his Taylor Made putter in the bag. For the bubbly Swede, winning the Masters was a dream come true, and now she could enjoy it. 'I was never nervous on the course,' she insisted afterwards. 'But when we had finished the round, I was shaking.'

For Nick Faldo, winning a second successive Masters had been just as pleasurable. Two years, two play-offs and two victories, all on the same hole; perhaps the committee at Augusta should consider rolling up the green and giving it to him for his garden in Surrey. As he was driven back up the tenth fairway in a motorised buggy, Faldo thought ahead to the presentation ceremony in Butlers Cabin. There would, of course, be no one to hand over the green jacket, but he had his own solution to the problem. 'I remember thinking how nice it would be if Nicklaus were still around to give me the jacket. He'd been the only other player to win the Masters twice in a row. It would have been a great touch, and I'm sure if Nicklaus had been asked he would have done it.' The suggestion was put to various people, but it didn't happen. Mr Hardin did the presenting as usual, and at least there was no problem providing the correct size of jacket this year.

As for Ray Floyd, there was nothing left but the pain. 'This would have meant so much to me, you can't imagine,' he said in the post-match press interview, his voice starting to break with the emotion. 'To be the oldest. To win another major. Nothing has ever affected me like this. At this stage of my life, how many chances are you gonna have? If you're twenty-five and you lose one, you still believe in yourself, you still believe you're going to get a lot more chances.' The par-three tournament hex had struck.

It took Nick Faldo five years to rebuild his swing, but it was only in the summer of 1990 that he felt truly at ease with his game. Throughout the late eighties he had continued to apply radical solutions should any part of his game come unstuck. Unscheduled visits to David Leadbetter in Florida were commonplace, but by the time the 1990 Open arrived in July, both agreed that everything was finally in place. Happy with his golf and settled in his private life, Faldo would prove almost unstoppable.

Having denied Raymond Floyd the opportunity to become the oldest major winner in history at the Masters in April, Faldo could not stop 45-year-old Hale Irwin from taking the prize at the US Open in June at Medinah. In what proved to be an incredibly frustrating week for Faldo, he played brilliantly but missed a ten-foot birdie putt on the very last green which would have given him a share of the lead. He was unable to join Irwin and a once-again-resurgent Mike Donald in their eighteen-hole play-off on the Monday, and it was a huge disappointment for the British golfer (especially as he had set his heart on becoming the first player since Jack Nicklaus in 1972 to hold both the Masters and US Open titles in the same year). Of course, the world is full of 'what ifs', but opinion favours the idea that Faldo would have beaten the 74 shot by both Irwin and Donald – a not exactly far-fetched notion considering his scoring average of 70.85 over the last twelve majors.

Despite his heroics at Medinah, Faldo would not have dislodged Norman from his number-one spot in the Sony world rankings even had he emerged victorious. He was firmly lodged at number two, and people were starting to ask how this was possible; the facts did not add up. In eleven major championships since the 1987 British Open at Muirfield where he had ended tied thirty-fifth, Norman had achieved only two top-four finishes (third in the 1989 Masters and tied second in the Open the same year); Faldo, in comparison, had finished in the top four seven times over the same period, winning three and losing a fourth in a play-off. If that was not number-one form then the wind never blows in Scotland.

Actually the wind was hardly blowing at all in Scotland as Nick Faldo and Greg Norman arrived at St Andrews to battle it out for the 119th Open Golf Championship. It came less than a month after the dramatic finale at Medinah, and the weather on the normally windswept east coast was more akin to Florida than the Kingdom of Fife. A prolonged absence of rain had left the venerable links looking threadbare and arid. Long-iron shots were bounding over bone-hard greens and bad bounces were commonplace. But just as the locals started to lick their lips in anticipation of the fun and games to come, a sustained period of typically Scottish weather in late June and early July left the course looking positively green and lush. It was a complete turnaround, and it left the ancient course virtually defenceless. Its only protection now was if the wind blew hard, but the forecast had already ruled that out by the time the tournament got underway on the Thursday. With the media predicting a record low winning score, a par of 72 would be little more than a figure on the scorecard – and so it proved.

Scheduled to meet with David Leadbetter at the Scottish Open the week before the Open, Faldo was in positive mood despite some intrusive interest from the tabloid press about his private arrangements that week. They got together on the Friday evening for little more than a two-hour 'fine-tuning session' which left his mentor suitably impressed. 'If Nick has a weakness it is that he tends to lose height in the swing,' Leadbetter said later. 'He has to watch that he maintains his correct posture so he can keep his swing on the right plane and not lose much width. But right now, Nick's in the mood. He's in the groove.' Signing off with a final round of 65 at Gleneagles the following Saturday, Faldo headed over to St Andrews to begin his preparations. On the Sunday afternoon, he played a few holes while Leadbetter walked alongside with a video camera. 'It all goes down in the memory bank,' Faldo had said. 'Hardly a day goes by when I do not write down my swing thoughts.'

Everything was falling into place, and for the first time in his career Faldo came into a major tournament expecting to win. Mentally and physically he was definitely 'in the groove', but there was always the odd unexpected distraction to deal with. One particularly noisy distraction was the one caused by Scott Hoch. In the days leading up to the Open, the combative American launched a personal attack on Faldo, saying how little credit he had received from the Englishman in the aftermath of their dramatic play-off for the 1989 Masters. Quite why Faldo was subjected to this carping criticism over a year after the event no one will ever know. As Masters champion, he had conducted himself well, but as always his relationship with the press was testy and often downright antagonistic, a fact to which this latest story, which was published under the banner headline FALDO IS A PLUNKER!, bore testimony. Then, with the tabloids eating up his every word, the outspoken Hoch referred half-jokingly to the two-time Masters winner's lack of popularity among his fellow professionals. It was a view many tabloid hacks were happy to expand upon, as shown by the following quote in one newspaper: 'Nicholas Alexander Faldo began life in a small council house in Welwyn Garden City. Sadly, it remains quite big enough to stage the party when he comes home in his green jacket. The friends of Faldo are few.'

It was all news to Nick Faldo, but, having been paired with Hoch for the opening two rounds at St Andrews, he chose to keep a diplomatic silence. Yet the story, understandably, did little to allay his long-held mistrust of the press, who always seemed to be 'on his back' each time he returned to Britain. (There had been an incident earlier in the year when Faldo was criticised for handing over his Masters green jacket for talk-show host Terry Wogan to try on. The show had barely finished before a tabloid journalist was on the phone to Augusta National to point out the breach in etiquette.)

Away from the sensationalist media, much of the pre-Open hype in the golfing press was focused on the expected showdown between Greg Norman and Nick Faldo. They had competed against each other in the Australian Masters earlier in the year in Melbourne, with the home favourite coming out on top. Norman had then missed the cut at Augusta and struggled home in fifth place at the US Open. So by the time he rolled into St Andrews more was expected from the Great White Shark, and where better to realise those expectations than the home of golf? Norman himself was upbeat about his chances of winning. Having suffered a cruel reversal the previous year at Troon, where he had shot an outstanding 64 in the final round only to lose in the play-off, he seemed determined to make amends. The flaxen-haired Australian wanted to put his growing reputation for last-minute disasters behind him, and was desperate to bag his second Open title (his first had come in 1986). The only thing he needed at St Andrews was a decent start.

Dogged by a run of poor opening rounds in recent majors, Norman finally got his wish. Striking the ball beautifully, he recorded birdies at the first, fifth, tenth, twelfth, fourteenth and eighteenth en route to an opening round of 66. He came within a whisker of driving the 316-yard par-four twelfth and the 354-yard par-four eighteenth, the fast-running conditions obviously suiting the big-hitting Australian, but Faldo hit back almost immediately. Playing just three groups behind Norman, he was also striking the ball wonderfully well. Three under par coming up the last, the tall Englishman surveyed his second shot from forty yards short of the pin. He chose to play a deft chip-and-run with an eight-iron through the Valley of Sin which protected the left quarter of the green. He saw the ball literally collide with the flagstick before disappearing into the hole for an eagle. Faldo punched the air in delight; the shot had transformed a good round into a great one, exactly the sort of outrageous good fortune you need to win the Open. Why, it even had Scott Hoch offering words of congratulation.

The second day too dawned bright and sunny with hardly a breath of wind. It would also provide another Faldo/Norman spectacular, but not before a number of lesser-known players had taken their turn in the spotlight. First to show was English professional Jamie Spence. Having come through both regional and final qualifying rounds, he shot a seven-under-par 65 for a two-round total of 137 which left him temporarily sharing the lead with Nick Price, Mike Reid and Ian Woosnam. Shortly afterwards, Payne Stewart and Craig Parry returned a pair of 68s to reclaim the top spot on the leaderboard, but the newspaper headlines were reserved for the titanic battle already shaping up between Faldo and Norman.

A good run of figures around the turn for Norman, including consecutive birdies at the seventh, eighth, ninth and tenth, was swiftly followed by a confidence-boosting eagle at the 567-yard par-five fourteenth. Another birdie at the par-four sixteenth put him six under par for the round (again) and twelve under for the championship, which is where he would eventually end the day. He was never an avid scoreboard watcher, but Norman could not have helped but hear the cheers going on behind him. Out in 32 after birdies at the second, the fifth, the sixth and the seventh, the new Masters champion drove the tenth for yet another birdie in what had become a real battle for the Ashes. Picking up two more birdies at the fifteenth and sixteenth, Faldo crept past the treacherous Road Hole with par before two-putting the last for a magnificent 65 and a share of the lead. It had been a wonderful contest to watch, and with Faldo and Norman paired together for the next day, it promised even more. 'I am playing well and putting well,' Norman told the press on Friday evening. 'When I get the ball on the green, I feel I am going to make the putt. As for a shoot-out with Faldo, it doesn't matter who I play.'

With the halfway cut falling at one under par, three strokes lower than it had ever been, defending champion Mark

Calcavecchia, Severiano Ballesteros, Curtis Strange, Tom Watson and, sadly, Arnold Palmer, playing in his last Open, would not be around over the weekend. Less mourned was the departure of Scott Hoch. He had looked certain to make the halfway cut with just two holes to play in the second round; then, like many others before him, he had crashed out of the championship after recording a nightmare nine at the Road Hole. Barely a word had passed between him and playing partner Nick Faldo for two days, and Hoch left St Andrews and Scotland vowing never to return. He would not be missed.

With fine weather set for the weekend, more low scoring was predicted, but quite how low nobody realised. First to show on the Saturday morning was Paul Broadhurst, who grabbed some headlines of his own with a fantastic 63, which equalled the lowest round ever shot in the Open's history. 'I was swinging so well I didn't think I could hit a bad shot,' said the Midlands-born pro, who was nursing a small cut over his right eye as a result of banging his head on the door of a telephone kiosk (he was in the kiosk on the phone to the R&A to see if he had made the halfway cut). After Broadhurst, it was the turn of the Australian Ian Baker-Finch, who had bittersweet memories of St Andrews having led the 1984 Open after three rounds only to watch his hopes disintegrate in the final round. On this day there would be no such disasters. He reached the turn in 29 and played the last nine holes in 35 for an eight-under-par 64, fifteen shots better than his nightmare round of 79 six years earlier. Afterwards, Baker-Finch admitted that his game plan had changed overnight after opening rounds of 68 and 72. Having watched the Faldo/Norman birdie-fest on television the day before, he had made a decision to 'go for everything' the following day. It had worked, but Baker-Finch's round was still considered little more than a side show compared with the main event going on behind him.

Given heavyweight billing once again in the morning papers, the head-to-head between Faldo and Norman over the closing rounds was predicted to be a real classic. The most eagerly anticipated day in recent major championship history, it was being compared with the legendary Nicklaus v. Watson clash at Turnberry in 1977. Four strokes clear of Payne Stewart and Craig Parry in joint third, it was thought the winner would come from one of these two players – but which one? Five-time Open winner Peter Thomson was in no doubt. 'Nick has been sensibly working on his rhythm and it's wonderful now. Greg, on the other hand, is a slugger. His swing can vary from one round to the next. It can be very difficult to make it repeat.'

Thompson was right. In pugilistic terms, Faldo had Norman on the canvas moments after the opening bell. Playing the par-four first, the gimlet-eyed Englishman hit a two-iron off the tee followed by a solid approach to sixteen feet. Then, almost before the Australian could catch his breath, Faldo calmly rolled his ball straight into the centre of the cup for an opening birdie, which Norman was unable to match. As they walked to the second tee, he already looked a little shell-shocked, and he made the decision to change tactics. Ditching the game plan that had served him so well over the first two rounds, he decided, like his fellow countryman Ian Baker-Finch, to attack. At the second, he made his new intentions clear by pulling out his driver when previously he had played an iron off the tee for position. Consequently, when it came to playing his second at the 411-yard par-four hole, he was totally out of position. Unable to get the ball close enough in two, he three-putted and fell even further behind.

It was the same story throughout the round, ball-striking errors compounded by tactical mistakes. Norman reached the turn in 36 compared with his playing partner's 33, and the difference widened to four shots at the par-four eleventh when Faldo holed yet another downhill birdie putt from fifteen feet. Now in total disarray, Norman drove into yet another bunker on the par-four thirteenth, which cost him a bogey. Two over par for the day, he dropped further shots at the fifteenth and sixteenth in what was rapidly becoming a horror back nine. Reeling on the ropes as first Baker-Finch then Woosnam and Stewart overtook him for second place, Norman cut a hapless figure as he walked on to the final green. Nick Faldo, in stark contrast, looked fresh, focused and in control. Playing remorseless golf, his thoroughly efficient round of 67 contained six birdies and just one bogey. If it had been matchplay, Faldo would have won 5 & 4, but this was the Open and Norman was too far back to mount a challenge the following day. Simply outclassed, it came as no surprise when he refused to give any interviews after the game.

The final day brought its own pressures for Faldo, who started his round five shots clear of the chasing pack. Rising early on what promised to be another sunny day, he was on the practice ground with Leadbetter shortly after breakfast. Describing it as last-minute 'fine tuning', he was back in his room at the Old Course Hotel by mid-morning hoping to catch up on some of the sleep he had missed out on the previous night. Later admitting to being 'all knotted up', he was in the unique situation of holding a large lead instead of having to come from behind, as in his previous major victories. 'There was much more pressure,' he confessed afterwards.

Payne Stewart, tied with Ian Baker-Finch on twelve under in second place, admitted he would have to 'shoot a low number' to have any realistic chance of catching Faldo. Talking in terms of a 64 or 65, he secretly hoped the championship leader would play defensively, and with a five-shot lead that was always possible. But Faldo was an experienced campaigner and knew the dangers of protecting a lead. 'I just have to keep it going for one more day,' he said after his third-round heroics. 'I have to stay in the same mode, play aggressively and keep going for it. Tomorrow, I will not be content to make pars, I want birdies.'

By 2.30 p.m., Faldo was on the practice putting green behind the grandstand that flanked the right-hand side of the first fairway. With Leadbetter standing quietly off to one side, he continued his routine of putting with just the right hand. Stroking putt after putt with his left hand tucked in his trouser pocket, he cut an almost disinterested figure, but it could not have been further from the truth. Filling in the minutes before his scheduled tee-off time of 2.48 p.m., he stopped for a brief chat with Ian Baker-Finch, his partner for the final round. It was the laid-back Australian who initiated the conversation, even managing to draw a warm smile from the reputedly humourless Englishman. Shortly afterwards, Faldo talked with veteran American pro Doug Sanders, who had also wandered over to offer his best wishes. It was a curious moment. Twenty years ago almost to the day at the 1970 Open, Sanders had notoriously three-putted the final green and been beaten by Jack

Nicklaus the following day in a play-off. If anyone knew how cruel the final round of the Open could be, it was Sanders. 'Hopefully,' one journalist remarked, 'meeting Sanders was not an omen of things to come.'

As at the Masters and US Open, there is always a special atmosphere on the final day of the Open, wherever it is being held, but when it is played at the Old Course at St Andrews that feeling is heightened immeasurably. The most legendary of venues, the spiritual home of golf, it literally bristles with all the great names of the past that have trodden its hallowed fairways. Earlier in the week, Faldo had stood alongside Jack Nicklaus at a gathering of former Open champions that included Seve Ballesteros, Arnold Palmer, Gary Player and Lee Trevino. Some, like Nicklaus and Ballesteros, had been fortunate enough actually to win at St Andrews. No doubt mindful of Gerald Micklem's words, Faldo now hoped to emulate them. 'The enduring truth is that winning at St Andrews sets even the champions apart,' his old friend had said. 'It lifts the truly great golfers away from the rest. There are Opens. And there are Opens at St Andrews. Therein lies the difference.'

Walking on to the first tee from the clubhouse steps, Faldo looked neither left or right. Taking his glove from Fanny Sunesson, he immediately drew out his two-iron and prepared to play. The memory of Medinah was still fresh in his mind, and he had no desire to miss out again. He was here to win, and nothing would deflect him from that purpose, not Baker-Finch, not Stewart, not anyone. As a breeze began to pick up from the west, Faldo followed his playing partner down the left half of the opening fairway. Playing first, he quickly served notice on the rest of the field by landing his second shot on the narrow shelf between the burn and the flagstick. Brave or foolhardy, depending on your opinion, it would have been entirely understandable had Faldo taken the safe option and played for the centre of the green. Instead, his ball came spinning to a halt fewer than four feet from the hole. He stroked it home for a simple birdie three, and in so doing stamped his authority on the final round in the most emphatic way possible. If five shots looked like a comfortable cushion, a six-shot lead looked almost impregnable. Nevertheless, the day was not without its drama.

As he cruised effortlessly to the turn in a one-under-par 35, Faldo's lead over Stewart had been cut to four after the American hit back with birdies at the fifth and sixth. Spectacularly clad in a colourful Stars and Stripes shirt and knickerbockers – 'dressed for a burial at sea' remarked Raymond Jacobs of the *Glasgow Herald* – Stewart spent the remainder of the round patiently working away at the deficit, and not without some success. In typical Muirfield style, Faldo seemed happy to accumulate pars all the way to the eighteenth. Stewart, on the other hand, was throwing everything but the kitchen sink into an all-out attack. With further birdies at the par-four tenth and par-four twelfth holes, he had reduced the gap to just two shots by the time he reached the thirteenth tee. It was getting a little too close for comfort for Faldo. 'When my lead was down to two strokes, it was pretty scary,' he admitted afterwards. 'Anything could have happened. There are so many deep bunkers, and if I had stuck in one of those and run up a score, I would have been in serious trouble.'

In the end, though, it was Payne Stewart who found 'serious trouble', not Faldo. His tee-shot at the par-four thirteenth found the aptly named Coffin bunker down the left half of the fairway. He was forced to play out sideways, which effectively buried any hope the American had of winning. Like Icarus flying too close to the sun, Stewart spiralled back down to earth in flames. Having registered his first bogey of the day, he failed to birdie the par-five fourteenth, then overshot the green at the Road Hole (the seventeenth) to drop yet another shot. And just to rub salt into the wound, he dropped a shot at the last after three-putting from the Valley of Sin. Having run up four fives in the last six holes, he stumbled home in 37 for a round of 71 and a share of second place with Mark McNulty, who had fired a best-of-the-day 65.

At least Stewart had given Faldo pause for thought. In contrast, Ian Woosnam, who never came to grips with the back nine all week, ended up tied for fourth place with American Jodie Mudd after closing rounds of 70 and 72 respectively. And a short time later it would be a story of missed opportunities for Ian Baker-Finch, whose round of 73 had simply fizzled out after a good start. He also finished joint fourth, alongside a resurgent Greg Norman.

So, when Faldo arrived at the penultimate hole with his six-shot lead restored for him, he could, in the words of the legendary Walter Hagen, have 'kicked off his shoes and smelt the flowers'. But Faldo is definitely no Hagen. Two under par for his round, he had no intention of gambling on what was justifiably seen as the toughest hole in championship golf. To constant reminders from Fanny Sunesson to 'take your time', Faldo drove his ball into the wide part of the fairway before nudging his second short and right of the green. Effectively playing the Road Hole like a par five, he then pulled out his putter for the third. Still some fifty feet from the cup, he aimed well away from the cavernous bunker guarding the front centre of the green. Three putts later, he walked off the green with the safest bogey in the Open's history. 'It was the smart play,' he said later. 'Anything can happen at the Road Hole and I would not like to have come to the last green needing two putts to win. I just wanted to walk up the eighteenth and enjoy it, look at the crowd, see people hanging out of the windows, lap it all up. It's every golfer's dream to win at St Andrews.'

How right he was. In comparison with a certain previous occasion on which he had walked up the eighteenth at St Andrews, this was a real dream. Back in 1987, he had been greeted with placards and catcalls having refused to finish out his Dunhill Cup match against Ireland's Des Smyth because of fog, showing little concern for the large crowd that had followed the match in freezing conditions. The incident had often been picked up and brandished as an example of his ruthless and competitive nature. Now, all that was forgotten as they followed him up the fairway like rats after a latter-day Pied Piper, clapping and cheering his every step. The Home hole green put one in mind of a packed Roman amphitheatre as thousands settled down to watch the last act in this virtuoso performance by Faldo. Moments later, he raised his arms aloft in triumph as his final putt gave him victory by five shots. His second Open win confirmed what everyone already knew: here was a British sporting hero everyone could be proud of.

Statistics rarely tell the whole story, but in this case it was different. With his final round of 71 added to his previous scores of 65, 67 and 65, his eighteen-under-par total established a new Open record. He had dropped just four shots all week and accumulated twenty birdies and one eagle. This perform- ance finally silenced the hurtful whispers that he had won his previous three majors almost by default, an idea promoted in the main by American writers. No one could deny the quality of this victory, but Faldo suspected he would still have his knockers. 'You want to play well, but you just can't take risks,' he said afterwards. 'I would have loved to hole some putts just to make life easier, but nothing much happened.'

As a measure of his huge popularity, the grandstands were still packed thirty minutes later when Faldo received the Open trophy. 'It's good to have my baby back,' he said, clutching the silver claret jug that represented his fourth major title in as many years. Humble in victory, he was happy to share the spotlight with the people closest to him. There was his wife, Gill, who had supported him through the worst years of his self-imposed swing changes; his children, four-year-old Natalie and one-year-old Matthew; and, of course, his faithful caddie, Fanny Sunesson. It was a moment to savour for all of them. Moments later, the Red Arrows Display Team screamed across the St Andrews sky trailing red, white and blue smoke. Wiping a tear from her eye, an emotional Gill Faldo later admitted, 'It was hard not to be moved by the whole spectacle of it.'

Nick Faldo left St Andrews knowing he now had a unique opportunity to equal Ben Hogan's record of winning three major titles in one season – not even Jack Nicklaus had done that. This time, however, not even he could mount a serious challenge on the PGA Championship at Shoal Creek Country Club in Birmingham, Alabama. The tournament went to Australian Wayne Grady. In truth, Faldo was suffering from a combination of the stifling heat and an end-of-year fatigue, recording roller-coaster rounds of 71, 75, 80 and 69 to finish seven over par and tied for nineteenth position. It was his worst finish in a major championship since the Masters in 1988, but his record since then had been quite exceptional. Starting with his play-off defeat in the US Open at Brookline, his majors record read as follows: second, third, tied fourth, winner, tied eighteenth, tied eleventh, tied ninth, winner, tied third, winner, tied nineteenth. Brilliant as well as consistent, it is a record that compares with any player this century, including the legendary Golden Bear himself.

In the end, winning the Grand Slam proved beyond him, as did finishing inside the top ten in the European Order of Merit, but his faultless golf game and ice-cool demeanour had undoubtedly made him the player to beat. He had played the greatest golf of his career, his performances at Augusta and St Andrews had impressed everyone, and in the months to come award followed award, plaudit followed plaudit. Already BBC Sports Personality of the Year for 1989, he again finished in the top three. Fêted by everyone from US President George Bush to Margaret Thatcher, he was recognised in the New Year's Honour List for services to British sport.

It had certainly been a long journey from a two-up, two-down council house in Welwyn Garden City, but Nick Faldo MBE had unquestionably arrived.

13. PUSHED TO THE LIMIT

After recording wins in the Masters and the Open in 1990, Nick Faldo was installed by September as the number one ranked player in the world, the first time any British golfer had ever achieved this honour. It served to fuel his insatiable desire for more major championship success. Faldo maintained a busy tournament schedule in Europe and the United States in 1991, finishing high up on the money list on both sides of the Atlantic. He was rarely outside the top twenty in any tournament he played, including the majors, and his consistency was undoubtedly his greatest strength. He had broken through the one-million-dollar barrier in prize money for the first time, but the frustration he felt at not adding to his tally of four major titles was obvious. 'You play the tour events for prize money. You play the majors for the trophies, the prestige and a place in the record books. I'm not saying I don't play to win prize money – I'm saying I want my name to be recognised in the world of golf. I want people to say in twenty, thirty, fifty years' time, they saw me play.'

Come 1992, he was determined to add another major to his haul. After a brief but reasonably successful trip to Singapore and Dubai in February, Faldo spent the rest of the first third of the year in America, managing a joint runner-up spot at the prestigious Players Championship in March. After that, in mid-April, it was on to the Masters, but having failed to make it three in a row in 1991, he ended another disappointing week at Augusta by finishing in joint thirteenth place.

It was after heading back to Europe that his season really started to take off. Commencing with a tied-third finish in the Benson and Hedges International Open at St Mellion in mid-May and ending with the same result in the Scottish Open in July, he put together a fantastic run of form, finishing among the top five in seven events out of eight on the PGA European Tour. He recorded a second consecutive victory at the Carroll's Irish Open in June, then two weeks later put up a strong challenge at the US Open at Pebble Beach only to fall back in the final round to finish joint fourth behind the eventual winner, Tom Kite. In short, Faldo was in great form in the two months leading up to the Open at Muirfield in July and it looked as if no one could stop him making it three titles in six years.

In contrast to the 1987 Open at Muirfield, Nick Faldo came into the 1992 Open confident about his chances of winning. Returning to the East Lothian course that had witnessed the first of his four major victories, he remarked on how it almost felt as if he were 'defending his title'. Yet despite playing his best golf since St Andrews in 1990 added to the fact that every department of his game was in good order, some niggling doubts had been voiced by the press about his ability to win another major. With just two European Tour victories under his belt since his spectacular double-winning season two years earlier, some journalists questioned his continuing desire to push himself to the absolute limits. Others were less forgiving, placing question marks over his competitive nerve – something Faldo took huge exception to.

According to the tabloids, the evidence was damning. At the recent Carroll's Irish Open at Killarney, Faldo had blown a four-shot advantage going into the final round before scraping through in a play-off against South African journeyman pro Wayne Westner. (Ironically, one newspaper had famously sent a reporter to the 1991 Irish Open to write a story about Faldo being all washed up – this just days before he won the tournament.) Then in June, the allegation had resurfaced after he lost the French Open having held a two-stroke lead with just five holes to play. Faltering with a four-over-par final round of 74 was hardly Faldo-like behaviour, they bleated in unison. It was all hugely upsetting to the man himself. He discussed the matter with David Leadbetter in the run-up to the Open, and the decision was made to keep his build-up deliberately low-key, with press and television interviews kept to a minimum. He was there to win, and nothing would get in the way of that.

When he arrived at Greywalls Hotel the Sunday before Open week, the wind was howling and, not surprisingly, the course and practice ground at Muirfield were completely deserted.

Contradicting the media's idea that he liked to take it easy, Faldo headed straight out on to the course accompanied by Fanny Sunesson. Swathed in layers of cashmere wool and waterproofs, he played four holes in the worst of the weather before heading off to the practice ground. The breezy sunshine of California a month earlier must have seemed like a distant memory.

A few days later, the 121st Open Championship began with barely a hint of wind. Quick to cash in on the benign conditions, Steve Pate and 49-year-old Raymond Floyd raised hopes for an American victory with seven-under-par 64s to lead the tournament. One stroke behind was the British pair of Gordon Brand Jr and 1991 US Masters champion Ian Woosnam. Seven under par with two holes remaining, Woosnam was looking at least to match the lowest-ever round at an Open of 63, but his hopes were dashed after a par–bogey finish.

Nick Faldo, meanwhile, made an inauspicious start. He hit his opening drive into a bunker on the first for bogey and was disgusted by his ineptitude. Nine holes later it was all forgotten as a superb eagle on the par-five fifth was followed by consecutive birdies on the eighth, ninth and tenth. Back in the old Muirfield groove, he then recorded another birdie on the thirteenth en route to a superb round of 66. He was later joined on that score by Lee Janzen, John Cook and 22-year-old South African Ernie Els, but the joint fifth place would keep his critics quiet for at least one night.

That evening, Faldo headed back out to the practice green between the tenth tee and eighteenth green, accompanied by David Leadbetter, video camera in hand. They continued to work on a new putting style that involved 'brushing' through the ball. Almost in imitation of a greenkeeper sweeping away autumn leaves, it was intended to improve his pupil's rhythm and timing – and boy did it work. Apart from the tense final round, Faldo would continue his good work on the opening day (he took just twenty-seven putts to get round) by ducking under the magical thirty barrier every time.

Friday, like the day before, dawned bright and breezy. Faldo, in increasingly confident mood, made a solid start with four straight pars followed by birdies at the fifth and sixth. Then,

Right A fresh faced Nick Faldo pictured with Seve Ballesteros during the Irish Open at Portmarnock in 1978. Rivals for many years to come, the Englishman once admitted, 'There was something magical about him.'

Below Looking to the future. Faldo playing a practice round with Jack Nicklaus and Tom Watson shortly before the start of the 1980 Open Championship at Muirfield.

Above With first wife Melanie in happier days at Tudor Cottage.

Left Back from the dead. After two years in the golfing wilderness, Faldo sinks the winning putt at Muirfield in 1987. His first Open Championship, he would go on to win two more in 1990 and 1992.

Left Working with David Leadbetter shortly before the Ryder Cup at Muirfield Village in 1987. One of the most successful player/coach partnerships in golf, they would win six major championships between them from 1987 to 1996.

Below To the victor the spoils. Faldo and family outside Buckingham Palace in 1988 after he was awarded the MBE by the Queen.

Left With the Open Championship trophy at St. Andrews in 1990.

Right Revealing his selection for the Champions Dinner at Augusta National in 1991. A long-standing tradition, the previous year's winner is invited to host an informal get-together of past winners and select the main course for the evening. Reflecting the culinary roots of the host, Faldo chose shepherd's pie in 1990 and steak and kidney pie in 1991. After winning his third Masters title in 1996, he went with traditional British fish and chips.

Right Double take. A smiling Nick Faldo poses with his Madame Tussauds waxwork in 1991.

Left He did it his way. Faldo shows off the silver claret jug after his Open victory at Muirfield in 1992. Moments earlier, he had surprised everyone by singing a few bars from Frank Sinatra's *My Way* before thanking the press from 'the heart of my bottom'.

Left Faldo and Fanny lining up a putt together during the 1994 Open Championship at Turnberry. A dream partnership, they enjoyed enormous success together for most of the nineties.

Right The calm before the storm. With Gill at the 1995 Ryder Cup at Oak Hill. Shortly after, news of his relationship with American student Brenna Cepelak would make headlines all over the world.

Right Commiserating with Greg Norman on the final hole of the 1996 Masters at Augusta. It had been a gruelling and hard fought battle, and Faldo had overturned a six-shot deficit to record his third Masters victory in eight years.

Left A walk in the woods. Brenna Cepelak tries to avoid the cameras at the 1995 Johnny Walker World Championship.

Left Passing on the baton. Faldo with Tiger Woods at the 1997 US Open at Congressional.

Below In relaxed mood with Valerie Bercher.

after dropping a shot at the next, he came to the par-five ninth needing a three-wood to reach the green. Playing what he later described as 'one of the best shots of my career', he landed his ball just three feet from the hole having faced 241 yards into the breeze. With the eagle putt a mere formality, Faldo was out in a four-under-par 32. Now just one stroke behind tournament leader Steve Pate, the remaining nine holes were equally impressive as he amassed four more birdies for a magnificent round of 64 – his best ever in an Open. It was a truly dazzling exhibition of pinpoint iron play and superb pressure putting, and it could, like Woosnam's round the previous day, have been even better. On the par-five seventeenth, Faldo had pulled his second shot wide of the green and was forced to settle for par instead of the birdie he might have expected. That said, Faldo could not have been more delighted. 'I just felt so good inside,' he said later. 'No matter what club I had in my hand, it always felt just right. Never before have I had such a feeling over a whole round. When you consider where we are and that every shot is marked in history, it really is a unique sensation.'

Faldo's two-round score of 130 beat his own Open record set at St Andrews in 1990 and gave him a three-stroke lead over Brand Jr and Cook going into the weekend. At the other end of the scoreboard, the halfway cut fell at 143. Muirfield waved goodbye to the evergreen Jack Nicklaus, who had missed only his second cut in three decades of Open appearances, and also saw off Fred Couples, Colin Montgomerie, Tom Watson and Seve Ballesteros. Not that Faldo even glanced that far down the list when he read the morning papers. For him, the third round was the only thing he wanted to think about. During a chat with David Leadbetter the evening before, both men had agreed that Faldo should look to consolidate his lead; ideally, that meant shooting at least a few shots under par which would increase the gap between him and second place and effectively shut out the rest.

Reaching the turn in a respectable one-under-par 35, Faldo might indeed have expected to increase his lead. Instead, he found himself in a real dogfight, with the unheralded American Steve Pate leading the charge. Storming through the front nine, Pate drew level with Faldo on fourteen under after a bogey on the tenth returned the Englishman to level for the day. The pressure was intense, and with Brand and Cook just two shots further back, Faldo kept telling himself to remain patient. He focused on the job in hand with barely a glance at the leaderboard for eight holes, and when he finally did look up at the scoreboard behind the eighteenth the news could not have been better. He had come home in 34 with birdies at the twelfth and seventeenth and his closest challengers had fallen away one by one. With most of them shedding strokes on the testing back nine, his lead was now four strokes over Cook and Pate, with Els, Brand Jr and Donnie Hammond two shots further back.

Reading the press and listening to the media, you would have thought Nick Faldo had the championship won, the winner's cheque for £95,000 banked and the silver claret jug packed away in the back of his car ready for the journey home to Surrey. Hoping to relieve some of the enormous pressure he felt, Faldo made conciliatory noises at his post-round press conference on Saturday evening. He assured everyone that he would 'take one shot at a time', and told them of how he 'hoped to do well', but no one really thought he could lose, and in truth, neither did he – an opinion later backed up by his nearest contender, Steve Pate, who said, 'I don't know anyone who I would less want to give a four-stroke lead to than Faldo.' But Faldo was right to sound cautious. On Sunday, John Cook, one of the lesser lights of the US Tour, gave the Pringle-clad Englishman the biggest fright of his life.

With such a large lead at the outset, the final round proved a particularly difficult one for Faldo. Aware of the criticism he would face if it all went disastrously wrong, he knew better than anyone what was at stake. If he lost, the tabloids would roll out the old 'Nick Foldo' headlines and his career would be (temporarily, at least) in ruins – such is the wafer-thin line between success and failure for many top sporting stars. Faldo took steps to shut out any negative thoughts from his mind; before the final round he took out a pencil, wrote in big letters on a scrap of hotel paper YOU ARE PLAYING FOR YOURSELF, and placed it in his pocket. It was something he would refer to on and off throughout the round.

On a cold, breezy day that threatened rain throughout, the quality of Faldo's play matched the low-key mood of the weather. He dropped a shot at the first after finding sand, and it seemed for a while that nothing would go his way. Striking the ball solidly enough from tee to green, however, Faldo compiled a front-nine score of 37 – one over par – which was bettered by Steve Pate, who shot a 36. It was obvious that Faldo was lacking the razor-sharpness of the previous three days, especially on the greens. It seemed that no matter how well he struck a putt the ball just would not drop. He missed opportunity after opportunity to stamp his authority on the tournament, and comparisons with Muirfield in 1987 were hard to avoid as he collected par after par.

Inevitably, a degree of frustration set in on the run home. As Pate began to struggle and there seemed to be no one else making a significant challenge, Faldo started playing defensively. And, protecting a three-shot lead with nine holes to play, he began dropping shots. On the par-four eleventh, for example, he pulled his approach left, and with the pin over on that side there was little chance of getting down in two. Two holes later he three-putted the par-four thirteenth, having left no more than a nine-iron approach to the green. Then, after hitting what he thought was a solid drive on the par-four fourteenth, the ball caught the breeze and plummeted into a fairway bunker for yet another bogey. The wheels had come off big-time, and Faldo could sense the awaiting journalists sharpening their pencils in anticipation of a spectacular collapse.

Walking to the fifteenth, Faldo knew he was facing the biggest crisis of his career and struggled hard to compose himself. He glanced up at the leaderboard; the name of John Cook now sat proudly at the top. It had been a remarkable turnaround for the American professional, who was at that time two shots clear of the field. After he had made an eagle at the par-five fifth, his round had been derailed somewhat at the ninth where he hooked his drive out of bounds. Following a calamitous double bogey, the notoriously edgy Cook suddenly relaxed and started picking up shots when everyone else was dropping them. He made birdies at the twelfth, fifteenth and sixteenth, and had picked up six shots on Faldo in six holes since the turn.

The tournament was now Cook's to win, but pressure often has a strange effect on a player, especially during the final round of a major championship – ask Greg Norman. Some players fall apart; others, like Nick Faldo, thrive on it. Even so, with four holes to play that day there must have been some niggling doubts. He had, after all, fresh in his mind some untypical errors he had made less than a month before, including a loss in the French Open when he should have won. Standing on the tee of the par-four fifteenth, Faldo berated himself for the position he had put himself in. The pressure was intense, but he was far from finished as he looked down the narrow fairway. Then, with almost messianic zeal, he outlined to himself exactly what was needed. 'I told myself I would have to play the best four holes of my life.'

Of course, thinking it and doing it are two totally different things. After a solid drive into the heart of the fairway, Faldo left himself with 164 yards to the flag into a crosswind. He discussed the shot with Fanny, then chose to play a three-quarter five-iron – exactly the type of shot he and Leadbetter had been working on earlier in the week. He executed it perfectly. The roar of the crowd behind the green told him what he wanted to know: the ball had come to rest a matter of feet away from the cup. Moments later he holed out for birdie and reduced the deficit to one. It was ample reward for the hard work that had been put in on the practice ground, and it would also prove to be a major turning point at the 121st Open.

Despite his heroics at the fifteenth, Faldo needed some help from John Cook, and on the par-five seventeenth he finally got it. Playing downwind, the American hit the green in two and looked to have the simplest two-putt birdie from around forty feet, or possibly even an eagle. If either had gone in Faldo would have been all but finished, but the pressure of the occasion got to Cook. To his credit, he managed to graze the hole with his first putt, but the ball still finished three feet away. As he came to the second putt, with Faldo at that time in trouble on the hole behind, it really was a case of 'this for the Open'.

The rest, as they say, is history. A nervy nudge resulted in a missed putt for Cook and, under the circumstances, a disastrous par. At the same time Faldo chipped and putted for his par at the sixteenth. Still one shot in the lead with the formidable eighteenth ahead of him, the ashen-faced American clattered his second shot into the crowd on the right and made bogey. Faldo, in contrast, struck a splendid four-iron into the heart of the seventeenth green and, unlike his rival moments before, two-putted for his birdie. Having been match point down, it was now advantage Nick Faldo coming to the last.

It was still advantage Faldo as he sized up his third shot from the back of the final green twenty minutes later. He hit a great drive up the centre of the fairway, followed by a thrilling three-iron that covered the pin for much of its flight, his ball landing hard and running through to the back of the green, leaving a treacherously quick downhill putt. It was definitely not the type of shot you want with the Open at stake. Needing to get down in two for victory, a tense-looking Faldo walked back and forth surveying the ground between his ball and the hole. When he did hit it, all the effort seemed to have been wasted. 'I'm sure many people thought my putt back towards the hole was going to finish short of the cup,' Faldo said afterwards. 'To tell the truth, so did I, but luckily I mishit the stroke and the ball released and trundled to within a foot of the hole.'

At last, something had gone his way. Having coaxed the ball to within inches of the hole, Faldo stepped up and rolled it in for par. Within an instant, a wave of emotion crashed over him. Breaking down, he stumbled across towards Fanny Sunesson, desperately trying to choke back the tears that had welled up inside him. The tension over those last few holes had been colossal. He was still emotional in the media centre a short time later. 'I have never felt so drained,' he said, dabbing away a few more tears. 'The whole thing knocked me for six. I was absolutely gone. I felt physically ill inside.'

Not surprisingly, John Cook felt the same after his closing round of 70. 'I was alive, dead, alive and then very much dead again. I've never gone through so many emotions during a round. That [second] putt on the seventeenth, I expected it to break a little, but it didn't. I didn't hit the stroke well, but at least it clipped the hole. The seventeenth was the key, and I guess I gave away a major championship.' Dignified in defeat, Cook joined Faldo for the presentation in front of the clubhouse a few minutes later. Having finished one shot ahead of Olázabal in third and three shots ahead of Pate in fourth, Cook could justifiably be proud of what he had achieved that day. Ultimately, his reward would be a place in the USA Ryder Cup team to face the Europeans at the Belfry fourteen months later (where, incidentally, he would face Faldo in the foursomes).

Using the new Rextar ball Faldo had helped develop with his sponsors, Bridgestone, he had finished with a round of 73 for a twelve-under-par winning total. Faldo had taken possession of the silver claret jug for the third time in six years, but he had been pushed to the limit in order to win, and it is reasonable to speculate what would have happened had he not won that day. Considering everything that had gone before, what effect would it have had on his career? Would there have been a big enough hole to bury his disappointment had the result gone against him? Even Faldo was not sure. 'I could have lost it all, right there, and that was a horrible feeling. I would have needed a big sticking plaster to heal the wound. At the end it just becomes a battle of the mind, a battle for control. You try so hard to do the right things, to relax, but the pressure takes over. It wears you to a frazzle.'

His hero Ben Hogan used to practise long into the evening because he wanted to know how he would hit the ball when he was tired. Faldo had done the same, and it had paid off. Mentally and physically drained on that nerve-tingling final afternoon, he had emerged triumphant. Nick Faldo was once again the Open champion. When the tall Englishman gratefully received the Open trophy from the hands of Douglas Foulis, club captain of the Honourable Company of Edinburgh Golfers, he confirmed once and for all his place among the legends of the game. The Faldo era reached its zenith at Muirfield that day. Forget Nick Price, forget Greg Norman, forget Seve Ballesteros; Faldo was the player who set the standards, and how they cheered him.

Michael Bonallack, secretary of the R&A, said afterwards, 'He is the greatest golfer we've ever had. He is the most complete professional I've seen since Ben Hogan. He is in a similar mould. He gives the impression that he is very aloof, but that's because he is so single-minded. He has devoted himself to the game.'

Mark McCormack, whose company IMG handled his business affairs, was also full of praise. 'Nick is potentially Ben Hogan. He is the person who attracts more awe and respect among all the golfers of the modern era. Somebody once asked Tommy Bolt if he thought Jack Nicklaus was as good as Hogan, and Bolt replied, "Nicklaus watched Hogan practise, but I have never seen Hogan go to watch Nicklaus practise." Well, Nick's on the way to becoming the Hogan of modern golf – the ultimate professional.' Tony Jacklin, three-time Ryder Cup captain, agreed. 'To dominate, as he did, when the standards are so very high is absolutely fantastic. Yet it really comes as no surprise because he is so single-minded and determined.' 'Nick is the champions' champion,' added Lee Trevino, winner at Muirfield in 1972. 'His ability to concentrate reminds me of Jack Nicklaus in his prime.'

Another thing Nick Faldo had in common with the legendary Golden Bear was that both men had won the Open at Muirfield and St Andrews. Unfortunately, that is where the similarities ended. Jack Nicklaus, as gracious in victory as he was in defeat, handled himself with dignity at all times. He knew what being a champion meant, and always acted accordingly. Sadly, as one now notorious incident confirmed, Faldo did not. With the entire golfing world looking on that cool July evening, he accepted the trophy and proceeded to make a complete idiot of himself. Not only did he burst into an impromptu version of Frank Sinatra's 'My Way', he chose that particular moment to settle some old scores, thanking the press from 'the heart of my bottom'.

At best his comments were ill-timed and ill-advised (as one tabloid hack said, 'If Faldo wanted to declare war on the press, he could not have picked a better way'); at worst they were petty and mean-spirited. Summing up the feelings of many people that day, Mark James recalled the incident in his book *Into the Bear Pit*: 'I remember cringing when he won the Open at Muirfield for the second time. He had won it brilliantly, and he was everybody's hero. Then he made a speech in which he thanked several people from the bottom of his heart and the press from the heart of his bottom before breaking into song. It was incredible. One minute you were admiring the guy completely, and half an hour later you were left wondering what planet he was from.'

James was not alone in feeling this way. Even Gill Faldo later admitted to 'cringing' with embarrassment at her husband's performance, but Faldo was unrepentant. Deeply upset at the coverage he had received in the run-up to the Open, he commented, 'It was just my way of saying [to the media] thanks for putting all that pressure on me. The younger generation thought it was wonderful. The older generation thought, what a bloody fool. It was tongue in cheek. Okay, the timing was probably wrong, but when the hell can you do it?'

The answer to that question is never. And if you do, you never try to justify it afterwards, as Faldo did. In the days that followed, his 'people' blamed his comments on the strain of the occasion, the stress of the week, not having won a major for two years, etc. One unnamed representative even talked in terms of what a witty joke Faldo had told at the press's expense. But, as Doug Sanders once said, 'A champion is not a champion because he wins, but because of how he conducts himself,' and Faldo had done himself no favours that day.

Not that it mattered to Faldo. After the Open he was on a major high for the rest of the year. After Muirfield, he took a much-needed holiday with Gill and his two children, Natalie and Matthew, before making a winning return to action in the Scandinavian Masters in mid-August. After that, he narrowly missed out on making it another double-major winning year after finishing in a four-way tie for second in the US PGA Championship at Bellerive. He ended up three shots behind Nick Price of Zimbabwe, but had good cause to regret a disastrous third round in scores of 68, 70, 76 and 67.

Returning to Britain in mid-September, he repaired some of the damage by winning the GA European Open at Sunningdale, following that up with solid performances in the Lancôme Trophy and Belgian Open. He then rounded off an already remarkable season by defeating a hapless Jeff Sluman by 8 & 7 in the final of the World Matchplay Championship at Wentworth in October. Faldo was becoming unbeatable, and even the indignity of being disqualified in the third round of the Million Dollar Challenge in Sun City shortly before Christmas after a scorecard mix-up made little difference to his buoyant mood. Neither did missing out on the top prize make too much of a dent in his bank balance. He had finished number one in Europe for the second time in his career, and become the first player to smash through the magical one-million-pound mark with total prize-money earnings of £1,220,540.

Another reason to be cheerful at the back end of 1992 was that hastily arranged meeting with the great Ben Hogan. With Dave Marr, former US Ryder Cup golfer turned BBC commentator, acting as go-between, Faldo was invited to join the great man for lunch in the grill room at the Shady Oaks Country Club in Fort Worth, Texas. It was a huge honour, the memory of which Faldo will cherish for the rest of his life.

After meeting Hogan, he was in obviously reflective mood. Repeating what he had said shortly after the Open in July, he said, 'I've always said that I will retire at the end of the decade. After what happened at the Open, I thought I might bring that forward a year or two. But I feel there are a few more majors left in Nick Faldo.'

Sadly, he was wrong on all counts.

14. MEASURING UP TO EXPECTATION

By the end of 1993, Nick Faldo was in analytical mood. He had come into the year on a wave of expectation, but it had turned out to be a case of well done but no cigar. He began the year in spectacular style winning the Johnnie Walker Classic on Singapore Island in February. Then, in July, he added the Irish Open to his growing collection of tournament victories along with a number of top-ten finishes in Europe and the United States. For the remainder of the season he played steady but unspectacular golf to finish a close second behind the new European number one, Colin Montgomerie, by just £60,000.

But it was in the majors that Faldo suffered his greatest disappointments. Even the birth of his third child, Georgia, in the third week in March failed to inspire a lacklustre Faldo at the Masters in early April, where he finished just inside the top forty. He played equally poorly to end up in joint seventy-second at the US Open at Baltusrol, New Jersey, in June. He rallied a month later, defending his title at the Open at Royal St George's, but finished a frustrating second, two shots behind Greg Norman. Then, after completing four rounds in the sixties in the PGA Championship at the Inverness Club, he missed out on the Greg Norman/Paul Azinger play-off by a single stroke. Close, but definitely no cigar.

In typical style, the press speculated on how much winning the Open at Muirfield the previous year had taken out of him both physically and mentally. Suggestions were again made that he had lost his competitive edge, but Faldo remained un-daunted. While in Jamaica for the Johnnie Walker World Championship in December, he outlined a fitness regime that would put Arnold Schwarzenegger to shame. Afterwards, he explained to the press his reasons for this and other changes he planned to make over the winter. 'My goal has always been to say to myself when I retire that I gave it one hundred per cent. I don't want to sit back when I am forty-five and say that I could have done more. There is surely no harm in trying to get the best out of yourself.' When questioned about his lacklustre last twelve months, Faldo gave an answer which confirmed the growing dissatisfaction he felt. 'It has obviously been disappointing. I haven't won the majors. Maybe it was faults in my technique.' And when asked by one intrepid journalist to elaborate on the reasons for his 'failure' in the majors that year, Faldo replied somewhat analytically, 'In 1992 when I was playing well, at least a dozen times [in a round] I would be inside fifteen feet. Then, obviously, when you are not playing as well, the numbers reduce by as much as half. If you are trying to shoot low scores you have got to be around the hole all the time. You've got to be making birdies and I haven't been doing that.'

He assured the waiting journalists that he and 'Led' were going to work hard over the winter to put that right, the focus inevitably turning to rumours about wrist problems. After countless hours spent bashing balls on the practice ground, Faldo had been diagnosed earlier in the season with an inflammation of the left wrist, possibly even tendonitis. Admitting that his wrist was 'not as good as I would like', Faldo went on to describe the intensive treatment he had undergone over the past few weeks, then, almost in passing, remarked, 'I have to be careful how much I do this week.'

On the Monday before the tournament, Faldo surprised everyone by appearing on the practice ground without his shoes and socks. He had first tried it out, he said, at the Ryder Cup three months earlier; it was an attempt to improve balance by removing excessive leg action in the down swing. The exercise had evolved from a David Leadbetter-inspired ploy that originally involved Faldo standing barefoot in a bunker, the idea being that if he used too much leg action he would slip in the sand and fluff the shot. 'You can get more of a sense of what your feet are doing,' Faldo explained self-consciously, already sensing the 'Twinkle Toes' headlines in the next day's tabloids. (Quite how his new shoe sponsors Mizuno felt about him appearing barefoot is anyone's guess.)

But a far more significant change came in his putting method. He had studied hours of video footage with David Leadbetter back in Florida during the summer in a desperate attempt to rediscover the exact set-up he had had when winning the Open.

That quest failed, so he began the tournament at Tryall with a reverse-grip, left-hand-below-right method. The news, when it broke, shocked hardened Faldo watchers throughout the world. Sure, they said, Bernard Langer had tried it, Curtis Strange and Fred Couples had even tried it, but Nick Faldo? The experiment only lasted three holes of the opening round, but the effect on his reputation would last much longer. When he finished the Johnnie Walker World Championship a distant sixth behind the winner, Larry Mize, Faldo was forced to defend the change, describing it as 'little more than something to work on'. The question now was, would he start the 1994 season with this new grip? The answer was yes.

Faldo began his 1994 campaign with some disappointing news. Number one in the Sony world rankings since July 1992, his reign had lasted a record-breaking 81 weeks. Now, as he prepared for his first tournament of the year in Thailand in February, he had slipped to second behind Greg Norman. Of no great importance in itself, it did put him under some pressure to put in a good performance at the Johnnie Walker-sponsored Classic in Phuket if he wanted to regain the top spot. In truth, it was pressure he could have done without so early in the new season. He missed the cut after rounds of 73 and 76, and that established a pattern of failure that proved hard to shake off over the first half of the year.

His ambition for 1994 was to become only the fifth player in history to win all four major championship titles, so he was targeting those that he had not already won: the US Open and PGA. Only Gene Sarazen, Ben Hogan, Gary Player and Jack Nicklaus had achieved this grand slam, but like most New Year resolutions, Faldo's would turn out to be a case of unrealised dreams and dashed ambitions.

He missed his second consecutive cut of the year at the Doral-Ryder Open in early March, but his season picked up considerably with a top-five finish in the Tournament Players Championship in Florida at the end of the month. Then, after another disappointing display at Augusta where he finished thirty-second, followed by another missed cut in the Memorial two weeks later, Faldo continued his climb back to respectability with a confidence-boosting second place in the Benson and Hedges International Open in early May. He was also runner-up at St Mellion in Cornwall, to his old rival Seve Ballesteros, and went one better the following week by winning the Alfred Dunhill Open at Royal Zoute in Belgium. His first tournament win in eleven months, it came after a tense play-off with rising Swedish star Joakim Haeggman. He completed rounds of 67, 74, 67 and 71 and credited his success to some swing changes he and David Leadbetter had made over the winter. He had also been inspired by the acquisition of a shortened putter, and boasted about regaining the putting touch he had lost over the previous six months.

At last, it seemed that the latest round of hard work was starting to bear fruit, and with the US Open beginning two weeks later, it could not have been better timed. Faldo had often stated a desire to play testing golf courses, and they did not come any tougher than the legendary 'monster' in Pittsburgh, Pennsylvania. So named by Ben Hogan after his historic victory there in 1953, Oakmont was a course Nick Faldo had long looked forward to playing, but his first impressions pre-tournament were fairly intimidating. Barely able to break 80, Faldo described it afterwards as 'the most difficult golf course I have ever seen'.

No particular surprise there. A typical US Open set-up, Oakmont demanded long, accurate tee-shots to small greens, which according to Faldo had some of 'the toughest slopes I have ever seen anywhere in the world'. Combined with narrow tree-lined fairways, punishing rough and often unpredictable bounces on the greens, this was a championship that would test the best players in the world. Whether or not Faldo was ready to take on such a challenge was an entirely different matter.

Despite his recent victory in the Alfred Dunhill Open, his overall game felt strangely out of sorts. Uncomfortable with his swing, uncomfortable with his short-game, it came as no surprise when he missed his first cut in a major since the 1986 PGA Championship at Inverness. He finished six over par for the tournament after rounds of 73 and 75, his problems beginning and ending around the greens. 'My game just wasn't consistent,' he admitted afterwards. 'One of the things I felt was weak was eight-irons and nine-irons into the greens. You've got to get those shots close to the pin all the time, but they simply were not there. I simply didn't play as well, or didn't swing as well, as before. You know, there is a fine line between shooting sixty-eights and seventy-fives.'

It was a similar story at the Open at Turnberry in mid-July. Following up a lacklustre 75 in the first round with an inspirational 66 in the second to make the cut, Faldo repeated the roller-coaster ride over the weekend with a 70 and a 64 for a total of 275, which left him tied for eighth place behind the eventual winner, Nick Price, on 268. After that, it was back to America and another exhausting round of tournaments to try to retain his US Tour player's card. Having notched up a creditable joint eleventh in the Buick Open the week before, he finished a very respectable joint fourth at the PGA at Southern Hills in Oklahoma thanks to his second and final rounds of 67 and 66 (the rampant Nick Price won again with an eleven-under-par score of 269). Then, nearly three weeks later, in early September, he made his way over to Switzerland for the Canon European Masters. This gruelling schedule seemed to have little impact on his form. In fact, he seemed to thrive on the arduous nature of it, as his performance at Southern Hills showed.

Away from the course, he was becoming more and more distant from the rank-and-file members of the PGA European Tour. He rarely socialised with anyone other than John Simpson during a tournament, and was perceived as arrogant and aloof. 'Throughout his career, Nick Faldo has made an art form of upsetting people,' said one unnamed professional, citing the 1991 Ryder Cup at Kiawah Island as a prime example of his less than accommodating attitude. There, Nick Faldo had been paired with out-of-form rookie David Gilford in the second-day foursomes. Faldo was suffering from his own drop in form prior to the highly volatile 'War on the Shore', and it surprised no one when they were soundly thrashed 7 & 6 by Paul Azinger and Mark O'Meara. What did come as a big surprise was the way in which the British press lambasted Faldo for his selfish behaviour in the match and his less than helpful attitude towards his shy, softly spoken playing partner.

Another European player who found Nick Faldo non-communicative was Frenchman Marc Farry. Farry was very much looking forward to playing with Faldo shortly after he won the 1987 Open, but Faldo barely spoke a word to him all day. Then, adding insult to injury, he walked off the final green without even shaking Farry's hand. Willing to write it off as single-minded devotion to his game, Farry partnered him again in the Lancôme Trophy at St Nom-la-Breteche not long after. They were joined in a three-ball by Eduardo Romero, and Farry remembers the talented Argentinian holing a full four-iron second shot for an eagle during the round. It was met with huge cheers from the appreciative crowd and backslapping from Farry and his caddie, but he noticed that Faldo remained standing off to one side, stony-faced and concentrating on his next shot. 'Don't worry,' said the highly experienced Romero to the shocked French player, 'he's always like that.' One newspaper journalist later reported, 'Faldo's idea of a good night is dinner for one on his hotel balcony.' Not surprisingly, David Leadbetter disagreed. 'I just think he was so wrapped and so focused. I remember Ian Baker-Finch played with him in 1990 at St Andrews in the Open and Ian was really upset that Nick never said "Good shot", "Boo!" or anything. Didn't say a word to him. I just said, "Well, you have to expect that from Nick – to him you didn't exist. You go play your game, he'll play his, and you meet at the end."'

At the British Masters at Woburn in mid-September, more mileage was added to the distant relationship between Faldo and his fellow European professionals. He took one look at the highly rated but relatively new golf course, and his frustration bubbled over into public criticism of the quality of European Tour venues compared with those on the PGA Tour in America. 'We have not made as much progress as America has made over the last ten years,' he said. 'We cannot do much about the weather, but we can about the courses. If we can make the golf courses irresistible we [the pros] can't help but play them. In the end it's down to money – money grows grass.'

Not surprisingly, these off-the-cuff comments angered many of his fellow players, including former Ryder Cup colleague Mark James, who immediately labelled Faldo a blatant hypocrite. Here was someone, said James, who complained about the lack of investment while simultaneously pocketing a small fortune in appearance fees. Money, he added, that could have been reinvested into the type of courses everyone wanted to play on. Citing the previous week's European Masters over the less than challenging Crans-sur-Sierre golf course in Switzerland, he went a step further and actually accused Faldo of only playing in tournaments where he received substantial amounts of appearance money. In fact, he said, the only reason Faldo had bothered to turn up was because of a lucrative sponsorship deal he had with a Swiss watch manufacturer. If Faldo wanted to play on 'better quality, more challenging layouts', perhaps he should start thinking more about his playing schedule rather than his wallet. 'I think a lot of the top players are dominated by money to a ridiculous degree,' James continued, pointing a finger not only at Faldo but other guilty parties like Ballesteros and Norman. James and others were also incensed that Faldo had taken his grievances to the newspapers instead of discussing them in private. 'We all thought,' said the Manchester-born professional, 'that if Faldo had a problem he should have brought it before Ken Schofield or the [Tournament Players] Committee rather than blurt it out in the press. That was just typical in my opinion.'

Having read the newspapers the next morning, Nick Faldo arrived for the second round in a foul mood, which darkened when he spotted James on the practice range. Faldo made a beeline towards his former Ryder Cup colleague, red-faced and fit to burst. Determined to have it out right there and then, the five-time major winner demanded an immediate apology. James was having none of it. Living up to his sobriquet of 'Jesse', he remained ice cool as the six-foot-three-inch Faldo towered over him menacingly. Reiterating what he had told the press the day before, including his inflammatory comments about Faldo only playing in certain tournaments because of the money, James stood back and dared him to do his worst. As for an apology, Faldo walked away empty-handed.

The 'Woburn controversy' obviously had a major effect not only on Faldo's performance but also on his general attitude towards playing in Europe. Unable to shrug off the bad feeling that had grown up between him and his fellow pros, Faldo ended the week in a sheepish thirteenth position after a not very surprising 74 in the second round, the day of the confrontation with James. Respected rather than liked, Faldo had never been the most popular player on the European Tour; now, relations were at an all-time low. 'Nick had a tendency to ignore people when he shouldn't and say the wrong things at the wrong times,' argued Faldo's former caddie, Andy Prodger. 'He's not trying to, but he just does.'

The following week Faldo was in Paris for the Lancôme Trophy. Insisting that his comments about European Tour venues were only ever intended to be constructive, he continued to dismiss Mark James' claim that his schedule was based on how much appearance money he received. Dogged by the press from the moment he arrived from London, Faldo had inadvertently opened a major can of worms and it was proving extremely difficult to put the lid back on. When rumours of possible disciplinary action by the European Tour were added to the mix, something had to give, and on the Wednesday before the tournament something finally did.

Arriving for a pre-tournament question-and-answer session with the press, Faldo seemed agitated and ill at ease. Giving off the impression that he would rather be anywhere else in the world than there, he was quickly ushered to his seat by the tournament press officer. He glanced nervously at the microphone set up on the table in front of him, acting as if he were about to be strapped to an electric chair. He flicked the microphone with his fingers to make sure it was on and looked around the room before taking a gulp of water from a glass in front of him. He was obviously preparing himself to say something unpleasant, but what? Within minutes we knew, as a tabloid journalist stood up and fired off the first question.

'Nick, can you just explain if the rumours about you going to play full-time in America next year are true?'

'Yes, they are,' said Faldo, agitatedly tapping the side of his glass with a biro.

'Was it a difficult decision for you to come to?'

'No. It was the easiest decision in the world after all the shit that has been thrown at me by you guys,' Faldo replied, staring at a couple of tabloid reporters sitting in the front row. He continued in the same accusatory vein. 'Last week I came in [to the interview room at Woburn] with the intention of saying something and you got the wrong end of the stick. That was the last straw. I have been misquoted for the last nineteen years and I am fed up with it. There is a small element you need to sort out.' He looked at the tabloid hacks again. 'If you want me to change, put your own house in order first.'

This outburst marked an all-time low in terms of Faldo's relationship with the British press. He headed straight back to the relative calm of America after a seventh-place finish at St Nom-la-Breteche, and later confirmed that one of the main reasons for turning his back on Europe was to get away from the tabloid press. 'They ask you simple questions,' he explained, looking for a measure of understanding, 'like what's the golf course like? And how are you playing? I might say, "Well, not so good, really, could be better." The next day the headlines say "Moaning Faldo"! I'm trapped. I can't say "No comment" and walk away. There is no doubt I can talk more freely in America.'

How did things reach this stage? It had been a long-running conflict dating back more than twenty years. Faldo was first criticised by the press for throwing away the lucrative golf scholarship at the University of Houston in the mid-seventies. Forgotten, if not forgiven, by the time he turned professional in 1976, perhaps the real turning point came four years later, at the Kenyan Open in March 1980. It was a fairly innocuous incident, but it was to have an immeasurable effect on Nick Faldo's attitude to the press over the coming years.

While partnering his long-time rival Sandy Lyle – who, incidentally, received no criticism whatsoever after failing his entrance examinations to the University of Houston – Faldo noticed that a sticking plaster had been placed on the top of Lyle's putter to stop the sun's glare from distracting him while he putted out. Unsure of the exact ruling, Faldo said nothing to Lyle but reported the incident afterwards as they signed their scorecards. Lyle had indeed broken the rules, albeit unwittingly, and was immediately disqualified for having 'altered the playing characteristics' of his club. Cast in the role of villain, Faldo pleaded his innocence, but the golfing press was not in sympathetic mood. What they really took exception to was the way in which Faldo had waited until Lyle had signed his card before saying anything. They contested that had Faldo mentioned it out on the course, then the likeable Scot would have received nothing more than a two-shot penalty.

Once he had been portrayed as some vindictive, win-at-all-costs competitor, the battle lines were well and truly drawn. In the decade that followed, the 'Kenya incident' would be used as a stick with which to beat Faldo every time he and Lyle were in contention for the same tournament – which in the late seventies and early eighties was fairly often.

Lyle and Faldo are polar opposites in temperament and nature: Faldo is focused, Lyle is laid-back; Faldo's success has been the product of many years' hard work, Lyle is the most naturally gifted golfer of his generation. They have been rivals throughout their entire golfing career, even as amateurs; of course the press were not beyond adding fuel to the fire with so-called quotes from Faldo criticising Lyle, and vice versa. Yet as Lyle would later comment, they would never be the best of friends. 'For what he has achieved I have a high regard for him. But the channels he has taken to get there have lost him a lot of friends. It's the tunnel vision he has. He's not the sort of person I'd drop in to see for a cup of tea.' The two men were never close, and were never likely to be, but the 'fierce' rivalry talked about in the press was often blown out of all proportion.

As a result of the 'Kenya incident' and others along the way, Nick Faldo's attitude to the press has always been a negative one. In the wrong mood, he can certainly prove temperamental, awkward and wholly self-centred. Even during his glory days of the early nineties he often gave the impression that he would far rather visit a dentist than talk to a golf journalist. But like many things printed in the newspapers, the truth always tends to get blurred along the way. For example, there is one well-known story from the early eighties concerning his former caddie Dave McNeilly that is often used to enforce the idea that Faldo is tight and mean-spirited. According to this tale, Faldo pulled up McNeilly about the state of his trainers.

'Isn't it time you bought yourself new ones?' Faldo asked, looking down at McNeilly's left shoe which had opened up at the toe.

'Yes,' replied McNeilly, 'I will when I'm less strapped for cash.'

With that, Faldo pulled out a wad of cash held together with an elastic band. 'I don't believe it,' McNeilly thought. 'He's going to pay for some new trainers.' Then, before he could catch his breath, Faldo removed the elastic band and handed it over. 'There,' he said, 'use that!'

Today, Dave McNeilly laughs about the incident, describing it as a private joke between the two of them that was taken seriously by the media. 'You cannot believe how many times I've heard that story repeated. While Nick was always careful with his money, he was always pretty generous to me.' Surely another myth put to the sword.

Another misleading impression perpetuated by the media concerns Faldo's on-course demeanour. Through the use of terms such as 'miserable', 'sour-faced', 'glum', 'fed-up', 'gloomy' and 'despondent' they have constantly reinforced the idea that Faldo is like that all the time, which is patently untrue. As many journalists have found out over the years, Faldo can also be charming, polite and occasionally downright funny. 'People say he could really afford to be more pleasant out on the golf course,' said David Leadbetter, 'but that's just not Nick's way. He focuses hard and just does what he has to do.'

This sunnier side often emerges in one-to-one interviews. Arouse Faldo's interest with an attention-grabbing question, usually about his golf swing, and he will gladly chat away with few, if any, glances at the clock. Away from the tabloid hacks, he can be surprisingly animated about a whole range of things, including fishing (his one great sporting passion other than golf), flying helicopters, golf-course design, fast cars, music and, increasingly in recent years, his Faldo Junior series for up-and-coming golfers. He may not fit everyone's idea of a well-rounded human being, but he has certainly proved over the years just how touchingly human he can be.

Nevertheless, Faldo has often been his own worst enemy when it comes to dealing with the press. Mark James once compared Faldo to Seve Ballesteros, describing him as 'very guarded, almost secretive', and he certainly is when it comes to talking about his private life. Notoriously thin-skinned about his off-course relationships, Faldo can be defensive to the point of rudeness whenever a journalist seeks to question him about one incident or another. Unlike tennis star Pete Sampras, who will maintain an icy silence whenever something personal pops up at a press conference, Faldo will do the exact opposite. Often following up a brusque reply of 'no comment' with a detailed reason why he is saying 'no comment', he will mumble and stutter until his patience finally snaps and he turns on the questioner. He then seems genuinely surprised when his victim writes something derogatory about him the following day. As David Leadbetter once explained, 'He's been burned a few times and puts up a wall.'

A 'wall' is an apt description when talking about a press briefing with Nick Faldo. In recent years, especially in Britain, he has developed the nervous habit of looking at anything other than the person he is talking too. He is a surprisingly shy and vulnerable character. More often than not he will gaze down at his hands, rub his nose, even finger the microphone until the question has been satisfactorily answered – body language that shouts in the clearest possible terms, 'Leave me alone!' Counting the minutes from start to finish, he will half-rise from his seat long before the press has finished grilling him and say, 'All right, then?' Rarely is anyone brave enough to say, 'One more question, Nick.'

In his defence, Faldo has often been quoted as saying that he wished to be judged on his record and nothing else, but, sadly, that's not the way of things in modern sport. Increasingly, readers want more than just facts and figures fed to them on a daily basis. They want an insight into the player's life, his or her personality, dreams and ambitions. In return, the rewards for top sportsmen in certain sports (including golf) are vast in terms of appearance fees and sponsorship deals. Perhaps Faldo should have been made to understand a long time ago that talking to the media is a responsibility for someone in his position, not a chore, and that dealing with them is the inescapable result of playing well and being successful.

But modern sportsmen do have more reason to be wary these days. 'We used to meet up in the bar for a chat,' said former columnist for the *Telegraph* Michael Williams in an item for *Golf*

World on the relationship between golfers and the press, 'while these days the players seem to get dragged away by their managers to discuss their latest contract. There was much more trust then than there is now. They are suspicious of all of us, largely because of the attitude of the tabloid press. The players have to be careful what they say.'

The largest-selling British newspapers are tabloids, and they compete with each other ferociously and relentlessly. The same applies to the golf reporters who work for them. While many are honest, upright citizens who have the best interests of the game at heart, there are others who like to take the truth, stretch it, rename it, give it a paint job and then, as Faldo believes, make the facts fit the story, not the other way round. This process was described by one American golf writer as 'journalism on steroids', and there are plenty of British pressmen who would agree with him. 'Before any money came into golf, they [the tabloids] weren't interested,' said Chris Plumridge, author of eight books on golf. 'With the money came the rat pack. They will stop at nothing – absolutely nothing. And if there isn't a story, they will create one. They are a disgrace.'

'We do tend to stereotype people a bit too easily,' confessed Dai Davies of the *Guardian* in the same piece in *Golf World*. 'Then we look for ways to prove our point. But what these players fail to realise is that all publicity is good publicity. People see a name and remember it; they don't always remember the finer details. I saw a couple of Americans following Faldo who said, "There's Nick Faldo and that's his wife caddying for him." They hear stories about him and stories about his wife, and put two and two together.'

In the coming months, people would be putting an awful lot of twos together.

15. DRAMA AT OAK HILL

After nineteen straight seasons playing tournaments in Europe, Nick Faldo quit the PGA European Tour and IMG announced that he had officially joined the PGA Tour in the United States and would play nineteen tournaments there. He would still play a small number of events in Europe, including the Volvo PGA Championship, the Scottish Open and the Open itself, but most of 1995 would be spent honing his game on the most competitive circuit in the world of golf. The apparent hastiness of the switch surprised many people, but, unbeknown to them all, his decision to play full-time in America had been made long before that.

As far back as February 1994, Faldo had discussed the possibility of moving over to the United States lock, stock and Mizuno golf clubs. It was while watching coverage of the Hawaii Open back home in Surrey that the idea had first been brought up. In short, Faldo was tired of playing in Europe. Returning to the same courses season after season, competing against the same players, he felt stale and for the first time in years was not looking forward to the new season. As for Gill, she seemed surprisingly open to the idea of splitting her time between Europe and America. The details of such a move remained to be worked out, but it was no secret that her husband preferred the practice facilities over there and by basing himself at Lake Nona near Orlando (Gill had never been there before) he could be much nearer his mentor, David Leadbetter, with whom he had been meeting up just once every four to five weeks on average – never enough for the ambitious Faldo.

Faldo discussed the matter a few days later with his manager, John Simpson, and the more he considered the possibility of playing full-time in America, the more excited he became. For the past decade, Faldo and other top European players had been limited in the number of tournaments they could play in America as 'foreign' players. In January 1985, as a result of a long-running battle between PGA Tour supremo Deane Beman and the notoriously stubborn Seve Ballesteros, it was ruled that all non-tour members would now be required to play a minimum of fifteen tournaments in a season or lose their playing privileges in the United States. It was an impossible situation for any European golfer who wished also to play a full schedule on his home tour, an underhand way of forcing star names like Ballesteros over to the PGA Tour on a full-time basis. (Prior to this ruling, Ballesteros, like Nick Faldo, could pick and choose what tournaments he wanted to play in based purely on Ryder Cup exemptions, sponsors' invitations and the rollover system that meant a good finish the previous week automatically qualified the player for the next.)

The ruling effectively presented 'foreign' players, including Greg Norman, with a take-it-or-leave-it ultimatum. If they decided not to play the full schedule, they would be restricted to just six events a year on the PGA Tour, not including the Masters, US Open and PGA Championship. Of course, that brought problems of its own, not the least of which was the enormous amount of extra travel involved. As Faldo had shown in 1994, top European players were often forced into the ludicrous situation of playing for two weeks in America sandwiched by three or four in Europe (not to mention being coerced into using up their six-tournament allowance if they wanted to play in warm-up events prior to the three US majors). The situation placed Faldo, Langer, Woosnam and the rest at a big disadvantage compared with their American colleagues. Was it any wonder that Ballesteros described the PGA Tour's ruling as a 'thoughtless decision that can only harm international golf'?

It was somewhat serendipitous that Nick Faldo's decision to apply for full US Tour membership coincided with the appointment of an enlightened new commissioner, Tim Finchem. A forward-thinking individual fully aware of the major role international golfers had to play on the PGA Tour, he slowly relaxed some of the more draconian restrictions put in force by the previous administration – a move no doubt inspired by Greg Norman's announcement in November 1994 that, with the support of Rupert Murdoch's Fox Television, he intended to start a World Tour of thirty events (including eight three-million-dollar events) which would involve the top thirty to forty golfers on the Sony world rankings list. (It never got off the ground, but the idea formed the basis for the World Series events introduced by the PGA Tour in 1998.)

These were fast-changing, exciting times, and Faldo desperately wanted to be part of it. He was fed up with the second-rate courses and practice grounds and, above all, the bloody awful weather in Europe. 'I chose to go to America because I wanted to play a lot more in January, February and March to prepare myself for the majors,' he said. 'Then I could work hard for nine months and the rest of the year I would be winding down. Plus the sunshine is great and the weather is a major factor.' After a year that had promised so much but delivered so little in terms of success in the majors, Faldo's growing frustration with the European Tour had been obvious – especially at Woburn in August. For any other player, top-ten finishes in both the Open and US PGA would have been more than acceptable, but for Faldo it was nothing but a disappointment. Even his victory in the Alfred Dunhill Open earlier in the season had brought little joy, as did the £523,320 in prize money he won by finishing eighth in the European Order of Merit (not to mention the cool quarter of a million dollars he won in America along the way).

In order to win more major championships, Faldo instinctively felt that he needed to improve his putting stroke, and to do that he needed consistent greens like those found on the PGA Tour in America. 'The greens here are different than in Europe,' he said. 'You've got to learn to putt on faster greens with more break, and that's part of the reason I want to learn to putt in the States.'

Nevertheless, the final decision to play full-time in America could not have been an easy one to make, for Faldo or his family. He and Gill decided to play it by ear. The first thing they had to do was find somewhere to live. Faldo suggested that Gill could follow him on tour with the help of a full-time nanny, plus a tutor for the children, but this was quickly dismissed as impractical. Instead, they decided to rent a home in Lake Nona from January onwards, with the intention that their two children, Natalie (eight) and Matthew (five), would stay at school in England, Gill splitting her time between Florida and the family home in Surrey (the possibility of educating them in two different countries was considered for a short time, but school terms did not match, and neither did the educational systems). The children would only be uprooted when a proper family home had been built at Lake Nona, which looked likely to be some time in the late summer of 1995 (a plot of land was bought in April). It meant at least six months of travelling back and forth between Florida and London, but it seemed like the ideal situation (unlike her husband, Gill never suffered from jetlag).

They both looked upon it as a new start; Gill would have the task of supervising the building and decoration of their new home while her husband headed out on tour. More importantly, they would get to spend a lot more time together as Faldo intended to head back to Florida in between tournaments, or, if that was impractical, Gill would fly out to join him wherever he was. Indeed, he had already intimated to his manager and long-time friend John Simpson that he believed a more settled family life would lead to a renaissance in his career, which ultimately it did.

After celebrating Christmas and New Year in England with his family, Faldo, accompanied by Gill, packed his bags and headed off for an extensive tune-up with David Leadbetter at Lake Nona. He was a little rusty after his winter break, but everything seemed on track as he prepared to head off to Arizona and the Northern Telecom Open.

Coming hard on the heels of the season-opening Mercedes Championship in California, the tournament was unusual in the fact that it was played over two courses: Tucson National and Starr Pass. Little more than a warm-up event for the Phoenix Open the following week, it was more a time for renewing old acquaintances and catching up on winter gossip – not that Faldo was one for doing either. The tournament was scheduled for 19–22 January, and Faldo arrived early on the Monday hoping to work on his game. On Tuesday, he had started his first practice round when an attractive but plainly nervous blonde-haired girl strolled up to him on the course. Her name was Brenna Cepelak, it was her twentieth birthday and she was a student at nearby Arizona State University. She was also a big fan, and it showed in every animated gesture. Brenna had been dared by her friends to ask him out on a date, and Faldo took the fumbling approach in good humour, along with her telephone number. Not ungallantly, he promised to telephone her and wish her a happy birthday, and that is exactly what he did.

Attending college on a hard-earned golf scholarship, Brenna Cepelak was a talented golfer herself. A member of the Arizona 'Wildcat' team along with her fellow 'stars' Ulrika Johansson and Heather Graff, she was part of a squad that had dominated intercollegiate golf in the area. Playing off a three handicap, she was highly rated by her golf coach Rick La Rose and looked to have a career in the professional game beckoning. But all that would fade into the background as her relationship with Nick Faldo blossomed beyond that first meeting. Over the coming twelve months plenty of reasons would be given as to just why their affair began. Maybe he was flattered by the attention. Maybe he felt the need for some entertaining and youthful company after a winter at home with the wife and kids. Whatever the reason, it would be the start of a relationship that would last well beyond any short-term fun and games. Faldo struggled hard to keep his new friend a secret. In the end that would prove impossible, but for now it was business as usual as he set about rebuilding his career.

After a solid enough start to his campaign at Tucson, where he finished tied twenty-fifth after rounds of 70, 70, 70 and 68, the next few months Faldo spent sharpening up his game in preparation for the Masters in April. In the first week in February he headed over to California for the AT&T Pro-Am tournament at Pebble Beach. He was joined there by Gill, who had flown over from Britain with a family friend.

He finished with rounds of 66, 72, 76 and 67, his ninth place at Pebble Beach boosting his prize-money earnings to just under $50,000 in just three weeks. Having missed the cut the following week at the Buick Invitational of California tournament, Faldo headed east to Florida with Gill, spending the last two weeks of February looking for a suitable plot of land around Lake Nona to build a new home and working on his game with David Leadbetter.

With Gill back in England, Faldo returned to action in the first week in March at the $1.5 million Doral-Ryder Open in

Miami. Striking the ball wonderfully well and putting even better, he crafted rounds of 67, 71 and 66 for a share of third place going into the final round. Trailing joint tournament leaders Greg Norman and Peter Jacobson by just three shots, he was not expected to win – neither, surprisingly, was Norman. Instead, the bookmakers made the in-form American the favourite on the strength of his back-to-back victories at Pebble Beach and the Buick Invitational. Faldo was in determined mood, however, and in a tense final round during which all three players batted the lead back and forth, Faldo managed to post a three-under-par 69, despite making a nervous bogey on the very last hole. In doing so he set the clubhouse lead on fifteen under par. Neither he nor anyone else expected it to be good enough to win, but it was. Edging out Norman and Jacobson by a single stroke, Faldo was as surprised as anyone to record his fourth PGA Tour victory, his first since the 1990 Masters. His decision to play full-time in the United States had borne rich fruit earlier than anyone could have imagined, and this was confirmed by a second-place finish at the Honda Classic a week later. In the words of the British press, the American lifestyle obviously suited him (not that Faldo was a fan of American culture or indeed Americans, describing them in private as brash and impolite).

A month later, he headed south to the Masters knowing that victory would take him to the top of the PGA Tour money list for the first time. Refreshed after a brief holiday with Gill at their rented home in Lake Nona, Faldo arrived at Augusta in confident mood. 'I've played eight tournaments and took the week off last week because I was getting a little tired,' he admitted at the pre-tournament press conference. 'But I came out here and I stayed out here. I'm very pleased with the way it has worked out.'

Another thing that 'worked out' was the unexpected way in which the American crowds took to him. American golf fans loved his knockabout style, the way he pretended to stumble on the green after missing a putt – in fact, everything about him. And Faldo responded in kind. Showing a hitherto unknown side to his personality, the Englishman found he could relax more during tournaments. Without the British press around, dogging his every footstep, he worried less about what he said and how he acted, or whether or not his ex-wife had popped up with another quote for him to respond to. Faldo had also gone out of his way to make friends on the US Tour, something he never did in Europe. One of his closest pals was Brad Bryant, a journeyman pro whom the American press had nicknamed 'Dr Dirt' because of his perpetually scruffy appearance. They shared a passion for fishing, and the two men were often seen heading off to the nearest lake in between tournaments. 'He fishes much like he plays golf,' Bryant said. 'He makes sure he has the right fly, the right rod, the right line. He's so precise about everything.'

In stark contrast to his reputation back in Europe – surly, ill-tempered, uncommunicative – Faldo was seen in the US as charming and witty, perhaps even funny (he was once described by Jacobson as the 'funniest Englishman since John Cleese'). His depreciatory humour wowed audiences from coast to coast, and in a sport lacking in real superstars he stood out head and shoulders above the rest. The PGA Tour had a real catch, so they were delighted when Faldo announced his intention at the Masters to carry on playing in America. 'Same thing,' he said when asked about his future plans. 'Leave the family at home, come over and play here.'

Quite what Gill Faldo thought about that comment as she watched her new Lake Nona home begin to rise from its muddy plot is anyone's guess. She continued to push forward with everything she and her husband had planned, dealing with American builders, plumbers and sanitary specialists, and at the same time making plans to bring her three children over to Florida during the school holidays in July.

But the rumours were growing. Speculation was rife in the days leading up to the US Open at Shinnecock Hills in June and continued through to the Open at St Andrews in July.

Gill was feeling increasingly uneasy about the situation. She decided to confront her husband about the rumours after the final round of the Open on Sunday evening. She asked him straight out whether he was seeing another woman, and he denied it completely.

Meanwhile, any dreams Faldo had had of winning his fourth Open evaporated on the Thursday after an opening round of 74.

To his credit, he hit straight back with a superb 67 to make the halfway cut, but that was as good as it got. A mere shadow of the player that had conquered St Andrews in 1990, the Englishman stumbled around the Old Course like a blind beggar fishing for change. Finishing with two 75s for a three-over-par total of 291, he ended up in joint fortieth place, adding another disappointing major championship performance to his joint forty-fifth place at the US Open and his joint twenty-fourth at the Masters.

Faldo headed back to London on a private jet with Gill. A few days later, he was back in America competing in the Buick Open at Grand Blanc, Michigan. Not that things got much better there. He ended the week tied for fifty-seventh place after roller-coaster rounds of 72, 67, 75 and 69, and it was the same story a few days later in the PGA Championship. Situated just outside the sprawling metropolis of Los Angeles, the Riviera Country Club course was a long-time favourite, but a lacklustre Faldo could do no better than joint thirty-first. Nick Faldo had run out of gas, and with just three weeks left to the final Ryder Cup qualifying tournament in Germany, the pressure, both on and off the course, was becoming intolerable.

Having drastically reduced his European Tour schedule at the end of 1994, Faldo was no longer able to qualify automatically for the Ryder Cup team on points. This meant that to make the team he would have to rely on a wild-card pick by European team captain Bernard Gallacher. Normally this would not have been a problem, but with serious question marks hanging over his form his selection was not the certainty it had once been, and Faldo knew it.

How different things had been a few months earlier. Having followed up his victory in the Doral-Ryder Open in March with a string of top-five finishes in the Honda, the Nestlé Invitational, the MCI Classic and the Buick Classic, Faldo had been a surefire pick to play against the Americans at Oak Hill that September. By the end of May there had even been talk of him becoming the first European to top the United States money list. Now he could hardly break into the top forty of any tournament he entered. There was also the problem of captain's picks. In previous Ryder Cups, nine players qualified automatically for Europe while the captain selected three others; now, the rules had been changed allowing the captain just two wild cards, bringing Europe into line with the United States. And with class players like Ian Woosnam, Mark James and Irishman Philip Walton dancing around the edge of automatic qualification, the mathematics were suddenly horribly complex.

Faldo, not surprisingly, thought the new system favoured the Americans, and lost little time in outlining his views at the Buick Open in August. Calling for a return to three picks instead of two, he said, 'They should move the goalposts. For the good of the Ryder Cup we must have our best guys. Simple as that.' When grilled about his crumbling form by the British press, Faldo's desperation was obvious for all to see. 'They knew I was coming to America, so in theory I was taking one spot – hopefully. That left just one real spot open. We're going to play a tough US Open-style golf course and we must have players who are familiar with that style of golf.'

In theory, that was true, but the only question now was whether Bernard Gallacher agreed with him or not. In the end, Faldo need not have worried. Along with Ian Woosnam, he was selected to make a record-tying tenth successive appearance in the Ryder Cup, but with the match less than a fortnight away he was forced to withdraw from the Lancôme Trophy in Paris with a wrist injury (he had jarred his right hand playing in an exhibition in Germany on the Monday of tournament week). Rumours quickly began to circulate about a substitute being brought in, but a spokesman for Faldo said his withdrawal was merely precautionary. 'There is nothing to panic about,' he added. 'Faldo will be practising all next week in Florida with his coach, David Leadbetter.'

He was not the only player with health problems. Having already lost 1994 Masters champion José-María Olázabal to a long-standing toe injury, Gallacher also had doubts about the fitness of Bernhard Langer, Seve Ballesteros and David Gilford, all of whom had complained of back problems in recent weeks. Like Faldo's damaged wrist, each of those complaints would turn out to be fairly minor, but in a European team boasting seven professionals aged 37 or over, it was a concern (Team USA was not much better, with five forty-year-olds in the final line-up and only Phil Mickelson aged under thirty).

Faldo's wrist injury actually became a convenient excuse to escape the attentions of the British press. Amid reports in the *Sun* newspaper that Faldo had asked his lawyers to work out the cost of a divorce settlement, it was left to his agent, John Simpson, to deny reports of an impending split between the couple. 'Nick and Gill are not getting a divorce,' said Simpson adamantly. 'This is a non-story.' With Faldo already in the United States, Gill flew out with the rest of the European team on the Monday before the match. In a week dogged by intrusive reporters she seemed determined to support her husband's efforts to win back the Ryder Cup.

In that respect, she was spectacularly successful: Europe completed one of the most unexpected victories in Ryder Cup history. Trailing by nine points to seven going into the final day, Faldo looked to redeem what had been a fairly poor week by his standards. He resumed his highly successful partnership with Colin Montgomerie, but any magic they had had two years before at the Belfry was now sadly gone. Faldo slipped to defeat in both his opening-day matches, his tortured state of mind best summed up by an incident in his morning foursome match against Tom Lehman and Corey Pavin. Already one-down, Faldo left his partner in deep rough on the par-four second after thinning a relatively simple pitch through the green. He then berated Lehman for holing his par putt after it had already been conceded. 'When I say it's good,' barked an annoyed Faldo, 'it's good!' Lehman got the message but had no intention of being intimidated by his more experienced opponent. 'I told him to speak clearly,' he reported afterwards. 'He claims he said a couple of times that my putt was good. I wasn't going to put up with any crap, especially after he stretches his arm out as if to say, "Put the ball in your pocket, you idiot!" I was hot.'

After winning the first three holes to establish a formidable lead, the British pair spent the rest of the round playing catch-up, finally achieving parity on the par-three fifteenth after Lehman's tee-shot hit a spectator before bouncing into thick rough. Coming to the final hole still with everything to play for, Faldo drove into the rough on the right. Monty had to pitch out into the centre of the fairway, which left Faldo with a straightforward wedge shot into a raised green. He dumped it into a sodden bunker, long and right. From there, the big Scot was unable to threaten the hole and had to settle for bogey. In contrast, the American pair found the green in regulation and, despite having to wait while excess rain water was sponged away, safely two-putted for par and a one-up victory. It was the first point on the board for the USA, and it established not only a pattern for Faldo but for the early part of the Ryder Cup. As Lehman said later, it was 'a statement that Europe's best team could be beaten'.

In their afternoon match against Fred Couples and Davis Love III it was a similar story. Montgomerie was playing solidly, but Faldo's putting kept letting them down at crucial times. Having missed a number of short putts in the morning match, most notably from three feet at the fifth, he looked tentative and edgy. He was unable to sink a vital six-footer on the par-four thirteenth for a win, and the Americans eventually ran out winners by 3 & 2.

Resisting the temptation to split them up, Captain Gallacher persisted with the Faldo/Montgomerie pairing in the opening foursomes on the second day. Nicknamed 'Snooty and the Blowfish' by some of the American golf writers after their ill-tempered display on day one, the British pair bounced back admirably with a 4 & 2 win over former Wake Forest University pals Curtis Strange and Jay Haas. But if the margin of victory was impressive, the quality of their golf certainly was not, nor had it been. Having played fifty holes in their first three matches, the so-called European dream team of Faldo and Monty had quite simply failed to deliver. Collectively four over par by this stage, it came as no surprise when they were split up for the afternoon fourball matches, Montgomerie going out with Sam Torrance and Faldo with Bernhard Langer.

Matched against Loren Roberts and Corey Pavin, the Anglo-German pairing was unlucky to lose. Renewing a Ryder Cup partnership that had worked so successfully at PGA National in 1983, where they won three matches out of four, they battled back from being one-down at the turn to all-level by the last. For Faldo it must have brought back memories of the previous day, but this time he managed to find the green in two with neither of the Americans threatening to make birdie. Faced with a straightforward putt from eighteen feet, Faldo must have fancied his chances of winning the hole, especially after Roberts two-putted for his par. Having missed the fairway off the tee, Langer was effectively out of the hole; Faldo and Pavin, equidistant from the cup, would decide the outcome of the match. Unlike his opponent, the tenacious American faced a treacherously quick downhill chip from the back of the green. Advantage Faldo – at least it was, until Pavin chipped his ball right into the middle of the hole. Amid scenes of utter chaos, the tiny American clenched his fist in celebration. 'I had the luxury of being able to have a free run at the chip,' he gasped later. 'I didn't care if it went ten feet past. It looked like it might pop out of the hole for a second, but it sank right down to the bottom.'

Poker-faced, Faldo waited until the noise died down before addressing his putt for a half. He surveyed it from all angles, but the putt, when it finally came, was a big disappointment. Never really threatening to go in, it rolled past the hole by some distance. It was his third defeat in two days; the 445-yard par-four eighteenth was not destined to go down in his top-ten list of most favourite finishing holes (at least for now). Worse still, it was a point Europe desperately needed. They were trailing by two going into the singles, a series of matches that traditionally favoured the USA. Things looked bleak for the visitors. 'Phone it in, mates,' said Woosnam to a gathering of British reporters. 'It's time to catch the Concorde home.'

Not surprisingly, American team captain Lanny Wadkins was on a real high at Saturday evening's press conference. 'Yeah, I'm real confident,' he said. 'I have twelve guys playing well, but this is golf and a two-point lead is not big enough.' Wadkins was right to be cautious. If the history of the Ryder Cup revealed anything, it was that anything can happen, and usually does. That was certainly the case at the Oak Hill Country Club the following afternoon as the tide finally turned in Europe's, and Nick Faldo's, favour.

Few Ryder Cup matches could be clearer in Faldo's memory than his epic tussle with Curtis Strange at Oak Hill in 1995. Yet for every winner there is a loser, and Curtis Strange must often have wondered how it ended up being him. Picked as wild card by his old university buddy Lanny Wadkins, Strange instinctive-

ly felt he had something to prove. No longer the player that won
back-to-back US Open titles in 1988 and 1989, his selection for
the Ryder Cup at Oak Hill had already attracted some carping
criticism from sections of the American press. Strange was
ranked outside the top fifty in the world, but Wadkins defended
his decision on the grounds that you needed an experienced
competitor like Strange when the going got tough – comments
he would regret by close of play on Sunday.

With Bernard Gallacher packing the middle order with his
most experienced players, Curtis Strange must have smiled at
the irony of finding himself up against his old rival Nick Faldo.
They knew each other well, and Strange must have thought he
had the psychological edge having beaten Faldo in that play-off
at Brookline to win the 1988 US Open. The match itself proved
to be a tense battle between two of golf's greatest tacticians.
With barely the width of a scorecard between them all the way
through, Strange nudged ahead for the first time at the par-five
sixth, only to be pegged back at the next after making bogey.
Having levelled the match, Faldo fell behind again at the
par-three eleventh, and Strange was still one-up as they reached
the penultimate hole. 'What I really remember about that day,'
said Faldo, 'was looking up at the scoreboard and doing some
quick maths with two holes left to play. I was in the eight match
[of twelve] and I suddenly thought, "Oh boy, my match is
important!" I thought if I could turn it around it would make a
big difference.'

Faldo was right, it would make a huge difference. The
previous hole had been halved with bogeys, but the quality of
the golf was unimportant as both men wrestled desperately for
control. Holding a narrow lead as he played his second to the
458-yard par-four seventeenth, Strange was the first to crack.
Accompanied by frenzied shouts of 'Fore right!' his approach
sailed wide of the green and handed the advantage over to
Faldo. Unfortunately, it was a fairly short-lived advantage as he
hit an equally poor approach that found the front left bunker.
After three shots, Strange was eight feet away putting uphill for
par while Faldo was a foot nearer on the same line. Strange
missed, Faldo holed, and the match was level with the
eighteenth left to play.

The atmosphere of the match had now changed considerably, in keeping with its importance to the overall result. Over the previous two hours, European fortunes had picked up considerably with unexpected wins for Howard Clark, Mark James, David Gilford and Colin Montgomerie. Europe had closed the two-point gap, so the Faldo/Strange match assumed a massive importance. It was no exaggeration to say that the destiny of the Ryder Cup now lay in their hands. Faldo, however, did not feel 'one hundred per cent' confident as he walked up to take his tee-shot. Twice already he had reached this point in a match only to lose out, and after pulling his drive into the left-hand rough it looked as if he was going to crash and burn again. With most of his team-mates watching from the sidelines, Faldo was forced to chip out within pitching-wedge distance of the hole, but his ball ran through the fairway into the first cut of rough. His problems were building by the second; with Strange assessing his options from the centre of the fairway after a wonderful drive, things could not have been much worse. 'I was trying not to think whether my match was going to be the turning point, but I could sense it,' Faldo said later. 'You really have to play from the heart.'

Watching from the edge of the fairway, Captain Wadkins, walkie-talkie in hand, must have been congratulating himself on his inspired choice of wild card. A few minutes later, however, his dreams were in tatters as Strange failed to find the green with his three-iron approach. Landing short and left, it left the double US Open winner with an impossible chip to a raised green out of ankle-high rough. Looking at the two lies, it was hard to know who had the more difficult shot.

Lining up his shot from 94 yards out, Faldo hit the most exquisite pitching-wedge shot of his career. The ball landed on the firm green and bounced twice before finally coming to a halt just six feet from the hole. Considering the enormous pressure he was under, it was a magnificent stroke. 'Playing that wedge was the most nervous I've ever been,' he admitted later. 'I just told myself not to hit it too hard, I didn't want it to go long. And coming out of the semi-rough was great because I didn't want it to spin back too much. It came out perfect. It's one of the best shots I've ever played, if not the best.' The pressure was firmly back on Curtis Strange, who scrambled his ball on to the green and somehow managed to stop it within eight feet. The applause both men received as they stepped on to the green was definitely deserved that day.

The end, when it came, was typical Faldo. He was unable to watch as his opponent lined up his putt. A loud gasp from the partisan crowd told him that Strange had missed. Now it was his turn. It was not the actual putt that won the Ryder Cup, but it might as well have been. Left with a hugely quick, right-breaking putt to take the match, the Englishman had never felt such pressure. 'Everything was shaking,' he said later. 'Everything except the putter.'

Having played such a brilliant approach shot, Faldo knew he had to capitalise on the golden opportunity he had carved out for himself. Stepping up to the ball, he fought hard to dismiss all the negative thoughts that were racing around in the back of his mind. What if I miss? What if the ball rolls past the hole and keeps on rolling? What if I three-putt? But he slotted it right into the heart of the cup and stood with his arms aloft in victory. Faldo, five-time major winner, the greatest pressure-player of his generation, had done it again. Speaking afterwards, he said: 'That was the greatest scrambling par of my life. It was as good as Muirfield in 1987. Actually, it was tougher, because if I miss it goes four feet past and I have to start negotiating with Curtis.' Perhaps the biggest compliment of all came from Seve Ballesteros, who said later, 'If I had to bet my life playing the last hole and trust someone, Nick Faldo would be my choice.' 'When Nick put that putt in at seventeen,' said an emotional Ian Woosnam, 'then won at the last, I knew then we had won the Ryder Cup.'

The tide had finally turned in Europe's favour. Faldo's victory over Strange by the narrowest of margins took the visitors ahead by 13 ½ to 12 ½. This meant the Americans now needed to win the Mickelson v. Johansson match and halve the Haas v. Walton match just to keep the cup alive. And with Haas two-down with two to play, that looked unlikely.

For the record books, it was Philip Walton who officially gave Europe a 14 ½–13 ½ victory after closing out Jay Haas on the last hole of their match, but everyone watching that day knew that Nick Faldo had made the difference. Reliving his experiences in that match, an emotional Faldo said:

> When everything was churning inside me going into those last two holes, I had to fight to keep my legs still. When I knew how important it was for me to win, I wondered, 'Can I still do it?' It is what you are supposed to do . . . it's what you train yourself for, going on to automatic and soaking up all the pressure. But when things haven't been going so well, you find yourself asking, 'Will it ever happen to me again?' Well, it did, and I'm so grateful I had the chance to contribute to the team. You just don't want to let anyone down. You see the guys working and suffering and really digging down, and then when it is all done you say, 'God, I'm glad I was able to be part of that.'

Over six decades, the United States had only lost the Ryder Cup six times, and only twice on home soil. Many experts blamed the defeat on the PGA Tour and its emphasis on winning prize money over winning tournaments. Out of twelve singles matches, five went down to the eighteenth hole; out of those five, the United States lost four and halved one, which placed a big question mark over their competitive nerve. The American press lambasted their fellow countrymen and their attitude. Without actually mentioning players like Faxon, Haas and Maggert by name, none of whom had won a tour event in the last two years, they pointed out how players had become 'lazy' picking up huge cheques every week for very little effort. Harsh criticism indeed, but perhaps the harshest of all was reserved for Lanny Wadkins' two wild-card picks, Fred Couples and Curtis Strange. Ignoring the strong claims of Lee Janzen and Jim Gallagher Junior, both of whom had won two PGA Tour events in 1995, Wadkins had chosen experience over youth and paid the price. The blame would fall squarely on his shoulders over the coming days and weeks. 'America lost the [Ryder] Cup in a week Nick Faldo made two birdies, Seve Ballesteros hit three fairways, and the European captain forgot Ian Woosnam existed,' wrote Rick Reilly of *Sports Illustrated*. 'America lost the Cup with the number-one player on the PGA Tour money list, Lee Janzen, sitting on his couch at home.'

Not surprisingly, a lot of his American colleagues agreed with him, concentrating particularly on the folly of picking Curtis Strange as a Ryder Cup wild card. Keeping his dignity throughout, the two-time US Open winner had come within one putt of being hailed as a national hero; now he would have more battles to fight. 'It's a frightening thought,' he said in the post-match press conference, 'how I'm going to feel when I wake up and realise we didn't win.' Golf fans' memories are long, especially when it comes to the Ryder Cup. The following March at the Honda Classic, a heckler shouted at Strange, 'Bogey, bogey, bogey! Ryder Cup choker!' Strange, coincidentally partnered by Nick Faldo that day, did his best to ignore the interruption but the Englishman was having none of it. Pointing out the heckler to tournament marshals, he demanded he be removed from the course, which he duly was. 'It was the worst thing I've seen in almost twenty years of playing professional golf,' said Faldo. 'He has no idea of the pressure of playing at the top of a sport.' Declining to discuss the incident, Strange would only say afterwards how 'appreciative' he was of Faldo's actions. But the scars from Oak Hill would live on long after the European team had headed home on Concorde, and not only for Curtis Strange.

Gill Faldo had also conducted herself with great dignity under extremely difficult circumstances. Less than a month before the Ryder Cup, on Bank Holiday Monday, 28 August, she had been told by her husband that he wanted out of their relationship. (A possible divorce was not mentioned until many months later.) Both of them had just flown back to England, she from Florida to see the children and he from the NEC World Series tournament in Akron with the express intention of telling her it was all over. For Gill, this was a nightmare come true. After twelve years of reasonably happy marriage, her husband was now leaving her and her three children for a woman half his age. Under any other circumstances, his decision would have been almost laughable, but knowing the enormous impact it would have on her children, her family and her friends when the press got wind of it, Gill kept her emotions tightly under control – at least when her husband was around. When he was not, the floodgates opened, with even HRH Prince Andrew drafted in as a marriage counsellor.

Shortly before being given the devastating news, Gill had gone upstairs to unpack Faldo's travel bag. (Since she dealt with his paperwork, it was commonplace for her to go through his bag and pick up his hotel receipts, etc.) It was there that she had come across some photographs that showed her husband on a fishing trip in Canada with his arm around a young blonde. Gill had thought at first that the woman must be the daughter of the local gamekeeper, and it was only when her husband delivered his bombshell that she made the link. The girl in the photograph was Brenna Cepelak, the twenty-year-old student from Arizona.

In the long days leading up to the Ryder Cup, an unreal calm existed in the Faldo household. As he went out to practise at nearby Wentworth, Gill would get on with her daily life almost as if nothing had happened. Midway through September, she declared her intention of going to the match in New York no matter what objections there might be from her wayward husband or anyone else. She reasoned that if she were to miss the Ryder Cup, the press would want to know why. Besides, she thought she *deserved* it. She travelled on Concorde with the rest of the players and their wives, comforted by the support of her many friends on the team, making the trip without her husband who was conveniently working on his game with David Leadbetter in Florida.

It was a terrible time for all concerned, but especially for Gill Faldo. With her every move photographed and written about as rumours grew apace about the state of their marriage, she dutifully greeted her husband on the tarmac on his arrival in New York with a kiss. She might have put on a brave face for the television cameras, but she spent much of the week sobbing her heart out in the privacy of their hotel room. Buoyed by a bottle of sleeping pills that gave her some respite from the hurt she obviously felt, she bravely accompanied her husband to the many functions that preceded the Ryder Cup. With the entire world looking on, they smiled, held hands and generally kept up the pretence that everything was fine. All week, Gill fought desperately hard to save what was left of her marriage, but with little or no success. On the course Faldo had publicly shunted her away in favour of embracing Seve Ballesteros after victory had finally gone Europe's way. Gill suspected that her husband knew that Brenna would be watching on television.

After the Ryder Cup was over, Gill and her husband flew back together on Concorde, barely speaking to each other. They headed back to the home they still shared in Surrey knowing it was now only a matter of time before the press published the story about Faldo and his new love affair. The situation was becoming intolerable for both of them. In the meantime, Gill still believed things could be put right if only she could talk to her husband about their problems. Sadly, she would find the time for talking long over. When, at the end of October, news of his adulterous liaison with Brenna Cepelak hit the headlines, the Faldos had already gone their separate ways.

John Simpson was given the thankless task of announcing their break-up on Monday, 23 October, adding, 'Gill and Nick request privacy for themselves, their family and friends.' Even as he said it, Simpson must have known what a pipe dream that would be. After all those long weeks of speculation, the news triggered a feeding frenzy in the tabloid press, news editors dispatching reporters to every corner of the golfing globe in search of a new angle on the story. At home with her children Natalie, Matthew and Georgia, Gill found herself literally under siege. Refusing to answer questions about a reported $11.8 million divorce settlement, she not only found journalists squatting outside her house all night but also noticed that some had even sifted through her rubbish. Desperate for a juicy quote, one persistent hack had left 27 messages on her answering-machine in one night alone.

So their marriage, predictably, ended in a blaze of publicity. One newspaper cruelly pointed out that their relationship had begun as an affair back in 1984, and had ended the same way. Faldo had expected the worst, 'and that's exactly what we got'. Genuinely surprised at the level of interest his break-up with Gill had caused, he later admitted, 'We had a month of hell, courtesy of the British tabloids . . . They listen in on phone calls, things like that. You ask for privacy and they watch Gill and the children at the house for a month.'

Little had changed by the time Faldo entered the Tour Championship at the end of October. A veritable army of press and photographers was waiting outside his hotel just outside Tulsa, Oklahoma, on the day he arrived. As his car pulled up, the media pounced, hardly giving the occupant time to get out. 'Nick, Nick, over here!' they shouted. 'Hold on, stop shooting!' their victim yelled back. 'I'm Nick Price, not Nick Faldo!' Never letting the truth get in the way of a good story, one tabloid ran a story the following day saying how the 38-year-old Faldo had flown to Tucson to be with Brenna Cepelak, shoving in a picture of him arriving to prove it. Coming hard on the heels of another report that stated how he planned to start a new life with her in America, the *Sun* newspaper described Brenna's so-called reaction at the news: 'Faldo's young mistress jumped for joy and said, "He's my dream lover."'

Unable to escape the media spotlight, Brenna was forced to quit classes at the University of Arizona a month later. Quite simply, the situation had become intolerable for her. She had been forced to hide in the boot of a friend's car on more than one occasion in order to escape reporters; two had even been arrested for disorderly conduct after barging into Brenna's ironically named Communications 200 class in late October. Charged with the little-known crime of 'interfering with the peaceful conduct of an educational institution', the hacks were sent for trial in January 1996, but by then Brenna had already had enough. 'Basically,' said Faldo, talking about the tabloid press, 'they go at you until you crack.'

Having said her goodbyes to her fellow players in the Arizona Wildcats golf team, Brenna requested that no information from her enrolment forms be released to the press (the Dean of Students office had already been asked for this information on numerous occasions). It was a sad moment for all concerned. A talented golfer and well-liked student, Brenna Cepelak would be missed, and not only by her fellow students. Interviewed for the *Arizona Daily Wildcat* newspaper, athletics director at the university Jim Livengood commented, 'I probably know more about it than I should. That's his personal life, and Brenna Cepelak's personal life, and those are decisions that people are allowed to make. I know she's a good person, I think an awful lot of her. If that turns into something, I hope it works out. She dropped her classes for the semester, but I hope she comes back to school here because she has a great future. She's a neat young lady.' Golf coach Rick La Rose was more forthright in his views, having lost three of his best players over the autumn period. 'We've had one player drop out, one transfer and one run off with Nick Faldo!'

For the next few months, the couple would be followed and photographed everywhere they went, bringing even more heartbreak to Gill back in England. Things were now mercifully out in the open. John Simpson's continual denials that anything was wrong between Faldo and his wife prior to the Ryder Cup in September, despite strong evidence to the contrary, appeared misjudged. Simpson was a loyal servant, but his consistent denials put Gill in the terrible situation of having to put on a brave face to support his words, making life far more difficult for her than perhaps it should have been. Nick Faldo, on the other hand, remained typically unrepentant, frequently complaining about the treatment he was receiving at the hands of the tabloid press. 'The very annoying thing is they can just make up a story and you can't do anything about it. You've got no recourse. You're powerless. You're just a victim.'

Nick Faldo a victim? In truth, he and Brenna had been spotted 'out' together on several occasions leading up to the break-up of his marriage, and the press had chosen to say nothing.

Saint or sinner, depending on your opinion, it does beg the question of how he managed to keep his wits about him at Oak Hill, especially on that dramatic final hole against Curtis Strange in the singles. What sort of person can shut out his personal life so effectively that he is able to perform at such an incredibly high level in a top-class sporting arena? Only Nick Faldo can answer that particular question. Certainly, in the past he has shown an uncanny ability to separate his private life from his very public one. Rarely has his golf suffered because of personal issues, no matter how upsetting they might have been at the time. Indeed, the opposite is often true, as demonstrated by the form he showed throughout the 1983 season. That year he won five tournaments en route to becoming the European number one, during the period when his relationship with his first wife Melanie was disintegrating into argument and recrimination.

Remarkably, the dramas of the back end of 1995 would have a similar effect on his game, and as his relationship with Brenna blossomed so did his career. Having been all but written off in certain sections of the British press, Faldo would bounce back better than ever.

16. THE COMEBACK KING

Despite the many disappointments of the past few years, Nick Faldo always believed that he had at least one more major championship in him. Having begun a strict fitness regime back in November 1995, the former two-time Masters winner arrived at Augusta in the second week in April looking strong enough to take on the world. Proving that six months is a long time in golf, as in politics, he also appeared far happier than he had the previous October at the Tour Championship when news of his relationship with Brenna Cepelak had first hit the headlines. The whirlwind of controversy that had greeted his decision to leave his wife and young children had given him the haunted look of someone who had just seen his world turn to ashes. Now, with everything out in the open, at least he could start building for the future, and for the 38-year-old Faldo that meant winning tournaments again, perhaps even another major. 'The majors are what motivate me,' he said. 'That and just winning.'

The signs for a Nick Faldo revival were already good. In the run-up to the Masters, Faldo appeared to have recaptured some of his old rhythm with a string of top-ten finishes including the Buick Invitational (joint eighth) and the Honda Classic (tied ninth), but his best result had come in the season-opening Mercedes Championship in January. He had qualified for the exclusive winner-only event via his victory in the Doral-Ryder Open the previous season and set about taking full advantage of his inclusion in the select field. Recapturing some of his former putting touch, he shot rounds of 70, 69, 68 and 67 at the La Costa Resort in Carlsbad, California for tied second place behind the eventual winner, Mark O'Meara. It was an impressive showing, but Faldo was still not completely happy with his game. 'By the time I get to Augusta,' he said confidently, 'I should be comfortable with everything.'

One month later his opinion had not changed. Two weeks before the Masters Faldo was in Ponte Vedra Beach competing in the Players Championship at Sawgrass. Coming into the tournament having recorded scores in the sixties in eleven of his last twenty competitive rounds, his confidence was high. When asked for the reasons behind this unexpected revival, Faldo talked about his improved putting, his work with David Leadbetter over the winter, the video analysis they had completed since February and even the new golf balls he had received from his Japanese sponsors, Bridgestone. Then, almost in passing, he gave the true reason. 'I think better,' he said, without any further explanation.

That had long been the secret of Faldo's success. Even in the dark, distant days of the mid-eighties when he underwent those revolutionary swing changes, he was able to compete because his mind was strong enough to handle everything at once, including the pressure of competition, as his long-time mentor Leadbetter confirmed.

He was a great thinker. He would manage his game very, very well. He was a great putter. He also worked the ball well – he was very good at hitting three-quarter shots and things of that nature. He was also a tenacious competitor, very focused and self-centred, as many of the top players are. Plus he had great rhythm in his swing, which was one aspect we were able to build on. He was always very auditory. He was always clicking his fingers and whistling. That is where his rhythm came from, I'm sure.

Then there was Brenna Cepelak. Having announced to the world that she was travelling with him full-time from the start of the year, he was now free to concentrate on his game and nothing else. Clearing his mind of all the niggling distractions that had seen him steadily slip down the world rankings since January 1994, Faldo could finally see light at the end of tunnel – and for once it was not an oncoming train. Then, out of the blue, came another problem.

Unable to complete his second round in the Players Championship because of rain, Faldo arrived early on the Saturday morning still hoping to make the halfway cut. With most of the round still to play, he warmed up on the practice ground in a damp, heavy mist before heading out on to the course. But he had only walked a few steps when he heard a loud crack. The pain was excruciating for the second or two it lasted, but it quickly wore off, leaving him with nothing more than a lingering stiffness in his neck and shoulders. Looking concerned, his caddie Fanny Sunesson asked if he wanted to continue. He did, a decision which could have been the biggest mistake of his career had he aggravated his condition. Instead, the biggest problems he faced were not being able to make a full back swing and not being able to track the roll of the ball on the green because it hurt so much to turn his head.

He added a three-over-par 75 to his first round of 70, and it came as no surprise to anyone when he missed the cut. Describing his neck problem as little more than a 'spasm', Faldo seemed happy with his overall game and dismissed any suggestion that he might not be at Augusta in a fortnight's time. 'My game is ready to blossom,' he said to some British reporters, 'and hopefully some good things are in store.' He knew how invaluable experience was at Augusta, and they did not come any more experienced than Nick Faldo. 'Experience pays dividends there,' he said. 'You have to know what you are doing out there. You have to know when to be aggressive and when to hold back. You can't miss a green and expect to get it up and down. The greens are too fast and too difficult. Out there you have to play pretty well. You have to hit great shots all the time. That's why it's such a great test.'

Nick Faldo then took an early flight to Orlando to link up with David Leadbetter, accompanied by Brenna. He arrived in Florida two days earlier than planned, but once there he and Leadbetter concentrated on fine-tuning his game for the upcoming Masters, especially his putting. Having reverted to a more traditional putting grip since the 1995 PGA Championship at Riviera, Faldo had briefly slipped into his more controversial left-below-right grip during the second round of the Doral-Ryder Open in early March. 'It was just too mechanical,' he said, giving his reasons for the change, but with Augusta just days away he mentally resolved to stick with his old method no matter what. Aided by a new Odyssey putter with a composite insert in the striking face, the improvement in alignment and ball striking was staggering. He had been asked by Leadbetter some weeks earlier to 'stand taller over his putts', and Faldo's putting at Lake Nona was as impressive as it had been all season. 'Lead noticed I was taking the putter back shut and lifting it too quick. He got me to stand as tall as I could to get the putter swinging like a pendulum with no wrists, just swinging it from the shoulders, which freed up my stroke. It made all the difference.'

Faldo was top of the PGA Tour putting statistics before the Bay Hill Invitational in March, and the dual change in putter and method would prove the key to his success over the coming four months. Not surprisingly, he arrived at Augusta National full of confidence. Yet it was not all wine and roses as he set about preparing his Masters challenge. He had finished outside the top twenty in all four majors the previous year, and many so-called experts were openly speculating that his best years were behind him. Faldo hardly gave them a thought. He still believed he had another major in him, so why should he worry? 'Everybody's been banging the drum,' he said shortly before the tournament began, 'criticising me that I have been getting too technical. But me and Lead just laugh. We'll carry on doing it our way.'

Experienced enough not to make any rash predictions that might add to the pressure, Faldo played down his chances all week. 'Lead just got me following through a little bit better,' he said about his week at Lake Nona, 'and that is really all I have been doing.' Leadbetter, who like Brenna Cepelak would accompany Faldo all week, was far more upbeat about his pupil's form. 'Everything is starting to come together,' he said knowingly. 'His personal life is settling down and it's helping his golf. He's had a lot of distractions but he's very settled now. I really think he could do something special this week.'

Another confidence-boosting addition to the Faldo armoury was a new hi-tech titanium-headed driver he had been using since Bay Hill. It gave him greater length off the tee and would prove to be a useful asset on the 6,925-yard, par-72 Augusta National course, especially on longer holes like the thirteenth and the fifteenth. From past experience, Faldo knew what a vital role these two par-five holes often played in determining the final outcome. 'You have got to do well on the par fives,' he said.

'You've got to be at least six under on those holes for the tournament to have any chance.'

Another interesting change in his pre-Masters routine was the amount of practice balls he was hitting, or lack of them. Since the start of his career back in the mid-seventies, Faldo had routinely hit hundreds of practice balls as if his life depended on it. That fervour had now been reined back in favour of promoting better tempo in his swing. 'Hit fewer shots but hit them better' was the new mantra, and who could argue with that? 'You can't win any golf tournament without feel and half-shots,' Faldo would say later, and he was right. Instead of pounding ball after ball down the practice range, Faldo's warm-up now comprised in the main a series of gently hit half-shots with a five- or a six-iron. Then, just before playing, he would hit the same clubs in the same order as he would during the round; for example, a driver and a seven-iron for the first, followed by a driver and a two-iron for the second, and so on.

Having already played the opening round cleanly in his head, Faldo stepped up on to the first tee, partnered by the larger-than-life figure of John Daly. The difference in style between the two men could not have been more marked: Faldo the tall, athletic and reserved Englishman who treated every shot with as much care as a dentist extracting a wisdom tooth, and Daly the rotund, chain-smoking, hard-living American who simply gripped it and ripped it. Yet below the professional surface they had more in common than many realised: each of them had won the Open, they hated speaking to each other and both were facing costly divorces.

It was Faldo who came out on top in the end, despite being out-driven by obscene distances on almost every tee. His three-under-par 69 was his best opening round at Augusta for six years. Daly, going well too, fell back to a one-under-par 71 when he hit a tree with his final tee-shot and double-bogeyed the eighteenth. As soon as the round was over he stormed off to the car park. A fearless spectator got an autograph out of him, but it was left to his second wife, Paulette, to explain the problem. 'This is a tournament he really wants to win,' she said. 'He has been working very, very hard pointing to this week.

He's really into it. He figures if he can just be close heading into Sunday he has a chance to win.' In contrast, Faldo was delighted with his opening round. 'I'm very pleased,' he said after signing his scorecard. 'It's my best round here in a long, long time. I played what I call "smart, aggressive, defensive". I played safe until I had the ball in the right spot then I tried to pick the birdies off.'

Knowing he needed something special to bolster this opening-day effort ahead of the weekend, Faldo went out on Friday and shot a 67. He was now in an excellent position going into the final two rounds. Daly, in contrast, played hot and aggressive golf and paid the price with a missed cut. When asked if playing with 'Wild Thing' had been a distraction, Faldo just smiled diplomatically and said, 'I just don't think about it.'

Like the rest of the field, Faldo had been forced from the start to chase the in-form Greg Norman. Having scored a course-record-equalling 63 on the opening day, Norman had followed it up with a 69 for a twelve-under-par total at the halfway mark. Yet few people knew how close the Australian had been to packing his bags on the Wednesday and heading home. Suffering from severe back pains and unable to make little more than a half swing, he had cut his practice round short. 'He was just so frustrated,' said his wife, Laura. 'It hadn't ever happened to him before. He kept saying, "Why now, of all times?"' On hearing the news, Norman's pal Fred Couples had dispatched his own back therapist, Tom Boers, to fix him up. When Norman outplayed her fiancé 63 to 78 in the opening round, Tawyna Dodds said to Fred half-jokingly, 'You picked a helluva time to make Greg feel like a million bucks!'

Faldo would probably have agreed. He partnered Greg Norman on Saturday, hoping to apply some pressure. In a real battle of the Ashes Faldo certainly had enough chances to close the gap but failed to take them time after time. For the Englishman, the turning point came on the treacherous par-three twelfth. Trailing by four strokes, Faldo watched as Norman stepped up to the tee, took one look at the hole, flubbed his eight-iron and dumped his ball straight into Rae's Creek. At the time leading the tournament on eleven under, Norman was now staring at a possible double bogey, or even worse.

Faldo had some doubts of his own as he prepared to play. 'I still had to hit the shot,' he said later. 'It was a difficult wind situation. It wasn't an eight-iron, it was a hard seven-iron, and I pulled it through the wind.' The ball sailed over the green, and Faldo left himself the toughest shot on the golf course: a downhill chip on to a green running away from him with water waiting to gobble up anything slightly over-hit. It was a nightmare shot to have to take, and he rebuked himself for having put it there.

Taking a few minutes to remove dozens of seed pods from around his ball, Faldo looked on as Norman, after taking a penalty drop, hit an eighty-yard sand wedge to within ten feet. It was still advantage Faldo, but the best he could do was run it down the slope to around twelve feet. After everything that had happened it was somehow inevitable that he would miss the next putt to make bogey, and Norman would hole to equal it. 'He made a great four and I had a very difficult chip,' Faldo summed up begrudgingly.

It was the same story for the remaining six holes of the third round. On the par-five thirteenth, Faldo missed an eagle putt from eight feet to close the gap by one. Two holes later, on the par-five fifteenth, he hit a perfect drive down the middle, while Norman pulled his drive and was forced to lay up. Moments later, Faldo hit his second to around fifty feet, while Norman hit a superb wedge over the water to within six feet for a possible birdie. Once again it was advantage Faldo, and once again he failed to take any advantage at all. Indeed, he took three putts to hole his ball and watched from the side of the green, tapping the putter head against the heel of his shoe, as Norman holed his putt and increased his lead. The frustration was beginning to tell, and by the time they walked off the final green, Faldo knew exactly which part of his game had let him down. 'I could have saved the day by making putts on twelve, thirteen, fourteen, fifteen and sixteen,' he said. 'I missed all of them, and the longest putt was eight to ten feet!'

After notching up a 73 to Greg Norman's 71, Faldo returned to his hotel with Brenna, hardly able to speak. He was trailing the Australian on thirteen under by six strokes going into the final round; the tournament was surely over. No one could give the Great White Shark six shots over eighteen holes and still expect to win. Give him the green jacket now, went up the call. In fact, it was quipped, he could probably play the last round in his green jacket and still win. But without a major win since the 1992 Open at Muirfield, Nick Faldo went into the final round of the 1996 Masters with little to lose. Victory certainly seemed out of reach, but few players in history can have been as intimidating to play against as Faldo. A cold-blooded competitor fashioned in the same mould as the legendary Ben Hogan, tough and uncompromising, he had dedicated himself over the past two decades to the science of tournament play. Meticulous in both practice and planning, Faldo had exhibited throughout his career an awesome will to win. One of the few players to translate strokeplay success into matchplay domina-tion, Faldo's head-to-head record in the Ryder Cup and World Matchplay events revealed just how hard he was to beat. Faldo knew it and Norman knew it. He was certainly not the player anyone would want breathing down his neck in the latter stages of a golf tournament. Indeed, despite the coming round being the final one of a US Masters, it turned out to be matchplay at its most brutal.

Just one stroke clear of American left-hander Phil Mickelson in third, Faldo nevertheless thought Norman would win his first Masters at a stroll. Throughout the week the blond-haired Australian had looked confident, yet going into the final round Norman must have had his doubts. He had been in winning positions at Augusta before and blown it, most notably in 1986 when he came to the last needing a par to tie Jack Nicklaus, only to take bogey. Indeed, Norman had now led going into the final round in seven major championships and won only once, at Turnberry in 1986 (Faldo, in contrast, had only once given up a final-day advantage, in the 1993 Open at Royal St George's – coincidentally losing out to Greg Norman and his final round of 64). Now, with a six-stroke lead, this normally attack-minded player would be forced to play defence.

For Norman, trouble started as early as the opening hole. After a nervy drive into right-hand rough, he failed to make the green with his second and dropped his first shot of the day. Faldo, in turn, made a regulation par four and the lead was immediately cut to five. At the par-five second, Norman looked to have recovered his composure after matching his playing partner's birdie to go back to thirteen under. Two solid pars at the third were followed by poor tee-shots by both men at the par-three fourth. Faldo found himself through the green, while Norman was in a bunker short and right. Chipping to around four feet, Faldo put the pressure on Norman, whose splash shot out of the sand finished at least double the distance from the hole. Minutes later, Norman missed and Faldo holed to reduce the deficit to four.

Norman twelve under, Faldo eight under.

Despite a bogey on the fifth, Faldo looked comfortable in his role as greyhound to Norman's hare. Repairing the damage with birdies at the sixth and eighth, he soon found himself on nine under. Treading water on twelve under, the Great White Shark was beginning to look uncomfortable as they reached the ninth.

From outside the ropes, the trained eye of David Leadbetter had noticed something different about Norman's set-up routine. As he lined up his second to the eighth, the Australian had lingered over the ball far longer than normal, seemingly reluctant to draw the club back. The result was a straight pull into the trees on the left. 'You could see what was different,' Leadbetter said later. 'On almost every shot he was taking eight to ten seconds longer over the ball. That second shot on eight he just stood there. He's over it and he doesn't move. He looks up a few times but he doesn't move! He's fidgeting, having one look then another look, and all the time the pressure is building up.'

This nervy pattern continued. After hitting a short-iron approach into the ninth, Norman looked on in anguish as his ball spun back down the green coming to a halt on the front edge. With Faldo on the green in regulation, Norman now faced a treacherous putt up a severely sloping green. Unlike his playing partner, the Australian failed to get up and down in two and recorded yet another bogey.

Norman eleven under, Faldo nine under.

As they headed off to the tenth, it was impossible to see from their expressions which of the two players had the two-stroke lead going into the final nine holes of the Masters. Head down and ashen-faced, Norman seemed totally preoccupied with his thoughts while Faldo marched on as impassive as ever. Yet even he would feel the strain of the occasion as they entered the back nine at Augusta. 'From ten, eleven and twelve,' he said, 'it was just so nerve-racking it was unbelievable.' At most major championships, especially at the Masters, commentators and television pundits inevitably trot out the hackneyed phrase about the 'tournament really starting on the back nine on Sunday', but one look at the intense expressions on the faces of Nick Faldo and Greg Norman would have told them that this was a battle that had begun back in the late seventies when they first started competing against each other. They had never been the best of friends; the next few holes would decide a lifetime of rivalry.

On the par-four tenth, Norman added to his problems by pulling his second shot left of the green. Faldo, in response, struck a solid nine-iron approach eighteen feet short of the hole. Lucky not to have run down a steep bank, Norman managed to chip up to within ten feet, leaving himself a twisting side-hill putt. A two-shot swing – a birdie and a bogey – was definitely on the cards. Faldo, putting straight up the hill, shaved the hole with his first putt before tapping in for par. Norman took extra time looking at the line of his crucial putt. Sadly, it made little difference. Under the pressure that was building all the while, Norman's putting stroke speeded up fractionally and he missed. Following the action on television, Nick Price, Norman's best friend on tour, left the clubhouse looking pale. 'I can't stand to watch,' he said, before heading to his car.

Norman ten under, Faldo nine under.

At the par-four eleventh, the scene of past Faldo triumphs, both men hit solid tee-shots down the fairway. Slightly shorter off the tee, Faldo hit first, and while he would not admit it, he pulled it slightly left. Heading straight for a flag that was cut just to the right of the pond, it pitched dead on line, just twenty feet short. Delighted with this outcome, Faldo winked conspiratorially at Fanny Sunesson. Had the shot been struck by John Daly you might have believed he'd gone for it, but Nick Faldo, the King of Cautious? Accompanied by enthusiastic calls of 'Go Greg!' Norman also erred on the side of safety. Hitting into the heart of the green, he ended fractionally inside Faldo. Things were so tense by this stage that the scene put one in mind of a World Championship chess match. The Englishman two-putted for his par, then ambled over to Fanny to watch his opponent's shot.

It was a vital stroke for Norman. It was possible that the next few seconds would decide the outcome of the tournament. Here was an opportunity to move two strokes clear with just seven holes remaining, the chance he had waited for, but it was a treacherously fast side-hill putt. The Australian lined up the putter face with his left hand while gently flexing the fingers on his right. Hoping to inject some feel into the stroke, he closed both hands around the grip and pulled back the putter head. Barely setting the ball in motion, Norman watched in agony as it rolled five feet past the hole. The speed of the ball shook him, and it came as no surprise to anyone when he missed the return to record yet another bogey.

Norman nine under, Faldo nine under.

The six-stroke lead Norman had enjoyed at the start of the round had evaporated; both players knew just how important the next few holes would be. Still with the honour, Faldo lined up his tee-shot at the par-three twelfth. Ignoring the flag positioned front right, he settled for the heart of the green, and found it. Breathing a sigh of relief, he turned to watch Norman.

Probably the last hole in the world anyone would want to face under such circumstances is the par-three twelfth at Augusta. Known as Golden Bell on the scorecard, it offers a narrow target set in an opening of high pine trees. Once again, Norman decided to gamble and paid the ultimate price. With Rae's Creek gently lapping the bank at the front of the green, his seven-iron came up fractionally short. The ball pitched on the bank fronting the green and looked for a split-second as if it might hold, á la Fred Couples in 1992, but luck had deserted the Australian and it slowly slipped away into the water.

Watching the drama unfold from the back of the green, Faldo, like everyone else, could barely believe what had happened over the past two hours. ESPN's Dan Patrick said on commentary, 'If he [Norman] blows this, it will be the biggest collapse in modern golf history.' As Greg Norman dropped under penalty, the word 'choke' was hanging in the air like a heavy mist. He successfully pitched on to the narrow green, and attention turned once again to Faldo. Would he also stumble under the pressure? The answer was an emphatic no as he calmly two-putted for par. Moments later, Norman missed his putt to record a confidence-sapping double-bogey. The Great White Shark was sinking fast.

Norman seven under, Faldo nine under.

'I knew that now I had the pressure,' Faldo said, describing his feelings on the way to the thirteenth tee. 'You just sense that all the attention is pointing at you.' And it got to him to begin with. After a poorly struck drive down the par-five thirteenth, Faldo left himself with a real dilemma. Having watched Norman lay up short of the creek from the pine needles on the right, he had exactly 206 yards left to carry the water and 228 yards to the pin. No problem under normal circumstances, but he had a tough side-hill lie and the five-wood he wanted to use seemed determined not to sit flat on the ground. More than once he drew out the metal wood from his bag, cast away the head cover and tentatively placed it behind the ball. No matter how many times he tried it still wouldn't sit right. 'I thought the shot was to hit my five-wood, but then I thought I didn't like the look of it,' he explained.

Faldo knew how costly a mistake could be at such a stage; instinct told him that he had to attack. His only other option was to hit a two-iron. For what seemed like an eternity, Faldo stood next to his bag, staring down the fairway with his hand resting on the clubs that would ultimately decide his fate. Finally, the decision was made. He pulled the two-iron from the bag. There would be no margin for error, and he knew it. 'I had to button it. If I don't hit it solid, it's in the water. But I felt good, so I obeyed that feeling.'

It was a shot that must rank among his best ever. Faldo found the green thirty feet left of the hole, and his relief was obvious. He subsequently two-putted for birdie, matching the scrambling pitch-and-putt birdie of Greg Norman. His pre-round ambition 'just to do everything a little better' was finally starting to pay off.

Norman eight under, Faldo ten under.

The birdie on thirteen seemed to settle some of Norman's ragged nerves. He had cut a forlorn, almost tragic figure over the past few holes, but, always far more comfortable chasing a lead than defending one, he was now beginning to fight back. The question was, how long would it last? At the fourteenth, Norman pulled his drive leaving an almost impossible approach to a back-left pin position. Nervously gripping the club over and over again as if the shaft had inexplicably grown thicker over the last few holes, he was forced to play right of the flag, eventually finishing on the putting green but some sixty feet away. It was a good shot, but he was left with a monstrous putt across the twisting green. The sick feeling lingered, but Norman had his support. Frank Williams, his long-time friend and manager, stood quietly in the crowd along with Norman's wife, Laura, and daughter, Megan. As mother and daughter held hands, it was difficult not to be moved by the concern etched on their faces. Like all of us, they wanted something positive to happen to lift the gloom. A few moments later they got their wish: after a firm hit, Norman's ball ran like a roller-coaster over two slopes, moving in both directions before finally coming to rest just inches away from the cup.

If ever two putts could be considered a victory, this was the moment. Norman had his par, but Faldo still had a chance for birdie after his superb eight-iron approach had landed twenty feet from the hole. Sadly, the quality of his putt failed to match that of his playing partner, and the ball barely dribbled up to the hole. As the players left the green as soon as Faldo had tapped in, there was a hushed but audible murmuring in the crowd. Could Norman win after all? Was it now Faldo's turn to tread water then sink?

Norman eight under, Faldo ten under.

This was the first time Faldo had been in contention for a major since his fourth-place finish in the 1994 PGA Championship at Southern Hills, and he had no intention of letting things slip. With four holes to play and millions of golf fans watching on television and waiting for the next twist in the saga, both players found the fairway at the 500-yard par-five fifteenth with solid drives. Norman pushed hard for a breakthrough, but his poorly struck second shot was fortunate to clear the water fronting the green; he was even more fortunate to stick on the slope just short of the putting surface to the right of the hole. Faldo, attacking the green with a four-iron, got a hard bounce and found himself over the back with yet another difficult recovery shot. Sensing the barest glimmer of a chance, the stiff-jawed Australian looked on as Faldo prepared to play. He faced yet another slippery downhill chip towards water, but the Englishman's execution of the shot could not have been better. He kept his hands ahead throughout the stroke and the ball landed softly on the highest part of the green before embarking on a winding journey down the twisting slope. The crowd roared its appreciation from the nearby bleacher as the ball got closer and closer to the cup, finally coming to a halt just a few feet away.

Now it was Norman's turn. From barely twenty feet away, the Australian hit a low, skidding chip that ran up the right-to-left slope, moved right in towards the flag, then somehow dived across the front left edge of the hole. Norman, like everyone else, was convinced it was going in. Realising within an instant that his ball was still above ground, he reeled back on his heels and fell dramatically to the ground. Seconds after he tapped in, Faldo holed his own putt for birdie. Honours even at the hole, game still on, but an emotionally drained Norman, still not quite believing that he wasn't walking away with an eagle, seemed to have little left to offer.

Norman nine under, Faldo eleven under.

At the par-three sixteenth, the nails which had been forged over the last seven holes were finally hammered into Norman's coffin when Faldo found the middle of the green on the 170-yard hole while the hapless Australian hit the worst six-iron of his life. Striking it inches fat, he saw the ball dive into the azure-blue lake short and left. It was a desperately tired shot, and any lingering hope he had of making a late comeback sank without trace. Faldo holed out for a par; Norman ran up his second double-bogey of the back nine and was finished.

Norman seven under, Faldo eleven under.

Holding a four-shot lead with two holes left to play, Faldo knew the tournament was his. 'It was over with after sixteen,' he admitted afterwards. 'That's what you practise hard for, to put yourself in that position. It takes a long time to learn how to enjoy it, but that's what you could say I'm doing it for. You want to put yourself in that position.' Now it was just a matter of making no stupid errors, and the five-time major winner was a past master of that particular strategy. 'I wanted to play sensibly and not make a mistake,' he said, 'and I managed to do that. I hit all the shots where I intended to hit them.' After he had notched up another par at seventeen, the final hole was little more than a victory march.

It was obvious to everyone that Norman was completely shell-shocked. He tapped in his final putt on the final green with little show of emotion. It had been a bruising encounter, and not for the first time in his career the Great White Shark had come off second best. But for Nicholas Alexander Faldo, winning the Masters could not have come at a better time. He had been without a major victory for nearly four years, and his career had been threatening to grind to an undignified halt. Vital putts no longer dropped, tournament victories had dried up and the tabloid press appeared far more interested in his tortured private life than in his golf. Twenty-four hours earlier he had seemed destined to finish among the also-rans. Now, after a thrilling last round, he could put all that behind him.

As the crowd continued to applaud, Faldo walked over to the hapless Norman hoping to offer a few words of comfort. After all, the former world number one had literally fallen apart in front of him and countless millions watching on television. With Norman close to tears, Faldo instinctively held out his arms and embraced him. 'I don't know what to say,' he said to Norman. 'All I know is I want to give you a hug.' For a few precious moments all past rivalry was forgotten. The scene revealed a side to Faldo few thought existed, least of all Greg Norman. For both players, the unexpected show of emotion obviously meant a great deal. In the press conference that followed, Faldo refused to elaborate on the words that had passed between them. As for Norman, all he would say was 'how much Nick had gone up in my estimation'.

For the record, Faldo had started the day six shots behind Norman and ended the day five ahead. A fifteen-foot birdie putt on the last gave him a 67, the lowest round of the weekend, and made his margin of victory among the largest in Masters history (beaten only by Cary Middlecoff in 1955, Arnold Palmer in 1964, Jack Nicklaus in 1965 and Ray Floyd in 1976). It was the sixth major title of Faldo's career, and the win meant that a European golfer had won the US Masters ten times in the last seventeen years. 'I'm just delighted to scratch another one up on the board,' said Faldo.

Despite his troubles, Greg Norman finished with two solid pars for a 78. Ever the Masters bridesmaid, he had to settle for his third runner-up spot in the last eleven years. Phil Mickelson shot a level-par round of 72 for third place, but he might have been playing on the moon for all it mattered. For weeks afterwards, it was Norman's spectacular collapse that captivated everyone and drew comment.

In truth, what happened to Norman was unbelievable. On the Sunday morning the championship was his for the taking; by the evening, all he could reflect on was a round that included five bogeys and two double-bogeys – and this just three days after tying the Masters and major championship scoring record with a 63! The final round saw an eleven-shot swing over eighteen holes; simple maths told him that a level-par round of 72 would have given him his first Masters title.

One poignant story comes to mind. After Norman's head-to-head battle with Faldo on the Saturday, he was sitting quietly by himself in Augusta's first-floor locker room, taking in everything that had happened. He had been the last man off the course, and he was still sitting there an hour later when the attendant turned out the lights and headed home. Norman had no idea of how to turn them back on, so he just sat there in the dark. Not long afterwards a friend came up to find him.

'Your last night in this locker room, Greg,' he said, pointing towards the champions' locker room just along the corridor.

'Damn, I hope so,' Norman replied.

Even the presentation of the green jacket was a surprisingly sombre affair. Conducted in a wake-like atmosphere, as though Norman had just been carried away in an ambulance, Ben Crenshaw, the presenter, said, 'Our sincerest feelings go out to Greg.' Faldo agreed. 'I do feel sorry for Greg,' he said, moments before pulling on his prize.

It was nearly dusk by the time Faldo came out of Butlers Cabin. Forced to wait while Brenna went back to their rented house to change for the traditional champions' dinner, he was in reflective mood. 'An amazing day,' he said to a few British journalists who had gathered around. 'I don't know how it happened. He had played so great. It was the strangest turn of events I've ever seen.' Still shaking his head in bewilderment, he admitted that he had not expected to win. In fact, he was so laid-back about his chances that, totally out of character, he had arrived at Augusta that morning thirty minutes behind schedule after getting caught up in a motor race on television.

Despite the hushed gloom in Butlers Cabin, it was a remarkably composed Norman who turned up at the post-championship press conference. 'I screwed up,' he said, fingering his shark sun visor. 'It's all on me, I know that. But losing the Masters is not the end of the world. I let this one get away, but I still have a pretty good life. I'll wake up tomorrow still breathing, I hope.' Wake up tomorrow? Certainly. Breathe? Definitely. Win another major? Possibly not. It had been a brutal lesson in losing, and only Greg Norman's nearest and dearest will ever know how he truly felt walking off that final green. In the end, it was left to Phil Mickelson to sum up what many of us felt. 'My heart goes out to Greg,' he said. 'The next week or two will be really difficult for him because some negative things will be written about him.'

If negative things were going to be said about Greg Norman's round, they would definitely not be coming from Nick Faldo. 'I don't want to comment, to be fair to him,' he said when asked what he thought had happened to Norman. Realising that the slightest mention of the word 'choke' would provide the tabloids with the headlines they craved, Faldo wisely and generously kept his silence. The furthest he went down that road was to say, 'I honestly, genuinely felt sorry for him. What he went through today was horrible.'

What about the pressure? they asked. Comparing it with the 'absolutely nerve-racking' tension of a Ryder Cup singles match, Faldo said it was the most pressure he had played under for a couple of years. 'The Masters exerts excessive pressure as it requires the highest degree of accuracy of any golf course. As the week goes by the screws get tighter. It's very tough . . . That's why I was pleased the way I finished. I went forward, which was great. That was the key thing. I got in that position and I kept going forward.' When asked for the secret of his success, Faldo credited both his putting and his decision to play full-time in the United States. 'I putted very well all week. I only three-putted once,' he said, adding that playing on manicured American courses had improved his putting. 'The greens here are different than in Europe. You've got to learn to putt on faster greens with more break – that's why I came to the States. You've got to get used to fifteen-footers with four feet of break.'

At the conference it was inevitable that the press – especially the Americans – would keep on returning to the subject of Greg Norman and his spectacular collapse. Deep down, Faldo knew exactly what they would say about his third Masters victory – that the Australian had handed him the title on a golden plate. Faldo got the hint, but didn't really care. After all, they had said the same about his last two Masters wins. 'I hope I'm remembered for shooting a sixty-seven and storming through today,' he said, 'and not just for what happened to Greg.' David Leadbetter agreed with his pupil. 'You don't want to see this happen, but you can't take anything away from Nick either. He's put it on Greg today. He's been relentless. Nick was going to go out and play well. All the headlines will be that Greg collapsed, but Nick had something to do with it.' Leadbetter and Faldo were the only two people who really knew what had gone into this win. 'I've been planning and preparing for this for six months since the [1995] PGA Championship,' Faldo said later. 'Now all that work has finally paid off. In some aspects I'm better than I was in 1992. Now I've got to find a way to steal the US Open.'

After competing in the Hilton Head tournament the following week, the new Masters champion returned home to England. He was welcomed back at Heathrow airport by crowds of well-wishers, and tributes continued to flood in. 'The response from everybody both here and in America has been very big,' said Faldo from his home in Surrey. 'Of my six majors, this might be the biggest in terms of public interest and attention.

Nine million people watched it here and I think I've met all nine million over the last three weeks.' It was not only members of the public who had something nice to say about Faldo. He also received notes from players, including Curtis Strange, which were complimentary about his victory at Augusta. 'The comments from players, some articles in America, have been really nice. The guys were saying my sixty-seven in the last round was a hell of a round under the circumstances.'

After the relatively warm weather of Georgia it was back to work in the wind and the rain of Britain. He interrupted his busy schedule to play two events – the Benson and Hedges International and the Volvo PGA Championship – and it was a welcome homecoming for the new Masters champion. It was during the Volvo tournament at Wentworth in May that a relaxed Faldo spoke again to the British press. Explaining how the pressure had been lifted by his victory after two years in the doldrums, he concluded, 'Whatever happens now, the season will have been a meaningful one.'

It was an attitude he carried through the Volvo PGA Championship. After workmanlike rounds of 67, 69 and 72, Faldo was just three shots behind joint leaders Mark McNulty of Zimbabwe and Costantino Rocca of Italy. For the final round there was a swirling breeze as Rocca set about making his challenge. With Faldo in the group ahead, the gregarious Italian seemed determined to deny Faldo his first win on home soil since the European Open four years earlier. Rocca, who had famously forced a play-off with John Daly in the 1995 Open at St Andrews after holing a huge putt from off the last green, took the lead with three holes remaining. It was game on, and everyone expected Faldo to come through with a late charge, but when he stepped on the gas the new Masters champion found that the petrol tank was empty. With two par-five holes left to play, Faldo required two birdies to put some real pressure on Rocca; in the end, he could do no better than par, which left him with a share of second place with fellow Briton Paul Lawrie after a round of 68.

Faldo took defeat on the chin. With the second leg of the grand slam at the US Open only three weeks away, he left Britain for Florida to work on his game with David Leadbetter.

'The most important thing is to get back and start swinging the club long,' said Faldo. 'With all this weather the swing has got shorter and shorter.'

From Florida, Faldo, with Brenna, headed to Westchester in New York and the Buick Classic, then on to the US Open at Oakland Hills near Detroit. Already installed as favourite by the British bookmaking industry, he was greeted by the news that veteran Lee Trevino had predicted that he could go on to threaten the eighteen major titles won by Jack Nicklaus. Faldo himself was dismissive. 'That's a long way off,' he said, trying to lessen the pressure. And the grand slam? he was asked by reporters. 'Well, sure, it's a possibility,' said Faldo with a smile to the eager reporters. 'All you got to do is win four!' If Faldo thought that one joke would satisfy the news-hungry journalists, he was wrong. They continued to question him about what it would take to win a grand slam. Faldo took it all in good spirit, then compared it to climbing Mount Everest. 'You have got to get everything right,' he said, 'physically, mentally, emotionally, health-wise, all sorts, then you have got another hundred and fifty other guys, you know, also trying to compete, so we all know how difficult it is, but it's a possibility.' A possibility, again? Not even Jack Nicklaus had talked about winning the grand slam in terms of it being a real possibility. Faldo immediately tried to backtrack and qualify his comments in case he was mistakenly seen as arrogant or boastful. 'The US Open is my next priority,' he said, latching on to a question about where he ranked the majors in order of importance 'I'd love to complete the four, simple as that.'

Shortly before he headed for the door, his relief at escaping was obvious. 'I'd hate to think what the media attention would be like if you did happen to do three and you were going for the last one,' he said, only half-joking.

Oakland Hills, situated in the suburbs of Detroit, is a typical US Open venue. Originally a Donald Ross design, it had been toughened up in the early fifties with enlarged greens and strategically placed bunkers. Add to that tree-lined fairways and thick grasping rough, and the 'monster' Ben Hogan so famously brought to its knees in the US Open of 1951 was back looking for more victims. In many ways it was a course that suited

Faldo's game perfectly. Similar in style to Oak Hill, the Ryder Cup venue where he defeated Curtis Strange on the final day, it required unerring accuracy off the tee, powerful long-iron shots and a masterly short game. All of which Faldo had in abundance.

Yet the new Masters champion never really came to grips with the course that week. Practice had gone well, but maybe it was just too soon after Augusta to raise his game again to such high standards. Perhaps talk of a possible grand slam had put him under too much pressure. Perhaps he just wanted to enjoy life a little more. Whatever the reason, he failed to live up to the high hopes he and everyone else had. Having finished in a disappointing tie for sixteenth place, Faldo continued his downward trend when he missed the halfway cut at the Western Open the following week. Blaming his lack of form on the windswept conditions he had endured in England in May, Faldo labelled it a temporary blip.

He decided to fly home earlier than he'd planned and headed off to Royal St George's on the south coast to put himself into 'links mode' for the upcoming Open at Royal Lytham. 'I knew it would have exactly the same conditions,' he said, 'and I could play with a relaxed attitude and get the feel of a links again.' With any thoughts of a grand slam now consigned to the dustbin, Faldo could prepare normally for the Open.

Scheduled for the second week of July, the championship was returning to the west coast venue where it had all begun for Faldo back in 1975, when he won the English Amateur Championship the year before he turned professional. From the moment he stepped out on to the golf course, he felt at ease. 'It was the first big one,' said Faldo, looking forward to the opening round on Thursday – his thirty-ninth birthday – 'as near as dammit the start of my career, and I have good memories of that.' He also had good memories of the last time the Open was played there, in 1988, when he'd made the play-off with Nick Price and Seve Ballesteros. 'What went wrong that day?' he was asked on the Tuesday. 'Wrong?' said a bemused Faldo. 'A guy named Seve shot a sixty-five, that's what went wrong!'

Like other Open venues such as Muirfield and Carnoustie, Lytham puts a high premium on accuracy off the tee. A flat, occasionally uninspiring course, its main feature, apart from the wind, is its severe sand traps. With cleverly positioned pot bunkers at 240 to 260 yards out and every green heavily guarded by bunkers as well, you have to be either a great driver or a genius out of the sand to be successful (as Ballesteros proved here in both 1979 and 1988). Yet it is also a fair course. Unlike the roller-coaster greens associated with the back nine at Royal St George's, the putting surfaces at Lytham are generally flat and bordering on medium-paced. It is widely known as a good ball striker's course, and if you play well from tee to green it is possible to make a good score, especially on the first twelve holes. Then, as you turn back, often into the prevailing wind, you have to hang on to it, especially over the last six. If there is a secret to playing at Lytham, that is it.

Having come so close to winning the US Open only weeks earlier, Tom Lehman came to the Open still searching for his first major. Just like the old movie saying, it had taken the 37-year-old fourteen years to become an overnight success. Lehman's transformation from struggling journeyman to number-one ranked golfer in the world (as he was soon to be), had been little short of miraculous. It was hardly a rags to riches tale, but Lehman had certainly experienced the many ups and downs of a tournament professional's life. Six years earlier he had been struggling just to make ends meet. His early career was spent travelling around America in a battered Volvo and playing golf in backwater tournaments where the first prize would often fail to cover his expenses. After that, repeated failure in the early eighties to retain his player's card had sent him into a ten-year tailspin of satellite tours and second-rate foreign events.

Trying to make the best out of what one journalist described as an 'agricultural' golf swing, Lehman had come within a whisker of giving it all up. But he persevered with golf on a shoestring budget and returned to the Hogan mini tour in 1992. With the pressure on him to succeed greater than ever, he finally got the breaks he deserved, winning three times that season. Having topped the money list with $141,936, the rejuvenated golfer regained his exempt status for the main tour the following season. The rest, as they say, is history. In his first year on tour since 1985, he notched up nine top-ten finishes, earned over half a million dollars in the process and finished a creditable twenty-fourth on the money list. He has hardly looked back since.

After thirty-six holes at Lytham, Lehman shared the halfway lead with the little-known Irishman Paul McGinley. Then, with Faldo and Ernie Els snapping at his heels in the third round, he blasted the field apart with a seven-under-par score of 64 – his lowest-ever round in a major. Game, set and match to the American. He now had a virtually impregnable six-shot advantage going into the final day. Or was it? With Faldo in second place, comparisons with the US Masters in April proved too tempting for the British tabloids. IT'S FALDO-OVER: NICK'S SIX DOWN – BUT REMEMBER AUGUSTA, TOM read one headline in a tasteless display of misguided patriotism. I'LL SPANK THE YANK: FALDO'S VOW TO TOPPLE LEHMAN screamed another downmarket back page with a photograph of a determined-looking Nick Faldo. 'It's the Ryder Cup all over again,' said one European player, referring to the Union Jack illustration which adorned one Sunday rag. More Blackpool pleasure beach than Royal Lytham, it was an undisguised attempt by the tabloids to rally fans behind the English star. Quite how they expected the Lancashire crowds to behave is anyone's guess, but the coverage must have left Tom Lehman wondering quite what he had done to upset everyone.

In reality, Faldo had said nothing to support such ridiculous headlines. In fact he had been avoiding the press since the start of the week after being tipped off by an estate agent about a couple of tabloid reporters who were booked into a private house next to where he and Brenna were due to stay (they changed their accommodation). After his third round he had agreed with the press that there were similarities with Augusta in that, yes, it was a major; yes, he was in second place; and yes, he was six shots behind the tournament leader. But that was as far as the comparison went. Or was it?

Three weeks earlier at the US Open, Lehman had stood on the seventy-second tee as joint leader and blown it big-time. In a decision that effectively cost him the championship, the six-foot-two-inch American had overruled his caddie on what club to tee off with. The highly experienced Andy Martinez advised a three-wood, but Lehman chose a driver, with which he hit his ball through the fairway and into a deep bunker. The resulting bogey meant that he finished runner-up to his friend Steve Jones. So how would he handle the pressure of leading the Open with eighteen holes to play?

One person who had no doubts that Lehman would win was Glen Frey, lead singer of the Eagles. In an odd coincidence, both Faldo and Lehman had received tickets for the group's London concert the week before. Accompanied by Brenna, Faldo had visibly winced halfway through the concert when Frey suddenly announced to the audience that they had a celebrity in the audience. Nick Faldo, a huge fan of the world-famous band, then cringed with embarrassment as Frey set about introducing this 'celebrity': 'One of our favourite guys, and a professional golfer . . . Tom Lehman! He finished second in the US Open, and we know he's going to win at Lytham. Go for it, Tom!' As Lehman stood up to take a bow, a ruffled Faldo did not know whether to laugh or cry.

He felt the same in the final round at Lytham. He had missed a handful of putts in his third-round 68, and continued the same way on Sunday. As Lehman stumbled around in 73, Faldo was unable to exert any real pressure as putt after putt stayed above ground despite some excellent ball striking from tee to green. In fact, it was a frustrating day all round for the Englishman as both Mark McCumber (66) and Ernie Els (67) shot excellent final rounds to overtake him for second place. Ending the Open in fourth place after a disappointing one-under-par 70, Faldo could only reflect on what might have been. The next morning, the British tabloids were forced to pay grudging tribute to the new champion, Tom Lehman. Typically, though, they still found time to take a side-swipe at Faldo: one headline read A SQUEEZE OF LEHMAN, referring to the sour taste left in the mouth of all home supporters. One tabloid even dared to criticise Faldo's efforts with the banner headline PUTTER FINGERS FALDO. 'He was very frustrated,' admitted David Leadbetter. 'He won't admit it, but at the back of his mind he was really cross with himself. Taking nothing away from Tom Lehman, but having put himself in position and done most of the hard work [to make a challenge], he did not finish the job. He felt it was one major that got away.'

Another major that got away was the US PGA Championship at Valhalla three weeks later. He had been in prime position after an opening round of 69, but his challenge simply evaporated in the humid Kentucky conditions. Closing out the tournament with scores of 75, 74 and 73, he finished in a disastrous four-way tie for sixty-fifth. 'It's been a week where nothing has happened,' he said when the tournament was over. 'I started well but didn't keep it up.' Unfortunately, this performance set the pattern for the remainder of the season, during which time Faldo blamed everything, from bad putting to competitive fatigue.

He had enjoyed a wonderful run early in the season, but 1996 did not end on the high note Faldo had expected. Talk of his imminent divorce from Gill was gaining momentum, one British newspaper publishing details of the proposed settlement. According to them, Gill would receive a $790,000 pension for her work as a director of Nick Faldo International, ownership of their $4.7 million mansion on the Wentworth Estate, plus a one-off payment of $6.3 million. In return, Faldo would keep their newly built Florida home, their chalet at Crans-sur-Sierre in Switzerland and all future income from tournaments and his four other companies. It certainly sounded tempting enough, but like most stories there was little truth in it. (Incredibly, the final settlement would not be agreed until June 1999.)

Whatever the rights and wrongs of his earlier decision to leave his wife and children, his relationship with Brenna Cepelak was proving to be a surprisingly happy one. Faldo looked relaxed in her company, and this had been reflected in his attitude both on and off the golf course. So why had standards slipped so much over the second half of the year? In September, Faldo was competing in the Lancôme Trophy in Paris and the Loch Lomond Invitational in Glasgow. Finishing joint twenty-fifth and joint thirty-seventh respectively, he struck the ball superbly well in both tournaments but was inconsistent on the greens. His final round of 77 at Loch Lomond was his worst score of the season; he seemed distracted, unmotivated. The only positive thing that could be said about his participation in these tournaments was the fact that they contributed £12,105 in prize money towards the £1.5 million home in

Surrey he bought a few weeks later. A five-bedroom residence with heated swimming pool, all-weather tennis court, snooker room, library and summerhouse, Faldo would spend the remaining months of the year furnishing it with Brenna.

Having predicted that Faldo would do 'amazing things on the back of his Masters victory', David Leadbetter, like many others, had been proved wrong. Sure, he won over $900,000 in prize money on the PGA Tour, but apart from the Masters in April there was very little else to shout about. In June at the US Open he was 'never close enough to the pin', in July at the Open he 'didn't play all that well', then at the PGA he struggled badly. 'The Masters was great and the rest of the year wasn't as good as I planned,' he said philosophically. 'It was disappointing that I couldn't do better.'

That Christmas, the British press homed in on Faldo's apparently uninterested attitude. In seven months he would reach his fortieth birthday, and speculation began about how long he would carry on. Just how motivated was Faldo? they asked. In the end, it was left to David Leadbetter to answer Faldo's growing band of critics.

> I think we have to keep things in perspective. Nick's season is all about four tournaments and any time he wins one of them it has to make it a very good year. Yes, there is not quite the consistency we hoped for, but what we have to recognise is that after twenty-one years as a pro it's very difficult for a player such as Nick to stay motivated if he is, say, ten shots off the lead at the halfway stage. He lives for the major championships and so he's not as 'up' as he would be for those events. When he is trailing by so many it is not easy to stay focused.

It was strange to hear Leadbetter talking about his pupil in terms of not being 'motivated' or 'focused'. After all, this was Nick Faldo he was talking about. He still ranked among the best golfers in the world, so whatever the tournament, whatever its importance, it was hard to imagine this most competitive of sportsmen not applying himself one hundred per cent. Faldo had built his career on cornerstones like motivation and focus. He could give lessons to Jack Nicklaus in motivation and focus!

So what had changed? At the Benson and Hedges tournament in May, Faldo had admitted 'giving up' in the teeth of the strong gales that buffeted the Oxfordshire course during his final round of 80 – quite an admission from a player who in the past would lean out of his hotel window during major championships and pray for conditions such as these. But like so many things in his life, that was then and this was now. Looking back, Leadbetter's comments heralded a subtle but significant shift in Nick Faldo's career. His coach's words were strangely prophetic because the seeds of his decline had already been sown. In the months and years to come, Faldo would no longer dominate tournaments through sheer force of will. No longer would the sight of his name on a leaderboard frighten his rivals into submission.

In many ways, his Masters victory at Augusta in April 1996 should have been the start of a whole new chapter in his career, one filled with tales of more major victories and even greater glory, one that confirmed his place among the legends of the modern-day game. Instead, analysts will in all probability look back, point to the back end of 1996 and say, 'That is where things started to slip, that is where his glory days finally came to an end.' Whether that is right or not is up to Faldo, but certainly for the remaining years of the decade he would make more headlines on the front pages of the newspapers than on the back.

17. TAKING ON THE TIGER

In March 1997, Nick Faldo arrived in Florida for the Doral-Ryder Open. Turning up five minutes early for his pre-tournament press conference, he stood off to one side as Tim Finchem took his turn at being grilled by the media. Looking on with detached amusement, he waved away any attempt to cut the PGA Tour commissioner short. 'The more he talks, the less I talk,' he remarked matter-of-factly.

In truth, nobody can ever remember a time when Faldo has been happy talking to the media. As one battle-hardened golf journalist once said, 'If it came to a straight choice between speaking to the press or practising barefoot on broken glass, it would be time to get the bandages out.' In Florida it was no different. The notoriously thin-skinned Englishman went straight on the offensive after being asked to confirm rumours that a wedding was on the cards with his girlfriend, Brenna Cepelak. Turning to the questioner with ill-disguised contempt, he replied, 'No, we've got to go through the first bit before the wedding. You have to go through the divorce first before the wedding. That's the next – not before, because it's not going to happen before. So, it's divorce next and then we will see what happens next.'

Angered by the news that his ex-wife Gill had just bought a four-bedroom waterfront house in Lake Nona with the interim payment of her divorce settlement, he was now in the difficult situation of having his girlfriend and soon-to-be-ex wife living just minutes away from each other. That said, Gill's move enabled him to see more of his three children, Natalie (10), Matthew (7) and Georgia (3), but it was an uncomfortable situation for all concerned, even though Gill and Brenna would never actually meet face-to-face. Having suffered the most turbulent eighteen months of his life, Faldo now seemed anxious to draw a line underneath it all and get on with his life. 'It's all old news now,' he said. 'Now some other poor individual will have them go through their trash.'

On the plus side, his relationship with Brenna was having a positive effect not only on his golf but on his overall attitude. Always eager to please, she attended many of his practice sessions at Lake Nona with David Leadbetter and would even offer advice if she noticed that something was wrong. Offering support and encouragement all the while, she would then follow his progress from beyond the ropes during tournaments, keeping as low a profile as possible. It was the same away from the course. In early February she had been out shopping on Rodeo Drive during the AT&T Pro-Am at nearby Pebble Beach when a journalist approached her asking for an interview. 'No thanks,' she said politely before walking away. 'I don't want to answer any questions.'

Faldo had agreed in January to have Brenna accompany him on tour, and he certainly benefited from having her around full-time. From the Mercedes Championship onwards he was noticeably easier on himself, less worked up about a bad round or tournament result. At the AT&T Pro-Am – an event he usually avoided like the plague because of its showbiz distractions – he got into the swing of things by offering to caddie for his pal, rock star Huey Lewis. Introducing himself to the crowd as 'Fannie' Faldo, he then donned an Ozzy Osbourne wig for the official photograph. This was Faldo at his relaxed, happy and entertaining best, and the fun did not end there. Before the Masters in April, he gave up a few days' practice at Lake Nona in favour of a short break with Brenna during which they visited the Daytona 500 car race and watched a space shuttle launch from Cape Kennedy. After a difficult start, they now seemed settled in their relationship, the Albuquerque-born co-ed bringing a sense of youthful fun into Faldo's well-ordered life. With her, he seemed a million miles away from his reputation as a hard-edged, sombre-faced automaton. 'I'm having a good time out there,' he confirmed. 'On and *off* the golf course.'

In addition to these changes in his personal life, Faldo had also decided to make significant alterations to his business affairs. In November 1996, with at least one eye fixed on the future, he had taken the momentous decision to split with his long-time management company, IMG, placing his affairs in the hands of his close friend and long-time manager John Simpson.

'I've no intention of becoming a businessman,' Faldo explained. 'My business is golf. I still feel there's a lot of good golf left in me but when my form declines, inevitably, then the name Faldo will still carry some weight for what has been accomplished.'

Faldo had been part of the IMG stable of top-class sportsmen since the mid-seventies, but no sentiment clouded the decision to leave and he and Simpson immediately set about making plans. His Masters victory had opened up a host of commercial possibilities, especially in the United States, and now they both wanted to cash in big-time. Acknowledging the debt he owed IMG, Faldo said the parting had been affable but that it was time for a change (according to the press, Simpson's departure from the company hurt Mark McCormack more than his star client leaving). 'I'm not the person I was,' Faldo said later. 'Things move on and change. It's inevitable.'

On the golf course, things were also looking up. At the end of February, Faldo entered the $1.4 million Nissan Open at the Riviera Country Club in Los Angeles. The former playground of Hollywood stars like Errol Flynn and Douglas Fairbanks Jr, the course, with its rolling fairways and clever bunkering, was always a stimulating test so early in the season. Formerly the LA Open, it had long been a popular stop on the West Coast swing, not to mention a challenging one. As Faldo said afterwards, 'This tournament has history and atmosphere. This is the sort of course I'm meant to win on.' Looking tanned and refreshed after a short break with Brenna the week before, he was eager to do well. 'You have to be happy off the golf course to be happy on the golf course,' he said, more than hinting at how difficult things had been over the past year or so. 'Things are sorting themselves out. Life's going good again.'

Another thing that was 'going good' was his golf. Over the winter Faldo had spent a lot of time with David Leadbetter working on a new, stronger grip that gave him more length off the tee. 'It's a more powerful position,' said his coach. 'We're trying to get a little more snap into his swing, a bit more pop to his shots. Nick's swing is kind of like a metronome, very calm. A little bit more speed, a little bit more leverage, will help.' In his desire for longer drives, Faldo had also been experimenting with a new Mizuno T-Zoid driver with a graphite shaft, with which he was able to hit the ball an additional ten to fifteen yards. Leadbetter admitted that the emergence of Tiger Woods had influenced the change. 'We've based Nick's whole game around control, and it's the biggest reason he's won six majors. But you look at the way Tiger is able to crash the par-fives and it's obvious that length is an asset. No question, Tiger has spurred people on. There's a new kid on the block, and we've got to put in that little bit extra.' Faldo, however, was more cautious. In a rare disagreement with Leadbetter, he contested that the grip change had improved the consistency of his back swing rather than increased his distance. He was also more reserved about Woods and his impact on the game. 'It's very difficult to tell yet if he's improving the standard of golf,' he said. 'But he has got the attention of us golden oldies. We'll have to play hard.'

Playing hard was exactly what Faldo had in mind as he approached the Nissan Open. As usual, Leadbetter accompanied him to the tournament at Riviera and spent the early part of the week fine-tuning his long-game. Forced to leave his pupil on the driving range on the Thursday afternoon, he said, 'If I see something on television I'll call.' Thankfully for Faldo, he never had to. Striking the ball wonderfully well from tee to green, Faldo made only four bogeys and one double-bogey in four superb rounds of 66, 70, 68 and 68. More significantly, he averaged just 26 putts per round using a new approach of 'get up to the ball, stop messing about and hit it'. In fact, he made it look so easy that it begged the question, why had he not won more PGA Tour events in the past? His twelve-under-par total over the tight, eucalyptus tree-lined course with its thick kikuyu rough was enough to edge local favourite Craig Stadler into second place by three strokes. Remorselessly accurate and unerringly steady throughout, Faldo could not have been happier with his performance. 'I feel I've learnt so much, especially over the last five years,' he said, shortly after winning his sixth US title. 'I've got to use it now.'

It was an impressive victory, especially with a number of quality players making a run at Faldo over the closing holes, including Scott Hoch, Fred Funk and Tom Purtzer. Another player who mounted a late challenge was the new wunderkind of American golf, Tiger Woods. Despite an understandable desire to get into contention so his father, Earl, recovering from triple heart bypass surgery at the nearby UCLA Medical Center, could watch him on television, Tiger was never really in the hunt, even with a final round of 69. Yet it had been a promising tournament for the twenty-year-old. 'Considering everything that is going on,' said Woods, 'it was hard to get a real deep focus because I was thinking about more important things than a round of golf.'

Fortunately, 'focus' had rarely been a problem for Faldo. The Nissan Open (and the first-prize cheque of $252,000) was just one part of his intensive preparation for the Masters in April. After that it was on to Doral and Bay Hill, and then the Players Championship at Sawgrass before joining Leadbetter for a week in Florida. It was a routine that had brought him success in the past and he could see little reason to change it. 'They used to write I was mechanical and boring,' he said. 'I'm delighted to say I'm getting close to that again. I'll be glad to get back to mechanical and boring.' He predicted that his game was 'very close' to the standard he wanted for Augusta, then, as a passing shot at his critics back in Britain who had been airing the idea that Faldo should make room for a younger player to come into the team for the forthcoming Ryder Cup match at Valderrama in Spain, he said, 'This week I played as solid as I've ever played. Who knows? Let's see if this is going to be the start of a good run this year.' Confident about his game and his chances of making the team on a wild-card pick, Faldo had some advice for European captain, Seve Ballesteros. 'If I was the captain and Seve had just won the LA [Nissan] Open he'd be on my team. That's my message to him.' Whether his old rival would take his advice was another matter.

With Ballesteros allowed just two captain's picks, there was a growing amount of pressure on the PGA European Tour to relent and allow him four. With José-María Olázabal recovering from a long-term foot problem and a number of top stars playing in America, the general feeling was that unless something was done, and quickly, Europe would be forced to field a substantially weakened team. Voicing the opinion of many, Colin Montgomerie had lobbied for two extra picks on the basis that it was patently unfair to penalise players like Faldo and

Jesper Parnevik for choosing to play full-time in America. Unfortunately for Monty, his view was firmly opposed by Ken Schofield, executive director of the PGA European Tour, whom in Faldo's opinion it would take a 'grenade' to shift.

The sticking point was the amount of tournaments Faldo and others needed to play to retain a place on the European money list. His own schedule was 23 or 24 tournaments worldwide, with fifteen or sixteen events played in America and only six in Europe – certainly not enough to retain his card even though the PGA European Tour had decreed that from January onwards the three US majors would count towards the final total. No matter how they calculated it, Faldo refused point blank to 'bust my buns' playing extra tournaments in Europe in the hope of qualifying automatically and relieving the pressure on Ballesteros. 'You can't go flying backwards and forwards to please everyone,' he said to his American audience. 'It's a lot further than you think.'

In truth, Faldo considered his place in the team a certainty whether one, two or ten picks were allowed. Unlike two years earlier at Oak Hill, when he was playing poorly and it was a toss-up between him, Parnevik and Woosnam to make the side, the pressure was no longer on in his opinion. 'If I'm playing well, I should be on the team,' he said in no uncertain terms. 'It's always been a priority making the team, but now I'd like to think I've got my record to help get me the last little leg-up that I need.'

Away from the tournaments and the pressure of Ryder Cup selection, Faldo was having an equally busy time. In February, he had travelled to County Donegal in Ireland to look at a number of potential sites where he could build his 'ultimate links course', but they had all fallen through. Then, shortly before the Doral-Ryder Open in Miami, news filtered through about a golf-course design project he had planned with the Marriott Hotel Group in Orlando, not far from David Leadbetter's Lake Nona complex. Building on the critical acclaim he had received for his Chart Hills course in Kent, Faldo was also designing a course in Asia as well as a major 36-hole complex in Portugal. 'A little artistic bit comes out in me,' he explained. 'It's great to go out and you want to create something and you want to do the best you possibly can, try and create some nice-looking holes and some challenging golf courses. I feed off good golf courses and enjoy the subtlety of the slopes and where you have to position the ball.'

During the Tournament Players Championship at the end of March, attention inevitably turned towards the Masters. When asked by reporters which player he thought would win, Faldo proved reluctant to answer, despite the insistent nature of the questioning. 'What about Phil Mickelson?' one asked. 'How about Lehman?' said another, before adding, 'And what about twenty-year-old Tiger Woods – can he win?' Fixing a steely gaze on his audience, Faldo knew exactly the quote they wanted. Tiger Woods was the hottest property in golf, and if the defending Masters champion said it was 'unlikely' that he could win first time out at Augusta, then the press would print a headline something along the lines of 'Faldo slates no-chance Woods'. Far too experienced to make that mistake, he said instead, 'I'll tell you what makes Augusta so tough. If you go out and play when you are relaxed, it is a piece of cake. When you go out and play it as the *Masters* and it's pressure time, that's when it's a tough golf course.' The press would not be put off. 'What about the media circus that surrounded him in Los Angeles?' demanded one journalist. 'Does it put you off, and do you have any sympathy for anyone partnering Woods?' Faldo struggled to find the right answer. 'If you want to keep on your own game, there is nothing worse than a lot of commotion going on,' he replied.

It seemed somehow inevitable that Faldo would draw Woods in the first round at the 1997 Masters. Yet even with this match-up, all the talk at Augusta was about the epic battle between Faldo and Norman the previous year. Unmatched in terms of sheer drama and raw emotion, the final round in 1996 had since gone down in Masters history as a classic, but not everyone saw it that way. 'Last year was the worst round of my life,' said Norman about his 78 that Sunday. 'I don't want to keep thinking about it. The eleventh, twelfth and thirteenth . . . I want to flush them out of my mind.' In order to do that, the Shark had had a session on the Monday with motivational speaker Tony Robbins. 'He reminded me who I am and how good I am,' said a determined Norman. Clearly, the Australian needed help to put the memories of last year behind him, but he had nothing but praise for the ruthlessly efficient Faldo. 'He put the pressure on me,' said Norman. 'He created it. He did all the things you have to do to win a major championship.'

Faldo, in contrast, needed little motivating and was eagerly looking forward to defending his title. When he was asked what advice he would give his old rival one year on from their bruising encounter, he simply shrugged and said, 'Play.' In Florida, Faldo had studied videotapes of the 1996 Masters purely to analyse head positions when he was putting. He had even persuaded the greens superintendent at Lake Nona to shave the greens to try to match the speed of Augusta (how the members felt about that has gone unrecorded). That part of his game successfully studied and logged, it seemed the rest of it was also in pretty good shape. 'On paper, it's way better right now than it was last year at this time,' said an upbeat Faldo after Monday's practice. 'Last year, I was still trying to fathom things out.'

In truth, his game had already, in his own words, begun to 'unravel'. His week with Leadbetter at Lake Nona had been a lacklustre affair, with Faldo easily distracted by his desire to spend 'quality' time with Brenna and his children over from England. For the first time in years, his desire endlessly to bash balls down the practice range was missing, and who could blame him? Looking back at him in the mirror each morning was Nick Faldo, reigning US Masters champion, a top-five ranked player in the world and winner of the recent Nissan Open in Los Angeles. At that stage of his career, what more did he have to prove? In his opinion, nothing. All he wanted to do now was step off the treadmill for a while, play with his kids and enjoy life.

It had been the same in 1992. After straining every nerve and sinew to win the Open at Muirfield, he had won four more events that year before closing out the season as European number one. He had reached some kind of a peak then, although he could not have known it. After that, his game gradually fell into decline and he won just four tournaments over the next four years. It was still a reasonable record for most professionals, but certainly not for Nick Faldo (it was his huge desire to arrest this decline that resulted in his Masters victory in 1996).

Five years later as he prepared to defend his title at Augusta, a similar, and perhaps more terminal, decline had already started to set in. It would have been hard to imagine at the time, but within two years Faldo would no longer be a contender at any tournament, let alone a major championship. From being the most feared golfer on the planet, he would take his place among the also-rans and the never-have-beens of world golf. 'So many little things crept in,' he would later admit. 'I don't know if it was mental, physical. How do you know?'

But as he prepared to 'fathom' out what meal to choose for the Masters champions' dinner on the Wednesday evening, all that was in the dark, distant future. By tradition (since 1952) the defending champ was invited by Augusta National Golf Club to host a dinner for past winners and to select the main course for the evening. Reflecting the culinary roots of the host, Faldo had chosen shepherd's pie in 1990 and steak and kidney pie in 1991. It was hardly nouvelle cuisine, although rare steak, fish and chicken were also made available for anyone who chose not to partake of the champion's fare. This year, he decided to go for fish and chips with a tomato soup starter (indeed, he requested that thirty pounds of cod be flown in from Grimsby especially for the occasion).

Meanwhile, in the press tent, Faldo's growing dislike of answering questions about Tiger Woods was becoming obvious. The constant topic of press interviews over the past few weeks, 'Tigermania', the Englishman made it perfectly clear, was something he could well live without. Faldo had already had his first opportunity to watch the tour's brightest young star at first hand during a practice round. 'He didn't say a word to me for the entire eighteen holes,' said Woods later. 'When we putted out on the last hole, Nick said, "I enjoyed playing with you."' On the Tuesday, Faldo was leaving the scorer's tent when it was officially announced that he had been paired with Tiger Woods in the first round (although it had been something of an open secret for some time, as the defending champion is traditionally paired with the US amateur champion, who this year happened to be Woods). Besieged by journalists sensing a good story,

Faldo pre-empted their questions by saying, 'Let's get one thing clear right from the start. I'm not talking about *him*.' Typically, one journalist tried to spin the question by asking him whether there was any particular player he wanted to put the jacket on. 'No,' said Faldo as he spun on his heels and walked away. 'I want it staying in my wardrobe. Simple as that.'

However, in the time left before the first round began, the subject of Tiger Woods was a difficult one to avoid. Son of an Afro-American Army veteran and a Taiwanese mother, Woods was not from what you would call typical golfing stock. He had picked up his first golf club at the age of two, and his stated ambition ten years later was to beat Jack Nicklaus's career record of eighteen major championships. He went on to win three consecutive United States Amateur Championships by the age of twenty, and his decision to turn professional heralded the biggest sponsorship deal in golfing history, at an estimated fee of $65 million.

Record sponsorship aside, Tiger Woods had found himself needing to win $140,000 in six weeks at the back end of 1996 to avoid PGA qualifying school in December. Typically, he needed only two events to win his player's card before going on to amass a quite remarkable $1,006,594 in prize money over the next seven weeks, a run that included three tournament victories. By the time Woods teed up at Augusta, he was virtually assured of a place in Tom Kite's Ryder Cup team later in the year. In April 1997, Woods was considered the hottest thing in sport. Hitting the cosy world of professional golf like a tornado, the athletic black youngster had featured on the front page of almost every sports-related magazine in the world. When he arrived at the course late on Tuesday and decided to play the back nine, the media centre emptied in a heartbeat. As he made his way out to the course surrounded by Pinkerton agents hired by the club, the news spread like wildfire and thousands of eager fans turned up to watch him practise. 'Tigermania', it seemed, had finally descended on Augusta National.

Moreover, the week following the 1997 Masters marked the fiftieth anniversary of black athlete Jackie Robinson breaking major league baseball's colour bar. It was a high-profile landmark in United States sporting history, and the occasion had the personal and very public backing of President Bill Clinton. With Woods looking to become the first black professional ever to win a major golf championship, the level of interest at Augusta was at fever pitch.

The 1997 Masters was always going to prove a particularly tough one for the locals. During the run-up to every Masters, race (and occasionally gender) is always a problematic topic of conversation at Augusta. The club is often roundly condemned for its lack of Afro-American members (black professionals were not even invited to compete until Lee Elder's historic first appearance in 1975). Set, as Augusta National is, in the southern state of Georgia, the majority of part-time waiters, bus boys, litter gatherers and green staff is taken from the local black community. All of them, without exception, come through a gate hidden away on the far side of the course, report for work, then leave the same way in the evening. Augusta hoped that by admitting their first black member in 1989 the tide of criticism might be halted. That has since proved to be a forlorn hope. The wheels on change of this kind inevitably move slowly.

Unfortunately, for this reason and others, not everyone was delighted to see Tiger Woods at Augusta. Since the Mercedes Championship in January, a number of his fellow professionals had expressed their disquiet about the media circus that often accompanied him, including Nick Faldo. 'You have to have strong mental powers to carry on playing how you want to play, rather than being caught into it,' he said. 'I think they need to keep their reins on it, because the media attention is getting too much. I think we're probably going to have to start making some new rules, where the photographers and where everybody can go. It's just too much commotion going on. It's not golf.'

Although it was annoying, most players, including Nick Faldo, realised it had little to do with Tiger Woods himself. Woods was, and remains, unfailingly courteous on and off the golf course to his fellow players. Indeed, opinion at Augusta was generally favourable, players like Greg Norman describing him as 'a breath of fresh air', while Payne Stewart commented, 'Tiger is the greatest thing to happen to this tour for a very long time.'

Even the Golden Bear himself said, 'I do not think there is anything in this game he cannot do.'

The golden rule on the opening day of any tournament, especially the Masters, is not to lose it. A lightning-quick start is always preferable – more tournaments are lost with a loose opening round of 75 than won with a spectacular final-round 65 – but experience shows that a player leading from the outset rarely wins the Masters; when Ray Floyd did it here in 1976, he was the exception rather than the norm. As Nicklaus said, 'You want to play well on the Thursday and Friday at a major, but you want to save your best golf until Saturday and Sunday.'

For anyone interested in golf, the Faldo/Woods pairing was an intriguing match to follow; the cold-blooded destroyer of Greg Norman a year before competing head-to-head with the charismatic black youngster from Long Beach, California. Teeing off at 1.44 p.m. local time, it was the first time they had played together competitively and the anticipation was intense. Yet just a few holes into the round, it was difficult to see how Faldo could hold on.

With Woods blasting it past the Englishman off almost every tee, it was almost embarrassing to see the difference in length between the two. Watched by one of the largest galleries in Masters history – over fifteen thousand – Faldo was out-driven at the first by sixty yards. At the par-five second it was almost eighty yards. Experienced enough to ignore it, Faldo kept his head down, speaking only to his caddie, Fanny Sunesson. Of more concern was how poorly both of them were playing. By the tenth, Faldo and Woods were five over and four over respectively. Struggling to control the ball in the swirling wind, approach shots were proving almost impossible to judge. It was the same on the putting surfaces. On a day on which former US Open champion Lee Janzen compared playing Augusta with 'walking through rattle snakes', the lightning-fast greens became even more treacherous as the breeze dried them out. Considering all the pre-tournament hype, things were not going well. The match was a dream-ticket pairing, but the way things were going neither player would be around come the weekend.

Then, almost without warning, all hell broke loose. A blistering series of birdies inspired by some scintillating iron shots brought Woods back in an amazing score of 30 – six under par. Loud cheers echoed through the pines. It was a remarkable display made even more dramatic by the score of his playing partner: a 75.

It had been one of the toughest opening days in living memory, and Faldo was not the only victim of the harsh conditions. The scoreboard was awash with bogeys, double-bogeys and worse. Greg Norman faltered with a 77, Ballesteros ended on 81, Pavin could only manage a 76, Lehman a 75 and Els a 73. After the traditional reorganisation of the pairings, Faldo returned on Friday knowing he needed something special to get back into the tournament. Woods had shown him what was possible, but Faldo began his round by dropping even more shots. By the turn he had taken 41 strokes; the possibility that he might miss the Masters halfway cut for the first time was now real. Two hours later, it was a certainty.

Come the weekend in any tournament, the noticeboards in the media centre are covered in press cuttings, often faxed through from Britain, so that journalists can see how much coverage their reports have been given in newspapers like the *Daily Mail*, the *Mirror* and the *Telegraph*. European golf's best player and the reigning Masters champion was now out of the tournament and the American press could hardly contain their joy at seeing Faldo humbled. It was a feeling not helped by one British tabloid headline pinned to the noticeboard which screamed FALDO AND NORMAN SELF-DESTRUCT!

Like the journalists, the hundred or so accredited photo-graphers at the course are also looking for a big winner on the Sunday. It is a popular subject of debate at any golf tournament. Everyone has his or her own preferences, but now, for once, the choice was clear. With Faldo, Norman and Ballesteros all out of the running, a win by Tiger Woods in his first major as a professional would be by common consent the dream end. Two days later, they got their wish. Woods had gone into the final round six shots clear of second place, so the comparison with Greg Norman's situation the year before was inevitable. The questions in the media centre the evening before had been predictable enough, but everyone at Augusta knew in their heart that Tiger Woods would not choke. Colin Montgomerie had framed the words that only moments before Woods had refused to speak: 'Woods is not Greg Norman. There is no way he is going to blow it. He is just playing too well.'

With Nick Faldo sitting out the action in his hotel, Woods proved Montgomerie right by putting on a faultless display. Four hours later, the golfing prodigy stepped on to the seventy-second tee needing par to break a host of records including the lowest winning total, the largest winning margin and countless others. The cheers that greeted his appearance on the final green proved to be just the start of the celebrations; the knowledge that Woods could take thirteen putts and still win did little to dampen the crowd's enthusiasm. After holing out his putt for par and a superb round of 66, he walked off the back of the eighteenth green and into the arms of his father Earl – and into Masters history. In keeping with tradition, a few minutes later Tiger Woods received his green jacket from Nick Faldo in a made-for-television ceremony in Butlers Cabin. A few days earlier Faldo had been well and truly beaten by the twenty-year-old Woods. The irony of the situation was not lost on the tall Englishman. As Faldo warmly shook Woods's hand, it was obvious that a new era had begun. The only question now was, would Faldo be a part of it?

The simple answer was no. The week after Augusta, Faldo headed south to the MCI Classic at Harbour Town. He ditched the Odyssey putter he had used to win the 1996 Masters for a Taylor Made model, but the change did not prevent him from missing back-to-back cuts for the first time in three years. 'If your stroke is bad,' he admitted after rounds of 74 and 75, 'you can be using anything.'

Having experimented with different putting methods in the run-up to the MCI, Faldo blamed his poor play at Augusta on a difference in speeds between his hands and the putter head. 'It's a fault I'd been getting away with,' he said, somewhat lamely. 'Now it doesn't look like I am. I need to change the hand action, but it's difficult when you've been stroking the ball for one way so long.' Colin Montgomerie, among others, thought Faldo was making too much of his troubles. 'Phil Mickelson, Brad Faxon and Loren Roberts are the best putters I've ever seen and they also missed the cut at Augusta. I wonder how much they're rebuilding. They just go back to their families, have a beer or whatever they do in America, and forget it.' Not surprisingly, David Leadbetter was more analytical about his pupil's putting difficulties. Describing him as a 'streaky putter', he said, 'Nick's full swing has great rhythm, but he tends to lose rhythm in his putting.'

He returned to England for the Volvo PGA Championship at Wentworth, and the Masters post-mortem began in earnest. After yet another Tiger Woods victory in the GTE Byron Nelson Classic the previous week, an animated Nick Faldo demanded that course designers create more punitive bunkers to trap the big-hitting American. 'He's got the game throttled,' said Faldo, complaining about Woods' massive advantage off the tee. 'He's playing a different golf course to the rest of us. At the present time, if there is a bunker two hundred and forty yards out, the rest of us have to play to avoid it. But he can blow his drive right over it. That gives him an extra seventy or eighty yards of fairway to hit to.' Faldo had 'enjoyed' a close-up view of the Woods power game at Augusta a few weeks earlier, and with Woods' average drive measuring over 320 yards, the concern in Faldo's voice was obvious. Suggestions had also been made that courses like St Andrews and Royal Troon, the latter the venue for the Open in July, would not be long enough to offer a real challenge to Woods. Faldo just shrugged his shoulders. 'It's amazing to think,' he said, 'that one man has come along and they are thinking of changing some very historic golf courses.'

At the 'historic' Wentworth, Faldo at least managed to recapture some of his old form, finishing joint second after rounds of 70, 67, 70 and 70. After following that up with a morale-boosting tie for third place in the Kemper Open two weeks later, Faldo headed for Washington DC to prepare for the US Open at Congressional. It would be an important championship for him; he desperately needed a good performance to put his career back on track. The last thing he wanted was a repeat of Augusta, but in one way that's exactly what he got.

The course at Congressional was a tough par 70 measuring 7,213 yards, the longest in US Open history. The Bethesda, Maryland course also had an unusual and somewhat controversial finishing hole for a major championship – a par three. This meant that the champion elect, instead of walking up the last fairway to the cheers of a huge crowd, was forced to walk over a bridge to the polite claps of a relatively small group of fans. Not that this was of any great concern to Nick Faldo. His mediocre play over the first three days – he recorded rounds of 72, 74 and 69 – left him languishing among the also-rans, which meant that for the final round he would be partnered by Tiger Woods.

Quite how Faldo took the news we will never know, but, still smarting from his last bruising encounter in the Masters, a pairing with Woods in the final round of the US Open must have been the last thing he wanted. As Faldo predicted, it was never going to be an easy afternoon. The problems began as early as the second hole. Amid constant shouts of 'C'mon Tiger!' one fan yelled sarcastically, 'This is all for you, Nick!' Faldo struggled to keep his concentration and tried to keep his head down, but there were long delays on every hole and he began to complain of the hold-ups caused by the excessive number of journalists, photographers, on-course TV reporters and armed security personnel scrabbling around inside the ropes. The situation was exacerbated when the two men were warned for slow play. Faldo was furious, especially after being told by a USGA official to make up the gap between him and the group in front or suffer a two-shot penalty.

Not surprisingly under these circumstances, the standard of golf from both players was poor. At the sixth, Faldo ran up a horrendous triple-bogey after pitching from the rough straight into water. On the next, the agitated Englishman asked security officials to reprimand a man who had snapped a photo on his down swing. Woods also struggled to find any rhythm under the 'humbling' conditions. He dropped three shots on the front nine but finally made a birdie on the twelfth – his first for nineteen holes. Signing his scorecard for a 72, he finished at six over par, ten strokes behind the eventual winner, Ernie Els. Nick Faldo, who scored 76 for an eleven-over-par total, proved less diplomatic than his partner. 'We paid for the media, for the press,' he said, moments before storming off to the clubhouse. 'We lost five minutes and they made us catch up. So that's my official statement, and that's it.'

A few weeks later, back in Britain, things had not improved on or off the course. In March, the R&A, looking to encourage a younger element into the game, had announced that under-eighteens would be admitted free to the 1997 Open at Troon. It was seen as a worthwhile initiative by all concerned, including the press and public. 'The classic example was Nick Faldo,' said Peter Greenhough, chairman of the Tournament Committee, 'who was stimulated to take up golf by watching it on television.' To be the inspiration for such a move was a wonderful endorsement of the six-time major winner, but by the time the Open rolled around in July, his image was taking a real battering.

The British red-top tabloids, constantly trying to out-headline one another, were again after Faldo's blood. The *Daily Mirror* splashed a story under the banner GILL FALDO EXCLUSIVE: I'VE BEEN BETRAYED AGAIN which detailed the torments Gill had suffered and on the subject of his marital infidelities left little to the imagination. It was a story similar in style to the NICK IS A NASTY S.O.B. headline that had greeted him at Royal Birkdale in 1991, and it received an unwelcome boost of publicity as the tournament reached the halfway stage.

Faldo was celebrating his fortieth birthday on the Friday of the Open, and speculation was rife that he was about to marry Brenna Cepelak. Despite the fact that his divorce still had to be finalised, the tabloids could smell a story, especially after Brenna was spotted wearing a gold band on her wedding-ring finger. Faldo, at the time the story broke struggling hard to make the cut in the windswept conditions, then noticed a photographer taking pictures of Brenna and the finger in question. 'You're here to take pictures of golf and nothing else,' roared Faldo, who reportedly began to poke the opportunistic photographer in the back with his putter and to threaten to have the snapper 'thrown out'. The effect of this on his concentration was devastating. He finished his second round with a 73, then added weekend rounds of 75 and 72 for a tied fifty-first placing – his worst finish in the Open for over a decade. When asked to comment about the incident, Faldo said curtly, 'I don't know anything about that,' and stormed off.

A month later, in the PGA Championship at Winged Foot, his mood had not improved and he missed his first cut in the event since 1986. His form had taken an alarming dip, and with the Ryder Cup at Valderrama only weeks away he was now in danger of not making the side. For the hero of Oak Hill, it was an unthinkable situation. Feeling downcast and out of form, Faldo desperately needed some good news, and in late August he got some. Moments after the dust settled on the BMW International in Munich, European team captain Seve Ballesteros announced that Nick Faldo and Jesper Parnevik would be his wild-card picks for the match the following month. Breathing a huge sigh of relief, it was only later that Faldo realised just how close he had come to losing his place after ten straight Ryder Cup appearances.

In the weeks leading up to the BMW, Ballesteros had been faced with a major selection headache. With just two captain's picks, it looked like a straight choice between Faldo, Parnevik and Olázabal. The argument for each player was strong, but with Faldo's dip in form, it looked like Parnevik and Olázabal would be given the nod. Either way Ballesteros felt the team would be severely weakened, but aided by a bizarre set of circumstances, he was able to include all three in his team (what Seve wants, he usually gets). But not everyone was happy. Indeed, far from it. The unfortunate player who perhaps suffered most as a result of Ballesteros's scheming was the talented but highly inexperienced Spaniard Miguel Angel Martín. Having qualified automatically for the Ryder Cup, he had suffered a problematic wrist injury which had seen him sidelined in the month leading up to Valderrama. Martín insisted that his wrist would stand up to the pressure, but Captain Ballesteros was unconvinced and demanded that he take a playing test in the immediate run-up to the match. Martín refused, and was ejected from the team. Returning to the Order of Merit, Ballesteros then selected the eleventh-placed man, who just happened to be José-María Olázabal. Problem solved. All the Europeans had to do now was concentrate on beating the USA.

Before the match had even started, Ballesteros had canvassed his players' opinions on pairings and sought their advice on tactics. At the first team meeting on the Monday he asked each man how many rounds he thought he was capable of playing.

Unlike Langer and Rocca, who felt their golf would not be up to it, Faldo volunteered to play all five. He had scraped into the side, so the last thing he wanted was to be left out of any of the action. Ballesteros then asked each man to write down the names of two players with whom he felt comfortable playing. Nick Faldo gave him the names of Ryder Cup rookie Lee Westwood and Colin Montgomerie; Westwood handed in Darren Clarke and Nick Faldo. Decision made. 'I thought there was enough chemistry to put them together,' said the Spanish maestro later about the Faldo/Westwood pairing. 'They played very well and were a bit unlucky that they did not win more points.'

Ballesteros was right on both accounts. With many so-called experts predicting an easy win for Team USA, the Faldo/Westwood partnership was instrumental in Europe's victory. Out on Friday and Saturday, they won two matches (including the prized scalp of Tiger Woods, who was playing with Mark O'Meara in the morning fourballs on the second day) and lost two, helping Europe to a five-point lead going into the singles. Ballesteros thought that the American captain, Tom Kite, would send his big guns out early. He was right. Saving his more experienced players to the end too, Ballesteros sent out Faldo in the penultimate match. If it was to be a pressure-cooker finish, at least he would have someone he could rely on.

Matched against the underrated American Jim Furyk, Faldo began his match in spectacular style, hitting his approach shot to within three feet at the first for a birdie. Furyk, however, was not easily intimidated, despite the fact that he was taking part in his very first Ryder Cup singles. In a seesaw match that saw both men taking the lead only to be pegged back, the turning point came at the 370-yard par-four thirteenth. Faldo, two-down at this point, signalled his comeback with a superb approach shot to within inches of the cup. Furyk, in reply, was short of the green in two, leaving himself a sloping right-to-left chip just to make a half. Having conceded Faldo's tap-in, Furyk paced out the distance between his ball and the hole. It was dead-on fifteen yards. As he lined up his shot, Faldo stood impassively on the pathway leading up to the next tee, putter in hand, staring impassively down at his shoes. Seconds later, the loud applause told him what had happened. Furyk had holed out, his two-hole advantage intact.

With just four holes remaining it was a real hammer blow, one that Faldo would do well to recover from. Having slammed the door in his opponent's face, the American opened it wide again at the next, pulling his tee-shot badly at the par-three fifteenth. Having committed the cardinal error of matchplay of not finding the green (it had found the left-hand bunker), he could only admire the way in which Faldo replied with an arrow-like four-iron to within twelve inches. It was a truly wonderful shot and, like his approach into the previous green, deserved to win, but once again Furyk had other plans.

Conceding the birdie, he shuffled his size-eleven feet into the sand before taking up his address position. Long seconds passed as he gently hovered the leading edge of his sand-iron over the ball. Glancing back and forth between the ball and the target, he took a final deep breath, lifted his ball over the bunker face in an explosion of sand and dust and watched as it rolled gently towards the hole. For a moment it looked as if it might miss the hole on the right, but it had just enough speed to keep it on line. In it dropped, and one hole later the match was over. The most experienced player in Ryder Cup history had been defeated by the least experienced, and in some style. 'If somebody said Jim Furyk would not only beat Nick Faldo but play like he was possessed by the ghost of Ben Hogan, dropping chip-in upon chip-in,' wrote one American journalist, 'you'd say, lay off the sangria.'

As the weather closed in, Nick Faldo made his way over to the eighteenth to watch the big Scot Colin Montgomerie close out Scott Hoch to secure the point that gave Europe victory. Faldo had certainly played his part in the glorious win, but having lost to Furyk and without Brenna around to help him celebrate at the victory dinner, the occasion was a touch flat for him (before the event it had been decided, in consultation with other members of the Ryder Cup team, that it would be politic not to bring Brenna along, especially as many other wives were good friends with Gill).

After the dinner, Nick Faldo was left to reflect on what had been an oddly disappointing year. In the end, not even Europe's narrow one-point victory at Valderrama could lift the gloom. Tournament golf had become hard work, major championship-winning performances a dim and distant memory. He and Leadbetter had been working on some changes over the second half of the season; perhaps they had failed to take hold? He resolved, not for the first time, to work even harder on his game, but even with this decision he managed to upset the sponsors of the Million Dollar Challenge in November, saying he was only in Sun City to 'work on a number of things'.

Faldo spent most of the winter working on 'things', to little effect. His lack of major championship success would continue in 1998, along with his steady slide down the world rankings. Something had to change, but what? As things turned out, the 1998 season provided some unexpected answers.

18. OUT WITH THE OLD

In many ways, the Nick Faldo story reads like a Hollywood blockbuster. More often than not it centres on the highs and lows of his playing career, but over the next eighteen months the focus would be on his off-course activities.

Had Faldo wanted a clue that 1998 might not be his year, he need not have looked further than the Doral-Ryder Open in March. As he blasted away at one end of the practice ground, Brenna was relaxing at the other. Thinking she was out of range, she was suddenly hit hard on the foot by a beefy hotel guest's ball aided by a strong tailwind. In considerable pain, she was off her feet for two days before finally limping out to rejoin her partner. Maybe she shouldn't have bothered. In a matter of months, Faldo would be giving Brenna her marching orders – permanently.

It was not the only change Faldo would make that year. He was forced to spend a substantial part of his season talking with lawyers and accountants, so it came as no surprise when his form took another dive, along with his prize-money earnings. He was slipping down the world rankings almost on a monthly basis, and something had to be done about it. The solution, when it came, surprised everyone, especially his long-time mentor David Leadbetter. After a business trip to the Far East that September, Leadbetter returned to his teaching complex at Lake Nona to find a letter from Faldo waiting for him on his desk. There was nothing too unusual about that – his management company often wrote to him confirming Faldo's movements – but this letter wished him all the best for the future and matter-of-factly told him that he was fired.

The news reverberated around the golfing world. Perhaps the best-known pupil/teacher match-up in the history of the game, theirs was a relationship made in heaven. Together they had amassed three Open and three Masters titles; their story was the stuff of legend. Before Leadbetter arrived on the scene, Faldo was a proven tournament winner and former European number one but a consistent failure when it came to the majors. He had sought help from various teachers, but none had inspired him with confidence like David Leadbetter. He had helped Faldo to remodel his swing, helped him to achieve his aim of winning major championships. Now it was all over and nobody really knew why, least of all his former mentor.

The pity of it all to me was I wished it had been done differently. That is the thing with Nick, he never seems to confront things head-on. If there was a problem with anything, he'd rather just get away from the situation, rather than say, 'Hey, this is the way it is . . .' If he had just come to me and said, 'Listen, David, we need a break. We've had a great innings. I need to sort some things out on my own here,' that would have been fine. I can take that. Nobody likes confrontation, and it's not the easiest thing in the world to say, 'Hey, this isn't working and that's not working,' but I think it shows strength of character if you can deal with it.

On reflection, there had been enough clues throughout the year to suggest a cooling in their relationship, but nothing that might actually lead to them splitting up. In fact, the situation seemed the exact opposite of that. Having ended the previous season in ninty-seventh place on the PGA Tour money list, Faldo had appeared rejuvenated by the idea of playing more tournaments in Europe, a decision wholly endorsed by Leadbetter. In fact, Leadbetter had suggested a return the year before in the hope that Faldo 'could build up some confidence'. Then Faldo won the 1997 Nissan Open and the idea was quickly dropped. A year later, Europe once again seemed the right choice, and Faldo signed up to play eight events there.

It was a decision that seemed to pay off immediately in terms of his confidence. He mounted a strong challenge in the Johnnie Walker Classic in Thailand at the end of January 1998, finishing joint eighth. He then followed his normal routine of playing half a dozen tournaments on the PGA Tour as a warm-up to the Masters in mid-April. He made the halfway cut in all but the Bay Hill Invitational, his form steady but unspectacular. He won just over $90,000 but finished no higher than joint eighteenth in the Players Championship at the end of March. Yet it was a surprisingly relaxed Nick Faldo who rolled up at Lake Nona a few days later looking to fine-tune his game with Leadbetter. Keeping up their normal pre-Masters routine, Leadbetter had allotted time to work on all aspects of his pupil's game, especially his putting. But to his obvious surprise he found Faldo strangely uncommitted when it came to working on his game.

> *Prior to Augusta, we had a week off and he was at Lake Nona and I think I saw him for maybe two one-hour sessions during the whole week. One of the other players I coach – Brandel Chamblee – even mentioned it. He was always under the assumption that Nick was a six-hour-a-day man. Instead, Nick would come down for a couple of sessions. He had his little boy Matthew with him and he would wander over and watch him hit a couple of balls, then go back. They also had Brenna on the cart. She'd be hitting balls, then he would be over there for an hour or so, then they would wander off. He did that two, maybe three times that week. Before, it would just be me and him. Now it was just a carnival atmosphere.*

The lacklustre attitude displayed by Faldo in Florida the week before the Masters resulted in his worst finish in Augusta for years. He crashed out of the tournament after rounds of 72 and 79, his dream of making it four green jackets in ten years in ruins. Things were not much better the following week at the MCI Classic. After opening the tournament with a solid one-under-par 70, he lost the plot completely with rounds of 74, 73 and 83. That final score was his worst competitive round for years, leaving him languishing among the also-rans in eighty-fourth position.

Then came better news. As part of the newly constructed World Golf Village in Florida, Faldo was to be inducted into the World Golf Hall of Fame. It was intended as a lasting tribute to his career, and Faldo was suitably overwhelmed. 'This is the greatest accolade a golfer can receive for his achievements,' he said during his acceptance speech, 'and obviously I am extremely excited and honoured to be included.'

It is unlikely that he felt particularly legendary in the weeks that followed, however. He put in a good performance in the

Mastercard Colonial late in April, where a final round of 66 lifted him into the top thirty, but a month later he inexplicably stumbled to a 74 in the final round of the Memorial tournament to finish well down the field. In between, he returned to Europe to play in the Murphy's Irish Open, early in May. Putting a loose opening round of 75 down to jetlag, Faldo fought back with middle rounds of 72 and 67 to go into the final round within seven shots of the tournament leader, David Carter. This was 'the Faldo of old', gushed the media. 'Grinding out a score and putting pressure on the leaders.' Unfortunately, the 'old' Faldo did not hang around long enough to make a challenge. He stumbled to a two-over-par final round of 74, any confidence he had built up over the past two days evaporating into the air like Irish mist.

Also at the beginning of May, his contract with Mizuno was up. Feeling it was time for a change, Faldo switched his allegiance to a little-known company called Adams Golf. He signed a lucrative deal on 4 May which involved his playing with their innovative 'Tight Lie' metal woods throughout the world in return for stock options and a significant role in future club design. For Faldo, it was a dream deal, and even though it would turn increasingly sour over the next two years, at least he was not afraid of throwing out the old and bringing in the new (and he would prove to be very good at this).

Faldo had been justifiably noted throughout his career for his consistency, and he reasoned that his periodic drops in form had a lot to do with his tortured personal life. He had hoped that by the start of the 1998 season many, if not all, of his problems would be behind him; instead, everything had quickly gone from bad to worse. Protracted negotiations with Gill over a suitable divorce settlement had seemingly faltered. Add to that the frosty silences that often greeted him on his visits to the family home in Surrey, the heartbreaking departures from his three children and increasing pressure from Brenna to make their own relationship more permanent, and you had a recipe for chaos. It was certainly not the ideal backdrop for playing good championship golf.

After missing the cut in the US Open at the Olympic Club in June after disastrous rounds of 77 and 72 (on a par-70 course),

Faldo returned to Britain early in July hoping to salvage something from his season. He intended to compete in an increased number of European tournaments, the first of these he was scheduled to play in being the £850,000 Standard Life event at Loch Lomond, a highly rated course 23 miles north-east of Glasgow. Unfortunately, things went badly for him from the outset. During a warm-up on the driving range before the pro-am, Faldo suddenly felt a twinge in his right elbow. Choosing to ignore it, thinking it little more than a slight strain, he continued to hit shots. Minutes later it felt so bad that he was forced to withdraw and head straight for the treatment centre. Determined not to let the injury spoil his preparations for the Open the following week, he returned to the range and hit a few more shots, but it was obvious that something was badly wrong. 'He's injured the tendon on the inside of his right elbow and traumatised a muscle,' said European tour physio-therapist Jon Shrewsbury when asked why Faldo had pulled out of the Standard Life event. 'We will give him treatment three or four times a day now. It involves ice, rest, electrotherapy and putting on a fibreglass cast.'

It was the latest setback in an increasingly miserable year. Not only had Faldo missed the cut in the first two majors of the year, he now looked likely to miss out on the third altogether. His career was in free-fall. He had just dropped out of the top one hundred on the US money list too, so things were looking black indeed. Moreover, he had just fallen to an all-time low placing of fiftieth in the world rankings at a time when the top 64 only got to compete in a lucrative series of World Series events planned for 1999. Not for the first time in his career, the pressure was really on. Unless he pulled his game together soon, it was possible he might not qualify for the money-spinning events at all.

The following week, Nick Faldo put his injured right elbow to the test at Royal Birkdale. He played a solitary practice round on the Tuesday, concentrating mainly on his long-game, and came through unscathed. 'My elbow is feeling great,' he said afterwards. 'I'm pleased and quite surprised. It was a little achy this morning, but on the last six holes I was hitting proper divots and I did not feel a thing. I hit most of the balls out of the rough. But I shall be trying to hit all the fairways when Thursday comes.'

Keeping to his word, Faldo struck the ball surprisingly well from tee to green but hardly holed a putt outside twelve feet in his opening round of 72. 'Didn't hit the ball badly,' he said, 'I just need a putt.' Unfortunately, little had changed by the time he came to the final green on Sunday. Rounds of 73, 75 and 75 meant that he finished a demoralising fifteen strokes behind the winner, Mark O'Meara (who won the tournament on level par). Once again Faldo featured in the tabloids, this time as the butt of a joke: 'What do a moped and Nick Faldo have in common? They both go putt-putt-putt.'

Faldo was still struggling as he entered the US PGA Championship a month later at Sahalee in Washington State. Without David Leadbetter around to offer advice, Faldo turned to Ben Crenshaw for a putting lesson after a lacklustre three-over-par opening round of 73. Crenshaw, one of the game's most renowned putters, spotted the problem immediately. Faldo, he said, re-gripped the putter just before takeaway which had the effect of knocking the club-face off line at impact. Faldo was impressed by this diagnosis, but he also knew that re-gripping the putter at address was something he had done for years. Indeed, fiddling with the putter at address, lifting it off the ground then back again, was one of his trademark moves. But, willing to try anything once, Faldo took Crenshaw's advice on board – to very little effect, despite declaring himself 'chuffed' with the improved feel he was getting.

'It had got to the point where it caused a fault,' Faldo said after finishing the tournament with rounds of 71, 72 and 73. 'It's very difficult to change your characteristics so I am chuffed with the way it has worked so far. At least I feel I have something constructive to work on. Before I was practising bad putts. No two putts were the same. Now I can hit the same stroke, the same putt time after time.' He finished in a disappointing tie for fifty-fourth, a massive eighteen shots behind first-time major winner Vijay Singh, but he preferred to concentrate on the positive aspects of his game. 'I really feel like I have hit something,' he said, somewhat unconvincingly. 'If I can just unchain myself from the putting thing, it's going to help my whole game. That is all I really needed. I am hitting the ball very well and now I have found the thing that has been holding my game back. This could be a great turnaround. This has been a long year and I know the results have been lousy, but if I can hit the ball like I did this week for the rest of the year that will do for me. I just need to be patient.'

The British press were unmoved by his pleas, and Faldo found himself in a similar situation to that of Sandy Lyle a few years earlier, with rumours that his game was in terminal decline gathering momentum. 'Scores do not lie,' remarked one golf journalist. 'The simple fact is that he made just two birdies in four rounds, and none at all in the last fifty holes! Sure he has a great record in the majors, missing the cut just seven times in sixty-seven attempts, but four of those misses have come in his last eight attempts!'

So what had caused this slide from being the most feared golfer in the world to the status of a distant also-ran? In some ways, tournament professionals are often the last to know why they perform well one day and badly on others. This is the real reason why top golfers surround themselves with highly paid gurus, while the rest are forced to make do with minor adjustments to their grip or stance, hoping that something good will come of it. According to popular myth, the rot had set in during the final round of the 1996 Open at Lytham. Paired with the eventual champion, Tom Lehman, Faldo had missed four birdies inside seven feet and never found his putting touch again. However, highlighting that one round was too simplistic a solution. For the majority, confidence seems to be the key to good golf, and Faldo was no different. Confidence enables the player to get in the 'zone' – an Americanism that describes a state of being almost hypnotically focused on the next shot. 'Confidence,' as Faldo once said, 'is the link to positive thinking, which in turn leads to an ability to block out distractions and concentrate on the task in hand. No matter what may be happening around you.' Faldo's problem wasn't so much that he wasn't in the 'zone', more that he wasn't even on the same planet.

The week after the PGA Championship in August, Faldo missed yet another halfway cut in the Sprint International, his fourth of the year. With Leadbetter still unavailable, Faldo headed over to his own Golf Institute at the Marriott Grand Vista Resort in Orlando where he asked head instructor Chip Koehlke (pronounced 'Kalkee') to take a look at his swing on the computer. Faldo was shocked by what he saw and asked the 34-year-old coach to make some suggestions. Instead of blithely nodding his head and offering a quick fix (which would have been entirely understandable under the circumstances), Koehlke, as Leadbetter had done over a decade earlier, set about restructuring the legendary Faldo golf swing. 'Chip showed a lot of bottle,' Faldo said, 'because he told me that in some cases I would have to do just the opposite to what I'd done for years if I wanted to improve.' Faldo had intended his visit to the Marriott to be little more than a flying one but, cancelling flight after flight, he ended up staying for four days. He could not have been more impressed with the quietly spoken American.

Eventually he returned to Europe to compete in the £800,000 Canon European Masters in Switzerland. Played in the scenic surroundings of Crans-sur-Sierre in the Swiss Alps, this rich man's playground provides a spectacular backdrop for one of the premier events on the European Tour. It is a popular venue with many players, including Faldo, but the beauty of its scenery was lost on him this time round as once again he started a tournament badly, missing the cut after rounds of 71 and 70. He decided to stay on in the Swiss resort to practise, but that was not his only reason for remaining in the country.

Earlier that week, Faldo had found himself in conversation with a petite blonde hostess named Valerie Bercher, who was employed by tournament organisers IMG to hand out promotional brochures. She had introduced herself to him 'Brenna style' during one of the practice rounds. Fortunately for the 41-year-old Englishman, that is where the similarities ended. Swiss-born, Bercher exuded a quiet air of charm and culture to which Faldo responded immediately. Compared with the ebullient, in-your-face personality of his current American girlfriend, she offered a pleasing and no doubt welcome alternative. Flattered by the attention, Faldo resolved to contact her again on his return to England, which he did almost immediately. Over the coming days and weeks they would stay in touch over the telephone. She talked about her life and dreams for the future while Faldo talked about his life and his desire to escape the past. They agreed to meet up again, which went some way towards strengthening his resolve to make other wide-ranging changes in his life — most notably ending his thirteen-year relationship with David Leadbetter.

According to Nick Faldo, the decision to split with his long-time swing guru had been on the cards for some time. He had discussed it with John Simpson, and the final decision was taken shortly after the PGA Championship at Sahalee in mid-August. The 'Dear David' letter that would cause so much controversy was posted a few weeks later. When the news finally broke in September, the telephone at Lake Nona ran red hot with enquiries from journalists wanting a scoop, but Leadbetter was in no position to give them one. He was unsure of the facts himself, and it would be months before he got the whole picture. All he could do at the time was refer to the letter he had received from Faldo, which basically said, 'In view of my recent poor form, I feel I should push on with somebody new. Thankyou, and goodbye.' 'It's disappointing when you work so hard with a player for so many years for it to end that way,' said Leadbetter. 'We had a good relationship as far as these things go. It was a bit of a shock.'

A bit of a shock? In the mid-eighties, David Leadbetter had put his growing reputation on the line by taking time out to remodel one of the best-known swings in the business. Since then he had stood at his pupil's side every step of the way as Faldo picked off six major championships in the space of ten years. When Faldo was inducted into the World Golf Hall of Fame, he credited Leadbetter for turning his game around. After such a long time together, the split must surely have come as more than a 'shock'; then again, as Leadbetter would later joke, 'At least our relationship lasted longer than either of Nick's two marriages.'

In the hectic weeks that followed, Faldo attempted to justify his actions. He complained bitterly that his coach had been unavailable when he most needed him, and cited the PGA Championship at Sahalee as a prime example. 'There's been a lack of communication for some reason. David wasn't at the

PGA, much to my surprise, and I haven't spoken to him for weeks. He's been off doing his own thing.' Leadbetter conceded that in recent times he had not spent as much time working with Faldo, but as for missing the PGA Championship in August – the first major championship he had missed since 1985 – the reason was simple: his father had been ill for a long time and had died that month, and Leadbetter had spent most of the year travelling between the United States and England offering support to his elderly mother. 'There was simply not enough time to do everything,' he said later.

Faldo, however, was having none of it. He could understand Leadbetter not showing up at Sahalee because of his family commitments, but according to him, that was not the whole story. What really got his blood boiling was the news that Leadbetter had been spotted on the practice ground at Royal Lytham with Si Ri Pak during the Women's Open. For someone as competitive and as single-minded as Faldo, this was inexcusable and tantamount to betrayal. He had slipped down to sixty-fifth place in the world rankings and was nearly off the sheet on the PGA Tour money list; *he* was the one who needed help, not the girl who could count herself among the top five women golfers in the world.

Another reason for their split might have been David Leadbetter's much-publicised link-up with Greg Norman in 1997. Butch Harmon, among others, had hinted that this might become a problematic issue given the past history of the two players, but Leadbetter had dismissed talk of a possible rift with Faldo as pure speculation. Yet in a revealing interview with *Golf World* magazine later the same year, he had outlined some of the assurances he had been forced to give Faldo before taking on Norman as a pupil. 'I said to Nick that he wouldn't get any less attention from me because I was working with Greg. Nick Price was the top player in the world two years ago and Faldo never said to me that you can't work with Nick Price because he's number one! These players don't think like that, they're all big boys. Besides, there's always the chance that something I have learnt from Greg might help Nick.'

Considering Leadbetter's later admission that Faldo needed 'constant reinforcement' during their time together, that he should have taken 'more of the responsibility' for his own swing, his comments in the magazine article take on a slightly hollow ring. Faldo was someone who demanded loyalty from those he worked with. It was an integral part of his complex and often demanding personality that he needed reassurance that he was at the centre of the universe of those around him (Gill Faldo had written in her 1994 book *Faldo: In Search of Perfection* that 'genius in any form is not easy to live with'). With Norman around, Faldo was obviously ill at ease. Whether Leadbetter realised it or not, the end of their relationship was in sight.

After the Canon European Masters in early September, Faldo invited Koehlke over to Paris to work on his game during the Lancôme Trophy. They concentrated on infusing more 'feel' into his strokeplay, and the effect was immediate: Faldo put in his best performance of the year, finishing joint sixth with rounds of 70, 71, 70 and a superb 65. 'I'd got bogged down, but now I've got something to play with,' said a delighted Faldo. 'Sunday's sixty-five in the Lancôme was a great feedback from what we were working on.'

After Paris it was on to Cologne for the Linde German Masters. Speaking before the tournament, Faldo could barely disguise his happiness at having found someone he could trust. 'Chip is a disciple of mine, has read my books and teaches my methods. He's read Hogan, the lot. It was silly that I should be going elsewhere when I had my own tried-and-tested system all set up for me. It was a big decision after thirteen years with Lead, but things happen like that. It was something I needed, a whole fresh new approach, which is great. It's given me a boost and what I'm working on is fun again.'

Things were going well, and John Simpson enthusiastically endorsed his client's decision to take up with Koehlke and dump Leadbetter. 'Being taught by his own academy coach is perfect,' said his manager, who not long before had openly speculated that the elbow injury that caused Faldo to pull out of the Loch Lomond event might have been a result of the 'tired method' Faldo and Leadbetter had been working on. As for the 'Dear David' note described as 'cursory' by Leadbetter, Simpson explained that away by denying that it amounted to a letter of dismissal. 'We wrote to David so that he was aware that Nick was intending to see one of his teachers at the Faldo Institute for a second opinion,' he said. 'We did not suggest that the partnership between David and Nick should come to an end.'

Leadbetter wholly disagreed with Simpson's spin.

> I think I know when I've been fired! I knew very well that he [Faldo] hadn't written that letter – his manager had written that letter. Nick's name was at the bottom of it. I do that. When I go away, I sign some letterheads and they [his administrative staff] fill in the rest. I'm sure that John Simpson wrote it out, then probably read it out over the phone to Nick and said, 'This is what I've written.' [Then Nick would say] 'Oh, that's fine,' and send it off. I know the phraseology that was used in the letter was the way John Simpson speaks and not Nick – 'regards to the family' type of thing. That was a dead giveaway!

A short time later, according to Leadbetter, Simpson had pulled him up just to make sure that he had actually got the letter, 'because obviously there was going to be some stuff in the press'.

From that point on, the argument between the two camps became increasingly acrimonious, especially when it came to a conflict of business interests between Leadbetter and Faldo. Only a matter of weeks before he received his marching orders, Leadbetter had been told about his pupil's involvement with Koehlke at the Marriott Grand Vista Resort in Orlando. He had always been suspicious about the apparent secrecy surrounding Faldo's decision to set up a golf academy on his doorstep, and Leadbetter admitted feeling 'irked' that Faldo had set up in direct competition with him. In fact, it was this incident that made him realise how little he really knew his former pupil – and how little he could trust him.

> He benefited a lot from me working with other players. Nick Price was probably the best guy who I ever had the chance to bounce stuff off. We did things together, experimented, worked things out and so on. So indirectly, Nick benefited from all my work. Then, when somebody told me, 'You know Nick Faldo is

*going to start his own teaching academy?' I said, 'Nah —
rubbish.' Then, blow me down, I see it in the newspapers! There
was going to be a Marriott–Nick Faldo Golf Institute and they
would be teaching 'his' philosophy and stuff! And he never had
the decency to even come and tell me. Not even a word.
Negotiations were going on, the thing had been signed and it
just came out in the press. I felt like an idiot. The subject never
came up — never. Even after that he wouldn't mention it. [On
the practice ground] it was just sort of casually, 'Yeah, well, I've
got to go and do this promotional thing for the Marriott.' It was
nothing. Even the other players thought, 'What the hell is this?'
All credit to Nick for having the name to be able to do that, and
I'm sure he charged them a fortune, but it was confusing to the
public, who said, 'Hey, who's teaching this? Are they your
teachers?' It was a great business opportunity for him, okay?
Maybe if he was with IMG they might have told me. But
because it was a John Simpson deal it was almost, 'Hey, we can
do this.' But not to even mention it! I mean, what was I going to
do? If you have a personal relationship then you've got to be
honest with each other. No matter what it is, if it's a marriage
or a sporting partnership, as this was. I've always given Nick
one hundred per cent and you're going to feel a little hurt.*

Then, as a passing shot at Faldo's new teacher Koehlke, he
added, 'Why would somebody of his calibre put his career, put
his golf swing in the hands of some guy who knew nothing
about what he was doing just because he worked for him and
read his books? I mean, basically the guy knew nothing. What
a decision! Do you think any other top player would do that?'

Speculating on the reasons for the split, Leadbetter said about
the Marriott deal: 'It was probably a factor. He might not admit
to that, but . . . I mean business is business. I understand that.
I owe him so much for what I have achieved in my career, but
golf to me is much more than just money. I would enjoy it just
as much if I didn't have a nice house, sold millions of books
and what have you. I've always just enjoyed doing it.' And these
weren't hollow words. It surprised many people when it was
revealed that Leadbetter had been paid $20,000 per annum in
1985, and that the fee had never been renegotiated. 'That really

just covered costs, flying here, flying there,' said Leadbetter.
'That went right through – all the way. Never went up. That was
it. It didn't bother me at all. Like I said, I didn't do it for the
money.'

Teacher and pupil had socialised, but not often, rarely
exchanging anything more than practice-ground confidences.

> I stayed at his house periodically and would go to dinner
> periodically, but Nick was always a very private person. He was
> very difficult to get close to. He has his circle of friends and we
> were always very cordial and we got on well together, but he
> wasn't what I would call a great mate where you tell jokes and
> stuff. But it was still a good business relationship. That was just
> the way it was. I think it's different for a lot of people to get close
> to Nick Faldo because he is so intense a lot of the time. I think he
> finds it difficult to get away [from golf], even with his family. He
> was always thinking about golf. I mean, golf was his life.

And for that reason, and that reason alone, Leadbetter lost his
job.

By the end of 1998, the Leadbetter/Faldo spat was at its
height. Downplaying the vital role Leadbetter had played in his
career, Faldo launched into a scathing criticism of the practice
'drills' he had been forced to undergo. Describing them as little
more than 'gimmicks', Faldo hinted that his drop in form was
directly attributable to them and other routines his former coach
had come up with. In an interview with *Golf World* magazine
published in December 1998, he said, 'Capturing the old
feelings is what it has been about, and that is why it is so
exciting because I know the old feelings work. That had been
one of the troubles with David because we were working on
something new to try and get back to the old and I was getting
deeper and deeper into trouble. The things we were working on
were really upsetting my tempo and I'm very much a tempo
player. I had to do something.'

Perhaps understandably, Leadbetter was once again fuming.

> It was these 'gimmicks' that really stirred his imagination and
> got things going. He would almost get bored with one thing so

we'd tweak it a little bit, put it a slightly different way and it was, 'Okay, that sounds good.' That is what you have to do as a coach. But when things aren't going well, it's these so-called 'gimmicks' that get the blame. In the end, I think it was just a combination of the fact that he wasn't playing very well and in 1998 I didn't have as much time to spend with him because I was spending a lot of time with my dad, who was very ill. My mind was somewhere else, and it was just one of those things that I probably wasn't giving him the attention that I normally did.

Describing his former pupil's words as a 'slap in the face', Leadbetter then refused to take any further part in what was an increasingly bitter transatlantic slang-fest, preferring instead to concentrate on the more positive aspects of their relationship. 'He has been good for me and I was good for him,' he said. 'There was a time when every player at a major would look over his shoulder and wonder what Nick was doing. I wish him well in the future. If he gets his focus back and starts putting well, I still think he can win. He's a very gifted individual.'

First it was David Leadbetter; a few weeks later it was Brenna Cepelak. The break-up was announced before the opening round of the Belgacom Open in October, inspiring the inevitable tabloid headline: BRENNA NICKED OFF! For once, Faldo seemed remarkably unconcerned as he breezed around the Royal Zoute course in 65. 'It is always sad,' he said casually, 'but these things happen.'

Brenna, who had been on a golf scholarship at Arizona State University when they met almost four years earlier, seemed to be taking the news remarkably well too. 'There are always regrets and heartaches when two people end the kind of relationship which Faldo and I experienced,' she said breathlessly, like a tragic heroine from a Mills & Boon novel. Sadly for Faldo, the apparent harmony of the split was not destined to last. When she found out about his burgeoning relationship with Valerie Bercher, the 23-year-old American decided she was not prepared to head off into the sunset just yet.

After finishing a respectable six under par in the Belgacom Open, Faldo returned to England only days before his marriage to Gill finally ended in divorce. The money-and-property settlement, thought to be worth around $12 million, still had to be settled, but at least his golf game was in better shape. After the season-ending Volvo Masters at Montecastillo in Spain, where he finished one over par for a joint thirty-sixth placing, Faldo was invited out to New Zealand to represent England in his first World Cup since 1991. It meant a long trip out to Gulf Harbour in Auckland in the middle of November, but it ultimately proved a successful one for both Faldo and his partner, the Irish Open champion David Carter.

Carter, a pencil-thin pro with a whiplash swing, was born in Johannesburg but had represented England in the Dunhill Cup only weeks before. He was nervous before play started that he might let the great man down, but there was something about the confident, easy-going 26-year-old that appealed to Nick Faldo, and it showed when they played together. With the more experienced man taking the lead, they finished eight under par between them, Faldo compiling rounds of 68, 70, 73 and 69 (eight under) to Carter's 73, 71, 76 and 68 (level par). Despite losing out by a single shot to American Scott Verplank for the individual prize, Faldo had won the trophy he came for. In a tense final day, he and Carter had managed to edge out Costantino Rocca and Massimo Florioli of Italy by the narrow margin of two strokes, with the USA in third. Faldo was thrilled with his first tournament win since the Nissan Open over eighteen months earlier. He had proved he could still cut the mustard; all he wanted now was to win another tournament on his own.

Having led England to victory in the World Cup of Golf, Faldo decided to stay Down Under and compete in the Holden Australian Open in early December. It was a decision he came to regret after opening up with a disastrous round of 77. Telling anyone who would listen that he could still compete at the highest level if only he could straighten his game out, his heartfelt plea reached the ears of 84-year-old Norman Von Nida. Legally blind, the Australian legend had 'spotted' Faldo on the practice putting green and ambled over uninvited. Faldo shook his hand and listened patiently as the three-time Australian champion told him his ball striking 'sounded all wrong'. Unable to see more than a blurred outline, Von Nida knew from the sound the ball made off the club-face that he was gripping the club too tightly with his left hand. 'He is such a fine player,' said the old man, 'I knew he would be looking for an answer.'

He certainly was, and with the help of Von Nida he found it. The following day he shot a magnificent 69 that catapulted him back into the reckoning. He went on to finish the week in fourth position and immediately credited the Australian octogenarian with this turnaround in fortune. 'Where was "The Von" when I was here in the eighties?' Faldo asked the waiting press. 'It all made sense. I make the left hand move first and it comes back too sharply. He got my right hand a little bit stronger to get my right elbow and right shoulder in the right place. That took a bit of adapting because it changed the swing a bit. I jiggled with things there. I hit balls last night at the range, trying to hit them with the least amount of pressure in my left hand. It was a new day again today.'

It was most definitely not a new day back in England. In fact, it was more like Groundhog Day when he arrived after his trip to Australia. While he had been away the news-hungry tabloids had broken the news about his relationship with Valerie Bercher, and there was worse to come. Having been told by Faldo that no other woman had been involved in their 'amicable' break-up seven weeks earlier, Brenna reacted badly to the news that he had been seeing his Swiss Miss for several months. She had been staying at Faldo's Surrey home while he was away, and had put her frequent lessons with him to good use by attacking his prize Porsche 959 with a Mizuno lob wedge, causing over £15,000 in damage. As one journalist later pointed out, 'at least she used one of his [former] sponsor's clubs'.

The manner of the splits with David Leadbetter and Brenna Cepelak went a long way to confirming everything people thought about Faldo, and he was accused by the media of being self-centred and cold-hearted. In PR terms the whole thing was a disaster. In the end, it was left to his latest love, Valerie Bercher, to put a more positive spin on things. 'Nick has a bad reputation for being a very cold man,' she said, offering a small but important insight into the man she loved, 'but I have found this to be completely untrue.' Then, having declared her feelings for the British golf star, she set about claiming credit for his recent run of good form. 'I hope I have improved his golf,' she said, referring to his recent World Cup triumph. 'Nick has been in a real mess for the last two years and I've decided to change his life.' As for improving his golf, she was probably right. Throughout his career, Faldo's best form on the golf course had often coincided with an upturn in his personal life. After all, Brenna had overseen his 1996 Masters triumph, two US Tour victories and (albeit on television) a spectacular performance in the singles against Curtis Strange at the 1995 Ryder Cup at Oak Hill.

Despite the furore, Faldo was remaining optimistic as 1999 approached. 'I still think I can win another major, I really do. It's been a long process getting back and I've got to take things step by step, but I'm only forty-one and I certainly think I've got the time. I've got to get back to winning again, getting on leaderboards and getting back into contention.'

Like the saying goes, 'Behind every successful man . . .'

19. END OF AN ERA?

After the 1998 PGA Championship, Nick Faldo outlined his plans to play a full schedule of tournaments in Europe the following season. 'The goal now,' he said, 'is Ryder Cup points.' Two weeks later at the BMW International in Munich, Mark James was appointed captain of the European team to face the Americans in Boston the following September. Never the closest of friends, the two men would now be inextricably linked over the next twelve months – and beyond.

The 1999 season had hardly begun before Faldo found himself under pressure. He played so badly in the first round of the Alfred Dunhill South African PGA in January that he threatened to 'walk the course'. Mark McNulty, his playing partner that day, agreed that it might not be a bad idea. 'He was hitting some shots like a rank twenty-four handicapper,' he commented unsympathetically. Down but not quite out, Faldo shook his head in disbelief before heading off to the practice ground. 'Golf,' he said, 'is a gentle reminder that you haven't worked hard enough.'

He followed these rounds of 77 and 76 with another disastrous performance in the South African Open a week later. Faldo was fast running out of answers. The break-up with Leadbetter was still a sore subject, his golf game was in limbo, and no matter how hard he worked with Chip Koehlke nothing seemed to improve. Worse still, this early-season form – or lack of it – had left his chances of making the Andersen Consulting Matchplay Championship in late February, the first in a series of lucrative World Series events open to the top 64 ranked players, hanging from a thread. It was vital to his Ryder Cup hopes that he made it into the select field. 'Obviously, it's a very big event with big Ryder Cup points,' he said. 'You want to have a big week there. If you have a good week, that's the equivalent of playing four tournaments in Europe because there's so much money.'

These new events were a good measure of how far Faldo had fallen. When they were first announced in September 1996,

Faldo would have been among the favourites to win the Andersen Consulting tournament scheduled for the La Costa Resort in Carlsbad, California; now he was struggling even to qualify. The pressure was on, and the maths was simple. At the end of January he was listed in sixty-fourth place in the world rankings; should he fall no further before 15 February, he would be off to La Costa with the rest of the world's elite. With that in mind, he decided to miss out the AT&T Pro-Am at Pebble Beach and the Buick Invitational in San Diego in favour of playing the Dubai Desert Classic in the second week of February. 'I'll have to have a good week,' he said, understating the importance of his first visit to the Arab Emirates in years.

Not surprisingly, there were players who hoped that Faldo, still regarded as one of the best matchplay golfers around, would not make it. The draw for the Andersen Consulting event was arranged in such a way that the top-ranked player played the bottom-ranked one, and so on. Since the Mercedes Championship in January it had become a fairly regular routine among the top hundred players on the PGA Tour to check rankings each Monday when they were released. Tiger Woods was riding high at number one, but David Duval in second place could just as easily be facing Nick Faldo should the rankings shift even fractionally. As for Faldo, his own place was equally precarious going into the Dubai tournament, with Sweden's Robert Karlsson just 0.8 points behind him in sixty-fifth spot. With every first-round loser at La Costa picking up a minimum of $25,000, Faldo knew how vital it was that he held on to that final position, and he put a positive spin on his form. 'I feel confident that things are close. That's the frustrating thing about this game. I've been far better than the results I've been getting.'

His results had certainly been inconsistent up to that point. As usual, there had been occasional flashes of the old Faldo genius, but they were both infrequent and short-lived. Not long ago he had been talking about slowing down; now, at the age of 41, he was playing a full schedule with plenty of hard practice in between – that is how much making the European Ryder Cup team meant to him. Despite his upbeat talk, making the select 64-man field was always going to be a close call. He missed the cut in Dubai after rounds of 75 and 74, offering his closest rivals a golden opportunity to overtake him in the world rankings.

Greg Turner, for example, needed to finish third on his own in the Australian Masters to dislodge Faldo. Tied for the lead at one point on the Sunday, he eventually wound up in a three-way tie for third (he was made first alternative at La Costa). And David Toms of the United States could have moved up to sixty-fourth by finishing in no worse a position than a three-way tie for seventh in the Buick Invitational the week before in San Diego. The unfortunate Toms had a fourteen-foot birdie putt at the last that would have given him seventh place on his own, but he missed and finished in a five-way tie for seventh. It was the same for Chris Perry, who had to finish second in the Buick to take the last spot in the Andersen event but, despite finishing with a gallant 66, ended in fourth place, five strokes behind runner-up Billy Ray Brown. Back in England, Faldo kept a close eye on all this action. He now relied on an elephant-sized favour from Jumbo Ozaki of Japan. Ozaki was a top-fifteen rated player, but he rarely travelled outside his home tour. He would have been perfectly entitled to take his place at the Andersen Consulting event, thus squeezing Faldo out by one, but PGA Tour officials quickly confirmed that he would not be playing at La Costa. By the skin of his teeth, the six-time major winner was in.

A week later, the provisional draw was made. The tournament organisers now had a first-round clash they could only have dreamed of a few months earlier: Nick Faldo v. Tiger Woods (Woods had consolidated his number-one ranking by winning the Buick Classic the week before). Number-two ranked player David Duval, who had taken the week off to go skiing in Idaho, would now play Stephen Leaney of Australia. Other notable first-round matches included Greg Norman against John Cook, Craig Stadler against Colin Montgomerie and, perhaps the pick of the bunch, Ernie Els against Paul Azinger. No pairing, however, was as tantalising as Woods against Faldo, the old maestro against the new kid on the block, the former undisputed king of golf versus the newly crowned youngster. Was it any wonder that the media couched the match in terms more fitting to a heavyweight boxing contest than a golf match?

To their credit, both Faldo and Woods stepped back from the hype and got on with their individual preparations. Up to this point they had only faced each other in regular 72-hole strokeplay events, so going head-to-head in a matchplay event was new territory for both of them (the nearest they had come to it was the second-day fourball match at Valderrama during the 1997 Ryder Cup, which Faldo had won). Even so, a curious rivalry had grown up between them over the past two years, neither giving nor asking for quarter from his opponent. Barely a word had passed between them on the rare occasions they had played together, which showed how much winning meant to both of them. On paper, though, it was a non-contest; Faldo and Woods were coming into the Andersen Consulting Matchplay Championship from opposite ends of the golfing spectrum. Fresh from his recent two-stroke victory in the Buick Invitational, Woods had widened the gap over Duval in the world rankings and now looked set to dominate the season; Faldo, in stark contrast, had missed the cut in two events that year already. But the two-time World Matchplay champion could still be a dangerous proposition for Woods, as his Ryder Cup record proved. 'Between two good professionals on their day,' said an optimistic Faldo shortly before his match, 'it's anybody's game over eighteen holes.'

In the end, brave words were never going to be enough to overcome the awesome form of Tiger Woods. Woods himself had made it to the final of the World Matchplay at Wentworth the previous autumn before narrowly losing to his good buddy Mark O'Meara. Against Faldo, he took an early lead and never let go, eventually defeating the hapless Englishman by 4 & 3. Faldo had failed to make the most of his opportunity, and this was the last World Series event he would play in for some time as his ranking began to move again in the wrong direction.

The run-up to the Masters in April was horrendous. Having gone out in the first round of the Andersen event, Faldo missed consecutive cuts in the Doral-Ryder Open and the Honda Classic. Then, in the Players Championship at the end of March at Ponte Vedra Beach, Florida, Faldo suffered a complete brainstorm. He made the cut with rounds of 71 and 75 to move into his first weekend of golf in over two months, then shot a disastrous third round of 83. He consoled himself with the world ranking points that would still come his way, but then came the worst news possible. Having unwittingly taken an incorrect drop, he was disqualified, and that meant no placing, no prize money and no points. Two weeks later at Augusta, the downward spiral was completed with horror rounds of 80 and 73, which added up to his third consecutive Masters cut. 'When things are going badly you practise as hard as you can,' Faldo said afterwards, 'trying to do this, trying to do that. Which is what I've been doing for the last couple of months. So maybe I have bogged myself down a little and not found enough time to totally switch off.'

Switch off from what – reality? At Augusta, his ball striking had been so poor that his driving average of 235 yards was exactly the same as 69-year-old Arnold Palmer. Worse still, Faldo had now made the halfway cut only once in seven events. Of course, pundits came forward to say how 'Nick is too good not to come out of this slump', but his record was proving otherwise. Question marks once again hung over his career. Was it really possible that Faldo would go the same way as other great players like Ian Baker-Finch, Sandy Lyle and Seve Ballesteros? Only time would tell.

A determinedly upbeat Faldo was beginning to sound like a broken old record as he insisted to anyone who would listen that his game was close to being at its best. 'Golf,' he kept saying, 'is a game of minor adjustments'; he was just weeks away from regaining the touch that had made him the best player in the world. 'This game is full of surprises,' he said philosophically, 'and I am constantly amazed by the very thin line between success and failure.' But people had stopped listening. Since his Masters victory exactly three years ago, Faldo had drifted off the leaderboard and settled down among the also-rans. The occasional bad round had now been replaced by the occasional good one; missed cuts were now commonplace. A small dip in form had become a slump, a slump had become a career-threatening crisis, and there seemed to be little he could do about it. Comparing his plight with that of former Open champion Ian

Baker-Finch, Gary Player commented, 'Nick was one of the greatest players in the world but the guy can't play at all now. When he makes a cut I am astonished.' Blaming over-coaching by David Leadbetter and others, he added that in his opinion Faldo was suffering from 'paralysis by analysis'. Not surprisingly, Faldo disagreed, saying that a vindictive media had misquoted Player just to cause problems. 'I don't believe Gary said that because he is one of my biggest fans,' he blasted back.

Prompted by the Gary Player quote, the press lost little time in contacting others for their thoughts on Faldo's plunge into mediocrity. 'Faldo is in a situation right now where he hasn't played well,' said PGA Championship winner Vijay Singh. 'People just look away from you after a while.' His old Ryder Cup partner Bernhard Langer was more sympathetic. 'Nick must be down because he was the greatest golfer in the world at the end of the eighties and into the nineties. I cannot pinpoint what his problems are but I am sure he will snap out of it. It's just a matter of time.' Peter Alliss was equally sanguine about Faldo's chances of arresting a slide that had seen him drop to a new low of eighty-ninth in the world rankings. Speaking at the Masters in April, the respected BBC commentator said, 'Faldo is in a terrible mess at the moment and I just don't understand it. I think it must be his nerves, and if your nerves go you're really finished. The longer you go without success the more difficult it is to come back again.' Greg Norman also chipped in with an opinion. 'I hate to see this happen to anybody, particularly a great player like Nick. There isn't a player in this game who has been at the top without hitting the bottom at one stage or another. It isn't a question of whether you like a guy or not, we all sympathise and empathise with him.'

Faldo was typically bull-headed. Rather than face facts, he chose instead to carry on implicating David Leadbetter. 'My swing got a little out of whack, a little out of time,' he said. 'I've got to firm up the main areas that are causing the mistakes and correct them. Then I have to work them in. It's been a little bit of a slow process.' The response from his former coach was not long in coming.

I'm sure there are a multitude of reasons [for his problems]. I think a lot of it started with his putting. He started putting poorly, and it put a lot of pressure on his long-game. You start missing those makeable putts, and you're not making the birdies. Then you try to hit it closer and miss the green and don't get up and down for par. It puts a lot of pressure on your long-game. What we did was keep things really simple, things like set-up, rhythm and so on.. He has obviously been a great putter throughout his career and I think it's tough when you have been a great putter then your putting goes off. All of a sudden, you get a negative reaction, and it goes right through your game.

Tracing his decline back to mid-1996, Leadbetter also believed that Faldo's decision to play full-time in America had eroded his confidence in the long term.

When he went to the States he had this aura about him. People would look at him and say, 'Wow! Nick Faldo!' He would go over there, play a couple of tournaments before a major and play maybe okay. He was just gearing himself up. Then in every major he was favourite to win. Whether he did or not was a different matter, but he was favourite to win because of his intensity, and his ability to play so well in those tournaments. Because of that he felt the other players treated him with that degree of respect, and they certainly did. That was something I think he lost when he started playing over there full-time. Because after a while, especially when he wasn't doing that well in regular tournaments, it was, 'We can beat Nick Faldo. What's the big deal? What's so special about this guy?' And I think whether subconsciously or otherwise he, to some extent, felt that too. So when these young kids are blowing it forty or fifty yards by him every time and putting the eyes out of the ball, I think it got wearing after a time.

On the subject of Faldo's future in the game, Leadbetter was equally forthright.

It's going to be a battle. I'm not saying he is 'done' because you can never say that about a guy like him because he could always find something and prove people wrong. It's sad. Some people bow out gracefully, some people don't. It's not like tennis, where you know you are a step slower, or you're losing in the first round and you think, 'I'd better get out of here.' Because in golf, there are always those little flashes that come back, but who's to say what mental damage this has done, not playing well for somebody like Nick for such a long period of time? I think he can get his technique back, but whether he can get his mind-set back is another thing.

Faldo, however, remained resolutely convinced that better days were just around the corner. 'You've just got to have good feedback,' he said about his lack of competitive success since the start of the year. 'You make some good swings, and you hit the shots you're trying to hit under tournament conditions. That gives you good feedback. That's really what you need to do after you haven't played well for a while. When you haven't played well for a while, all you've seen is negatives.'

Someone else who was giving him negative feedback was European team captain Mark James. Under the newspaper headline JAMES WARNS FALDO OVER CURRENT FORM, it was made clear to Faldo that unless he regained his form soon he would not be making it twelve consecutive Ryder Cup appearances. Speaking just days after Faldo missed the cut at Augusta, James confirmed that his team for Brookline would comprise only in-form players; there was no room for nostalgia. 'We have too much strength in depth for me to hand a wild card to someone playing on a wing and a prayer,' James said, somewhat harshly. 'If a player like Nick Faldo is on form then I want him in the side, but if he's not on form then I wouldn't consider him an asset.'

Talk about kicking someone when they are down! With ten automatic qualifiers and two captain's picks, it was common knowledge that Jesper Parnevik, playing full-time in the United States, would definitely receive one of the wild cards. That left Faldo in a large group of contenders for the final spot, including Ian Woosnam, Bernhard Langer, Andrew Coltart, Thomas Bjorn, Patrik Sjoland, Per-Ulrik Johansson and Sergio Garcia. Of course, some of these could still qualify automatically, but others would not. In many ways, Ryder Cup selection was the golfing version of Russian roulette: ultimately, only one player would survive, and Faldo hoped it would be him. The problem was, the man holding the gun was his old adversary 'Jesse' James.

During his post-Masters interview, James added that Faldo would have to improve his position in the Ryder Cup points table by at least nineteen places to have any chance of playing at Brookline. At that time Faldo was down in thirty-ninth place; perhaps James' comments were meant to spur him on, perhaps their purpose was to soften the blow should he ultimately have to leave him out. Whatever the truth, Faldo was having enough difficulty notching up a top-twenty finish or placing *anywhere*, let alone the European Order of Merit. 'I can't see myself giving a wild card to anyone not in the top twenty by the time the team is chosen,' James reiterated. 'And if I have enough experience in the side then I expect to stay within the top thirteen or fourteen.'

Faldo's next problem was inconsistency. After a brave and confidence-boosting display in the Benson and Hedges event at the Oxfordshire, where he partnered Mark James en route to opening rounds of 68 and 69, he slipped to a third-round 73 which wrecked any ambitions he had of a comeback victory. On the back of that, Faldo's fragile confidence started to evaporate. The following week at the Deutsche-Bank at St Leon Rot, he closed out the tournament with a horrible final round of 79 after earlier scores of 71, 75 and 73. Finishing no fewer than 25 shots behind the eventual winner, Tiger Woods, a dejected Faldo returned to England in May to prepare for the Volvo PGA Championship at Wentworth.

The Surrey venue had always been a personal favourite. Faldo was a long-time member of the club and there was no layout in Europe he knew better or liked more than the famous West course. It was here he hoped to kick-start his season, but after an opening round of 74 he was once again forced to defend his reputation in front of the headline-hungry British press. 'Physically I'm good, mentally and technically I'm still good,' he insisted. 'So it's just a matter of piecing it all together and then hopefully my confidence will return.' But confidence can take a real battering when things aren't going for you. After another mediocre performance and a fifty-ninth place, Faldo followed it up with yet another in the English Open at Hanbury Manor a week later. With Ryder Cup selection looming like a dark shadow over the rest of his season, even Colin Montgomerie's welcome comments about how an 'eighty per cent Faldo would be on my team' failed to lift his sagging morale. With only ten weeks left to the final qualifying event in Munich, things were looking increasingly desperate, and for the first time in his long career Faldo began to contemplate the possibility that he might not make the team.

He returned to America to prepare for the US Open knowing that he needed a good performance. A decade earlier, Pinehurst No. 2 would have been tailor-made for him. A narrow, tree-lined layout with lightning-fast greens, it was exactly the type of testing course he had once thrived on. Now it was just a struggle. Before the tournament, Faldo recalled an incident in London where a van driver had leant out of his window and shouted, 'Nick, sort it out! We need you!' A few weeks earlier at the B&H, Faldo had told the story with a broad smile on his face. Now, as he retold it, he looked like someone who had run out of answers. Sort it out? Faldo only wished he could.

A combination of wayward approach shots and poor putting resulted in a four-over-par round of 74, which left him struggling to make the halfway cut. Thankfully, the rest of the field was finding it equally tough, and after twelve holes of the second round Faldo was level par for the day and looked set to make it to the weekend. Then disaster struck in the form of four bogeys in the last six holes, leading to his sixth cut in the last ten major championships.

Faldo, still desperately searching for a late spurt in form, headed back to Britain and entered the Standard Life tournament at Loch Lomond the week before the Open. Buoyed by the introduction of yet another new coach in Mitchell Spearman, Faldo worked hard on his game, and for the first time in months it actually paid off. Combining some solid ball striking with some half-decent putting, he breezed around the Weiskopf-designed course like the Faldo of old with rounds of 68, 70 and 68. Then came the sting in the tail that had plagued him all season. In a good position to challenge for the lead, he stumbled to a disappointing last round of 74. It was scant reward for all the work that had gone before, but it was still his highest finish in six months, and with the Open at Carnoustie beckoning, beggars definitely could not be choosers.

With a combination of high winds, high rough and fairways so narrow that players and caddies were forced to walk down them single-file, Carnoustie proved to be the monster that everyone predicted, certainly the most testing major champion- ship of recent years. 'This is a golf course that'll find you out if you're a little low on confidence, and Nick's fighting battles on two fronts,' David Leadbetter said about his former pupil's chances. 'He's got his own internal fight as well as the fight with the golf course. And this golf course is a strong enough opponent without having to worry about anything else.' Faldo began his campaign with a couple of pars before a bad run meant that he reached the turn seven over par. To his credit, he then knuckled down in horrendous conditions and managed to complete the back nine in level par, including a birdie three at the extremely difficult seventeenth. Normally a 78 in the opening round of any event, never mind the Open, is the signal to book your flight for Friday evening; this time, however, Faldo was in exalted company as some of the best players in the world struggled to get to grips with the ferocious Angus links.

The weather conditions improved the next day, but Faldo's game did not. On a course where anything less than perfect ball striking is severely punished, he struggled gamely but ultimately failed to better his first-round score. In truth, nothing went horribly wrong, but neither did anything go right. It wasn't outright murder so much as death from a dozen cuts – or, in Faldo's case, a cut after a dozen small deaths. At the short thirteenth, he and his playing partners, Davis Love III and Jim Furyk, had reasonable putts for birdie. Faldo was the only one to miss. Then, on the downwind, downhill par-three sixteenth he drove into the bunker, and after a good recovery missed another one. Then came the final nail in the coffin when he drove straight into the burn off the seventeenth tee. Coming off the eighteenth green, Faldo summed up his performance in four words: 'Played lousy, putted lousy.'

That eight-over-par round of 79 left him at fifteen over par for the tournament. Despite the conditions it was never going to be good enough, and Faldo missed his first weekend at an Open in 24 years. It must have been cold comfort when local favourite Paul Lawrie came through to win in a play-off having finished the tournament at six over par. Davis Love had made clear his relief at not having to play over the weekend, but Faldo, to his credit, had never once stopped trying. Never once had he stopped his endless practice swings. Never once had he stopped looking for something that would turn his game around.

In terms of majors played in 1999, it was now strike three. Before Carnoustie Faldo was fifty-third in the Ryder Cup rankings, and he had hoped that a good finish in the Open would be his passport to Brookline. Things were now looking hopeless. He discussed his options with John Simpson, among others. He had entered just two more ranking tournaments before the cut-off point of 22 August, but even with a win at the Smurfit European Open in Ireland he would still not make the grade. The only real chance left to him was the PGA Championship at Medinah in the second week in August, and even then he would probably have to win it. 'The longer you go through this phase, the tougher it is,' said Leadbetter about the excessive strain Faldo was putting on his game in order to make the Ryder Cup. 'It gets to the point where you put a bit of pressure on yourself to perform and then, as every week goes by, it gets worse. It's sad. You don't like to see any player, especially Nick, who has been Great Britain's greatest, not compete as he has in years gone by.'

Britain's greatest player – and its richest, if you believed one survey published in a daily newspaper at this time – headed for the K Club for the European Open at the end of July. His performance there was solid rather than spectacular. He did enough to finish in the top thirty with rounds of 70, 73, 70 and 70, but very little else. Now it was a case of Medinah or bust.

Faldo began his campaign in Chicago on a positive note with three birdies in the first nine holes, moving smoothly into the weekend with a pair of solid 71s. His third round started well too with a level-par front nine followed by a birdie at the tenth to take Faldo into the top ten on the leaderboard. The astonished gasp from the large contingent of British press in the media centre told the whole story. Was it really possible that the former world number one could roll back the years and, at a crucial time in his career, win his first PGA Championship, or would it all finish in tears and frustrating failure again? In the end it was something of a mixture of the two. Faldo frittered away shots at the twelfth, fourteenth, sixteenth and eighteenth for a third-round score of 75. It was the same up-and-down story on the Sunday: a double-bogey at the par-three second was quickly followed by birdies at the fifth, sixth and seventh to bring him back to level par for the tournament. For his many fans watching on television back in Britain, this was wonderful stuff. It was beginning to turn into a vintage Faldo performance. He scrutinised each shot as if it were his last, grinding out shot after shot, edging ever nearer to the top of the leaderboard. Then he three-putted on the par-three thirteenth and fell out of contention. The double-bogey punctured his balloon of concentration, and a dispirited Faldo stumbled back to the clubhouse with two late bogeys for another 75 and a disappointing tie for forty-first – a massive fifteen shots behind the winner, Tiger Woods.

True to recent form, Faldo remarked afterwards, 'A couple of shots really hurt me, but at least my game is way more positive.' Not a tournament seemed to have gone by in recent months without Faldo hinting at a comeback in form. But things were truly desperate, and with just a fortnight to the final Ryder Cup qualifying event in Munich, Faldo was reduced to trying to talk himself into the team. 'In a month's time I'll be playing really well,' he said after his final round at Medinah. 'We've got a pretty young team of rookies and nobody has got more experience than I have. I feel I'm a good team member and I feel I'm good on the course with a rookie. I've done a good job with the young guys helping them play their best.' (Whether or not David Gilford would have agreed with that last mark was questionable.)

But Mark James was far more interested in the form of Sergio Garcia and the other Ryder Cup rookies Faldo had offered to partner than in Faldo's curriculum vitae. In that respect, he would not be disappointed. The nineteen-year-old Spaniard had catapulted himself into James' team after his sensational second-place finish at the PGA, while Miguel Angel Jiménez (joint tenth), Jean Van de Velde (joint twenty-sixth), Paul Lawrie (joint thirty-fourth) and Andrew Coltart (joint sixty-fifth) had all performed well. When asked before he left Chicago whether he'd made his decision, James was typically coy. 'I have, yes,' he said enigmatically. Perhaps more revealing in this respect were comments he had made earlier in the week. 'The situation, as Nick knows, is that to be considered for selection you have to show some form. I would love to have an on-form Faldo and an on-form Woosnam and an on-form Seve on the scene. If they're not going to be in there, they are not going to be there. There comes a time when everyone has to move over, and if it's this year then so be it.'

How big a clue did anyone need that Faldo would not be picked? Yet with Garcia having qualified automatically, the competition for wild-card picks had been thinned down; theoretically, the door had opened for Nick Faldo. After everything that had happened, there was still a slim chance he could make it, and as attention turned to the BMW International in Bavaria, Faldo was not without support. There was a rather inexperienced look about the European team, and some sections of the media began to campaign for the inclusion of Nick Faldo, a battle-hardened veteran of eleven Ryder Cup matches. In many respects it was a convincing argument. The potential side to represent Europe in the US's back garden had little or no Ryder Cup experience whatsoever.

By the time the European Tour pitched up at Golfclub München Nord-Eichenried a week later, speculation had moved up several notches from reasoned discussion to fevered debate. Especially when Nick Faldo decided to travel back from the United States to play in the event. 'The Ryder Cup has been a big part of my life,' he said before leaving for Germany. 'I would love to be there again.'

So who was Mark James likely to select as his wild cards? Sweden's Jesper Parnevik, at that time twelfth in the Ryder Cup standings, had already been given the nod by James at the PGA Championship and was spared the long journey back to Europe. His inclusion was kept a closely guarded secret, but it was assumed by everyone that he would play, especially after his victory at the Greater Greensboro Open in April. So to whom would the final wild card go? Assuming that James did not pick himself – and all season he had refused to rule that out – the sensible money was on Bernhard Langer, Robert Karlsson, Andrew Coltart or Nick Faldo. Of course, if Langer, the local favourite, were to qualify automatically by winning the BMW International, it might simplify matters enormously. Langer would then be ahead of Andrew Coltart and Robert Karlsson in the table; surely James could not then omit a player with Faldo's experience?

Still convinced that a good performance might be enough to tip the balance in his favour, Faldo made the perfect start with a season's-best opening round of 67 followed by a 73 to make the cut. Then all hell broke loose after he shot a lacklustre 72 on the Saturday, but it had little to do with how he had played. As Faldo came off the final green, it was obvious that something was wrong and it did not take the media long to find out what. Standing in the entrance to the scorer's tent with his fingers picking nervously at the flap, Faldo recounted what had happened the previous evening at the Munich Sheraton.

He had come across Mark James in the hotel foyer, and decided to press the European Ryder Cup captain on the matter of his wild-card selections. At the time James was on his way to dinner accompanied by his wife Jane; he was polite to Faldo but in no mood to talk shop in such a public place. Faldo, like everyone else, would have to wait, but having already lived for six months with the threat of missing out on the Ryder Cup, Faldo would not be brushed off quite so easily. Insisting that James there and then clarify his particular situation, Faldo asked, 'What if I win this week? Would that be enough to get me in?' James' answer took Faldo completely by surprise. Looking at Faldo with ill-disguised annoyance, the European captain said without hesitation, 'No, even if you win it's unlikely that you will get a pick.'

As he told the story it was obvious just how much the news had upset Faldo. Almost inevitably, as more journalists headed over from the nearby media centre, his mood turned from disappointment to recrimination. 'I'm gutted,' he said. 'One line that James threw at me was the killer. It was the one saying that even if I won, I was unlikely to be picked. That's the one line that knocked me over. I only hope he's got some more motivating lines for the rest of the team.'

It was never going to end there. James was immediately asked for his comments about Faldo. 'I don't think this should be made public,' he said with growing unease. 'Nick's come to me for clarification and suddenly he doesn't want to hear what I've got to say to him. He complained when I didn't speak to him and now he doesn't want to hear what I had to say. If I say nothing he's not happy, if I say something he's not happy.' The verbal ping-pong had started, the battle lines well and truly drawn in what was destined to become a long-running saga.

This was just the latest chapter in a fairly turbulent relationship. Faldo and James had made their Ryder Cup debut together at Royal Lytham in 1977. They were destined never to be bosom-buddies from the outset, but it was more a personality clash than any outright dislike. Like everyone else they had their occasional spats, but it was the 1979 Ryder Cup match at the Greenbrier that first saw them really at loggerheads.

James and his co-conspirator Ken Brown had spent most of the opening ceremony looking bored and generally making a nuisance of themselves while the rest of team, including Faldo, looked on with ill-disguised displeasure. From there it was all downhill. They informed team captain John Jacobs that they would play together or not at all, and team member Tony Jacklin was all in favour of having James and Brown bundled on the next plane back to London. Thankfully, the problem effectively disappeared after an injury to Mark James in the opening fourballs which ruled him out for the final two days. But the effect on team morale had been devastating and the subsequent 17–11 defeat was largely ascribed to the devilish twins. Both men have since put their actions down to youthful indiscretion, but Faldo always did have a long memory.

A lot of water flowed under Swilcan Bridge, but the relationship between the two remained polite rather than friendly. That is until 1994, when Faldo complained bitterly about the poor quality of the courses being used on the European Tour. Citing that as his main reason for joining the PGA Tour, he also slammed the practice facilities and generally upset many of his fellow players, including Mark James. A staunch defender of European golf, James publicly attacked Faldo, saying that he should stay and change things rather than snipe from abroad.

'What he doesn't like,' James once said, 'is somebody standing up to him.' Indeed, as characters the two men are just too different. Compared with the intensely private Faldo, 'Jesse' James is a laconic figure who hides a boyish sense of fun underneath a serious, almost forbidding exterior. Quick-witted with a keen sense of the ridiculous, he can be hard to fathom at times. When James says one thing, he often means something totally different, and for anyone fortunate enough to interview him, this can prove very confusing. Yet above all he is the most trusted man on tour. When he says he will do something, he does it; when he says he will not do something, he will not do it. And if he said Faldo was out, then Faldo was out.

Not surprisingly, Faldo felt that despite his near-terminal slump to 192nd in the world rankings, he still had something to offer the team at Brookline. After all, he was not playing all that well when he took on and beat Curtis Strange in the crucial singles at Oak Hill only four years earlier. But as far as Mark James was concerned a Faldo win in Germany would only take him to twenty-second in the final standings and that was never going to be enough. 'I said all along that it was unlikely I would go further down than the top twenty in the table,' said James resolutely. 'It wasn't written in stone, but that was my thinking.'

The problem was that Faldo never believed him and couldn't accept his decision. He could understand Woosnam or Langer being left out because they had failed to make the grade, but surely the same did not apply to him. Then, in a moment of typical Faldo-like petulance, he accused James of not telling him 'a dicky bird' since May. Having shifted the blame to his own satisfaction, Faldo then said how he 'could have done with a week off' had he been told he was not in the running at Medinah the week before. On hearing these comments, the statuesque Jane James summed up the feelings of many when she said, 'He's nothing but a big cry-baby!'

The rest of the BMW International in Munich unsurprisingly turned out to be an uncomfortable time for both men. Despite shooting a final round of 67, Faldo spent much of the latter half of the weekend giving off-the-cuff press briefings to journalists he had previously despised. Insisting that he was 'worn out' after playing both the American and European tours in the hope of making the Ryder Cup, he summed up his frustration with the muttered comment, 'I wasn't even close to getting a pick.'

Meanwhile, Mark James continued to play the diplomatic card. Forever stressing the positive aspects of the situation, he said how much he admired the effort Faldo had made 'trying to get his game in order', adding that he expected Faldo to win more majors and play in future Ryder Cups – just not this one! Insisting that his final selection would not be made until the Sunday evening, as planned, he gave a wry grin when asked if he had plans to hold further meetings in the foyer of the Munich Sheraton.

In many ways the official announcement, when it finally came, did little to placate an increasingly upset Faldo. Irishman Padraig Harrington had muscled his way into the team after his second-place finish at the BMW International, behind the eventual winner, Colin Montgomerie. This meant that Robert Karlsson had been pushed out of the automatic top ten, despite finishing joint ninth himself. It now seemed that the final wild-card place was between Langer and Karlsson, but James went for Andrew Coltart. The news of this unexpected selection brought an audible gasp from the media. 'It was a desperately difficult decision,' James said. 'Jesper [Parnevik] is one of the world's top twenty players and to go there without him was inconceivable. But Coltart, Karlsson and Langer were all very close [for the last pick]. Bernhard has been a rock of the European team for many years, but his form since the US Open has not been so good. I was gutted to have to tell Robert he was not in the team, but I think Andrew has played the best since the US Open.'

As the press conference continued it became increasingly obvious that Faldo had never been in the reckoning as far as Mark James was concerned. Ultimately his lack of form throughout the season had been his undoing, and although James admitted that Faldo had undergone a mini-resurgence over the past few weeks, in his opinion he had finished far too far down the Ryder Cup rankings to be considered. In the end, Captain James said he had 'too much respect for the young players' to overlook them in favour of a more experienced professional. 'In my experience,' said James to anyone who might question his choice, 'experience is overrated.'

With a groundswell of sympathy building for Faldo's plight (as early as April his former Ryder Cup partner Lee Westwood was convinced he should play, saying, 'A Ryder Cup without Nick Faldo would be a weaker European team'), James felt honour-bound to offer some extra words of comfort. 'He's done everything right to try to get his game back,' he said unconvincingly, 'and I admire him professionally enormously. But the fact is that there's a limit to how far down the list you can go, and if you pick someone when their form is not good enough then I don't think you're doing them any favours. I've been in the situation in the Ryder Cup of being in the team and not being on form, and it's not a nice experience.'

But preferring the relatively untested Coltart over battle-hardened players like Faldo and Langer left James wide open to criticism from the press, especially as Coltart's inclusion raised the number of rookies in the European side to seven compared with just one for the USA (and that was the world number two David Duval). Writing in the *Daily Express*, journalist Martin Hardy summed up the general feeling about Faldo's omission from the team. 'It is still staggering that the obsessive, cranky instinct for winning that so dominated his life for so long – and provided British sport in particular and European golf in general with the presence of an authentic superstar – should now be so lightly dismissed by a team which, between its twelve members, can boast of a mere three majors – precisely half of Faldo's haul.'

In the week following his surprise selection, Andrew Coltart became embroiled in the 'experience versus youth' debate that was raging in the British golfing press. Never one to shun an argument, the feisty 29-year-old Scot delivered a damning put-down to his critics, including Nick Faldo. 'I think he was a great benefit to the team two years ago, but Nick hasn't really done anything in the last couple of years. He's been beaten and bettered by other, younger players. Maybe other players aren't in awe of him as they used to be and he's no longer one hole up standing on the first tee in the minds of his opponents.' Then, in a radio interview for the BBC, the outspoken rookie spelt it out again, loud and clear. During a discussion of the merits of sending over a European side without Faldo, Langer, Ballesteros or Woosnam, he commented, 'Without sounding too cool or harsh, I think these guys are cracking on a little bit and maybe it's time to stand aside and let some younger guys take over. You can't go on for ever.'

Considering how exhausted he felt after the BMW, Faldo might have agreed with him. Having worked so hard to make the Ryder Cup and failed, and with the prospect of another gruelling five-week run on the PGA Tour, Faldo had just about had enough. 'I don't need this,' he said. 'I just kept thinking, "You're working hard and you're not getting anything out of it." By the end of the Open I said to myself, "Christ, I've still got twelve more tournaments to play to get this year over, then I'm going to explode."'

After Germany, Faldo headed over the Alps to Switzerland, where he narrowly missed the cut in the Canon European Masters at Crans-sur-Sierre. And when asked about the forthcoming match in Boston, he was surprisingly upbeat about Europe's chances. 'The Americans always look strong on paper and it's been like that for the last few times, but we've still won. We must go there with the attitude that we have all to gain and nothing to lose. They still have to win it, so we must turn the pressure on them.' It seemed that he was already beginning to accept that he had not played well enough to warrant a place in the European team, and he surprised everyone by offering his help to the rookies on the team. After all, was there another player who knew more about playing in the Ryder Cup than Nick Faldo? 'I don't want to tread on any toes,' he said, 'but there are a few tips I could give our team, especially the newcomers. I'll get in touch with them to see if I can help or answer any questions they may have.'

After his mini-sojourn in Europe, it was back to North America to fulfil the minimum criterion of fifteen tournaments to keep a PGA Tour card. Starting at the Canadian Open at Glen Abbey, he began positively by recording his first top-ten finish of the season. The eighth place and the cheque for $77,500 gave

Faldo just the boost he needed, both mentally and financially. It also went some way towards proving a point to Mark James, but from there it was a case of grinding out the rest of the year. This meant making even more cuts, keeping his card and building up some much-needed confidence.

Yet where Faldo goes, controversy is never far behind. After his morale-enhancing third round of 67 at Glen Abbey, the six-time major winner was invited into the media centre to talk to the press. Nothing special in that, except that Faldo inexplicably chose the occasion to make a withering verbal attack on his former Ryder Cup partner Colin Montgomerie. Speculating on the reasons why the European number one had not played more tournaments in the United States, Faldo said, 'I don't know what he wants. I'm surprised he hasn't done something different as a challenge. But he likes to earn his fat cheques each week, and there is no harm in that . . . if you're motivated by that. A few are. Most of us go for ten claret jugs.' Having criticised Monty for his big-fish-in-a-small-pond attitude, Faldo went on to compare the 36-year-old Scot with Jumbo Ozaki, who had won more than a hundred tournaments but only one of them outside Japan. 'He's great in his own backyard, he's comfortable, happy,' he continued on the subject of Montgomerie. 'He knows he's only got to play half-decent and he's going to be there. Even if he plays badly, he's the sort of guy who turns around a score the next day and gets himself into contention. He's in the comfort zone and I think he just enjoys it. He goes out and wins a couple of hundred thousand each week and goes home. I'd be comfortable if I did that every week.'

Monty, who had just set a European record with over £1.6 million in prize-money earnings, was understandably upset by Faldo's comments, especially since he had said two weeks earlier that he had no intention of playing full-time on the PGA Tour because of family commitments back in Britain. But coming as it did just three weeks before the Ryder Cup in Boston, Faldo's attack seemed to have wider implications. By criticising Europe's top player, Faldo had criticised the European team – at least that was the way it was seen by Mark James, who interpreted Faldo's off-the-cuff remarks as a deliberate attempt to undermine morale.

Speaking at the Lancôme Trophy at St Nom-la-Breteche, Monty tried to calm things down by saying that he would clarify things with Faldo when he saw him next. Aware that Faldo could have been misquoted or had his comments taken out of context, he said, 'I've always considered Nick and I to be good friends and I'm equally sure something has been made of nothing and that his comments were not meant to harm anybody in the European Ryder Cup team.'

With just a week to go before the match at Brookline, a potentially explosive situation had been diplomatically defused. Montgomerie, like everybody else, hoped that peace would now prevail. Sadly, as Mark James' controversial book about the Ryder Cup would show, it did not.

The 1999 Ryder Cup was a memorable affair, and not for all the right reasons. Trailing by four points going into the final day, the Americans fought like tigers, and as the tide of the match turned so did the mood of the New England crowd. From certain defeat came the merest sniff of victory, and with it an atmosphere of nationalistic fervour. As the singles matches progressed, enthusiastic applause was replaced by chants of 'Go USA!' and 'You're the man!' A provocative mixture of high-fives, low-fives and noisy American wives, it was not a day any European will remember with pleasure. No one could deny that it was a remarkable fight-back by the Americans, perhaps the best in Ryder Cup history, yet the brilliance of their golf will forever be overshadowed by the boorish behaviour of their players and the crowd.

In truth, Team USA enjoyed the prospect of winning back the trophy a little too much. As the scoreboard turned red signalling home-team advantage, they simply lost the plot. By the time they danced a victory jig en masse right across the seventeenth green, things had already gone badly wrong. The Ryder Cup tradition of fair play and comradeship had been replaced by clenched-fist salutes, high-octane aggression and barely transparent gamesmanship. Who was to blame? It did not matter. Who actually won? Nobody cared. The most important question at the time was, how had things been allowed to go so far?

Expressing the sense of outrage felt by many, the *Daily Telegraph* said that the Americans 'not only indulged in the worst excesses of triumphalism during and after the match, but also turned in a repulsive display of bad manners', no doubt referring to the incident on the seventeenth green. Michael Bonallack, secretary of the Royal and Ancient Golf Club of St Andrews, the guardian of golfing tradition, likened the atmosphere at Brookline to 'a bear pit'. 'I felt embarrassed for golf,' he said afterwards. 'It went way beyond the decency you associate with proper golf. I love the Ryder Cup and I don't want to see it degenerate into a mob demonstration every time we play it.'

Nick Faldo agreed. As the dust settled on the Battle of Brookline, he voiced his concern at the direction the Ryder Cup was taking. 'It has become too much life and death,' he said. 'Let's get back to the bottom line. This is twenty-four guys going out and playing. Sure, you are going to play really as hard as you can on the golf course. But when you come off, the goal is you can sit at the bar and talk. "Hey, the three-wood you hit was an awesome shot!" If we get back to that level, then great.' Wise words indeed, although no one could recall a time when Nick Faldo had sat in a bar and said to a playing partner, 'Hey, the three-wood you hit was an awesome shot!'

A month later, in October, Faldo improved on his eighth place in Canada with a top-five finish in the Michelob Championship at Kingsmill. There he had revealed a much more relaxed attitude towards his game, although, surprisingly for this popular visitor to American shores, he had been heckled during his second round of 70. It had happened on the par-four eighth, moments after he three-putted for a double-bogey. As Faldo picked his ball out of the cup, a spectator shouted, 'Why don't you let her putt for you?' pointing at his pony-tailed caddie Fanny Sunesson. Coming less than two weeks after the Ryder Cup, where the crowd had abused various members of the European team along with their wives, it could have proved a difficult moment, but Faldo brushed it off with a joke. 'Be careful,' he said, waving his fist in mock threat, 'I weigh two hundred and thirty pounds, so don't mess with me.' Speaking about the incident later, Faldo was still in a jokey mood. 'He was probably right. Fanny probably would have holed it.'

In the end, Faldo shrugged off this minor distraction to break par in every round. His seven-under-par total (70, 70, 70 and

67) made up for consecutive missed cuts in the Texas Open and Buick Challenge at the end of September (tournaments, incidentally, which coincided with the Ryder Cup match at Brookline in Massachusetts). It was a confidence-boosting performance, and he was delighted with it. 'If I get my putter worked out I think I'm going to get back in the winner's circle,' he said afterwards. 'I'm really pleased with the way I'm striking it. I did everything a lot better tee to green. It drives me mad playing badly. It infuriates me because I know I can do better. That's why I've been grinding away. I don't want to roll over just yet.' Faldo was still a long way from his best, but the confidence was starting to trickle back. 'I was trying to hit shots that I was not comfortable with,' he said, attempting once again to explain the reason for his extended dip in form. 'I was putting too much pressure on myself. I was trying to hit perfect shots every time. I kept saying to myself, "Come on, if you want to be a decent player you've got to be able to hit this."'

As happened during the recent Ryder Cup, Faldo's personal life continued to attract press interest. In November 1999, normally a quiet month in the golf calendar, Faldo announced his engagement to Valerie Bercher – something that had been on the cards for some time. Since their first meeting at the Canon European Masters in Switzerland in August 1998 they had been virtually inseparable, the 26-year-old Swiss Miss offering him support and encouragement throughout his problematic campaign to make the Ryder Cup. She had been his constant companion on tour since April, and Faldo credited his gradual rise in form to her calming presence. 'Thanks to Valerie's love and support,' he gushed, 'I am happier than ever and we are both very excited about our future plans together. This one's going to last.'

Sadly for Faldo, another partnership failed to survive the year. Shortly before the Australian Open in Sydney at the end of the year, his long-time caddie Fanny Sunesson suddenly announced that she wanted to quit after a decade's service. She had been a permanent fixture in his often turbulent life, the only one to survive the occasional night of the long knives that saw two wives, one girlfriend, one high-profile coach and several lesser-name teachers depart for ever. Throughout it all

20. STORM IN A RYDER CUP

Nick Faldo entered the new millennium with renewed confidence. 'I'm quite excited about 2000,' he declared. 'I want to be in contention, to be in the winner's circle again, and it's going to happen. I think there is another major in me and I still want to get back into the Ryder Cup team. I am starting to climb the ladder again.'

When Faldo spoke, publicly at least, he invariably talked positively in terms of winning major championships. Yet his career had been in virtual free-fall since his Masters victory four years earlier and there had been only occasional signs of recovery. To make matters worse, his former swing guru David Leadbetter had gone, his long-time caddie Fanny Sunesson had gone, and despite working harder on his game than many players half his age, many experts now considered him a spent force. As Faldo began his twenty-fourth year as a tournament pro, questions were still being asked about how long he could keep going. The answer was an emphatic 'For as long as I want.'

In the centenary US Open at Pebble Beach in June, Faldo rolled back the years to set up an unlikely challenge to the brilliant Tiger Woods. He was building on a solid run of results since the Australian Open at the end of 1999, and things were slowly starting to turn around. More significantly, he was starting to putt better, and for Faldo that was the key. Yet despite the improvement in his overall game he was realistic enough to know that to win was now an uphill struggle.

A lot of guys have got better odds of shooting sixty-fives as they can reach the par fives in two, which immediately reduces the course to par sixty-eight or sixty-nine. Where I'm hitting a three- or two-iron for my second shot they're taking mid-irons and reducing the margin of error. I can combat that by swinging it the best way I can and using a bit of technology such as a longer driver, but the key is the short-game. If I can get it up and down better than most then I still have a chance.

At Pebble Beach, he did get it up and down better than most. Although he, like the rest, would finish a country mile behind the awesome Woods, his campaign was deemed a triumph of tactical brilliance. Plotting his way around the testing 6,846-yard course like a chess grandmaster, he knew exactly when to gamble and when not to. Wrapped in a cocoon of concentration that even a lengthy fog delay could not puncture, he shot an opening-day 69. It was a classic. While players of the calibre of Sergio Garcia and David Duval stumbled around blindly in 75, Faldo doggedly held on to the end – an attitude that stuck with him all week.

Hanging on to the advantage he had secured for himself, he ended the tournament in a four-way tie for seventh place, his best performance in a major since his fourth place in the 1996 Open at Royal Lytham. With Tiger Woods in such sparkling form it was never likely that Faldo would win, but success can be judged in different ways. For the rookie, it is about making the cut; for the journeyman pro, it's all about making enough money to keep your card; for Faldo, it was all about staying in contention for as long as possible, which is what he did, well into the third round. After that, Woods was out of sight and everyone was playing for second spot. Holing pressure putt after pressure putt on that tense final day, Faldo gave a vintage performance, and if anyone needed reminding just how great a competitor he truly was, this performance was it.

Faldo had made seven cuts out of ten on the PGA Tour leading up to the US Open, including his first in the Masters since 1996, and this went some way towards justifying his decision to work with Swedish sports psychologist Kjell (pronounced 'Shell') Enhager. Faldo had been introduced to Enhager by Fanny Sunesson after missing the cut in the Open at Carnoustie in July 1999. The Swede had already worked with a number of European players including Per-Ulrik Johansson and Joakim Haeggman, and with Nick Faldo his first task had been to help him to relax more, to see things more positively. Faldo was always prone to periods of self-doubt, so Enhager wanted far less emphasis on improving the golf swing and more emphasis on improving the mental aspects of his game. Then, as Faldo slowly gained in confidence, Enhager began to analyse how he acted when things went well for him so he could remind Faldo when things were going badly. Dealing with everything from body language to positive speech patterns, it was all about breaking with negative modes of behaviour and preventing them from being reinforced. Ever the perfectionist, Faldo had arranged to spend some time in Ireland so that he and Enhager could work closer together with minimal distractions. 'I spent a week on the golf course with him,' said the Swede, 'building a picture from every movement and every word he said.'

Something must have come of it. Coming into the US Open, Faldo had talked about clearing his mind of the obstacles that had held him back over the past few years. While never directly referring to his turbulent private life: his divorce from Gill, his acrimonious split from David Leadbetter and the very public departure of Brenna Cepelak, it was obvious what he meant. Now, with the help of Enhager (who also stepped in for bagman Murray Lott at Pebble Beach after the Australian returned home to Sydney to be with his pregnant wife), he finally believed he could see light at the end of the tunnel.

In the end, it all came down to focus. Nick Faldo, like many great champions, had always worked towards a goal, whether it was breaking 80 for the first time, rebuilding his swing or winning the Open. His problems had started when he effectively ran out of targets at which to aim. Sure there were other major titles to win, but life is never as simple and clear-cut as that. As most of us know, life has a way of getting in the way of ambition, especially if your personal life intrudes on your career to the extent that it did for Nick Faldo. 'It's so difficult to regain your confidence,' Faldo remarked, 'and it's so frustrating to know you were once number one. But getting back to playing well comes so slowly. You start on the range, then hope to take it to the course and have a good round or two. Then you want to get into the top ten on the weekend, then the top three. I'm prepared to do all that. I've put in an awful lot of work.'

In many ways the lack-of-focus problem could be traced back to his Masters victory at Augusta in 1996. Following the defeat of Greg Norman in such a devastating manner, Faldo's focus had shifted entirely. Having achieved his goal of winning his first major after a four-year drought, he started to look at what didn't work in his game instead of concentrating on what did work. 'I'd been getting into little knots with my routine and visualisation,' Faldo explained. 'When you're playing well, you stick to the same things and everything stays in sequence.' In terms of unravelling those knots, Enhager proved to be a lifesaver. 'You need to focus all your energy on what you are trying to achieve, and if your energy has been burnt up off the course you are going to struggle,' the Swede explained. 'At this level you play as much with your heart as your mind, and if your heart is somewhere else it is a problem.'

The most obvious change was in Faldo's on-course demeanour. Light years away from the sour-faced, round-shouldered figure of the past two years, he now strode upright down the fairway with renewed confidence. Before Enhager's input he had remarked that every course was beginning to look like 'eighteen bear traps', and that his only thought was 'How can I avoid getting my ankles bitten off?' Now it was more a case of, 'I have an opportunity to go out and make some birdies. Let's see what happens.'

Away from the golf course there had also been a miraculous change. As his world ranking had plummeted off the scale, so had his overall mood. In press interviews, constantly asked to explain what had gone wrong, he had become increasingly monosyllabic. When he had spoken at any length it was only to trot out the party line about 'how things are getting better' and 'I'm working hard on my game and should be seeing the benefits any day', but now that had all changed. It was as if someone had let the sunshine into his cell. He was much more relaxed, even to the point of joking with interviewers, and this time it was not an act. In the space of six months he had evolved into a far more laid-back and positive individual. Having scraped along the bottom for so long, he had discovered at last some peace of mind, and it showed. When asked whether Faldo could now regain his old form, his new guru was typically forthright. 'I'm very optimistic,' he said. 'But it's not a question of trying to regain what he had before. The things he accomplishes from now on will be accomplished by the new Faldo, not the old one.'

Although the 'new' Nick Faldo appeared remarkably upbeat, there was still enough baggage from the 'old' one to make life uncomfortable. At Pebble Beach he was quizzed by the media about the controversial remarks made about him in Mark James' new book about the 1999 Ryder Cup, *Into the Bear Pit*, serialised in the *Daily Mail* at the end of May. When asked whether he would be lodging an official complaint, Faldo just shrugged his shoulders and said he had no plans to do anything apart from play golf. But this decision was soon turned on its head as he became embroiled in an increasingly bitter argument with the 1999 Ryder Cup captain.

The book, written with the help of *Daily Express* journalist Martin Hardy, dealt with some of the more controversial incidents that had occurred during the Ryder Cup at Brookline. Effectively lifting the lid off this particular Pandora's box, it criticised the American team's behaviour and, in particular, the invasion of the seventeenth green during the Justin Leonard/ José-María Olázabal singles match, which left James 'speechless with rage'.

Speechless was right. In the immediate aftermath of the Battle of Brookline it had been noted how little James had had to say on the behaviour of the Americans. As the British tabloids fell over themselves to criticise the unsporting manner in which the Ryder Cup had been won, the European captain kept a diplomatic silence, even at the post-match press conference on the Sunday evening. 'Perhaps he's saving it all up for a book,' one hack whispered somewhat prophetically as dusk settled on the Country Club.

Perhaps predictably, *Into the Bear Pit* received a hostile reaction in the United States after its publication in May (especially since James had just been appointed vice-captain to Sam Torrance for the 2001 Ryder Cup at the Belfry). Among those most upset was Tom Lehman, who was described in the book in less than glowing terms. The 1996 Open champion had, in the words of James, broken 'the hundred metres record in an effort to get to Leonard' on the seventeenth green that day. Lehman, in turn, was less than complimentary when he was asked for his view on James' literary efforts. 'I think it's really low class,' he said. 'I hope he feels good about it. I guess every good story needs a villain and I'm glad he's found me. I hope he feels good about making money out of taking shots at other people's character and integrity. And I think he ought to be proud that he's dragging the Ryder Cup through the muck.' Harsh stuff indeed, but Faldo and Lehman were not alone in receiving a tongue-lashing from Mark James. David Duval was also blasted for his rabble-rousing display on the final day. 'Had I not known better,' James wrote, 'I would have sworn he was on something.' And having taken pot-shots at various players, including mentioning captain Ben Crenshaw's habit of kissing the ground in celebration, James also criticised the crowd, the stewards and even the garish shirts Team USA wore that Sunday. 'They exemplified the difference in dress taste between our two continents. Had I laid out anything similar in front of my own team on the final morning, I would have been asked to seek therapy.'

Ultimately, though, it was the verbal assault on Nick Faldo that grabbed most of the headlines. James lambasted Faldo for a number of reasons, not least of which was his stinging criticism of European number one Colin Montgomerie in the run-up to the Ryder Cup. James chose to see the 'fat cheques' interview as an attack on team morale. 'The outburst came at such a crucial time,' he wrote in the book, 'that I can only think it was deliberately designed to undermine the team's challenge. In the eyes of the team it was unpardonable.' No matter whether Faldo was quoted correctly or not (he later said he hadn't been), James was in no mood for excuses. Having questioned Faldo's patriotism, he then threw doubt on his suitability as a future leader of the European team.

Faldo has said in the past that he would like to be Ryder Cup captain, but I think that will depend a lot on his relationships with the players. A lot of them do not like him because he has been critical of the European Tour, tends to keep himself so much to himself and tends not to acknowledge people. Somebody the players do not particularly get on with will probably not make a good captain, and unless Faldo's relationships with others improve I doubt he can ever be elected. Just because he has achieved what he has does not automatically qualify him for the captaincy.

Not surprisingly, others agreed with him. 'You ask any of the guys out here about Faldo and you won't hear many kind words,' said Jamie Spence, member of the European Tour Players Committee. 'I'm not saying he has to be Mr Happy all the time, but he never even says, "Hello, how are you doing?" to anybody. Jesse [James] is a very well-liked and respected guy, the sort who anyone would like.'

Despite the backing he received from some of his fellow players over his remarks about the six-time major winner, James was unprepared for the furore that would erupt over his comments about Faldo and his good-luck note. 'Nick Faldo had sent a good-luck letter. Similar missives from the likes of Seve and Ian Woosnam had been pinned on our noticeboard and were much appreciated. This one was not pinned up, because I took one look at it and could not believe that Faldo had sent it. Not only had he had a serious barney with me relatively recently, but he had also slagged off Monty just before we came to Boston.' He went on to say that he had thrown it in the bin shortly before the match began.

A relatively minor incident in the scheme of things, it would prove to be the most contentious issue of all. Faldo took huge exception to Mark James' actions. Having sent the letter in good faith, he had expected it to be read by all the players, so when he found out that it had been unceremoniously binned, he was fuming. After all, there was nothing in it that could have been construed as offensive or even mildly controversial. He immediately sent a copy of the letter to the press.

16th September 1999

To the 1999 Ryder Cup captain, Mark James, and the European team, the Country Club, Brookline, Massachusetts.

As Tony Jacklin said to me: 'Good luck and play well goes out of the window. Just win.' I believe you can bring the Ryder Cup back to Europe again where it belongs. I am right behind you and will be supporting the team throughout the event, even though it is from 2,000 miles away.

My very best wishes to each of you. Above all, enjoy it.

Nick Faldo

Whatever Mark James thought of Faldo on a personal level, it quickly became obvious that he had underestimated the hostile reaction his actions would provoke. 'Faldo could be a jerk,' shouted the golfing press, 'but what right had James to throw away a good-luck message from him or anyone?' The reasons behind James' actions exercised press and public alike for weeks after the story broke in the *Daily Mail* serialisation. So why did he throw it away? There might have been some festering animosity between the two men, but that was hardly a valid explanation. To gratuitously betray a confidential note for profit was almost unforgivable in many people's opinion. Faldo had been wronged, but Mark James was unrepentant and stuck by his version of what had actually happened on the day in question. 'Faldo's good-luck letter was typed and I think had his signature at the bottom. My first inclination was to throw it away, but first I decided to seek the views of a few other people, including some of the players, and everyone's reaction was the same: bin it. I had no hesitation in accepting their advice. There was no room on our noticeboard for someone who was not one hundred per cent behind us.'

Over the following weeks, the sports pages of every newspaper, magazine and internet site in Britain groaned under the weight of letters supporting Nick Faldo. He was a hero to countless thousands, and having him vilified like that was patently unfair. Feelings were even more entrenched after the *Daily Mail* published a photograph of him with a headline emblazoned above it asking the question, IS THIS THE MOST HATED MAN IN BRITISH SPORT? The answer was obviously no. While many agreed with Mark James' savaging of the Americans' behaviour at Brookline, dishing the dirt on someone who was not even present in Boston went beyond the pale. Nick Faldo, whatever his faults, had contributed enormously to the European cause and the public rose to his defence in overwhelming numbers. Now Mark James was on the back foot.

In the aftermath of the Ryder Cup, some question marks had been raised over some of James' less than sound tactical decisions during the match. Working on the principle that victory has a thousand mistresses while defeat has none, the press wanted to know how Europe could have gone into the last day with a seemingly unassailable 10–6 lead and still lose. More specifically, why had Captain James not blooded his three rookies until the final nerve-racking singles round?

The most vocal of his critics in this respect was Jean Van de Velde. Having qualified for the team after his runner-up spot in the 1999 Open at Carnoustie, the likeable Frenchman found himself relegated to the role of cheerleader for most of the match. Forced to sit out the opening two days with team-mates Andrew Coltart and Jarmo Sandelin, he could only watch from the sidelines as his colleagues attempted to retain the trophy. In many ways it was a near impossible role to play for all three rookies. With the foursomes and fourball matches going on a few holes ahead, they would often practise without a soul in sight. 'Part of the Ryder Cup, but not part of it,' as Van de Velde remarked later.

When they did get out on the course for real, they found themselves totally unprepared for the firestorm that greeted them (unlike the American players, all of whom had tasted the volatile atmosphere by the time the singles rolled around). Facing a pumped-up USA team and a highly partisan New England crowd, all three were soundly beaten out of sight. Europe lost, and it all should have ended there except that Mark James' book brought into question some of his decisions, including one obvious one. If he had no intention of playing the inexperienced Andrew Coltart before the singles, why on earth did he not select either Nick Faldo or Bernhard Langer when he had the opportunity? Either player would have given him more options in the foursome and fourball matches, and that's what most Ryder Cup captains want. All except Mark James, it seemed.

With the Ryder Cup controversy ringing about his ears, Nick Faldo returned to Britain in July for the Open at St Andrews. During the warm-up the week before at the Standard Life event at Loch Lomond, it became increasingly difficult to avoid commenting on the book and, more specifically, the good-luck note incident. Wasting little time in repeating his criticism of his former Ryder Cup colleague, Faldo made it clear that he considered it unforgivable that James had not only written about the incident in a book, but had sought to justify his actions by involving other players. 'I thought, we all thought, there was a code of conduct,' he said shortly after arriving. 'I'm sure the committee feels it was a breach, but for some reason they don't want to act on it. That's my main issue. If that's allowed, if that's not a breach of the code of conduct or bringing the game into disrepute, then I don't know what is.'

Faldo was not alone in thinking that Mark James had transgressed. Irish World Cup player Paul McGinley also believed he had gone too far. 'As someone who represents us,' he said shortly after the book was published, 'I regret that Mark James should have decided to write a book and launch such a vicious attack on Nick Faldo. It is uncalled for and not something I would expect from a Ryder Cup captain.' Another establishment figure who was forthright in her criticism of James' actions was former Solheim Cup captain Mickey Walker. 'What Mark James has done is unforgivable,' she said. 'I used to be a fan of his, but no more. When you are appointed captain of the Ryder Cup, or Solheim Cup, it is a privileged position and those of us fortunate to experience it should never abuse it.'

What Faldo also wanted to know was how someone could write so scathingly about the American team, then expect to take a significant role in the 2001 Ryder Cup at the Belfry. Determined to see the matter through, he boasted about the support he had received from many other players in his quest to have James resign. 'He has broken confidence and lost trust,' he said defiantly. 'I have spoken to others who feel the same way.' One player who certainly did 'feel the same way' was Bernhard Langer. 'I thought our chairman would have been more diplomatic than he has been,' he was quoted as saying in the *News of the World*. 'I think it is very negative and a bad thing. I don't think it helps the future to say bad things about the Americans. I think that has stirred up a lot of anger on the American side. I think we need to get back to recognising that the Ryder Cup is a game, and I don't think it will be easy for Mark to be vice-captain facing the Americans.' Predictably, Jean Van de Velde agreed. Speaking to the *Sun* newspaper, he said, 'I do not think he can represent us as a chairman or as Ryder Cup deputy. Once you lose the respect of your fellow players, there is no way you can continue to act on their behalf. And if you cannot be trusted not to betray a confidence, the only way to proceed is through the door marked WAY OUT. I hope he will realise this is not some kind of witch-hunt. We are calling for Mark to go because we feel it is best for the game – and the Ryder Cup.'

Yet despite all this support, Faldo's call to have James censured went unheeded. 'Anyone found to be in breach of the code of behaviour would face a fine or suspension,' said PGA European Tour spokesman Mitchell Platts, before outlining what provisions had been set aside for disciplinary action under the tour's own rules. 'The handbook deals specifically with competitions and therefore, in this context, we would not regard it as a breach of tour regulations.' And Mark James was still in defiant mood. 'I am just laying out the facts and I think they speak for themselves,' he said after Platts' announcement. 'Nick probably does not like them, but I stand by what is in the book. I think it's balanced.' When asked if he might consider resigning from his new post as vice-captain for the 2001 match at the Belfry if Faldo made the side, James was equally resolute. Commenting on whether or not his presence would harm team morale, he said, 'I would imagine the captain might speak to me if he thought that.'

For his part, Sam Torrance, the new Ryder Cup captain, was steadfast in his support of his long-time pal. 'Mark did a magnificent job at Brookline and I'm not going to criticise him. I want him at the Belfry. If he has told lies then I'm sure there will be trouble, but not if he's told the truth. I don't see anything wrong in a captain writing a book.' He did, however, confirm that the issue *might* be discussed at the next meeting of the Tournament Players Committee – a meeting coincidentally scheduled for the Wednesday of the week of the Loch Lomond event. 'I've never known the agenda in advance,' he said. 'But if it's brought up we will discuss it and if there is a certain view among players then that will have to be looked at.'

Unsurprisingly, an 'outraged' Nick Faldo disagreed with Torrance's defence of James. Reiterating his call for James to resign from both his chairmanship of the European Tournament Players Committee and his post as Ryder Cup vice-captain, he explained to *The Times*, 'It has to be discussed now by the Ryder

Cup Committee. Even if what has happened has not been a disciplinary issue, here is a captain who has gone too far. Tony Jacklin did a book and Bernard Gallacher did one too. They were never a problem, now there is a problem. There has to be some guidelines for the future. The players have to have some sort of confidence that the captain is not going to squeal on them as to what goes on in the team room.' To some this continued call for James' head seemed petty, but to others it was natural justice.

Then Torrance, extraordinarily, admitted he had not actually read *Into the Bear Pit* or any of the comments published in the *Daily Mail* serialisation, and then said, 'But this has absolutely nothing to do with the Ryder Cup.' Nothing to do with the Ryder Cup? It was an astonishing comment from the new captain. If he really thought that, he should have made it his business to read Mark James' book the moment it was published rather than rely on anything James had told him about its content. Perhaps then he might have come to a different conclusion. He might even have understood why Nick Faldo was so upset.

With the Mark James controversy at its height, the Tournament Players Committee meeting was always going to be a potentially awkward affair for all concerned. The day before it sat, James was still in fighting mode. 'I would like to get this matter sorted because Nick keeps going to the press and whingeing – as he always does. He slags off the press one minute, then the next minute, if he's got a cause, he'll go to them and ask them to support him. It's not doing any favours to anyone, all this constant whingeing. So I'm quite happy to have it heard by the committee.'

The following day, James *was* asked to defend his less than complimentary comments about Faldo; everyone else at the meeting wanted the issue resolved as quickly as possible too. But with media speculation building to a fever pitch in the days leading up to the meeting, reaching a satisfactory outcome was never going to be easy. In an effort to appear scrupulously neutral, the views of Van de Velde and Langer were presented in their absence by Ken Schofield, executive director of the European Tour. In the end, the decision, somewhat surprisingly, was that James had not acted outside his remit as Ryder Cup captain. As Schofield later pointed out, 'Mark had complete freedom to write a book having stepped down as captain.' Convinced his argument with Faldo was little more than 'a storm in a tea cup', James agreed with the committee that it was in everyone's interest to bury the hatchet (the only question remaining, presumably, was where to bury it). 'There is no doubt,' a vindicated James said, referring to Faldo's ongoing efforts to discredit him, 'he's running a big campaign here.'

It certainly was a big campaign. In a radio interview with the BBC the day before the meeting at Loch Lomond, Faldo had once again aired his view that James had 'overstepped the boundary' in his criticism of him and other players in his book. 'If it's a storm in a teacup, why is it ending up in front of the Players Committee? And it will probably end up in front of the Ryder Cup Committee as well.'

Despite being partly cleared, James' position as vice-captain of the 2001 Ryder Cup team was still under threat. Pre-empting the outcome of a simple majority vote on whether he should stay or not, James said he would resign from his vice-captain's role 'if the players wanted me to go'. In the end, James was given the full and unanimous backing of his committee (much to the surprise of Van de Velde and Langer, who immediately demanded to see the minutes from the meeting). Describing the whole affair as 'very negative', Faldo was equally nonplussed that James should have been allowed to remain in the room when the issue of his conduct was being discussed. 'It was a bit difficult,' he said, 'for a committee trying to make a decision on whether to discipline someone when he was sitting right there!' Angry and upset, Faldo still believed, as did others, that James had clearly contravened tour regulations, which demand that a player is 'obliged not to attack, disparage or criticise a fellow competitor'. Moreover, Faldo's demand that James resign his position as chairman had not even been discussed, let alone voted on.

However, despite the 10–0 vote, it transpired that James had not escaped censure completely. The issue had dented the reputations of all concerned, so it was strongly urged that the two men resolve any outstanding issues between them, with the pressure to make the first conciliatory move squarely placed on Mark James. It seemed Faldo might get his apology after all.

James sought out Faldo in the players' lounge at Loch Lomond the following day, hoping he might prove amenable after an excellent opening round of 67. That was his first mistake. His second was to bring up the issue at all. Faldo, who was enjoying his lunch at the time, was in no mood to discuss reconciliation and brushed away any attempt by James to discuss the matter. 'I don't think this is the time or the place to be honest,' he said to the press afterwards. 'I think we should keep it away from the golf course, and if he wants to talk to me then maybe we should make arrangements to speak after the Open.'

A week later at St Andrews, Faldo seemed equally reluctant to talk about anything other than playing golf. Buoyed by the huge public support he had received, he now wanted to concentrate on proving that his major-winning days were not over. 'To be honest, I am taking things step by step,' said Faldo, who was due to celebrate his forty-third birthday on the Tuesday. 'I came here in 1990 with the intention of winning it. But I am in a different state now. I am out there enjoying it and I have a great opportunity. I still have the drive and the enthusiasm and the dedication to get out there and just keep doing it. Maybe it will happen one more time.'

He certainly seemed relaxed enough to win. In fact, he was conducting a real charm offensive, smiling his way through the made-for-television Champions Challenge on the Wednesday. A million miles away from his image as a golfing automaton, his good humour even extended to Tiger Woods and the possibility of him breaking Faldo's record winning score in 1990. He jokingly wagged his finger in the direction of the tournament favourite, saying, 'I don't care about Tiger beating Jack's [Nicklaus] records, but if he beats my eighteen under I will be very upset.' In the end, Tiger did, and Faldo wasn't. Having witnessed what he was capable of at Pebble Beach the previous month, Faldo knew his score was well within reach, and so it proved.

Yet it was not all sweetness and light from the three-time Open winner. Frustrated by the incredibly slow pace of play in the opening two rounds, Faldo found time to take a verbal swing at the huge media army following the Woods match just ahead. Pulling away from shot after shot as photographers and reporters scrambled around inside the ropes looking for a good vantage-point, he found his patience was tested to the limit.

Slow play had been a problem at all recent major championships, but at St Andrews the problem reached a nadir. It took Faldo six hours to play his opening round. There was not only time to smell the flowers, but to plant some more and watch them wilt on a stiflingly hot day. Faldo, who often plays his golf to a waltz rather than a quickstep, demanded action, but as always, slow players were timed but not fined. Certainly the Old Course with its double greens and shared fairways did not lend itself to a sprint, but golf was never meant to be this slow. As Justin Leonard commented later, 'For professional golfers to take six hours to play eighteen holes is pathetic.'

Having survived the cut, Faldo ended the weekend in a creditable tie for forty-first place. While he was not exactly delighted with this performance, it was a decent enough showing after his ninth place at Loch Lomond, and it was definitely a platform to build on. Yet there was only ever going to be one winner. 'It's almost as though guys will pick Tigerless events to play in to have a chance to win,' Faldo predicted afterwards.

With all the bonhomie coming out of the Nick Faldo camp during the Open, it was hoped that any problems resulting from Mark James' book would quietly die a natural death. However, it soon became obvious that Faldo, who was writing a book of his own with veteran Sam Snead, had no intention of letting the issue drop quite so easily. 'When someone says things like that about you, it's hard to just say forget about it,' he said. 'If he [James] wants to clear his conscience then that's fine, but it's very difficult.'

In true vaudevillian style, this was a story set to run and run. Faldo maintained the pressure on the committee to have Mark James thrown out of the next Ryder Cup, and he finally got his way at the beginning of August. After a meeting at Wentworth, the decision was taken by six members of the Ryder Cup Committee with five other senior European Tour and British

PGA officials that James should go. They asked Sam Torrance to break the bad news and to make it clear that a dignified exit by his vice-captain would benefit all concerned. 'The last thing we need,' said Torrance afterwards, 'is for added controversy which might adversely affect our build-up to the Ryder Cup.' (Quite right. A dismayed Torrance had previously described the effect the spat was having on his Ryder Cup preparations thus: 'You'd need to be in Outer Mongolia to get away from it, and even then you probably wouldn't.') While the news did not come as a surprise for James, who was on holiday in Spain, it must have been a difficult call for both men. Torrance, an emotional character, never wanted to lose his long-time buddy, but in the end he had no choice. 'Mark and I agree that there seems no end in sight to the controversy,' said Torrance. 'Therefore, the most sensible course of action for all concerned is for Mark to stand down, which he has agreed to do.' Ian Woosnam was announced as James' replacement.

It was the right decision. The last thing anyone wanted, least of all the PGA European Tour, was to have to publicly censure James for his behaviour and risk losing both a Ryder Cup captain and vice-captain on a matter of principle. Or, as one committee member put it, 'It would be better for Sam if there are no problems at all. He has had enough to contend with being captain without having to deal with all these outside issues.'

The day after, Faldo gave his own opinion on the news. 'I don't take any sense of victory from this,' he said during the International Tournament at Castle Pines, Colorado. 'I am sure James' position as chairman of the Tournament Players Committee will [also] have to be questioned.' The war of words, it seemed, was not over yet. Returning to the issue of the good-luck note James had notoriously thrown away, Faldo now accused the former Ryder Cup captain of fabricating the story for financial gain. Questioning James' statement that he had the 'full support' of the European team when he destroyed the note, Faldo said on BBC radio, 'That's a major issue for me, because in his book he says he showed the note to everybody, tore it up and threw it in the bin. But the facts, I've now discovered, are that only two people were present and neither of them were in the team. I now know that he has fabricated a story for the sake of his book, for him to gain financially out of it at my expense.'

Talk about going over old ground! Yet once again, Faldo had his supporters. 'The fact that Jesse threw away a good-luck note from a past champion is not good,' said Jamie Spence, 'and I'm sure in hindsight he either wouldn't have thrown the note away or wouldn't have said what he did with it. I just think the situation with Faldo has been going on for years.'

It certainly had, and bad blood was still flowing, despite James' resignation. Still piqued by the fact that the PGA European Tour had failed to address the personal attacks published in *Into the Bear Pit*, Faldo demanded further disciplinary action. Like a dog with a bone, he was not letting go that easily. 'I've still got a case here which I would like dealt with,' he said from Colorado. 'If that's not a breach of the tour's code of conduct, I don't know what is.' Schofield, like the rest of the European Tour, was unsympathetic. 'If Nick wants to pursue this, that is a matter for him, but for the past decade we have run the tour in an adult way, for adults and by adults.'

Faldo was now in danger of pushing it too far. He repeated his call for disciplinary action in the press, only for Neil Coles, chairman of the PGA European Tour, to remind him that disciplinary action worked both ways. It was time to build bridges and mend fences – especially if Faldo harboured an ambition to be the captain of a future European Ryder Cup team – as the tide slowly began to turn against him in the press and in the country at large. Having enjoyed huge support at the start of his campaign, Faldo increasingly found himself in a minority as players rallied around their former captain. 'I'm very disappointed,' said Darren Clarke. 'I think Mark James was a fantastic captain. He wrote a book to try and give an inside view of what went on [at Brookline] and there was nothing that particularly bad in that. You have a certain person who took great offence to it and decided, even though he spends his time in America, that Mark James should not have anything to do with the Ryder Cup.' Colin Montgomerie also described himself as 'saddened that it has come to this'. He believed that James had done a 'great' job of captaining the 1999 Ryder Cup team under difficult circumstances, and was happy to say so. Lee

Westwood, who had originally supported Faldo's inclusion in the side, offered a more balanced view of the controversy. 'If you read the book,' he said, 'he [Mark James] is more than complimentary about Nick and I think he has been very hard done by. I think it's a great shame that some people have been baying for his head.'

Westwood was right; Mark James' book does have a number of positive things to say about Faldo – for example, when he refers to Faldo's loss of form leading up to the match at Brookline. 'I was particularly sad that Faldo was going through a rough patch, because I knew that a Faldo playing well would be a huge asset to the team. Nobody amasses a Ryder Cup and individual record like his without having a great deal to offer.' On Nick Faldo the individual: 'You can say bad things about Faldo, but there is a lot of good there, and I have always found if you asked for advice he gave it.' On Faldo playing in future Ryder Cup matches:

> Let there be no misunderstanding: Faldo is hugely talented and has kept himself in good shape. He has the desire and will to search endlessly for the right stuff to make a comeback. I hope he does, because if he qualifies for the next team, I am sure it will be to the benefit of the European team. I am sure Faldo thinks that I do not want to see him play in the Ryder Cup again, but that, as I have said, is simply not true. I have a lot of admiration for him as a player and would love to see him up there again challenging for the game's big prizes.

After the soft soap, however, came the scrubbing brush. Knowing that anything critical of Faldo is always good for a headline, James could and should have refrained from some of the more personal comments. If there was an error on his part, it was to throw all the less than complimentary remarks about Faldo together, which made it easier for people to get the impression that he was out to discredit his former Ryder Cup team-mate. Then again, if Nick Faldo had actually *read* the book before commenting on it – something, like Torrance, he failed to do – he might have acted differently. But as one person so aptly put it, 'Nick doesn't do books.'

In the middle of August at the US PGA, Faldo began to show the effects the controversy had had on him. His opening round of 79 at the Valhalla Golf Club in Kentucky saw him scrambling around the course like a rookie. In serious danger of missing his first cut in a major championship that year, he recovered brilliantly with a four-under-par round of 68 to scrape in by one. With Woods on course to make it a hat-trick of majors – which he duly achieved after a play-off with journeyman pro Bob May – Faldo did his own cause no harm with weekend rounds of 69 and 73, lifting himself up to a seven-man tie for fifty-first place. At least he could return to Europe with his head held high.

In September, the final act of the *Into the Bear Pit* controversy was played out between Nick Faldo and Mark James in Paris during the Lancôme Trophy. It was the first time they had played in the same tournament since the book was published. After some minor sparring in the press leading up to the event, a brief face-to-face encounter took place on the practice ground on the Wednesday. This was followed by another conversation later the same day, also instigated by James, and it was agreed by both parties to say no more on the matter. It was hardly a kiss-and-make-up session, but it was certainly time to put the argument behind them – for ever. 'As far as I'm concerned,' said Faldo, 'it's over and done with. I want to put this situation behind us. Golf is bigger than all of this and it is not doing anybody any good.' Mark James agreed. 'I think it's the end of the matter,' he said. 'We agreed there are two sides to every argument, but we've cleared the air. We don't want this to be an ongoing argument between us and I'm sure it won't be. It's a satisfactory conclusion to the matter.'

European golf breathed a collective sigh of relief.

In October 2000, Nick Faldo was asked to compete in the World Matchplay Championship at Wentworth. Winner in 1989 and 1992, he joined a select twelve-man line-up that included the cream of European golf. Delighted about this last-minute call-up, his first appearance in the event after a six-year gap, he joked with the press, saying, 'They always invite a young, up-and-coming player and I appreciate being considered.'

The huge crowds that turned up to watch his opening-round match against Darren Clarke only had eyes for Faldo. They cheered every well-struck iron and sympathised with every missed putt. And though he failed to provide the perfect storybook ending, few went away disappointed – except, of course, Faldo himself.

It was a disappointment that would linger into the following season, and perhaps beyond. He played a full schedule of European events throughout the latter half of the 2000 season, his desire to make the Ryder Cup side to face the USA at the Belfry in September 2001 appearing stronger than ever. He talked a good fight in his quest for automatic qualification, but as the task grew ever harder his confidence began to take a tumble. In January 2001, Nick Faldo, one of the world's most successful golfers with six majors to his credit, finally admitted that his best playing days were behind him. Speaking during the Alfred Dunhill Championship in South Africa, he said, 'I'm at an age where I'm not sure where I've come from, or where I'm going. I've given my all to golf for twenty-seven years. I'm in a transition phase as a golfer and laying the building blocks for my next career. As a golfer, I have to admit that the consistency has gone. In fact, the only consistency I have these days is inconsistency.'

21. OUT WITH THE OLD, IN WITH THE NEW

Nothing ever stands still in the life of Nick Faldo.

Married in July 2001 to Valerie Bercher, it was noticeable how much he had changed. With a ready smile and quick wit replacing the tough, winner-take-all attitude of previous years, he no longer wore the haunted, slump-shouldered look of previous years. More positive, he now looked forward to the future rather than battling with his often torrid past. Joking with his fellow competitors, he would play-act with the crowd. Not that long ago all he ever talked about was swing changes and winning majors. Now he saw life in terms of enjoying each round, each shot and each day. It was a remarkable transformation.

Aided by the welcome return of the other woman in his life, caddie Fanny Sunesson, even his relationship with the media had improved. Press conferences, once a fierce battleground between Faldo and scandal-hungry journalists, now involved little more than good-humoured jousting on both sides. Notoriously thin-skinned during his major-dominating years, the days when a tabloid hack could provoke a reaction with a barbed word or comment were thankfully long gone.

So what had changed? According to Faldo he had spent the past few years putting his affairs in order and, having done so, his life was all the better for it. That said, not every change was easy to make, with the hardest of all concerning his former business manager, confidant and two-time best man, John Simpson. With a new wife and new home in the pipeline, Faldo was in the mood to make even more wide-ranging changes. Feeling that his famous name could perhaps be better exploited in the wake of multimillion-dollar sponsorship deals for players like Tiger Woods and David Duval, he increasingly toyed with the idea of a change of management.

Simpson, no doubt seeing which way the wind was blowing, argued that Nick needed to win tournaments to improve his standing, but his client disagreed. Arguing that far less famous players than he were taking a fortune out of the game, Faldo wanted to know why he was not receiving his slice of the increasingly lucrative pie. Something had to give and it surprised no one when they announced their decision to part company in May 2000. Within days it was announced that Faldo had made a nostalgic return to the company that had managed his affairs as a teenager, IMG.

In the weeks that followed Faldo preferred to concentrate on his plans for the future. While never quite admitting that his best playing days were over, he told the press that he would now spend less time playing tournaments and more time developing other business interests like Faldo Design and his Junior Series. A consummate competitor, only time would tell whether this restricted schedule would be enough to maintain his interest in things like Ryder Cup qualification.

Reducing his playing schedule to the bare minimum for 2001, Faldo admitted that he would have to play 'great in all the events I have entered to have any chance of making it into the Ryder Cup'. Knowing that he might have to rely on a wildcard pick from Sam Torrance to get into the side must have brought back mixed emotions for the 43-year-old golfer. Having come so far in his career and achieved so much, the future was uncertain and even a few words of encouragement from Torrance would fail to lift the gloom: 'Nick is probably the greatest golfer we have ever produced,' he commented. 'If he can get his game half in shape he will be in the team.'

Considering what had happened with his predecessor, Faldo probably wished he could have that in writing.

The period immediately leading up to his marriage was a surprisingly emotional one for Faldo. With a wedding to arrange, a new house to move into and an 'Elysian-style' garden party to organise there were rarely enough hours in the day to even think about golf, no matter play it.

Leaving most of the minutiae to Valerie, his tournament performances throughout the first half of the 2001 season reflected his up-and-down state of mind. Tied for third in the Alfred Dunhill Championship earlier in the year in South Africa, he missed the cut at Augusta National aided by a miserable second round of 81. Then with Fanny Sunesson back in the Faldo fold from April, after a brief time with Notay Begay III, Sergio Garcia and Fred Funk, it was off to Europe in May and the Volvo PGA Championship at Wentworth. A long-time favourite hunting ground of his, Faldo probably knows the famous Burma Road course better than any player alive and this was reflected in a second-round six-under-par 66.

Currently fortieth on the Ryder Cup table, Faldo knew that he would miss valuable point-scoring opportunities when he headed back to the PGA Tour in America immediately after this event and would not return to Europe until July for the Scottish and British Opens. 'My schedule is set in stone and I can't change it,' he said, in the hope that it would take the pressure off for the last two rounds.

It did. Standing over an eagle putt of forty feet on the twelfth for a share of the lead in the final round, the resulting birdie brought Faldo within a single stroke, having started the day seven shots back. Driven on by a record Wentworth gallery and golden memories of the 1996 US Masters, a birdie on the seventeenth was followed by an anticlimactic pulled second shot at the par-five last. Followed by a stubbed chip it left him with a disappointing par and a round of 67.

It was never going to be quite enough as Oldcorn was able to raise his game sufficiently with birdies at the twelfth, seventeenth and eighteenth to deny both Faldo and Angel Cabrera. Nevertheless, it was a delighted Nick Faldo who addressed the media afterwards. 'It was like the good old days,' he said having moved to eighteenth on the Ryder Cup table and just eight places from the automatic spots. 'It was just like it used to be . . . I really enjoyed getting on a roll and feeling the heat again.'

Something Faldo was not excited about was closing rounds of 74 and 75 at Southern Hills in the US Open. Dropping him down the leaderboard faster than John Daly finishes off a hamburger, his poor form extended to the British open at Royal Troon a month later when he missed the cut after a 75 and 71; these two poor tournaments effectively put paid to any lingering Ryder Cup hopes.

Heading south to Windsor, Nick Faldo must have reflected how much his life had changed since meeting Valerie Bercher during the 1997 Canon European Masters in Crans-sur-Sierre in the Swiss Alps.

The impact 'V' had on his life was quite remarkable and he saw something in her that eventually brought out the best in him. This was no golf groupie or tournament camp follower. This was a smart, independent young woman who listened to his stories, sympathised with his disappointments but above all gave him enough room to be himself. The transformation was astonishing and when they finally got married in a London registry office on 28 July, in front of a small group of close and loyal friends, it was as though the rest of his life had just begun.

In many ways it had.

22. IN THE BLACK AT BETHPAGE

In the aftermath of the events of 11 September 2001, no sporting event was affected more than the Ryder Cup. As the world struggled to come to terms with the terrorist attack on the World Trade Center buildings in New York, the PGA of America and PGA of Europe were thrown into confusion. Forced to decide whether the match, scheduled for the Belfry two weeks later on 28–30 September, should be cancelled or not, it was a decision fraught with difficulty.

Faced with a massive security headache should the match go ahead or even be delayed for a month as was suggested, a disturbing silence descended on both organisations, leaving the media to speculate wildly on the outcome.

It came as a relief to all concerned when the decision was made to postpone the 34th Ryder Cup for twelve months until September 2002. From this point on the biennial match would now be played in even years and not the odd as it had done since 1927. Both teams would remain the same as selected and in recognition of this, all signage at the Belfry would stay the same proclaiming this to be the '2001 Ryder Cup'.

With question marks still hanging over whether or not to play golf tournaments while the dead were still being buried in New York, Faldo, Woosnam, Torrance and young Australian Adam Scott received unexpected invitations to compete in the Cisco World Matchplay Championship at Wentworth in October. With the USA on a heightened state of alert and security stepped up at every major airport throughout the world, a number of top American players had dropped out, leaving the event with a distinctly European feel about it.

Not that Faldo, who won the event in 1989 and 1992, found it a particularly comfortable tournament to play in. Drawn against Ryder Cup player Padraig Harrington in the first round, he lost by 9 & 8, admitting afterwards that he was thoroughly demoralised by the defeat. He commented to waiting reporters, 'It's time to get my chainsaw out and have some fun in the garden. It's demoralising and it makes me wonder what the hell I am doing out here.'

The game of golf was proving a fickle mistress. Having performed well in the final major of the season in Atlanta, where an opening round of 67 had put him among the leaders in the US PGA before eventually falling back into a tie for 51st, he had felt confident about his chances at Wentworth. That was before the rising Irish star had gone around in 63 in the morning.

Another trip to Virginia Water in October for the Cisco World Matchplay saw Faldo run up against another young gun in the shape of New Zealander Michael Campbell. This time it took 43 holes over two days to decide the first-round match; having started at 9a.m. they called it a day in the gathering gloom at 6.05p.m. only to return at 8.15 the following morning. It was the longest match in the championship's 39-year history.

It was a far more satisfactory return to the Wentworth five months later when he finished twelve-under-par and fourth in the Volvo PGA Championship. But having failed to secure a top-two finish and earn an automatic spot in the US Open, he now faced the dilemma of whether to try qualifying or not. It would be his 61st consecutive major appearance – a world record – and opinion was split as to whether such a legend should join the young bunks, club pros, has-beens and never-will-bes on the qualifying merry-go-round. Thankfully the 'will he – won't he' debate was settled two weeks later when an official invite from the United States Golf Association popped through his letter box.

With the US Open scheduled for the testing Black Course at Bethpage State Park in Farmingdale, New York, Faldo was enjoying a rich vein of form. His strong finish at Wentworth was just one of six top-fifteen finishes in 2002. It had been his best start to a season in years and he wanted it to carry on, but Faldo played down any chance of winning by admitting in the round of pre-tournament press interviews that he was not the player he once was. 'I was tearing my hair out up until about two years ago wondering what happened to my game and could I get it back,' he told the assembled hacks. 'It took me a while to realise that I was never going to get it back. I couldn't be what I once was and that's that . . . I'm older, have more interests away from the golf course and don't have the time or desire I once did.'

The week began quietly with a level-par round of 70, but fell away in the second after a rain-affected 76. Then came the fireworks. Getting the best of the weather, Faldo shot a 'best-of-the-day' 66 in the third round that did more than just get him on a leaderboard, it got him within shouting distance of tournament pacesetter Tiger Woods. Just two-over-par through 54 holes on one of the longest and toughest US Open courses ever, the former world number-one was ecstatic.

The elements were in place for a classic finish – the world's number-one player, Tiger Woods, being chased to the wire by one of his closest pursuers for that title, Phil Mickelson, and a veteran warhorse in the shape of Nick Faldo. Hoping the wind might blow hard enough to give him a chance, experience told him that another 66 might be good enough, but it was not to be. Ending with a closing round of 73, there was simply not enough gas in the tank to chase a rampant Woods, who finished the tournament at three-under – eight strokes ahead of Faldo, who tied for fifth place. Finishing top European and with his best display in a major for six years, at least it secured him a spot in the next year's US Open.

Regardless of what happened at Bethpage, Woods did not seem overly worried about a resurgent Faldo taking his thunder at Muirfield, but he may have considered asking his advice. 'One of the greatest compliments I heard, was that Tiger watched tapes of me winning at St Andrews in 1990 before he won there in 2000,' Faldo revealed on his return to Britain. 'So I bet he's been watching tapes of me winning at Muirfield. I'll see if he's worked out the secret.'

If there was a 'secret' to winning at Muirfield then the two-time Open winner was going to keep it to himself, but that was about all he was staying silent about. Returning to the scene of his Open Championship triumphs in 1987 and 1992, a buoyant Nick Faldo was in reflective mood and chose a number of interviews, including one with top US magazine *Sports Illustrated*, to open his soul or in some cases vent his spleen.

Speaking about his contentious relationship with the British media he referred back to his notorious, 'I'd like to thank the media from the heart of my bottom' speech during the trophy-presentation ceremony at Muirfield in 1992. 'In light of what had been written about me, it was a tongue-in-cheek little stab,' said Faldo, the wide-eyed innocent. 'It's amazing how many guys took offence.'

Oh really? Then, showing how little he had learned from the episode, he said that if he won again at Muirfield in 2002 he might give the same victory speech again! 'Because you can't win with them,' he opined. 'If you're super nice, they say it's all a public relations exercise. If you speak the truth, they slay you.'

Like many top British sportsmen, the myopic view he had towards the media was clouded by his own insecurities. Faldo had devoted himself single-mindedly to golf for years and it annoyed him when they wanted to know more about the man behind the mask. It was a vicious circle. The less he wanted to tell them, the more they wanted him to reveal. Then when he refused to play their game he was described as unemotional, dour and robotic. But that was all in the past. Everyone agreed that he was far more 'media savvy' since marriage had brought stability to his private life and – dare we say it – the grumpy Nick Faldo was no more.

He admitted that his personality had been 'stifled' during the bad years where he suffered the breakdown of his marriage, other relationships and a major loss of form, but it would not be Nick Faldo without the occasional pot shot being taken at the expense of others. Regarding his first wife, Melanie, he told Sports Illustrated, 'We were very happily married for eight months. Unfortunately we were married for four and a half years.'

And finally, regarding the damage inflicted on his beloved Porsche by his former squeeze Brenna Cepalek: 'It was a very special car. It was so high tech. It was made of plastic. The club kept bouncing off. It wouldn't leave a dent. I auctioned it off last year. It was a nice end to that part of my life.'

With his golf and personal life now on the upswing, Faldo was ready and eager to tackle Muirfield again. 'I feel like I'm in the most exciting time of my life,' he said shortly before the Open began. 'I have a beautiful new relationship and the potential to make some incredible things happen. People think it's this amazing transformation. I'm not a new guy now. I'm just able to be me.'

If a happy and contented home life translated into on-course success then Faldo was right to feel confident, but like the 47 Nigerians granted visas to enter Britain to take part in the Open pre-qualifying tournament who failed to turn up, Faldo's new-found golf game also went absent without leave. Suffering from the aftereffects of a bad cold that had seen him pull out of the European Open in Dublin two weeks earlier, he lacked consistency, seesawing between a second-round 67 and a third-round 76. Finishing the week in a disappointing tie for 59th, it was followed by a similar performance in the US PGA a month later at Hazeltine – home to Tony Jacklin's US Open victory in 1970 – where he ended up tied 60th.

A season that had promised so much was now ending on a low note, but there was always the rescheduled Ryder Cup at the Belfry to grab his attention. Invited by Sky Sports to join its regular commentary team, it must have felt strange passing opinions on an event in which he had invested so much blood, sweat and tears over the years but the consensus of opinion was that he did a surprisingly good job and it did not go unnoticed – especially in the United States.

Staged at the Belfry for the fourth time since 1985, the match finally went ahead with security still of paramount concern, with over a thousand volunteer stewards patrolling the course alongside large numbers of heavily armed police. In the end the decision to play the match was vindicated and to the delight of all, including the patriotic Faldo, the match had lost none of its competitive edge as Europe eventually ran out winners by 15½–12½.

More importantly, the game of golf could now move on.

23. BACK TO THE FUTURE FOR FALDO

Nick Faldo, 45 years old and without a win since the Nissan Open in 1997, was surprisingly upbeat about the 2003 season. Describing his mood as 'inspired' he had successfully reversed a downward trend in 2002 by turning in some noteworthy performances, not least of which was his fifth-place finish at the US Open. Changing his diet over the winter months, he worked hard on his fitness, his diet and his technique. 'At this stage of my career,' he said, 'my attitude is to just really give it a go.'

Give it a go he did. With teaching professional Jeremy Bennett in tow, he finished 33rd at the Masters but failed to hole any significant putt over fifteen feet all week. A missed cut at Olympia Fields in the US Open in June was disappointing but the Open Championship at Royal St George's a month later went 'Back to the Future' as Faldo turned on the style in vintage fashion.

Promising to give the Open 'one more blast', it brought a curious smile to his face when asked by a journalist how it would feel to become the oldest winner of the Open Championship since Tom Morris Snr at Prestwick back in 1867! Celebrating his 46th birthday on the Friday of the tournament, the champagne looked to have gone flat as he found himself ten-over after six holes of the second round. From that point, though, things picked up considerably and with four holes of the final round to play he had dragged his score back to level par. Rising to fourth place on the ever-changing leaderboard, the last time he had been in such an exalted position so deep into a major was at the 1996 Open at Royal Lytham. Back then he had failed to put any pressure on the eventual winner, Tom Lehman; now, he was within striking distance of Thomas Björn and surprise leader Ben Curtis.

The atmosphere was electric as people realised that he might actually do it. But his tilt at glory was short-lived as a touch of mental weariness tripped him up over the closing holes. Glancing up at the scoreboard on the short walk to the fifteenth tee, he noticed that Curtis was five strokes ahead of him on five-under! It was a shock and led directly to a poor tee shot that found a fairway bunker. Sparking a flurry of three successive bogeys, he was unable to take advantage of slips by both the leading players.

As he walked up the eighteenth fairway to record a one-under-par 70 and end the tournament in a creditable tie for eighth position, he raised the arm of popular caddie Fanny Sunesson to huge applause from the appreciative gallery. Moments later the huge scoreboard above the main grandstand flashed up 'Faldo for King' – and the resulting roar could have seen him resident in Buckingham Palace before the end of the day.

In the post-tournament briefing Faldo announced he was going to give his career 'everything' from now on, including planning a schedule to give him the best possible chance of qualifying for the 2004 Ryder Cup at Oakland Hills, Michigan. 'My big goal now is to really work on my stamina,' said a tired-looking Faldo. 'At my age it affects me and I slowed up a bit.'

In typical style he offered no excuses for his own shortcomings and even stopped long enough to offer his congratulations to the new champion, Ben Curtis. What he did not mention was how his final-round preparations had been disrupted when his mother Joyce had been rushed into hospital the night before after a worrying health scare.

There was far better news the following week as Valerie gave birth to a baby daughter, Emma Scarlett Faldo.

These were wonderful times for the charismatic Englishman, and his decision to miss the US PGA Championship at Oak Hill was symptomatic of his new attitude. Preferring to spend more time with his new family he limited his schedule to a bare minimum, even turning down an invitation from Colin Montgomerie to compete in the Seve Trophy in Spain, which pitted a Britain & Ireland team against another from Continental Europe.

In December Faldo was honoured by the Professional Golfers' Association for his outstanding services to British and European golf. Receiving the inaugural PGA Recognition Award, PGA chief executive Sandy Jones said: 'Since becoming our youngest ever Ryder Cup member at the age of twenty in 1977, Nick has continually set new standards of professionalism as well as records . . . His career achievement of winning three Opens and three US Masters, not to mention an unrivalled Ryder Cup record, positioned him as Britain's best golfer of all time. But it is his dedication and commitment to the game which really sets him apart as the professional's professional.'

But Nick Faldo is not someone who rests on his laurels. Around the same time, he bought Bartragh Island, 360 acres of spectacular links land on the Atlantic coast of County Mayo in the West of Ireland with only the River Moy separating it from the mainland. Not surprisingly, salmon thrive in the estuary and Faldo aims to show the locals how to play golf in return for a few tips on fishing – his favourite hobby. In the long term, he believes there may be the potential for his fast-growing company, Faldo Design, to create an exceptional links course on the island.

In March 2004, he announced the launch of Faldo Management, a new company set up to manage the affairs of professional golfers and guide the careers of promising young amateurs. As for his own career, he made no secret of his desire to add to a record 25 points from an unprecedented 11 Ryder Cup appearances by making the European team to face the USA at Oakland Hills later in the year. (His last match was at Valderrama in 1997, but it seemed a stint as television pundit at the 2002 event at The Belfry had reignited his passion for the event.)

'You've got to have goals in life,' he told BBC Sport. 'Otherwise you sit there and become a vegetable.'

It was not the only Ryder Cup ambition he had. Targeting the captaincy in Ireland in 2006, he insisted he still had plenty to offer current skipper Bernhard Langer as a player, but despite scheduling more events in Europe, the odds were always against him. Wearing spectacles for the first time in the opening round of the Deutsche Bank Open in May, not to mention trying out the belly putter so favoured by Colin Montgomerie, age was obviously catching up fast on the 46-year-old. Despite a closing round of 66 at the Volvo PGA Championship at Wentworth at the end of May, Faldo was not among the top fifty in the world that received an automatic invitation to the forthcoming US Open.

He knew that if he wanted to compete at Shinnecock Hills he was going to have to jump on a plane and go play in a qualifying tournament. Make no mistake, there were plenty of 'star' name golfers that would not have done it, but Faldo knew that if he was going to make the Ryder Cup team, he *had* to play.

Of course, the case for the six-time major winner, who had received an exemption for the 2002 US Open and used it to finish in a tie for fifth, was not difficult to make. Having competed in a record 65 consecutive major championships – until his record-breaking streak had ended after the British Open last year – his US Open record was impressive enough, including a playoff loss to Curtis Strange at The Country Club in 1988 and four other top-ten finishes. But there was a deafening silence from across the Atlantic and a short time later he arrived at Lake Nona in Florida, his home base for many years, and prepared to join the 763 other players at 13 venues across the United States vying for 79 spots.

It proved an interesting experience as Faldo added a three-under 69 on Tuesday to his 70 of the previous day. Finishing joint first, it was enough to secure him one of the three places available from a field of sixty. 'I'm very proud of myself,' he said afterwards. 'Five under par is a blooming good result for this day. I'll definitely go home and crack open a bottle of the good stuff to celebrate this one.'

Having qualified for Shinnecock Hills, Faldo must have wondered why he bothered after rounds of 81 and 70 left him beyond the cut line. Following a missed cut in the Masters (76–75), his season was beginning to unravel and it got worse at the British Open at Royal Troon where he shot 76 and 77. Never at any point in his professional career had he missed successive cuts in the Masters, US Open and British Open and it left him with absolutely no chance of making the European Ryder Cup team for September. It was that realisation that brought a final parting of the ways between Faldo and his caddie, Fanny Suneson. Announcing the decision shortly before the British Open got under way, the 35-year-old Swede had expressed her desire to quit working full time at the end of 2004 to spend more time with her husband Eric Rogers (whom she married on the same day that Nick married Valerie).

'I've had some great times with Nick,' she said after their swan song at Royal Troon. 'It was an honour to be alongside him for four of his six major wins.'

Having mapped out a hectic programme in the faint hope of clinching a Ryder Cup berth and failed, reality slowly began to dawn on one of the most competitive sportsmen ever to play the game. Shorter off the tee than most, an erratic putter and unable to concentrate at the level required, he was just not competitive over four rounds any more. When pushed, Faldo trotted out the familiar line that he would not still be playing if he didn't think he could win. The truth was that by the end of 2004 he was channelling his legendary single-minded focus in other directions – most notably his new family, Faldo Design, Faldo Junior Series and a host of various business interests. Tournament play did not hold the same thrill it once did and despite a fifteenth-place finish at the Hong Kong Open in December, Faldo insisted, 'I am planning to play a lot less next year. There are several things I'm focusing on, like course building and my junior series – and that means I will not play as much.'

Like his contemporaries Greg Norman, Seve Ballesteros and Curtis Strange, Faldo knew that his glory days were long behind him, and while he still clung to the dream of a final shot at that elusive seventh major, it was probably never going to happen and he knew it. It was time to expand his horizons and it was not long before other doors began to open. In February 2005, Faldo found himself sitting in the ABC commentary booth at the Nissan Open in Los Angeles. By a strange coincidence it was the tournament that had provided his last victory on the PGA Tour in 1997, so when the opportunity arose to share the tower on the eighteenth with his old sparring partner Paul Azinger he jumped at the chance. Striking up an immediate rapport with Azinger and co-host Mike Tirico, it could not have come at a better time: 'I'm in my thirtieth season as a pro and I was getting a bit jaded,' said Faldo. 'I always kept saying that I would like to have a bit of a breather but I have a knack for this. I don't want to get too personal, but if something happens out there, they want me to say my opinion. I've been there. I can speak from "I felt this" or "I did that".'

It would not be the only job he was offered in 2005. Along with Ian Woosnam and Sandy Lyle, he let it be known that he would like to be considered for the post of Ryder Cup captain at either the K Club near Dublin in 2006 or Louisville in 2008. With Lyle finding support from his fellow players and the media thin on the ground, it was expected to be a straight choice between Faldo and Woosnam, with the Welshman seen as favourite for the match in Ireland and the Englishman a strong candidate for America. As the decision drew nearer Faldo began to get nervous describing it as 'quite amazing' that no one had even called him in to discuss his plans. 'It's not a job you officially apply for,' he confided. 'You just throw your name out in the wind.'

While a formal job interview may not have taken place, someone got the message that Faldo wanted the job. Announcing their decision at the Dubai Desert Classic in March, Woosnam was duly appointed European captain for 2006 and, in an unprecedented move, Nick Faldo was appointed captain for 2008.

Revealing the support Faldo had within the game of golf, never in the 77-year history of the Ryder Cup had the selection committee named a captain so far ahead of the actual competition. Faldo was understandably ecstatic saying, 'The Ryder Cup is one of the most exciting competitions in the golfing calendar and never fails to inspire both team members and spectators alike. With eleven previous appearances, I have so many fond memories of my time as a player and am honoured to be joining the list of great names that have captained the European side in the past. Having played under five different captains, I've picked up a few tips along the way and hope that I can draw on my own experiences to guide the European side to victory.'

Captaining the European team will surely complete the circle for Faldo in much the same way it did for Seve Ballesteros at Valderrama in 1997. Since making his Ryder Cup debut at Royal Lytham in 1977 as a promising twenty-year-old, no single professional has done more to raise the standard of European golf than him. Three Masters titles, three Open Championships, former world number-one, a Ryder Cup veteran and now a future Ryder Cup captain, no one deserves his success more than Nick Faldo. Emotional, difficult, determined and single-minded – all these words have been applied to Faldo over the past three decades. Above all, he is a hugely patriotic man. No one before or after will be prouder to captain Europe and be more determined to win the Ryder Cup than he. Certainly, no player on either team will be held in greater respect and esteem.

'Sometimes I wish I could turn the clock back and set out on a pro career with the knowledge accumulated over the past twenty years,' Faldo once said. 'The next best thing is to pass on all that information to the next generation.'

At the 2008 Ryder Cup he will get that opportunity.

Looking back, it is easy to forget just how long Faldo has been around the tournament scene. The greatest British golfer of his generation, few players have dominated the world game as he did in the late 80s and early 90s. Competing alongside players half his age for the past decade or more, he now uses metal-headed drivers, graphite-boron shafts and titanium-filled golf balls. When he first started in the mid-70s, he used persimmon-headed woods, steel shafts and small-size British golf balls – antiques by modern standards. He began his career competing against legendary names like Lee Trevino, Tom Weiskopf and Johnny Miller. In the 80s, he battled alongside Jack Nicklaus, Tom Watson and Curtis Strange. In the 90s it was Greg Norman, Seve Ballesteros and Paul Azinger. Today it is Phil Mickelson and the awesome Tiger Woods. Throughout his career he has shown that nothing is beyond him if he wants it badly enough. For Faldo, that has *always* been the key.

Tough, uncompromising and totally dedicated to his chosen profession, Faldo once said that he hoped people in fifty years time might remember that he was simply a great golfer. Having plotted his career from a shy junior at Welwyn Garden City to the giddy heights of British Open and US Masters glory, I am absolutely convinced they will. Whether they will remember him with the affection reserved for a Seve Ballesteros or a Jack

Nicklaus is perhaps less certain. Respected rather than loved, esteemed rather than adored, it is more likely that Nick Faldo will stand alongside players like Ben Hogan and Gary Player in the pantheon of golfing legend. Yet even that opinion has mellowed over the last few years as a new generation of golfers see Faldo the shoot-from-the-lip media man, Faldo the successful golf course designer and Faldo the soon-to-be Ryder Cup captain.

Whatever the future holds, I look forward to writing the next chapter in this most fascinating life story.

FOR THE RECORD

AMATEUR
1975
English Open Amateur Strokeplay Championship (Brabazon)
The Berkshire Trophy
English Amateur Championship
British Youths Championship
South African Special Strokeplay Championship

PROFESSIONAL
1977   Rookie of the Year (Europe)
1977   Skol Lager Individual (Europe)
1978   Colgate PGA Championship (Europe)
1979   ICL International (Africa)
1980   Sun Alliance PGA Championship (Europe)
1981   Sun Alliance PGA Championship (Europe)
1982   Haig Whisky TPC (Europe)
1983   European Number One (European Order of Merit)
1983   Paco Rabanne French Open (Europe)
1983   Martini International (Europe)
1983   Car Care Plan International (Europe)
1983   Lawrence Batley International (Europe)
1983   Ebel Swiss Open European Masters (Europe)
1984   Sea Pines Heritage Classic (US)
1984   Car Care Plan International (Europe)
1987   Peugeot Spanish Open (Europe)
1987   Awarded MBE
1987   *The 116th Open Golf Championship (Europe)*
1988   Peugeot French Open (Europe)
1988   Volvo Masters (Europe)
1989   *The Masters (US)*
1989   Volvo PGA Championship (Europe)
1989   Dunhill British Masters (Europe)
1989   Peugeot French Open (Europe)
1989   Suntory World Matchplay Championship (Europe)
1989   BBC Sports Personality of The Year
1990   *The Masters (US)*
1990   *The 119th Open Golf Championship (Europe)*

1990   Johnnie Walker Classic (Hong Kong)
1990   United States PGA Player of The Year
1991   Carroll's Irish Open (Europe)
1992   Carroll's Irish Open (Europe)
1992   *The 121st Open Golf Championship (Europe)*
1992   Scandinavian Masters (Europe)
1992   GA European Open (Europe)
1992   Toyota World Matchplay Championship (Europe)
1992   Johnnie Walker World Championship of Golf (US)
1992   European Number One (European Order of Merit)
1993   Johnnie Walker Classic (Europe)
1993   Carroll's Irish Open (Europe)
1994   Alfred Dunhill Open (Europe)
1994   Nedbank Million Dollar Challenge (Africa)
1995   Doral-Ryder Open (US)
1996   *The Masters (US)*
1997   Nissan Open (US)
2004   PGA Recognition Award
2005   Nominated European Ryder Cup captain for 2008

WEEKS AS WORLD NUMBER ONE
2 September 1990–mid-October 1990 (six weeks)
3 February 1991–31 March 1991 (eight weeks)
March 1992 (one week)
19 July 1992–30 January 1994 (81 weeks)

TEAM

Ryder Cup	1977, 1979, 1981, 1983, 1985 (winners), 1987 (winners), 1989 (trophy retained), 1991, 1993, 1995 (winners), 1997 (winners)
Alfred Dunhill Cup	1985, 1986, 1987 (winners), 1988, 1991, 1993
World Cup of Golf	1977, 1991, 1998 (winners)
Four Tours World Championship	1986, 1987, 1990
Hennessy Cognac Cup	1978 (winners), 1980 (winners), 1982 (winners), 1984 (winners)
Double Diamond	1977

CAREER LOW SCORES
1981   62 Hawaiian Open *T-40* 70-62-72-77 = 281
1983   62 Lawrence Batley International *WIN* 71-69-64-62 = 266
1986   62 Panasonic European Open *4* 62-72-71-69 = 274
1988   62 Peugeot Spanish Open *T-3* 68-67-62-68 = 265

1992   62 Bell's Scottish Open *T-3* 69-62-69-65 = 265

1993   63 Open 2 69-63-70-67 = 269

1978   64 Braun German Open *11* 64-73-70-71 = 278

1990   64 Panasonic European Open *T-4* 68-70-64-68 = 270

1990   64 Independent Insurance Agent Open *T-15* 70-73-64 = 207

1992   64 GA European Open *WIN* 67-66-64-65 = 262

1992   64 Open *WIN* 66-64-69-73 = 272

1994   64 Open *T-8* 75-66-70-64 = 275

1995   64 MCI Classic *T-4* 74-64-70-68 = 276

1996   64 Buick Invitational *T-8* 69-70-70-64 = 273

THE OPEN

2004   Royal Troon – Tron, Ayrshire, Scotland – par 71, 7,175 yards, *CUT*
76-77 = 153 (+11)

2003   Royal St George's – Sandwich, Kent, England – par 71, 7,106 yards,
T-8 76-74-67-70 = 287 (+3)

2002   Muirfield – The Honourable Company of Edinburgh Golfers, Gullane,
East Lothian, Scotland – par 71, 7,034 yards, *T-59* 73-69-76-71 = 289
(+5)

2001   Royal Lytham & St Annes – Lytham, Lancashire, England – par 71,
MC, 7,115 yards, 75-71

2000   Old Course, St Andrews – St Andrews, Fife, Scotland – par 72, 7,115
yards, *T-41* 70-71-75-71 = 287 (−1)

1999   Carnoustie – Carnoustie, Angus, Scotland – par 71, 7,361 yards, *CUT*
78-79 = 157 (+15)

1998   Royal Birkdale – Southport, Lancashire, England – par 70, 7,018
yards, *T-42* 72-73-75-75 = 295 (+15)

1997   Royal Troon – Troon, Ayrshire, Scotland – par 71, 7,079 yards, *T-51*
71-73-75-72 = 291 (+7)

1996   Royal Lytham & St Annes – Lytham, Lancashire, England – par 71,
6,892 yards, 4 68-68-68-70 = 274 (−10)

1995   Old Course, St Andrews – St Andrews, Fife, Scotland – par 72, 6,933
yards, *T-40* 74-67-75-75 = 291 (+3)

1994   Turnberry (Ailsa Course) – Turnberry, Ayrshire, Scotland – par 70,
6,957 yards, *T-8* 75-66-70-64 = 275 (−5)

1993   Royal St George's – Sandwich, Kent, England – par 70, 6,860 yards, 2
69-63-70-67 = 269 (−11)

1992   Muirfield – The Honourable Company of Edinburgh Golfers, Gullane,
East Lothian, Scotland – par 71, 6,970 yards, *WIN* 66-64-69-73 = 272
(−12)

1991   Royal Birkdale – Southport, Lancashire, England – par 70, 6,940
yards, *T-17* 68-75-70-68 = 281 (+1)

1990   Old Course, St Andrews – St Andrews, Fife, Scotland – par 72, 6,933 yards, *WIN* 67-65-67-71 = 270 (−18)

1989   Royal Troon – Troon, Ayrshire, Scotland – par 72, 7,067 yards, *T-11* 71-71-70-69 = 281 (−7)

1988   Royal Lytham & St Annes – Lytham, Lancashire, England – par 71, 6,857 yards, *3* 71-69-68-71 = 279 (−5)

1987   Muirfield – The Honourable Company of Edinburgh Golfers, Gullane, East Lothian, Scotland – par 71, 6,963 yards, *WIN* 68-69-71-71 = 279 (−5)

1986   Turnberry (Ailsa Course) – Turnberry, Ayrshire, Scotland – par 70, 6,957 yards, *5* 71-70-76-70 = 287 (+7)

1985   Royal St George's – Sandwich, Kent, England – par 70, 6,857 yards, *T-53* 73-73-75-74 = 295 (+15)

1984   Old Course, St Andrews – St Andrews, Fife, Scotland – par 72, 6,933 yards, *T-6* 69-68-76-69 = 282 (−6)

1983   Royal Birkdale – Southport, Lancashire, England – par 71, 6,968 yards, *T-8* 68-68-71-73 = 280 (−4)

1982   Royal Troon – Troon, Ayrshire, Scotland – par 72, 7,067 yards, *T-4* 73-73-71-69 = 286 (−2)

1981   Royal St George's – Sandwich, Kent, England – par 70, 6,829 yards, *T-11* 77-68-69-73 = 287 (+7)

1980   Muirfield – The Honourable Company of Edinburgh Golfers, Gullane, East Lothian, Scotland – par 71, 6,926 yards, *T-12* 69-74-71-70 = 284 (level)

1979   Royal Lytham & St Annes – Lytham, Lancashire, England – par 71, 6,822 yards, *T-19* 74-74-78-69 = 295 (+11)

1978   Old Course, St Andrews – St Andrews, Fife, Scotland – par 72, 6,933 yards, *T-7* 71-72-70-72 = 285 (−3)

1977   Turnberry (Ailsa Course) – Turnberry, Ayrshire, Scotland – par 70, 6,875 yards, *T-62* 71-76-74-78 = 299 (+19)

1976   Royal Birkdale – Southport, Lancashire, England – par 72, 7,001 yards, *T-28* 78-71-76-69 = 294 (+6)

THE MASTERS

2004   Augusta National – Augusta, Georgia – par 72, 7,290 yards, *CUT* 76-75 = 151 (+7)

2003   *T-33* 74-73-75-73 = 295 (+7)

2002   *T-14* 75-67-73-72 = 287 (−1)

2001   Augusta National – Augusta, Georgia – par 72, 6,985 yards, *MC* 75-76

2000   *T-28* 72-72-74-75 = 293 (+5)

1999   *CUT* 80-73 = 153 (+9)

1998   *CUT* 72-79 = 151 (+7)

1997   *CUT* 75-81 = 156 (+12)
1996   *WIN* 69-67-73-67 = 276 (−12)
1995   *T-24* 70-70-71-75 = 286 (−2)
1994   *32* 76-73-73-74 = 296 (+8)
1993   *T-39* 71-76-79-67 = 293 (+5)
1992   *T-13* 71-72-68-71 = 282 (−6)
1991   *T-12* 72-73-67-70 = 282 (−6)
1990   *T-WIN* 71-72-66-69 = 278 (−10); beat Ray Floyd in a sudden-death play-off: Faldo 4–4, Floyd 4–5
1989   *T-WIN* 68-73-77-65 = 283 (−5); beat Scott Hoch in a sudden-death play-off: Faldo 5–3, Hoch 5–4
1988   *T-30* 75-74-75-72 = 296 (+8)
1985   *T-25* 73-73-75-71 = 292 (+4)
1984   *T-15* 70-69-70-76 = 285 (−3)
1983   *T-20* 70-70-76-76 = 292 (+4)
1979   *40* 73-71-79-73 = 296 (+8)

Note: course length 6,925 yards until 1999, when it became 6,985 yards

THE US OPEN

2004   Shinnecock Hills – Southampton, New York – par 70, 6,996 yards, *CUT* 81-70 = 151 (+11)
2003   Olympia Fields (North Course) – Olympia Fields, Illinois – par 70, 7,190 yards, *CUT* 75-75 = 150 (+10)
2002   Bethpage State Park (Black Course) – Farmingdale, New York – par 70, 7,214 yards, *T-5* 70-76-66-73 = 285 (+5)
2001   Southern Hills, Tulsa, Oklahoma – par 70, 6,973 yards, *T-72* 76-70-74-75 = 295 (+15)
2000   Pebble Beach – Pebble Beach, California – par 71, 6,846 yards, *T-7* 69-74-76-71 = 290 (+6)
1999   Pinehurst (No. 2) – Pinehurst, North Carolina – par 70, 7,175 yards, *CUT* 74-74 = 148 (+8)
1998   The Olympic Club (Lake Course) – San Francisco, California – par 70, 6,797 yards, *CUT* 77-72 = 149 (+9)
1997   Congressional – Bethesda, Maryland – par 70, 7,213 yards, *T-48* 72-74-69-76 = 291 (+11)
1996   Oakland Hills – Birmingham, Michigan – par 70, 6,974 yards, *T-16* 72-71-72-70 = 285 (+5)
1995   Shinnecock Hills – Southampton, New York – par 70, 6,944 yards, *T-45* 72-68-79-72 = 291 (+11)
1994   Oakmont – Oakmont, Pennsylvania – par 71, 6,946 yards, *CUT* 73-75 = 148 (+6)

1993 Baltusrol (Lower Course) – Springfield, New Jersey – par 70, 7,152 yards, T-72 70-74-73-72=289 (+9)

1992 Pebble Beach Golf Links – Pebble Beach, California – par 72, 6,809 yards, T-4 70-76-68-77=291 (+3)

1991 Hazeltine National – Minneapolis, Minnesota – par 72, 7,149 yards, T-16 72-74-73-72=291 (+3)

1990 Medinah (No. 3) – Medinah, Illinois – par 72, 6,996 yards, T-3 72-72-68-69=281 (−7)

1989 Oak Hill – Rochester, New York – par 70, 6,902 yards, T-18 68-72-73-72=285 (+5)

1988 The Country Club – Brookline, Massachusetts – par 71, 7,010 yards, T-WIN 72-67-68-71=278 (−6); lost to Curtis Strange 75 to 71 in an eighteen-hole play-off

1984 Winged Foot (West) – Mamaroneck, NewYork – par 70, 6,930 yards, T-55 71-76-77-72=296 (+16)

THE US PGA CHAMPIONSHIP

2004 Whistling Straits – Haven, Wisconsin – par 72, 7,514 yards, T-49 72-70-74-74=290 (+2)

2003 Oak Hill – Rochester, New York – par 70, 7,134 yards [Did not enter]

2002 Hazeltine National – Chaska, Minnesota – par 72, 7,360 yards, T-60 71-76-74-78=299 (+11)

2001 Atlanta Athletic Club, Duluth, Georgia, par 70, 7,213 yards, T-51 67-74-71-70=282 (+2)

2000 Valhalla – Louisville, Kentucky – par 72, 7,167 yards, T-51 79-68-69-73=289 (+1)

1999 Medinah (No. 3) – Medinah, Illinois – par 72, 7,401 yards, T-41 71-71-75-75=292 (+4)

1998 Sahalee – Redmond, Washington – par 70, 6,906 yards, T-54 73-71-72-73=289 (+9)

1997 Winged Foot (West) – Mamaroneck, New York – par 70, 6,987 yards, CUT 75-78=153 (+13)

1996 Valhalla – Louisville, Kentucky – par 72, 7,144 yards, T-65 69-75-74-73=291 (+3)

1995 Riviera – Pacific Palisades, California – par 71, 6,956 yards, T-31 69-73-70-67=279 (−5)

1994 Southern Hills – Tulsa, Oklahoma – par 70, 6,824 yards, T-4 73-67-71-66=277 (−3)

1993 Inverness Club – Toledo, Ohio – par 71, 7,024 yards, 3 68-68-69-68=273 (−11)

1992 Bellerive – St Louis, Missouri – par 71, 7,024 yards, T-2 68-70-76-67=281 (−3)

1991   Crooked Stick – Carmel, Indiana – par 72, 7,295 yards, T-16 70-69-71-76=286 (−2)

1990   Shoal Creek – Birmingham, Alabama – par 72, 7,145 yards, T-19 71-75-80-69=295 (+7)

1989   Kemper Lakes – Hawthorn Woods, Illinois – par 72, 7,217 yards, T-9 70-73-69-69=281 (−7)

1988   Oak Tree – Edmond, Oklahoma – par 71, 7,015 yards, 5 67-71-70-71=279 (−5)

1987   PGA National – Palm Beach Gardens, Florida – par 72, 7,002 yards, T-28 73-73-77-74=297 (+9)

1986   Inverness Club – Toledo, Ohio – par 71, 6,982 yards, CUT 76-71=147 (+5)

1985   Cherry Hills – Englewood, Colorado – par 71, 7,089 yards, T-54 70-77-73-74=294 (+10)

1984   Shoal Creek – Birmingham, Alabama – par 72, 7,145 yards, T-20 69-73-74-70=286 (−2)

1983   Riviera – Pacific Palisades, California – par 71, 6,946 yards, CUT 74-77=151 (+9)

1982   Southern Hills – Tulsa, Oklahoma – par 70, 6,862 yards, T-14 67-70-73-72=282 (+2)

INDEX